China and the World

China and the World

Chinese Foreign Policy in the Post-Mao Era

edited by Samuel S. Kim

Westview Press / Boulder and London

Published in 1984 in the United States of America by Westview Press, Inc., 5500 Central Avenue, Boulder, Colorado 80301; Frederick A. Praeger, Publisher

Library of Congress Cataloging in Publication Data
Main entry under title:
China and the world.
  Bibliography: p.
  Includes index.
  1. China—Foreign relations—1976-   —Addresses,
essays, lectures. I. Kim, Samuel S., 1935–   .
DS779.27.C4873 1984   327.51   84-11852
ISBN 0-86531-556-6
ISBN 0-86531-557-4 (pbk.)

Printed and bound in the United States of America

10   9   8   7   6   5   4   3   2

CONTENTS

List of Tables and Figures....................................... vii
Preface ix

Part 1
Theory and Practice

1. Chinese Foreign Policy Behavior, *Samuel S. Kim* 3
2. On a Slow Boat to Where? Analyzing Chinese
   Foreign Policy, *Davis B. Bobrow and Steve Chan* 32
3. The Domestic Political Dimensions of China's
   Foreign Economic Relations, *Susan Shirk*................... 57
4. International Systemic Constraints on Chinese
   Foreign Policy, *Michael Ng-Quinn* 82

Part 2
Interactions

5. China and the United States: The Limits of
   Interaction, *Steven I. Levine* 113
6. China and the Soviet Union: "Principled, Salutary,
   and Tempered" Management of Conflict, *Chi Su* 135
7. China and the Second World, *Donald W. Klein* 161
8. China and the Third World: In Search of a
   Neorealist World Policy, *Samuel S. Kim* 178

Part 3
Policies and Issues

9. Soldiers and Statesmen in Conflict: Chinese Defense
   and Foreign Policies in the 1980s, *Paul H. B. Godwin*...... 215
10. The Political Economy of China's Turn Outward,
    Bruce Cumings.. 235
11. Chinese Policy in Multilateral Financial Institutions,
    William Feeney 266

12. The Role of Science and Technology in China's
     Foreign Relations, *Denis Fred Simon* 293

Part 4
Prospects

13. China's Foreign Policy Options and Prospects:
     Toward the 1990s, *Allen S. Whiting* 321

Bibliography... 335
About the Contributors 346
Index... 349
Other Titles of Interest from Westview Press................... 355
About the Book and Editor....................................... 356

TABLES AND FIGURES

Tables

7.1 Prospects for Second World Assistance to China........... 174

8.1 Proportion of Trade with Third World Countries in China's Total Value of Imports and Exports, 1950–1982 195

8.2 A Chinese View of Hegemonic Decline and Multipolarization Based on Changing Proportions of World GNP, 1970–1990................................... 204

11.1 China's Comparative WBG Quotas/Shares/Subscriptions ... 273

11.2 World Bank Projects, Loans, and Credits for China 278

11.3 Comparative Cumulative IBRD/IDA Lending Operations ... 281

11.4 China's Comparative WBG Voting Power.................. 283

Figures

1.1 A Model of the Chinese Foreign Policy System.............. 6
1.2 Matrix for the Study of Chinese Foreign Policy Behavior.... 12
2.1 Matrix for Chinese Foreign Policy Analysis 35

PREFACE

It is commonplace nowadays to hear, and even faddish to say, how many great changes have occurred in post-Mao China. Has Chinese foreign policy also undergone a great change or even a transformation in the post-Mao era? To what extent have the basic values, norms, interests, and structure underpinning Chinese foreign policy been reaffirmed, revised, or repudiated since the death of Mao Zedong in September 1976?

Paradoxically, every turn and twist in Chinese politics has been accompanied by the compulsive projection of foreign policy—in striking contrast with domestic policy—as a policy of principled constancy and continuity. An "exceptionist," "exemptionalist" mentality is evident in practically all important official pronouncements. The 30,000-word document enunciating the official reassessment of Mao Zedong at the Sixth Plenum of the Eleventh Central Committee of the Chinese Communist Party, issued in late June 1981, deals almost exclusively with domestic politics, exempting the history of China's foreign relations from public criticism. Only a few pages of *Deng Xiaoping wenxuan, 1975–1982* [The selected works of Deng Xiaoping, 1975–1982], published in mid-1983, have anything to say about foreign (open-door) policy. This highlights one of the many source and methodological problems in the study of Chinese foreign policy.

This volume is the final product of a collaborative effort that was started a few years ago in the hope of clarifying some central issues in post-Mao Chinese foreign policy. Twin panels on "Chinese Foreign Policy in the 1980s" at the 1983 International Studies Association (ISA) Convention, held in Mexico City, Mexico, in April 1983, served as catalyst and focal point in bringing together scholars of diverse intellectual heritage, methodological inclination, and normative orientation in their common search for the elusive and changing interface between China and the world. The draft papers presented and discussed at the ISA panels, plus several additional papers, were revised and restructured to incorporate individual and collective criticisms and to account for further developments in Chinese foreign policy during the second half of 1983. All the chapters were completed late enough, I believe, to grasp a firm sense of the changes and continuities underpinning the foreign policy of the post-Mao era (1976–1983).

Without being too rigidly bound by the requirements of any particular perspective and methodology, the authors of this volume seek to answer the following questions: How does China relate to the outside world in the post-Mao era? To what extent, and in what specific ways, has the nexus between China and the world remained constant or changed, and why? What are the future implications and prospects for both?

With this broad concern in mind, this book combines theory and generalizations with some specific empirical case studies. The mandate of each contributor was to address, within the scope of his or her assigned chapter, several key questions and puzzles that are of theoretical and practical value to both students and policymakers. First, what are the wellsprings of Chinese foreign policy? Specifically, what is the relative weight of domestic/societal factors as opposed to external/systemic ones in influencing or circumscribing foreign policy options and directions? Second, what are the changes and continuities that characterize the Chinese foreign policy of the post-Mao era, and what are their sources? In Parts 2 and 3 of the book, the contributors identify the underlying patterns of China's interactions with the major global actors (the United States, the Soviet Union, the Second World, and the Third World) and China's policies on specific international issues and problems. Third, what is the extent of word/deed disjuncture in Chinese foreign policy? Several chapters probe and explain the discrepancies between ideal and real, between policy pronouncements and policy performance, and between intent and outcome in Chinese foreign policy. The task is neither to chant nor condemn the official script and score but to describe and compare in different issue areas, toward other actors, and over time the extent of theory/practice incongruence and to proffer adequate explanations. The concluding chapter identifies and assesses China's foreign policy options and prospects in the years to come.

This volume is an outgrowth of our experience in teaching Chinese foreign policy and international relations courses over the years. In response to a growing concern over the lack of significant development in the field of Chinese foreign policy, as well as over the continuing gap between China specialists and analysts of world politics, the Joint Committee on Contemporary China of the Social Science Research Council and the American Council of Learned Societies sponsored a three-day workshop on Chinese foreign policy in mid-August 1976 at the University of Michigan in Ann Arbor, where some twenty-two specialists addressed themselves to this problem. An invisible college of "bridge builders" has gradually grown out of this conference, providing a renewable network of intellectual resources and collaboration. This volume represents a modest step toward remedying the dialogue of the deaf between China scholars and world politics analysts.

Several specific acknowledgments are in order. Throughout the preparation of this volume I received invaluable help from Allen S. Whiting, who, along with contributing the final chapter, always offered sound advice and counsel. For diverse reasons, a number of scholars could not contribute to this volume, but I wish to acknowledge with thanks Gavin Boyd, Lowell Dittmer, June T. Dreyer, Edward Friedman,

Melvin Gurtov, Harry Harding, James C. Hsiung, Jonathan Pollack, Thomas Robinson, and Peter Van Ness for their contributions in the early stages of the project and in many other ways. Since 1979 I have had the benefit of critical dialogue with a number of PRC international relations scholars in China and the United States. Even though their participation in this project has been minimal (many do not even know the project exists), it may not be inappropriate to single out those individuals who have been of particular help: Dong Zujie, Guo Simian, Rong Zhi, Wang Tieya, Wu Guosheng, Xue Mouhong, Zhang Ruizhuang, Zhao Baoxu, and Zhao Huian. I am indebted to Monmouth College for a faculty creativity grant and for some released time away from teaching for the 1983–1984 academic year, which supported this and other research projects. It has been a great pleasure to work with Westview Press in the production of this book. Special thanks are due to Lynne Rienner, Byron Schneider, Lynn Arts, Michele McTighe, Miriam Gilbert, and Holly Arrow for guiding this manuscript through the various stages of the production process. The usual disclaimer still holds—that the editor and contributors alone are responsible for the views and interpretations presented in the book.

Samuel S. Kim

Part 1
Theory and Practice

CHAPTER 1

CHINESE FOREIGN POLICY BEHAVIOR

Samuel S. Kim

INTRODUCTION

Perhaps because of the sheer physical size and societal dimensions of China, only the parts can be grasped, never the whole. China seems to be in such a state of constant but ambiguous motion that one can never fully understand what makes it tick. Alternatively, China is still viewed through anachronistic or shaded glasses, perhaps, or is made a scapegoat for the outside observer's misconceptions, misperceptions, and miscarried expectations. Or China specialists may be languishing in an academic cul-de-sac because they have never prepared a proper road map (paradigm).

Whatever the real reason, the study of Chinese foreign policy has been advancing in divergent directions in an atheoretical, noncomparative, and noncumulative manner. A comprehensive bibliography on Chinese external affairs published in 1973 listed no less than 2,085 entries.[1] The decade since 1973 witnessed a more dramatic increase in Western scholarly monographs on Chinese foreign policy, accompanied by numerous state-of-the-field review essays and articles. Yet we are still some distance from capturing the multifaceted and elusive nature of Chinese foreign policy.

For example, consider the range of conflicting assumptions and conclusions about both the continuities and the changes that mark Chinese foreign policy—one of the major puzzles in the field. For some time, debate on this question of tradition versus modernity was divided into two schools of thought: the *exotica sinica* "continuity" school, which stresses the essential uniqueness and inscrutability of Chinese behavior ("a single Chinese nebula in the western world's firmament"); and the revolutionary "discontinuity" school, which argues that the lines of continuity with traditional China have been broken.[2]

More recently, the change/continuity controversy has split into three sharply divergent forms. From one pole of the conceptual spectrum, Thomas Robinson argues that "a general policy orientation, once adopted or forced upon the regime by circumstances, never continued for more than four or five years at most" and that "changes were not only relatively frequent but radical, moving within a relatively short time between pugnacious intervention, one-sided alliance commitment, total isolation, extreme involvement and reversal of alignment."[3] From the opposite pole, Michael Ng-Quinn emphasizes the structural constraints of the international system dominated by the superpowers, arguing that "Chinese foreign policy has been largely consistent since the end of World War II" and that "there is relative continuity in Chinese foreign policy amidst leadership changes even in the post-Mao era."[4] Harry Harding presents a third, dialectical perspective: "What has remained relatively constant thus far, in other words, are the fundamentals of China's foreign policy: its basic organizing principles, its general goals, and its style. What has changed, in contrast, are China's policies toward specific issues and its relationships with particular countries."[5] The basic scholarly disagreement on the "what" question, let alone on the "why" question, is also attested to by the conflicting periodization of the history of PRC foreign policy.[6]

In the interest of improving the scholarly quality of Chinese foreign policy analysis, this chapter develops a behavior-centered, multivariate, multimethod analytic framework based on the following core assumptions:

- The post-Mao principle of "seeking truth from facts" serves a useful point of departure
- The complex empirical reality of Chinese foreign policy need not be limited to the eye of the beholder: A social science approach can supplement impressionistic observations
- Chinese foreign policy is most amenable to empirical analysis during the "behavioral/implementation" phase described below
- Given the intricate nature of Chinese foreign policy, no single concept, method, or dimension is adequate to describe and explain it
- Human behavior tends (1) to be patterned around only a few values; (2) to change over time; (3) to be goal-oriented and future-oriented; and (4) to have diverse cultural forms and manifestations
- An understanding of China's international behavior can never transcend the limits and possibilities of the concepts and data used to describe it and the theories or models developed to explain it

The behavior-centered approach proposed in this chapter attempts to integrate the field of Chinese foreign policy into the larger framework of concepts, theories, and methods in comparative foreign policy and international relations and to develop a more orderly and systematic body of knowledge about Chinese foreign policy.

THE RELATIVE EFFICACY OF A
BEHAVIOR-CENTERED APPROACH

Chinese foreign policy covers a wide though nebulous domain. For analytical convenience and clarity, we may conceptualize Chinese foreign policy as a system of human actions, a system with its own structure, values, norms, and processes. Figure 1.1 presents an idealized, multi-dimensional model of Chinese foreign policy, with each behavioral dimension divided into interconnected, interacting sequential phases.

The most serious obstacle to a cumulative, comparative, and policy-relevant study of Chinese foreign policy has been inadequate conceptualization and operationalization. Priority should be accorded to conceptualizing Chinese foreign policy in discrete measurable units of analysis. Too often, students of Chinese foreign policy have put the cart before the horse, plunging into explanatory analysis without specifying a priori the dependent variables (x, y, and z) to be explained. Theories or models designed to explain the variations in a state's behavior must follow, not precede, the empirical specification of a given foreign policy behavior.

A state and its behavior are vague, abstract concepts. As a legal entity in international law, the state per se is incapable of making and implementing foreign policy decisions. Only members of foreign policy elites, acting on behalf of that state, are capable of pursuing goal-directed behavior. The leadership approach proposed by Robert C. Tucker is helpful here. In contrast to the traditional realpolitik method, Tucker conceptualizes politics in terms of how political leaders perform three related functions: diagnose a situation, prescribe a course of action, and implement policy.[7] The behavior-centered approach attempts to minimize the vagueness and mystique of "state behavior" by focusing on discrete, empirical units—the foreign policy actions of political leaders in various contexts and issue areas.

The nexus between states as dominant international actors and the external environment is at the phases of policy pronouncement and policy performance (Figure 1.1). The behavior-centered approach encourages an empirical inquiry into the reciprocal interaction between China and the outside world. As defined by the "event data" movement, an international event involves an action by an international actor toward one or more direct targets or indirect objects. This is the basic empirical unit for the description, comparison, and evaluation of the patterns and parameters of international interaction.

Perhaps its most important comparative advantage, the behavior-centered approach facilitates comparative analyses of Chinese foreign policy behavior in various issue areas toward different actors over a period of time. This method makes it possible to conceptualize and operationalize concrete and expressed external actions and activities in

6

FIGURE 1.1
A Model of the Chinese Foreign Policy System

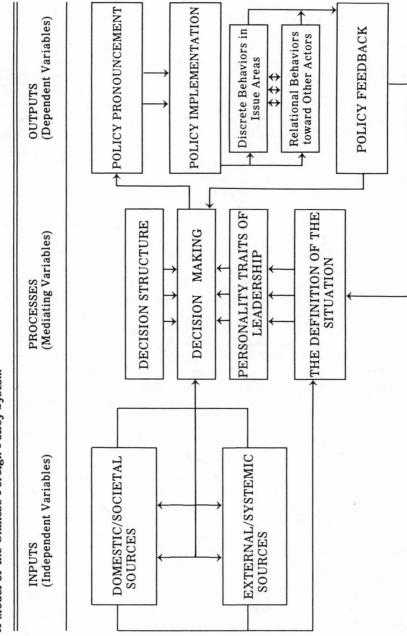

order to deal with three major puzzles in the study of Chinese foreign policy: (1) How constant or changeable is Chinese foreign policy behavior compared over time? (2) How unique and particularistic or general and common is Chinese foreign policy behavior compared with other nations? (3) How wide is the gap between ideal and real, between policy pronouncements and policy performance, and between intent and outcome in Chinese foreign policy?

The first puzzle of constancy versus change can be addressed by the use of a comparative/diachronic analysis. Human behavior has both a spatial and a temporal dimension; it is amenable to comparisons across time. A diachronic analysis should ask: What discrete, manifest behavior at what level or in what domain has changed over what intervals in time, at what rate, with what outcomes or consequences? Foreign policy continuity (or rigidity) can be measured by the consistency with which manifest behavior toward the same actor, issue, or problem recurs with the same mix of instruments over a given period of time. To the extent that policy behavior demonstrates a recurring pattern of consistency across different historical periods, there is a sound empirical basis for inferring a stable determinant for such behavior.

Specifically, we may compare (1) general Chinese foreign policy behavior, (2) issue-oriented or function-specific Chinese foreign policy behavior, such as conflict, voting, bargaining, or treaty behavior, and (3) actor-oriented Chinese foreign policy behavior toward individual or collective international actors—e.g., the United States, the Soviet Union, Japan, the Group of 77, the Non-Aligned Movement, the EEC, or international organizations. Such comparisons over time may reveal the extent to which the basic pattern of Chinese foreign policy has been maintained, revised, or transformed. The degree of continuity in Chinese foreign policy orientation could be confidently inferred from the results.

The inclusion of China in the Comparative Research on the Events of Nations (CREON) serves as a point of departure in addressing the second puzzle—the question of the unique/common nature of China's foreign policy. Based on foreign policy events of thirty-eight nations for thirty months over a ten-year period (1959–1968), the CREON project has produced a comprehensive body of cross-national data and findings on foreign policy behavior, analyzed in terms of substantive problem areas, target scope of action, goal properties, instruments, commitment, specificity, independence/interdependence of action, acceptance/rejection, and affect (cooperation/conflict).[8] CREON's reliance upon *Deadline Data on World Affairs*, a global but still Western-dominated chronology of international events culled primarily from major newspapers and wire services throughout the world, is a weakness,[9] and 1959 to 1968 is hardly a typical or representative period in the history of PRC foreign policy. Nevertheless, the CREON project provides a useful repertoire of empirical concepts, measurements, and referents for the behavior-centered approach.

The third puzzle—concerning the extent of word/deed disjuncture—can be approached by drawing a conceptual distinction between the ideals, principles, and orientations expressed in policy pronouncements and the actual conduct of foreign policy. As if to accentuate the word/deed disparity of their adversaries and to minimize their own discrepancies, the Chinese have repeatedly asserted that deeds are the critical test for describing and evaluating Soviet conduct—and more recently, U.S. conduct—while insisting that they themselves always mean what they say and are resolute and unyielding on their "principled stand."

At the level of policy pronouncements, post-Mao China's projected self-images of domestic and foreign policy are in sharp contrast. The latest post hoc verdict of the past CCP congresses suggests that at times even *past* Chinese domestic policies, often characterized by turmoil and discontinuity, cannot be confidently interpreted. At the same time, the projected self-image of Chinese foreign policy is one of unvarying constancy and continuity marked by the habitual use of "always" (for the Five Principles of Peaceful Coexistence, independence, world peace) and "never" (hegemonic ambition or behavior).[10] Of course, these self-serving pronouncements should not be accepted at face value.

A word/deed (or intent/result) dichotomy exists in all human political behavior—an inevitable corollary of the differential capabilities of human imagination and rhetoric (which can easily transcend temporal and spatial bounds) and human behavior (which cannot). The real task is not to establish the difference between words and deeds, but rather to describe and compare in different issue areas, toward other actors, and over time the extent of incongruity between pronounced values and norms and actual conduct and to proffer adequate explanations. Peter Van Ness's systematic analysis of the theory/practice discrepancy in Chinese support for wars of national liberation, although limited to the years 1965 to 1967, still stands out as a trailblazing work.[11] Like any other behavioral dimension, the word/deed dichotomy needs to be assessed in a cross-national frame of reference.

Given the dominant bias in mainstream behavioral science research against employing a normative framework in defining and evaluating social reality, a bias that is especially strong in the United States, the behavior-centered approach may easily be misunderstood as another faddish methodological claim. It rejects the assumption that a fact/value (and science/ideology) distinction is logically possible, theoretically necessary, and axiologically essential. Instead, the behavior-centered method assumes that normative and empirical approaches are dialectical and can be complementary. There is no such thing as pure (i.e., value-free and culture-free) scientific or social fact. On the other hand, facts do not speak for themselves nor do they add up to a theory. It is theory that makes sense out of facts.

The behavior-centered approach is compatible and complementary with problem-solving, policy-relevant, and value-realizing approaches.

Instead of directly assuming Chinese values from policy pronouncements, the preferred approach would be to infer them indirectly from various types of manifest foreign policy behavior. Specifically, foreign policy goals and values can be discerned by examining and identifying the main targets and beneficiaries of Chinese foreign policy behaviors in various domains. The increasing globalization of Chinese foreign policy also provides a firm empirical basis for a more disciplined and systematic inquiry into China's global role in the realization of world order goals and values.

What about the lack of "pertinent documents" that is customarily asserted by many analysts? The oft-heard complaint has some validity for the study of Chinese foreign policy decision making. Ironically, however, some of the best ground-breaking works in the field have dealt with Chinese decision making by showing how an alternative data base can be built on post hoc inference of motives and perceptions of Chinese foreign policy elites from their manifest conflict or crisis behavior.[12]

The problems of documentary paucity have been greatly exaggerated. At the same time, the availability of documents and data may easily tempt us to take the shortest methodological path, following what Abraham Kaplan called the law of the instrument: "Give a small boy a hammer, and he will find that everything he encounters needs pounding."[13] Those who follow the behavior-centered approach must beware of the self-fulfilling law of the instrument, lest they too eagerly and blindly count every individual "tree" buried in the available behavioral and empirical data, or uncritically equate qualitative significance with quantitative weight.

For the behavior-centered approach, Chinese foreign policy may be defined as an aggregate of purposeful external actions and activities designed to affect the international situation or behavior of other international actors in the pursuit of some values, interests, or goals. When defined in this way, there can be no valid complaint about the lack of "relevant data." A large and ever-increasing repertory of empirical and behavioral referents is generated by the objects/targets of China's expanding diplomatic, military, economic, cultural, technological, and legal practices.

The behavior-centered approach has several weaknesses. First, covert foreign policy activities—and inaction—tend to slip through the conceptual and empirical net. However, covert Chinese "intelligence" activities may be assumed to be an insignificant part of the total repertory of external actions and activities, as there has as yet been no known case of Chinese spies being caught or expelled by a host country.[14] China's covert activities, such as "support" for Thai Communist insurgents, illicit third-party trade with South Africa and South Korea, the secret joint operation of a Sino-American surveillance facility in Xinjiang to monitor Soviet missile tests, and "assistance" for the Pakistani nuclear program, cannot be kept hidden for too long.[15]

Second, the behavior-centered approach is not well suited to the "cognitive mapping" of the belief systems of political leaders and their impact on the decision-making process.[16] Based on the assumption that the domestic and foreign policies of any given state are strongly conditioned by the belief systems of its key decision makers—an assumption that is particularly pertinent to Chinese political culture—cognitive mapping addresses such questions as: What are the belief systems of decision makers? How do these belief systems influence the determination of policy choices? What will happen if there is an increase or decrease in certain variables or properties of the decision makers' cognitive maps? The behavior-centered approach can only indirectly infer decision makers' belief systems based on their manifest foreign policy behavior.

Finally, the behavior-centered approach is plagued by the clear and continuing possibility of reciprocal interaction between the status and image of the foreign policy actor and the normative presuppositions and perspective of the observer. A recent sociopsychological study has even suggested that "the actor must have no physical characteristics, such as clothing, beard, long hair, color, stigmata, the like, that could affect the labeling process apart from the act itself."[17] Likewise, a cross-cultural study of aggression has shown the meaninglessness of describing one culture as more or less aggressive than another, given the difficulty of establishing value-free external criteria of conceptualization and operationalization.[18]

These disadvantages can be countered by relying on a variety of empirical and behavioral referents, by using a variety of concepts and methods, and by examining a variety of Chinese foreign policy behaviors across time, in different contexts, and toward different targets.

DESCRIBING CHINESE FOREIGN POLICY BEHAVIOR

In order to grasp general Chinese foreign policy behavior, one must first typologize and describe the more specific external activities, then explore the relationships across different types of behavior in search of patterns of consistency and regularity. This typology can be constructed in a variety of ways. The organizational structure of the Chinese Ministry of Foreign Affairs follows the almost universal division of labor between geographical and functional areas of specialty. If the logic of this structure is followed, the search for consistent patterns may be limited to external influence activities directed toward major individual and collective actors—the United States, the Soviet Union, the Second World, and the Third World. Or the search may focus instead on a few select issue/problem areas—military-security, economic-developmental, monetary-financial, and science-technology.

Issue-specific or problem-solving typologies of Chinese foreign policy behavior come in many permutations. If Chinese foreign policy is conceived in terms of foreign policy instruments (the means and capabilities of foreign policy actors in the implementation phase), Chinese activities may be typologized along the continua of diplomacy (persuasion), economic sanctions (rewards and punishments, such as the extension or withdrawal of foreign aid), promotion/propaganda (cultural-scientific-educational exchange, the use of international legal norms, and the projection of normative and symbolic capabilities), and military force. Concerning the behavioral characteristics of Chinese foreign policy, manifest external activities may be conceptualized and operationalized in dialectical terms: positive versus negative; short-term versus long-term; substantive versus symbolic; conflictive versus cooperative; initiative versus reactive; bilateral versus multilateral; low politics versus high politics; independent versus interdependent; withdrawal versus enmeshment; and low-risk versus high-risk.

Or one could take a case-study approach, selecting a particular type of foreign policy behavior (e.g., relating to bargaining or negotiating, conflict or crisis, voting, treaty, commitment or alignment) within a systemic context or level for a given period to achieve a detailed and concentrated analysis. Alternatively, a set of behaviors may be selected (e.g., verbal, voting, consultative, administrative, and financial behaviors in an international organization) for empirical analysis.[19]

The sheer volume of foreign policy activities necessitates careful formulation of concepts and clear demarcation of the boundaries between types of behaviors. For the development of sound and empirically supported descriptions of, and generalizations about, Chinese foreign policy behavior, the observer needs concepts that facilitate comparisons of conduct over time, across nations, in different problem areas, and toward different actors. Figure 1.2 presents a matrix for the comparative study of Chinese foreign policy behavior. It is designed to facilitate comparative analyses to address the three puzzles of Chinese foreign policy mentioned above and to measure variations in both the pattern of relationship and the type of activity.

Based on the assumption that a decade constitutes a sufficient time frame to reveal the basic pattern of constancy or change in a nation's foreign policy, Chinese foreign policy behavior is divided into decades. (Of course, this is an arbitrary periodization designed to reveal long-term patterns and trends in Chinese foreign policy. To date, Chinese foreign policy reorientation has followed more closely a four-to-five year cycle.) For the first three decades of such policy behavior, there are forty-eight cells in the matrix (the 1980s and 1990s are included for forecasting purposes). After each cell has been filled using the existing literature of Chinese foreign policy, the degree of consistency or variation over time, across the issue areas and targets, and across other nations can be determined.

The matrix can be used for quantitative or qualitative comparison by measuring or observing any significant changes in the following types of behavioral properties: (1) level of external involvement (e.g.,

FIGURE 1.2
Matrix for the Study of Chinese Foreign Policy Behavior

Orientation Typology \ Issue/Problem Typology	Period	Diplomatic/ Political	Military/ Security	Economic/ Developmental	Functional/ Promotional	Inductive Generalization
Autarky	1950s					
	1960s					
	1970s					
	1980s					
	1990s					
Self-Reliance	1950s					
	1960s					
	1970s					
	1980s					
	1990s					
Interdependence	1950s					
	1960s					
	1970s					
	1980s					
	1990s					
Dependence	1950s					
	1960s					
	1970s					
	1980s					
	1990s					
Inductive Generalization						

the numbers of target parties and the level of military, economic, cultural, scientific, and legal activities); (2) distribution of foreign policy activities (e.g., the allocation of foreign policy agents, resources, leadership time, messages, and goals/values); (3) direction of foreign policy activities (e.g., shifts in direct targets and indirect objects); (4) pattern of instrument use; (5) numbers of international commitments (i.e., international agreements and treaties); and (6) degree of foreign policy autonomy.

Autarkic Behavior

Autarky is characterized by an extremely low level of external involvement in all four issue areas and an extremely high degree of self-centeredness and autonomy. It is a self-imposed retreat into the protective cocoon of state sovereignty. The number of international agreements is at a minimum, limited largely to the establishment of pro forma diplomatic relations. Nonalignment and noncommitment are the hallmarks of autarkic foreign policy. Given the low level of external involvement, the direction of foreign policy activities tends to be anomic and the pattern of instrument use may not be discernible except through indirect inference from domestic promotional/propagandistic activities. The foreign policy of China during the most intense phase of the Cultural Revolution (1966–1968) comes close to this behavior model.

Self-Reliant Behavior

As the Chinese have repeatedly stressed, self-reliance is not autarky. Self-reliant behavior follows the general, flexible principle of maximal self-realization. The level of external involvement is still generally low, although there is an uneven distribution of foreign policy activities. The logic of a self-reliant foreign policy stresses the maximization of internal autocentric development, the minimization of external dependency, and the long-term transformation of the capitalist world economy.[20] Nonalignment and noncommitment minimize the costs and vulnerabilities of asymmetrical interdependence or dependence. Diplomatic and promotional instruments are more salient than military and economic instruments in a self-reliant foreign policy. Foreign trade is carried out as a necessary balancing factor in the development process—largely to eliminate certain sectoral weaknesses, and foreign debts are consciously avoided or minimized by balancing imports and exports and by rejecting foreign borrowing. The foreign policy of China during the periods 1963 to 1965 and 1969 to 1977 is suggestive of this behavior model.

Interdependent Behavior

Interdependent behavior is characterized by deep and extensive involvement in all kinds of international transactions. Instrument use is most prominent in the economic domain. High commitment to the existing world order and close alignment with one major global actor are the hallmarks of interdependent foreign policy. As distinguished from international interconnectedness, international interdependence refers to a balanced and equitable dependence in which actors share the benefits, costs, and consequences of their transactions in goods (and bads), services, capital, knowledge, and rule making. Interdependence exists where actors of more or less equal "power" are engaged in the joint management of their mutual dependence. Despite the rhetoric of global interdependence, however, an interdependent foreign policy is largely limited to relationships between the core industrial countries. The foreign policy of post-Mao China provides a point of departure for testing this behavior model.

Dependent Behavior

Dependence is an adversely asymmetrical relationship—in the vivid metaphor of China's UN ambassador in 1974, Huang Hua, one "between a horseman and his mount."[21] The level of involvement is extremely high, but the distribution of external activities is unevenly concentrated in another state or group of states. By excessive commitment to and alignment with one side, a dependent foreign policy erodes self-control and self-direction despite a state's formal autonomy. The dominant or hegemonic state defines the parameters of acceptable behavior, and at times it may actually force key decisions upon the dependent state by exercising its sanction power. The security and welfare of the latter are precariously contingent upon an external heavy hand beyond its control. The foreign policy of China during the lean-to-one-side period (1949–1958) approximates this behavior model.

The four-category behavior typology is a variation on the simple independent/interdependent typology, with autarky and self-reliance representing extreme and moderate independence, and interdependence and dependence representing symmetrical and asymmetrical interdependence. This distinction focuses on the relational characteristics of foreign policy behavior and uses the degree of autonomy as the ultimate test of a state's foreign policy behavior. Of the thirty-eight nations whose foreign policy behavior was examined by the CREON project for the period 1959–1968, China displayed the most independent behavior, scoring "independent" 68 percent, "interdependent" 10 percent, and "mixed" 22 percent of the total sample.[22]

From the CREON project's findings, we can further propose three types of interaction as the most important parameters of Chinese foreign policy behavior: relations with the two superpowers; relations with international organizations, especially the United Nations; and relations with the Third World. During much of the 1959–1968 period China was nonaligned, following a dual-adversary strategy; hence China's independence may be considered a function of its nonalignment. During the same period, China was excluded from the United Nations and many other international organizations, which limited the number of its international agreements and commitments. The Third World began to emerge as an important component of Chinese foreign policy during this period. Given the normative commitment of the Third World to geopolitical nonalignment and national independence, and its incapacity to impose any serious constraints on the PRC, China's independent foreign policy behavior and its expanding ties with the Third World as a global actor can be described as mutually complementary rather than conflictive. All three factors have combined to increase China's unilateral, nonaligned, and initiative actions, decisively shifting the overall normative weight of Chinese foreign policy in the direction of independence.

Based on the assumption that human or national behavior tends to be patterned around a few goals and values, the horizontal axis of Figure 1.2 allocates all external Chinese foreign policy activities into four domains according to the nature of the problem or issue that the Chinese government seeks to address. This issue/problem typology facilitates comparative analysis and hypotheses. What is the distribution of Chinese foreign policy activity across potential targets and issue/problem areas? Why are certain targets and issues more salient than others in manifest Chinese foreign policy behavior? Under what conditions does China change or shift the distribution and direction of its foreign policy targets and objects?

Space is reserved on both the vertical and horizontal axes for inductive generalization on various dimensions of Chinese foreign policy. The aggregation of discrete behaviors provides an empirical basis for identifying patterns of foreign policy behavior. Proceeding on the basis of issue/problem typologies and descriptions, the structure of Chinese foreign policy as a whole can be more confidently delineated.

EXPLAINING CHINESE FOREIGN POLICY BEHAVIOR

Once the "what" question has been answered, the "why" question can be addressed. Exploring the causal relationships of independent variables located in the predecisional policy input phase with the dependent variables made manifest in the policy implementation phase clarifies the linked processes that produce foreign policy behavior. Why is Chinese foreign policy behavior what it is? Why has the reorientation from one type of behavior to another type occurred? What factors, sources, and determinants lie behind the making and implementation of foreign policy or account for the major shifts and changes in the development of foreign policy?

A recent critique of the literature identified and classified explanatory approaches to Chinese foreign policy among seven imperatives: historical legacy, Mao's domination, factional politics, national interest, ideology, capability, and multicausal analysis.[23] All possible explanations and causal claims and theories embodied in these approaches can be reclassified into three broad categories of domestic/societal, external/systemic, and domestic/external linkage factors affecting the foreign policy decision-making process (see Figure 1.1). A few approaches in each category will be discussed.

Domestic/Societal Factors

The search for domestic factors to explain foreign policy action or change assumes that such policy is an extension or externalization of domestic politics. Even a cursory review of the literature suggests that the overwhelming majority of Chinese foreign policy specialists, deeply rooted in the area studies tradition of idiographic description and analysis, focus on a variety of domestic factors in the search for a fitting explanatory model. Not surprisingly, there is also growing consensus in the related field of Soviet foreign policy–making not only that "domestic sources" have become more important and decisive but also that linkages between domestic and foreign policy issues have intensified in the post-Stalin era.[24] A recent cross-national study of the foreign policy "restructuring" of Bhutan, Tanzania, Canada, Burma, China, and Chile concluded that domestic factors, defined in terms of the perceptions, values, preferences, and objectives of key decision makers, now have assumed critical importance in all cases except Canada.[25]

Of the domestic factors, traditional political culture is most resistant to causal linkage with foreign policy behavior. Theories of national tradition and culture (or national character), which have had a checkered history, have recently fallen into disrepute. Yet proponents of the traditional political/cultural legacy approach (mostly belonging to the *exotica sinica* continuity school referred to earlier) insist that there is no better way to comprehend and explain the present-day international conduct of the People's Republic than by reference to the tradition of imperial China. To do otherwise, in the words of its most eloquent spokesman, John K. Fairbank, "is truly to be flying blind."[26] Proponents of this approach have advanced several variations on the theme of the political culture paradigm to explain Chinese political behavior.[27] Transplanting the Western Machiavellian-Hobbesian image of human nature as nasty, selfish, aggressive, and rigid to the Chinese political scene, Lucian Pye explains the dynamics of Chinese politics solely in terms of culturally rooted factionalism. Policy outcomes have no role in this single-factor behavior model except as a barometer for the long cycle of the rise and fall of competing factions.[28]

The traditional political culture approach has several problems. Like any monocausal, deterministic theory, it risks the danger of trying to explain everything—and nothing—by a single factor. If there is no variation in Chinese behavior (and this seems to be an implicit assumption in the political culture paradigm) then nothing needs to be explained. However, variation in behavior is the puzzle that explanation seeks to solve. Culture is subject to ongoing historical change. The foreign policy tradition of imperial China, a recent study has shown, is not as Sinocentric, unvarying, and rigid as much of the literature has suggested. Instead, enough cases have been discovered in the history of traditional Chinese foreign policy to show divergent and competing patterns of external behavior, ranging from expansion and integration to disintegration and coexistence.[29]

Even German sinologist Jurgen Domes, who engages in factional analysis to a fault, concedes that all successive intraelite confrontations and factional differentiations among the leadership have not been, for the most part, concerned with foreign policy issues, nor has he found any evidence that even *current* post-Mao Chinese policy toward the Soviet Union is under dispute.[30] Yet a PRC scholar makes exactly the opposite point: "Powerful forces inside China are moving Beijing to discuss seriously an independent foreign policy, neither pro-Washington nor pro-Moscow. And this is the general course Chinese foreign policy is likely to follow in the years ahead."[31]

Without denying some influence of factional politics on some foreign policy issues (especially resource allocation, where bureaucratic and regional stakes are high), some argue that Mao's domination offers a more potent "domestic" explanation for the redefinition and restructuring of China's strategic behavior during the first three decades of PRC foreign policy.[32] Foreign policy restructuring is rarely a response to the importunings of domestic factions.[33]

Of course, the political culture approach can shed some light on the conceptual and stylistic aspects of Chinese foreign policy, such as the tendency to define national power in terms of rectitude and to project and transpose the domestic model or rules of the game into the realm of international relations. But the more critical question of how, in what ways, and to what extent the cultural influence of foreign policy behavior is expressed (rather than modified) in the larger social and institutional contexts of foreign policy–making and world politics still remains.

The linkage between domestic politics and manifest foreign policy behavior during a specified period seems a more promising path to take. China's domestic politics, whether defined in terms of national interest, group or factional politics, or leadership, seems to provide the only possible explanation for the autarkic behavior displayed during the most intense phase of the Cultural Revolution. There is broad, if not unanimous, agreement on this point.[34]

External/Systemic Factors

Until recently, the comparative foreign policy literature has been primarily concerned with the linkages between domestic/societal sources and resultant external behavior. This domestic (Sinocentric) bias is even more pronounced in the study of Chinese foreign policy. If the breakdown of consensus politics in the United States and China's self-imposed isolationism provided a rationale for the domestic/societal approach in the 1960s,[35] the alarming realities of the larger global environment have highlighted the importance of external/systemic factors. A series of UN-sponsored single-issue global conferences in the 1970s have revealed the systemic pathology and its impact on the foreign policy behavior of states.

Since the mid-1970s, prodded by the global problematique of increasing interdependence and fragmentation and by the widening gap between global reality and mainstream research, several contending macrostructural systemic approaches have emerged as serious alternative models in international relations research. Comparative foreign policy also has been affected by this trend. In search of the "lost paradigm," scholars in this area have begun to incorporate a world-system perspective, moving in the direction of "a more judicious balance between quantitative and qualitative, historical and current, case-study, comparative, and statistical research designs."[36]

Practically all systemic approaches proceed on the assumption that the external behavior of states is shaped in varying degrees by external/ systemic factors. No state is an island; every state is part of a larger world environment that provides opportunities as well as constraints on state behavior. According to this approach, the system itself defines the role, position, status ranking, and norms of its interacting units (states); the reactions of member states to systemic variables are similar and thus predictable.[37] To borrow from Rousseau: The state is born independent and equal but everywhere it is in systemic chains. At times, the systemic approach moves perilously close to environmental determinism.

Notice how two leading system theorists of sharply divergent normative orientations see the linkage between systemic variables and foreign policy behavior. The "world-system" approach, exemplified in Immanuel Wallerstein's macrostructural and macrohistorical investigation of the emergence of world capitalism, views the international system as essentially based upon a global division of labor, in which an exchange of unequal value takes place between core, peripheral and semiperipheral areas. Even the "so-called socialist states," argues Wallerstein, "are in fact socialist movements in power in states that are still part of a single capitalist world-economy."[38] For Kenneth Waltz, a system theorist of the more traditional realpolitik variety and a prominent proponent of bipolarity as a system stabilizer, the international system is composed of a structure and interacting parts. The structure of this system acts as a "constraining and disposing force," producing a systemwide similarity in foreign policy behavior or what he calls "process and performance." As a result, the behavior of states as interacting units and the outcomes of their behavior become both explainable and predictable.[39] In both cases, however, the impact of systemic variables is conceptualized as deterministic rather than probabilistic and differential.

What are the principal external/systemic factors influencing Chinese foreign policy behavior? International values/norms and international structure can be singled out as the principal systemic factors, on the assumption that human behavior, including the behavior of the state, is conditioned by the values, norms, and structure of a given society. The international system may also be conceived of as a sort of society with its own values, norms, and structure.[40]

International values provide standards of desirable and preferable state behavior. But how—and where—do we find empirical evidence of values in a multicultural international society? A careful, systematic analysis of the policy pronouncements and policy performance of state actors in various normative domains of international relations, and of the progressive codification of some commonly shared values (e.g., the UN Charter), provides preliminary clues. International norms are specific prescriptive or proscriptive rules of state behavior appropriate to a particular role or situation, elaborated or codified in accordance with the value system of the global society. They vary greatly in scope of codification and degree of precision or effectiveness. International norms may appear in the form of written bilateral and multilateral treaties and conventions, unwritten international customs and usage, hortatory resolutions and declarations of international organizations and conferences, and even unilateral self-restraint. International values and norms, which are often used interchangeably in international relations research, act as a socializing agent for state behavior.

A number of studies have addressed the influence of international values and norms, defined largely in terms of international law, upon the conduct of Chinese foreign policy during the Maoist era.[41] Yet China's "great legal leap outward" has occurred since 1978. We may take Chinese behavior in international organizations as a point of departure for this type of explanatory approach. Because the Third World exists as a global actor only in the context of international organizations, this behavior largely overlaps and complements Chinese behavior toward Third World countries. To what extent, and in what specific ways, do international organizations and norms affect Chinese foreign policy behavior? How many norm-defying and treaty-violating actions have been committed in spite of the constraints of international law? How many actions have been prevented by the constraints of international legal norms? In an analysis of Soviet treaty compliance between 1918 and 1957, the Soviet infidelity ratio was estimated at less than 1.2 percent of 2,457 treaties.[42] How would China's treaty compliance compare with the Soviet record?

International structure reflects the composition and stratification of the interacting units. The nature and scope of interactions—a function of the number and type of actors participating in the social process—suggest an empirical image of international structure. The distribution of certain rights and responsibilities conveys a normative image of international structure. International structure defines the role, position, and status of each interacting member. The distribution of power and the ensuing status drive are generally assumed to be the most critical systemic factors affecting the foreign policy behavior of states.

Small states, given their size and dependency, are especially vulnerable to external/systemic pressures. Yet the restructuring power of the international system is such that China too lies within the range of systemic penetration. Whether China's reintegration into, and reformation by, the capitalist world-system is a matter of choice or necessity is another question.[43]

To what extent and in what way can it be said that Chinese foreign policy behavior is shaped by "power" (in contrast to ideological) considerations? The problem with this general line of inquiry lies in the elusive and multifaceted nature of power in contemporary international relations. As the faces of power change, so does the definition of power or powerlessness. At one time, the resort to military force was regarded as a sure sign of national power. At present, however, it is more likely to be perceived as a reminder of national frustration and aggression, a symptomatic expression that a nation has indeed lost its influence (and power) in the conduct of its foreign policy. As Algeria and Vietnam have demonstrated so convincingly, even in war David can sometimes stalemate, or even defeat, Goliath.

With some risk of oversimplification, one can identify two basic kinds of power in contemporary international relations: material power and normative power. Material power refers to conventional national capabilities based on measurable economic, military, demographical, and technological factors; normative power (often neglected in the systemic approach) is the ability to define, control, and transform the agenda of world politics and to legitimate a new dominant paradigm.

This dual conception of power reveals a paradox in Chinese policy. During much of the Maoist era, when the notion of normative power was still in its infancy in world politics, China made a virtue out of weakness by defining "national power" as a sum total of both material and normative power.[44] During the post-Mao era, however, when the notion of normative power has become an integral part of global politics, this conception of national power has been abandoned. The post-Mao leadership increasingly defines national status in terms of material power.[45]

Starting from the widely accepted premise that the distribution of "power" in the international system (and China's status in the system) is the most critical variable affecting and explaining foreign policy behavior, a number of writers in the field of Chinese foreign policy have attempted to capture the quintessence of that policy by combining the national interest (power) approach with the response-to-external-stimulus approach.[46] The resulting amalgam has made a significant contribution to understanding the impact of the superpowers upon the reorientation and restructuring of Chinese foreign policy. At times, the external/systemic impact has constituted a "preemptive strike" against domestic politics. As Roderick MacFarquhar has shown, the principal reason for Mao's lack of attention to domestic affairs in 1959–1960 was the preemption of the Chinese political agenda by Sino-Soviet relations.[47]

Yet an external/systemic model based on national interest considerations has several problems. First, it is more relevant to crisis and strategic behavior than to routine and low priority political behavior. A 1969 WEIS (World Events Interaction Survey) study concluded that conflict behavior in the international system is not the dominant type; instead, there is an even balance among three general classes of behavior: cooperative behavior (33 percent); conflict behavior (31.5 percent); and participatory behavior (35.5 percent). A later empirical study based on the same WEIS data detailed a similar distribution of foreign policy behavior: cooperative action (5.3 percent); participation (46.8 percent); diplomatic exchange (16.9 percent); verbal conflict (18.4 percent); non-military conflict (8.0 percent); and military conflict (4.6 percent).[48] Utilizing data from the WEIS project, Dina Zinnes concluded that the action-reaction model provided "unbelievably and almost universally poor fits."[49]

Second, the motives behind Mao's restructuring of Chinese foreign policy should not be reduced to a predictable reaction based solely on the national interest or on realpolitik considerations. Mao's evolving image of contradictions in the international system played an equally important part in Chinese foreign policy change. Third, the response-to-external-stimulus model is a poor fit for the Sino-Soviet arms race. The Sino-Soviet arms race showed neither an exponential curve nor an S-shaped logistic curve to follow the logic of the action-reaction model, obviously because of the nonsystemic intervening variables. In short, the problem with this type of external/systemic approach is its inability to account for the different reactions of states to the same systemic variables caused by the intervention of nonsystemic variables during the foreign policy–making process.

An alternative approach is to apply rank (status) disequilibrium theory, a variant on the power hypothesis. This theory posits that in a stratified social system, members of the system react to disequilibrium, and especially to perceived status inconsistency resulting from the difference between achieved and ascribed statuses, in similar ways. The theory can be conceptualized and operationalized at a dyadic or a systemic level. Approached in this way, the accelerated modernization drive in the post-Mao era suggests several explanatory hypotheses. The drive could be primarily motivated by (1) an intense status drive—the drive to make China a strong and powerful country by the year 2000 and thus to bridge the gap between ascribed and achieved status; (2) the pressure of a born-again realism (and opportunism) to take advantage of systemic opportunities and payoffs by becoming a de facto partner of world capitalism; or (3) Maoist strategic realism, seeking to maximize long-term self-reliant development by minimizing or neutralizing short-term systemic constraints and penalties.

Domestic/External Linkages

The factors that influence Chinese foreign policy behavior may not fall neatly into the dichotomous categories of domestic/societal and external/systemic variables. Both sets of variables involve structural as well as cognitive elements, and they interact during the decision-making process. Which factors in the linkage between domestic and external variables are more relevant to decision making is a matter of elite perception. "If men define situations as real," as W. I. Thomas once put it, "they are real in their consequences."[50] If we follow the logic of this "cognitive behaviorism,"[51] the "operational environment" of external/systemic constraints or opportunities cannot have any significant meaning or influence for Chinese foreign policy unless or until it is perceived and acted upon by key Chinese decision makers within their own "psychological environment." Chinese foreign policy is seen as the product of an ongoing encounter between decision makers' perceptions of needs, interests, and values and their perceptions of reality.

There is some evidence that Chinese leaders view domestic and external variables in a mutually interactive manner. Two examples may suffice here. In making a public declaration of the open-door policy as "another turning point in Chinese history," Deng Xiaoping said: "To accelerate China's modernization we must not only make use of other countries' experience. We must also avail ourselves of foreign funding. *In past years international conditions worked against us. Later, when the international climate was favourable, we did not take advantage of it. It is now time to use our opportunities.*"[52] In a paper presented at the symposium, "China's Future Position in Asia," sponsored jointly by the Tokyo Colloquium and the *Yomiuri Shimbun*, Pei Monong, senior researcher and deputy director of the Chinese Institute of International Studies, also argues that the future role and position of China will be determined by internal developments and external events.[53]

To note the substantial interaction between domestic and external variables is not to explain how and why the two intermix under certain circumstances and not under others. Another puzzle is why and how one set of variables predominates over the other in one problem area but not in another. One writer "solves" this problem by assigning "the weighted average" of domestic, great power, and systemic factors to Chinese foreign policy orientations.[54] However, a particular model or theory for explicating foreign policy behavior in one issue-problem area or in one historical period may prove unsatisfactory for explaining such behavior in another issue-problem area in the same or another historical period.

An understanding of the pattern of linkages between domestic/ societal and external/systemic factors calls for closer attention to mediating variables during the decision-making phase. As shown in Figure 1.1, mediating variables intervene between predecisional independent variables and postdecisional dependent variables to lay the analytic-cognitive basis for the decision makers' definition of the situation and for the authoritative formulation of foreign policy goals and strategies.

The virtually unexplored notion of circular feedback may be a crucial component in explaining whether Chinese foreign policy behavior is adaptive or maladaptive. How does the Chinese foreign policy system handle "heat" and "flak" coming from both domestic and foreign audiences? Such difficulties may stem either from "intolerable" actions by other state actors (e.g., the Dutch and U.S. arms sales to Taiwan, the Soviet invasion of Afghanistan, or the Vietnamese invasion of Kampuchea) or from negative reactions to China's own foreign policy behavior (e.g., the growing reputation of post-Mao China as a system-supporting power and the peripheralization of the Third World). Is there a homeostatic self-critical and self-correcting control system in the Chinese foreign policy process? Or does each input prompt a more intense recurrence of earlier behavior through an amplifying feedback system?

During the critical period between the Opium War (1839–1842) and the allied military expedition to Beijing in 1860, China's "barbarian specialists" became more sensitive to the caprices of the Court than to the objective demands of the actual situation, memorializing to the throne what they believed the emperor wanted to hear rather than what he needed to hear. Even though none of them shouted that the emperor had no clothes, ironically enough, few barbarian specialists fared well during the interwar transition period. This was a positive feedback system which functioned by intensifying the cognitive rigidity of the foreign policy elite.[55]

We can safely assume that the contemporary Chinese foreign policy system also has its own feedback process. Whether the substance is positive and amplifying or negative and homeostatic is not subject to empirical analysis. After extensive field interviews with officials of the Chinese Ministry of Foreign Affairs (MFA) and related organizations, one scholar acknowledges: "It has been nearly impossible to obtain information about *how* decisions are taken and by whom, how communications are routed from the field to Beijing and vice versa, and how a Chinese MFA official evaluates the field performance of a given ambassador or embassy."[56]

Conceptually, the post-Mao principle of seeking truth from the facts represents a negative, homeostatic feedback better suited for adaptive foreign policy behavior. Insofar as that process concerned Sino-Soviet relations, Wang Youping, the Chinese ambassador to Moscow during much of the 1970s, provides a revealing post hoc admission that for a variety of reasons, his embassy always reported what the home audience wanted to hear. The Soviet Union was caught in a double bind of domestic and external difficulties from which there was no exit. Wang now proposes a more "realistic" approach, exposing and evaluating all the facts and reaching a consensus through a step-by-step incremental process.[57]

At any rate, the changes and shifts in Chinese foreign policy since late 1981 theoretically provide a fertile ground for formulating a variety of domestic/external linkage hypotheses for both qualitative and quantitative analyses. Each source, whether domestic or external, should be viewed in a probabilistic rather than a deterministic manner to limit the range of permissible and possible foreign policy behavior choices that can be made in a given period.

THE FUTURE OF CHINESE FOREIGN POLICY BEHAVIOR

The method that should be stressed in considering the future of Chinese foreign policy behavior is *forecasting*, not *prediction*. As Nazli Choucri put it: "A prediction is generally made in terms of a point or event; a forecast is made in terms of alternatives. A prediction focuses upon one outcome, a forecast involves contingencies."[58] The unmanageably large number of known variables includes: the magnitude of the unknowns, the volatile nature of political phenomena, the resistance of available data to controlled experiment, the elusiveness of values in quantitative analysis, the complex and mysterious interaction between domestic/ societal and external/systemic factors, and the pronounced tendency for discontinuous shifts and changes in the contemporary international system. Consequently, the study of both foreign policy and international relations is unlikely to profit from prediction.[59]

The recent history of foreign policy/international relations research is replete with examples of erroneous predictions and glaring failures to anticipate major events. A few cases may suffice. Writing in 1960, Karl Wittfogel flatly declared that the idea of a Sino-Soviet break was "palpably absurd."[60] Ithiel de Sola Pool predicted in 1965 that "major fighting in Vietnam will peter out about 1967; and most objective observers will regard it as a substantial American victory."[61] In the grandiose long-term trend projection of *The Year 2000*, Herman Kahn and Anthony Wiener failed to anticipate such major international events as the ecological movement, the oil crisis and the transformation of the international petroleum regime, or the global stagflation of the 1970s.[62] A 1965 survey of some 171 foreign policy specialists (from U.S. government agencies, academia, and the media) showed an accuracy rate or level that was hardly better than one might expect from random chance.[63]

These examples underscore the hazard of prediction as well as the need for sensitivity to countervailing trends. A forecast can help to foster a better understanding of the future of Chinese foreign policy by identifying the range of behavior in a specified problem area or toward a specified target. A forecast based on a knowledge of recurring patterns in the history of Chinese foreign policy and the relationship between known variables can also help in developing contingency plans (in policymaking and in research design) for alternative future events. When "exploratory forecasting" (extrapolation of various alternative trends) and "normative forecasting" (restructuring of preferred and probable futures) are combined, there is a greater likelihood of depicting "possible futures."

In speculating about the possible futures of post-Mao Chinese foreign policy behavior in the 1980s, the open-door policy and its impact on foreign policy legitimation can be considered the centerpiece of the present inquiry. If Leonid Brezhnev has "brought foreign policy home to the USSR,"[64] as Alexander Dallin argues, Deng Xiaoping's open-door policy may be said to have brought Chinese foreign policy to the home audience. By widening the eye of the needle to let all kinds of "necessary" goods and bads pass through the gateway of China's nexus with the capitalist world in the name of "modernity," however, the post-Mao leadership has also opened a Pandora's box for foreign policy legitimation.

The ever-increasing linkage between domestic and foreign policy means that a nation's external behavior—and its perceived legitimacy or illegitimacy—directly affects the legitimacy of political leaders at home. In an age when national independence, equality, anticolonialism, and antihegemonism represent major international values, more and more Third World leaders are seeking political legitimacy at home through foreign policy behavior. In the context of the North-South dialogue or the confrontation arising from the New International Economic Order (NIEO), "the most vigorous support for Third World demands for regime transformation has come from countries where such policies contributed to domestic political legitimacy."[65]

The born-again independence and nationalism movement, coupled with renewed linkage with the Third World and "equidistance" from the two superpowers since late 1981, can be hypothesized as a function of the self-correcting feedback process designed to minimize the illegitimacy fallouts from an open-door (and thus dependent) foreign policy. *The Selected Works of Deng Xiaoping, 1975–1982*, published in mid-1983, has little to say about foreign policy with the exception of a belabored legitimation of the new open-door policy.[66] In keeping with Deng's open door, several post-Mao historical schools also began to rewrite accounts of the historical Open Door of 1900 in Sino-American relations. The ultimate intent of this new debate among Chinese historians is suggested in their appeal for "an upgrading of our knowledge of and research on the outside world to correspond with the new status of our country in international society"[67] and their attempt to seek a more legitimizing "fit" between China and the capitalist world-system.

Can the Chinese leadership restructure the open-door policy so as to let the "goods" in and the "bads" out in their quintessential quest for political legitimacy in the post-Mao era? Can the renewed attempt to balance and integrate "material civilization" and "spiritual civilization" succeed without stirring another big wave of the two-line struggle between party and deviationist policy?

The behavior-centered approach simply cannot avoid engaging in forecasting, because every Chinese foreign policy behavior is goal-directed and future-oriented. Explaining Chinese foreign policy behavior necessitates exploratory forecasting of both domestic/societal and external/systemic trends to establish empirically feasible parameters for various alternative futures. It is to be hoped that the kinds of typologies and procedures outlined in this chapter for describing and explaining Chinese foreign policy behavior will provide a reliable foundation for a more disciplined speculation about the future prospects of post-Mao Chinese policy options and directions.

NOTES

I acknowledge with appreciation the critical comments of William Feeney, James C. Hsiung, Steven I. Levine, Peter Van Ness, and Allen S. Whiting on an earlier draft of this chapter.

1. See Roger Dial, *Studies on Chinese External Affairs: An Instructional Bibliography of Commonwealth and American Literature* (Halifax, Nova Scotia: Centre for Foreign Policy Studies, Dalhousie University, 1973).

2. For further discussion on the two schools, see Robert Boardman, "Themes and Explanation in Sinology," in Roger L. Dial, ed., *Advancing and Contending Approaches to the Study of Chinese Foreign Policy* (Halifax, Nova Scotia: Centre for Foreign Policy Studies, Dalhousie University, 1974), pp. 3–50; John K. Fairbank, ed., *The Chinese World Order* (Cambridge, Mass.: Harvard University Press, 1968); Samuel S. Kim, *China, the United Nations, and World Order* (Princeton, N.J.: Princeton University Press, 1979), pp. 90–93; Mark Mancall, "The Persistence of Tradition in Chinese Foreign Policy," *Annals of the American Academy of Political and Social Science* 349 (September 1963):14–26; and Ross Terrill, ed., *The China Difference* (New York: Harper & Row, 1979); quote in the text is taken from John K. Fairbank, "The State that Mao Built," *World Politics* 19 (July 1967):665–666.

3. Thomas W. Robinson, "Restructuring Chinese Foreign Policy, 1959–1976: Three Episodes," in K. J. Holsti et al., *Why Nations Realign: Foreign Policy*

Restructuring in the Postwar World (London: George Allen & Unwin, 1982), p. 134.

4. Michael Ng-Quinn, "The Analytic Study of Chinese Foreign Policy," *International Studies Quarterly* 27 (June 1983):204, 211.

5. Harry Harding, "Change and Continuity in Chinese Foreign Policy," *Problems of Communism* 32 (March-April 1983):18–19.

6. Compare and contrast the following works on this point: Joseph Camilleri, *Chinese Foreign Policy: The Maoist Era and Its Aftermath* (Seattle: University of Washington Press, 1980); Harding, "Change and Continuity in Chinese Foreign Policy"; Robinson, "Restructuring Chinese Foreign Policy"; and Michael Yahuda, *China's Role in World Affairs* (New York: St. Martin's Press, 1978) and *Towards the End of Isolationism: China's Foreign Policy After Mao* (New York: St. Martin's Press, 1983).

7. Robert C. Tucker, *Politics as Leadership* (Columbia: University of Missouri Press, 1981).

8. For details, see Patrick Callahan, "The CREON Project," in Patrick Callahan, Linda P. Brady, and Margaret G. Hermann, eds., *Describing Foreign Policy Behavior* (Beverly Hills, Calif.: Sage Publications, 1982), pp. 31–51.

9. On the global political economy data, for example, the CREON data cannot match the periodic publications of the World Bank and International Monetary Fund in quality, reliability, and usage. In their careful study of Chinese crisis behavior, Davis Bobrow, Steve Chan, and John Kringen also discovered major differences in both the total number of events and their distribution in three event data sources: CREON data based on *Deadline Data on World Affairs*; the *New York Times Index*; and *Renmin ribao* [People's daily]. Based on this finding, they caution against the use of CREON data and suggest "that we should develop historical event data files from the perspectives of the national subject of analysis before we attempt to locate statistical patterns in and to build models of its past behavior." Two minor objections may be raised here: first, the above criticism is not as valid in the comparative, crossnational study of foreign policy behavior in the implementation phase; and second, the CREON event data sources include *Renmin ribao*, Xinhua [New China] News Agency, and *Peking Review*, although the combined total of these three Chinese sources amount to only 0.5 percent of the total CREON sources. See Davis Bobrow, Steve Chan, and John A. Kringen, "Understanding How Others Treat Crises: A Multimethod Approach," *International Studies Quarterly* 21 (March 1977):217.

10. See Hu Yaobang, "Create a New Situation in All Fields of Socialist Modernization—Report to the 12th National Congress of the Communist Party of China, September 1, 1982," *Beijing Review* [hereafter cited as *BR*], No. 37 (September 13, 1982):11–40; Deng Xiaoping's public declaration during the visit of UN Secretary-General Perez de Cuellar, in *BR*, No. 35 (August 30, 1982):7; Qi Wen, "Correctly Understand Our Country's Independent Foreign Policy," *Hongqi* [Red flag], No. 21 (1982):24–28; Pei Monong, "The Future Position of China in Asia," *Shijie zhishi* [World knowledge], No. 10 (1983):2–4; and Foreign Minister Wu Xueqian's interview with the French journal *Politiqué Etrangère* in *Shijie zhishi*, No. 13 (1983):2–4.

11. Peter Van Ness, *Revolution and Chinese Foreign Policy: Peking's Support for Wars of National Liberation* (Berkeley: University of California Press, 1971).

12. See Davis B. Bobrow, Steve Chan, and John A. Kringen, *Understanding Foreign Policy Decisions* (New York: Free Press, 1979); Bobrow, Chan, and Kringen, "Understanding How Others Treat Crisis"; Steve Chan, "Chinese Conflict

Calculus and Behavior: Assessment from a Perspective of Conflict Management,"
World Politics 30 (April 1978):391–410; Melvin Gurtov and Byong-Moo Hwang,
China Under Threat: The Politics of Strategy and Diplomacy (Baltimore: Johns
Hopkins University Press, 1980); Allen S. Whiting, *China Crosses the Yalu: The
Decision to Enter the Korean War* (New York: Macmillan, 1960) and *The Chinese
Calculus of Deterrence* (Ann Arbor: University of Michigan Press, 1975).

13. Abraham Kaplan, *The Conduct of Inquiry* (San Francisco: Chandler,
1964), p. 28.

14. The CREON study's finding on the distribution of China's foreign policy
instruments is also suggestive. In an eight-category typology of foreign policy
instruments, the largest concentration was on "diplomatic" (63.7 percent of the
total) and the smallest on "intelligence" (0 percent of the total). See Charles
Hermann, "Instruments of Foreign Policy," in Callahan, Brady, and Hermann,
Describing Foreign Policy Behavior, Table 7.3, p. 167.

15. To cite one example, Beijing's withdrawal of support for the Thai
Communist revolutionary movement has recently reached the point of shutting
down the insurgent radio station, the Voice of the People of Thailand, which
had been transmitting from China for years. *New York Times*, July 4, 1983, pp.
1–2.

16. For further elaboration of this approach, see Robert Axelrod, ed., *Structure
of Decision: The Cognitive Maps of Political Elites* (Princeton, N.J.: Princeton
University Press, 1976); Jeffrey A. Hart, "Cognitive Maps of Three Latin American
Policy Makers," *World Politics* 30 (October 1977):115–140.

17. James T. Tedeschi et al., "A Reinterpretation of Research on Aggression,"
Psychological Bulletin 81 (September 1974):557–558.

18. R. T. Green and G. Santori, "A Cross Cultural Study of Hostility and
Aggression," *Journal of Peace Research* 6, 1 (1969):13–22.

19. See Samuel S. Kim, "Behavioural Dimensions of Chinese Multilateral
Diplomacy," *China Quarterly*, No. 72 (December 1977):713–742.

20. For further elaboration, see Samuel S. Kim, "The Political Economy of
Post-Mao China in Global Perspective," in Neville Maxwell and Bruce McFarlane,
eds., *China's Changed Road to Development* (Oxford: Pergamon Press, 1984), pp.
213–232; and Friedrich W. Wu, "Socialist Self-Reliant Development Within the
Capitalist World-Economy: The Chinese View in the Post-Mao Era," *Global
Perspectives: An Interdisciplinary Journal of International Relations* 1 (Spring
1983):8–34.

21. General Assembly Official Records (GAOR), Sixth Special Sess., Ad Hoc
Committee, tenth meeting (18 April 1974), para. 15.

22. Margaret Hermann, "Independence/Interdependence of Action," in Callahan, Brady, and Hermann, *Describing Foreign Policy Behavior*, pp. 251–253.

23. Friedrich W. Wu, "Explanatory Approaches to Chinese Foreign Policy:
A Critique of the Western Literature," *Studies in Comparative Communism* 13
(Spring 1980):41–62.

24. For the most complete exposition of the domestic sources of Soviet
foreign policy, see Seweryn Bialer, ed., *The Domestic Context of Soviet Foreign
Policy* (Boulder, Colo.: Westview Press, 1981).

25. Holsti et al., *Why Nations Realign*, p. 208.

26. John K. Fairbank, "China's Foreign Policy in Historical Perspective,"
Foreign Affairs 47 (April 1969):449. See also the works listed in note 2 above.

27. See Richard H. Solomon, *Mao's Revolution and the Chinese Political
Culture* (Berkeley: University of California Press, 1971); Simon Leys, *Chinese*

Shadows (New York: Penguin Books, 1978); Ramon H. Myers and Thomas A. Metzger, "Sinological Shadows: The State of Modern China Studies in the United States," *Washington Quarterly* 3 (Spring 1980):87–114; and Lucian Pye, *The Dynamic of Chinese Politics* (Cambridge, Mass.: Oelgeschlager, Gunn & Hain, 1981).

28. Pye, *Dynamic of Chinese Politics.*

29. Michael Ng-Quinn, "China and International Systems: History, Structures, Processes," (Ph.D. diss., Harvard University, 1978). In the study of Soviet foreign policy, as Alexander Dallin perceptively notes, " 'political culture' has repeatedly become the residual category that has served as the catchbasin for everything that could not otherwise be explained." Alexander Dallin, "The Domestic Sources of Soviet Foreign Policy," in Bialer, *Domestic Context of Soviet Foreign Policy,* p. 356.

30. Jurgen Domes, "Domestic Sources of PRC Policy Toward the USSR," in Douglas T. Stuart and William T. Tow, eds., *China, the Soviet Union, and the West: Strategic and Political Dimensions in the 1980s* (Boulder, Colo.: Westview Press, 1982), pp. 25–38.

31. Edmund Lee [pseud.], "Beijing's Balancing Act," *Foreign Policy,* No. 51 (Summer 1983):28.

32. For the Mao-domination thesis, see Holsti et al., *Why Nations Realign,* pp. 204, 208–209; John Gittings, *The World and China, 1922–1972* (New York: Harper & Row, 1974); Samuel S. Kim, *The Maoist Image of World Order* (Princeton, N.J.: Center of International Studies, Princeton University, 1977); Michel Oksenberg, "Mao's Policy Commitments, 1921–1976," *Problems of Communism* 25 (November-December 1976):1–26; and Yahuda, *Towards the End of Isolationism.*

33. Holsti et al., *Why Nations Realign,* p. 210.

34. See Harding, "Change and Continuity in Chinese Foreign Policy"; Kuang-sheng Liao, "Linkage Politics in China: Internal Mobilization and Articulated External Hostility in the Cultural Revolution 1967–1969," *World Politics* 28 (July 1976):590–610; and Robinson, "Restructuring Chinese Foreign Policy."

35. For an elaboration of this point as the operational premise of a major interdisciplinary study of the domestic sources of foreign policy, see Rosenau's introduction in James N. Rosenau, ed., *Domestic Sources of Foreign Policy* (New York: Free Press, 1967), pp. 1–10.

36. Pat McGowan and Charles W. Kegley, Jr., eds., *Foreign Policy and the Modern World-System,* Vol. 8, *Sage International Yearbook of Foreign Policy Studies* (Beverly Hills, Calif.: Sage Publications, 1983), p. 9.

37. This line of argument is most fully developed in Evan Luard's study of seven historical international systems. Evan Luard, *Types of International Society* (New York: Free Press, 1976).

38. Immanuel Wallerstein, *The Capitalist World-Economy* (New York: Cambridge University Press, 1979), p. 280.

39. Kenneth N. Waltz, *Theory of International Politics* (Reading, Mass.: Addison-Wesley, 1979), pp. 79–96.

40. For recent PRC scholarly articles on the normative and structural changes in the international system, especially on the ideological isolation and relative power decline of the superpowers causing multipolarization trends, see Zhang Zhen and Rong Zhi, "Some Reflections on the 'Policy of Detente'," *Guoji wenti yanjiu* [Journal of international studies], No. 4 (1982):18–23; Xing Shugang, Li Yunhua, and Liu Yingna, "Soviet-American Balance of Power and Its Impact on the World Situation in the 1980s," *Guoji wenti yanjiu,* No. 1 (1983):25–31,

63–64; "Surging Tide of the Times—The Non-Alignment Movement," *Guoji wenti yanjiu*, No. 2 (1983):3–9; and Li Dai, "The Impact of Current World Economic Crisis on International Relations," *Hongqi*, No. 7 (1983):31–34.

41. See James C. Hsiung, *Law and Policy in China's Foreign Relations: A Study of Attitudes and Practice* (New York: Columbia University Press, 1972); Jerome Alan Cohen and Hungdah Chiu, *People's China and International Law: A Documentary Study*, 2 vols. (Princeton, N.J.: Princeton University Press, 1974); and Samuel S. Kim, "The People's Republic of China and the Charter-Based International Legal Order," *American Journal of International Law* 62 (April 1978):317–349.

42. Jan F. Triska and Robert M. Slusser, *The Theory, Law and Policy of Soviet Treaties* (Stanford, Calif.: Stanford University Press, 1962).

43. For the restructuring impact of external/systemic variables on Chinese foreign policy, see Camilleri, *Chinese Foreign Policy*; Bruce Cumings, "The Political Economy of Chinese Foreign Policy," *Modern China* 5 (October 1979):450–452; Edward Friedman, "On Maoist Conceptualizations of the Capitalist World System," *China Quarterly*, No. 80 (December 1979):836–837; Gittings, *The World and China*; Ng-Quinn, "The Analytic Study of Chinese Foreign Policy"; Michael Ng-Quinn, "Effects of Bipolarity on Chinese Foreign Policy," *Survey* 26 (Spring 1982):102–130; and Jonathan D. Pollack, "China in the Evolving International System," in Norton Ginsburg and Bernard A. Lalor, eds., *China: The '80s Era* (Boulder, Colo.: Westview Press, 1984).

44. See, for example, "On Protracted War, May 1938," in *Selected Military Writings of Mao Tse-Tung* (Peking: Foreign Languages Press, 1966), p. 198; *Renmin ribao* editorial, November 25, 1957, p. 1; and Mao's statement on the occasion of the U.S.–South Vietnamese invasion of Cambodia, "People of the World, Unite and Defeat the U.S. Aggressors and All Their Running Dogs," in *Peking Review*, Special Issue, May 23, 1970, p. 9.

45. For elaboration see Kim, "The Political Economy of Post-Mao China."

46. See Lowell Dittmer, "The Strategic Triangle: An Elementary Game–Theoretical Analysis," *World Politics* 33 (July 1981):485–515; Harold C. Hinton, *China's Turbulent Quest*, rev. ed. (Bloomington: Indiana University Press, 1972); Ng-Quinn, "Effects of Bipolarity" and "The Analytic Study of Chinese Foreign Policy"; James Reardon-Anderson, *Yenan and the Great Powers: The Origins of Chinese Communist Foreign Policy, 1944–1946* (New York: Columbia University Press, 1980); Allen S. Whiting, "The Use of Force in Foreign Policy by the People's Republic of China," *Annals of Academy of Political and Social Science* 402 (July 1972):55–66; Van Ness, *Revolution and Chinese Foreign Policy*; and Donald S. Zagoria, "Ideology and Chinese Foreign Policy," in George Schwab, ed., *Ideology and Foreign Policy* (New York: Cyrco Press, 1978), pp. 103–116.

47. Roderick MacFarquhar, *The Origins of the Cultural Revolution*, Vol. 2: *The Great Leap Forward, 1958–1960* (New York: Columbia University Press, 1983).

48. Charles A. McClelland and Gary D. Hoggard, "Conflict Patterns in the Interactions Among Nations," in James N. Rosenau, ed., *International Politics and Foreign Policy*, rev. ed. (New York: Free Press, 1969), pp. 711–724; and Stephen A. Salmore and Donald Munton, "An Empirically Based Typology of Foreign Policy Behavior," in James N. Rosenau, ed., *Comparing Foreign Policies: Theories, Findings, and Methods* (Beverly Hills, Calif.: Sage Publications, 1974), p. 344.

49. Dina A. Zinnes, "Three Puzzles in Search of a Researcher," *International Studies Quarterly* 24 (September 1980):321.

50. W. I. Thomas, *The Child in America* (New York: Knopf, 1928), p. 572. Robert K. Merton asserts that this famous statement of Thomas has now become

"a theorem basic to the social sciences." See Robert K. Merton, *Social Theory and Social Structure: Toward the Codification of Theory and Research* (Glencoe, Ill.: Free Press, 1949), p. 179.

51. "Cognitive behaviorism" is the term that Harold and Margaret Sprout used to distinguish and explain the relationship between "the psychological environment (with reference to which an individual defines choices and takes decisions) and the operational environment (which sets limits to what can happen when the decision is executed)." Harold Sprout and Margaret Sprout, "Environmental Factors in the Study of International Politics," in James N. Rosenau, ed., *International Politics and Foreign Policy* (New York: Free Press, 1961), p. 109. For a recent ground-breaking work on the role of perceptions in international relations, see Robert Jervis, *Perception and Misperception in International Politics* (Princeton, N.J.: Princeton University Press, 1976).

52. Deng Xiaoping, "Why China Has Opened Its Door," in Foreign Broadcast Information Service, Daily Report, China, February 12, 1980, p. L3; emphasis added.

53. Pei, "The Future Position of China in Asia."

54. Robinson, "Restructuring Chinese Foreign Policy," p. 155.

55. For further discussion of the traditional Chinese foreign policy system, see Kim, *China, the United Nations, and World Order*, Ch. 1, pp. 19–48.

56. Daniel Tretiak, "Who Makes Chinese Foreign Policy Today (Late 1980)?" *Australian Journal of Chinese Affairs*, No. 5 (1981):138.

57. Wang Youping, "A Talk at Meeting of Chinese Ambassadors," *Guang jiaojing* [Wide-angle lens] (Hong Kong), No. 91 (April 1980):30–31.

58. Nazli Choucri, "Key Issues in International Relations Forecasting," in Nazli Choucri and Thomas W. Robinson, eds., *Forecasting in International Relations: Theory, Methods, Problems, Prospects* (San Francisco: W. H. Freeman and Co., 1978), p. 4.

59. For further analysis and elaboration, see Samuel S. Kim, *The Quest for a Just World Order* (Boulder, Colo.: Westview Press, 1984), Ch. 8, pp. 301–342.

60. Karl A. Wittfogel, "A Stronger Oriental Despotism," *China Quarterly*, No. 1 (January–March 1960):33–34.

61. Quoted in Ralph Pettman, *Human Behavior and World Politics* (New York: St. Martin's Press, 1975), pp. 113–114.

62. Herman Kahn and Anthony J. Wiener, *The Year 2000: A Framework for Speculation on the Next Thirty-Three Years* (New York: Macmillan, 1967).

63. Lloyd Jensen, "Predicting International Events," *Peace Research Reviews* 4 (August 1972):1–65.

64. Dallin, "The Domestic Sources of Soviety Foreign Policy," p. 350.

65. Stephen D. Krasner, "Transforming International Regimes: What the Third World Wants and Why," *International Studies Quarterly* 25 (March 1981):144.

66. See Deng Xiaoping, *Deng Xiaoping wenxuan, 1975–1982* [The selected works of Deng Xiaoping, 1975–1982] (Beijing: Renmin chubanshe, 1983); and Qin Hao, "A Correct Policy Compatible with the Necessity of Historical Development," *Renmin ribao*, July 29, 1983, p. 5.

67. Luo Rongqu and Jiang Xiangze, "Research in Sino-American Relations in the People's Republic of China," in Warren I. Cohen, ed., *New Frontiers in American-Eastern Relations* (New York: Columbia University Press, 1983), p. 8. For details see also Michael H. Hunt, "New Insights but No New Vistas: Recent Work on Nineteenth-Century American–East Asian Relations," also in Cohen, *New Frontiers*, pp. 17–43.

CHAPTER 2

ON A SLOW BOAT TO WHERE? ANALYZING CHINESE FOREIGN POLICY

Davis B. Bobrow
Steve Chan

INTRODUCTION

Surely most analysts of Chinese foreign policy can only sigh at the prospect of still another essay on the state of the art of their subject. Indeed, our initial reaction to the invitation to write this chapter paralleled W. C. Fields's view of a free trip to Philadelphia: the shorter the better. After all, the state of sinology has been the subject over the years of a substantial number of essays by China specialists, outsiders, and in-and-outers like ourselves.[1] The general themes of these articles provide a familiar litany of criticism and flagellation. Furthermore, assessments of the state of the art almost inevitably open oneself to charges of self-glorification, self-deception, or both. The judgmental overtones are at least implicit, with no obvious mandate for the assessors to assume the role of a judge or scorekeeper. Finally, there is the nagging possibility that this sort of essay calls to mind the old joke about lawyers and law teachers. Those who can analyze Chinese foreign policy do so, and those who cannot write about the state of the art.

Why, then, have we gone ahead? First, China matters too much in world politics for us to be content with less than the best possible analysis. This importance is of course largely a consequence of how large China looms in the perceptions of others. Certainly, U.S. foreign policy designs in the past decade, with their often naive emphasis on the "China card," support our view. Chinese foreign policy has played and continues to play no less a role in Japan's foreign policy. The economic and political-military importance of the Asian Pacific further contributes to the status of China, at least to the extent that the Asian newly industrializing countries (NICs) affect the world economy and the future international system. The Soviet Union more than matches the United States in treating Chinese foreign policy as fundamentally important to the pursuit of Moscow's security and power objectives.

For the foreseeable future, there is no obvious rival to China as the champion of the interests of the developing countries as a class, or as a potential future great power by the middle of the next century. None of this explains in objective terms why China should loom so large, or whether great-power status will actually be achieved. Indeed, one of the more important questions about Beijing's foreign policy involves the extent to which the Chinese have created or abetted inflated attributions of importance, and if so, through what stratagems and for what reasons.[2]

Second, Chinese international activities and postures pose some intriguing puzzles. As puzzle solvers, we are naturally attracted by the challenges to theory provided by China's asymmetries in aggregate political, economic, demographic, and military characteristics. The challenges to method posed by abundant public propaganda or guidance and yet enormous gaps in many other kinds of information have intrinsic interest for problems of empirical evidence and inference. Also, change provides social science inquiry with both a source of fascination and endless fodder for intellectual revisionism. The Chinese have surely provided observers over the last several decades with at least superficially dramatic foreign policy alterations. Moreover, the combination of China's longevity as a political and cultural system and the experience of traumatic revolution through civil war provides abundant fuel for arguments about the sources of its foreign policy and about the degree of continuity and change. Accordingly, China offers a stimulating and demanding challenge to prevalent concepts and methods in Western academic studies of foreign policy. State-of-the-art reflections on the analysis of Chinese foreign policy have broad implications for the analysis of foreign policy in general.

If we are to assess analytic products, we also need to be aware of the sociology of analysts as a group or collection of professionals. Some battles couched in the language of debates about analytic payoffs are really fought over stakes involving the relative intellectual and political status of groups or "clubs" of analysts. Obvious cleavages between U.S. sinologists, for example, have involved acceptance or rejection of the legitimacy of the Communist regime and more recently, differences between the younger generation, which is oriented toward field work, and the scholars of the decades before U.S.-PRC normalization, who worked at a distance. Among serious writers on Chinese foreign policy, some are China specialists and others are international relations generalists using China as a case. More recently, a growing number have strong ties to both groups. Finally, one must remember that many U.S. writers on Chinese foreign policy have been advocates of particular policies toward China and targets of Beijing's persuasion to advance Chinese foreign policy. Of course, when an analyst's status rises and falls with foreign judgments of China's international importance, he or she may be a less than perfect judge of what that importance has been, is currently, or will be in the future.

It is unfortunate, though hardly surprising, that these sociological splits have been accompanied by a number of rather unrewarding and unresolvable controversies. We therefore preface our discussion by stating several positions that we hold but shall not debate. First, the Communist regime in Beijing exists. Its "right" to exist is irrelevant to the analysis of its foreign policy. Second, it makes obvious pragmatic sense to follow Allen Whiting's injunction to "remove analysis from the category of exotic inquiry and embed it firmly in the comparative and generic study of world politics."[3] One should use whatever ideas and methods help one to answer questions about Chinese foreign policy. The less satisfied we are with answers produced by traditional ideas and methods, the more it seems reasonable to try out conceptual and methodological tools borrowed from other social science work. Despite limitations, these tools are useful when their areas of strength help to compensate for the weaknesses of more standard approaches.

Third, we view China as unique in some respects and not in others. The dichotomy between unique and typical is oversimplified. The issue can be addressed more usefully in scalar terms (more or less) than in categorical terms (either-or). Moreover, it depends on what we want to know about Chinese foreign policy, and at what level of specificity.

Fourth, we also find some other familiar dichotomies (e.g., Chinese versus Communist, continuity versus change) equally unenlightening. In part, this is because both sides of the dichotomy contain a diversity of phenomena so rich that either side is capable of supporting almost any foreign policy behavior or ex post facto rationale. Finally, questions about the international importance of China and about Chinese foreign policy in relation to the foreign policy of other world actors cannot be answered by treating China in isolation. China must be looked at comparatively and contextually.

The rest of this chapter addresses the analysis of Chinese foreign policy with respect to the two concerns mentioned earlier: policy import and intellectual challenge. We trust the reader will understand by now that our discussion does not imply that the study of Chinese foreign policy is in worse shape than the study of most other states' foreign policies, or that our own previous work on China provides an ideal model that only requires emulation, extension, and refinement.

FOREIGN POLICY ANALYSIS:
CONTENT AND PURPOSE

The analysis of Chinese foreign policy can address a variety of subjects for a variety of purposes. Distinctions are important in establishing priorities, applying appropriate criteria, and coming to grips with the implications of numerous realistic constraints on analysis. Any simple set of distinctions naturally blurs complexity, but perhaps the price is

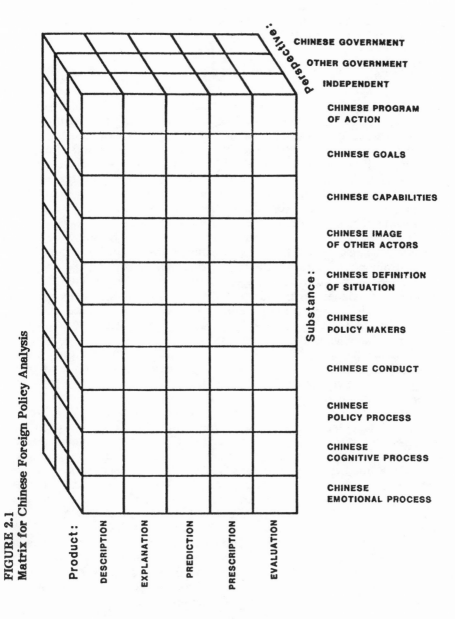

FIGURE 2.1
Matrix for Chinese Foreign Policy Analysis

Perspective:

CHINESE GOVERNMENT

OTHER GOVERNMENT

INDEPENDENT

Substance:

CHINESE PROGRAM OF ACTION

CHINESE GOALS

CHINESE CAPABILITIES

CHINESE IMAGE OF OTHER ACTORS

CHINESE DEFINITION OF SITUATION

CHINESE POLICY MAKERS

CHINESE CONDUCT

CHINESE POLICY PROCESS

CHINESE COGNITIVE PROCESS

CHINESE EMOTIONAL PROCESS

Product:

DESCRIPTION

EXPLANATION

PREDICTION

PRESCRIPTION

EVALUATION

worthwhile for facilitating discussion. Figure 2.1 uses a cube to portray three dimensions in analyses of Chinese foreign policy: *substance* (what do we want to know about), *analytic product* (what sort of answer do we seek), and *perspective* (whose concerns do we try to address). All analyses must necessarily take a position(s) on each of these questions.

Substance

We define a *policy* as a program of actions (be they of omission or commission) chosen to achieve particular goals during a particular time period. The actions envision the use of particular capabilities to affect specific actors in a specific situation. Current and projected situations are themselves likely to affect policy goals and means. Of course, governments do not have goals or decide means: The responsible officials do, and they may or may not agree about goals, means, or situations. Furthermore, the actual conduct of their government may or may not follow the chosen or intended program of actions.

A *foreign* policy is a program of actions intended to influence actors outside a state's jurisdiction. The pertinent goals and situations may range from purely internal to largely external. We doubt that they are ever exclusively external. A government may engage in conduct that influences foreigners in the absence of a foreign policy, independent of a foreign policy, or in contradiction to its foreign policy. And even the actions called for by a state's foreign policy may have consequences that are neither expected nor desired.

The harsh reality is that analysts of Chinese foreign policy, like analysts of many other governments, will rarely have timely and comprehensive knowledge of the chosen program of actions. The problem is instead to determine what we can about the other elements just mentioned, in order to arrive at more or less well-informed and intellectually warranted inferences about foreign policy. To summarize, these other elements are (1) goals or objectives, (2) perceived capabilities, (3) identity and image of foreign actors, (4) identity and definition of prevailing and pending situations, (5) identity and status of decision-making individuals or institutions, and (6) actual conduct. The key elements also include processes—cognitive, emotional, political, and administrative—that link and intervene between these elements in the course of policy formation, adoption, and implementation.

Goals provide the impetus and criteria for choosing programs of action, and public proclamations are obviously an important source for inferring foreign policy goals. Yet one need not be an expert on China to question the sufficiency of public pronouncements as a basis for analytic judgments.[4] Proclamations often present broad values, vague timetables, temporary compromises, and mask the hard choices to be made. Verbal affirmation can be a substitute for actual resource allocation. In a political economy of scarce resources (time, money, expertise, status, patience), current and future Chinese leaders face tough allocation choices of how much by when of what for whom.

Their task is to find an "acceptable" policy. Serious internal discussions about goals must be concerned with setting relative rather than absolute priorities, and with preventing shortfalls beyond some minimum levels of acceptability. The issues center on what the Chinese leadership can afford to postpone or defer, for how long, and at what cost. From this perspective, a small number of key questions about Chinese goals emerge. When do proclaimed goals represent pledges or portents of resource allocation, and when are they substitutes for actual allocation? What are the yardsticks for goal achievement, and in particular, where are the signs for shortfalls so great that they limit the pursuit of other important goals? Which goals will be seriously pursued, and which are simply instrumental or tactical devices to secure acquiescence and political latitude at home and abroad?

Whatever the goals and objectives of Chinese foreign policy, their implications for programs of action are shaped by Chinese officials' perceptions of the available *capabilities*. Surely the most interesting sense of capabilities involves subjective judgments about what China and its institutions are capable of (as opposed to capabilities as conveyed by military or economic statistics). In the military area, what actions do Chinese leaders feel are possible because of China's nuclear forces, and what do they rule out because of China's largely obsolete conventional forces? In the economic area, questions of continuing importance involve the perceived ability of China to absorb foreign capital and technology and to compete successfully in external markets. In making these and other estimates, "skill" assets are as important as more tangible resources. To what extent do Chinese leaders believe they can correctly anticipate and take advantage of internal or external developments? To what extent do they believe they can persuade or convince foreign elites to behave as China desires? As we come to understand tangible and skill capabilities as viewed by Chinese officials, we are in a better position to weigh their relative importance in Chinese judgments. The "price" or conditions that Chinese leaders will accept for gaining some additional capability naturally reflect the difference they expect the new capability to make for China. As we develop a basis for comparing independent capability assessments with Chinese perceptions of capabilities, we can better gauge when and where Beijing's foreign policies will be overconfident or unduly cautious, and what risks will be considered acceptable.

Of course, Chinese foreign policy involves some picture of *external actors*. The list of external actors that looms large to Chinese elites need not resemble the membership list of the United Nations or be consistent over time. The Chinese have publicly provided some formulations to classify foreign countries (e.g., the theory of three worlds). Yet major questions remain about the extent to which such taxonomies figure in the formulation of Chinese foreign policy. Even if they provide a central framework for foreign policy judgments, the overlapping categories in Chinese public discussions leave open the issue of which taxonomy takes priority for which state, and what the indicators of impending change are. The categories of, for example, "Second World" and "developing countries" are sufficiently broad and vague to allow a foreign actor to be classified differently in various situations.

Which countries do the Chinese treat as unique entities for foreign policy purposes? How do they approach countries with overlapping membership in multiple categories, such as the anti-Soviet, right-wing, newly industrializing countries of Brazil, Chile, or South Korea? What is the niche for and image of nonstate actors such as liberation movements, international organizations, and multinational corporations? What behavior and attitude proclivities do the Chinese attribute to particular foreign actors? What processes are seen as determining others' behavior and attitudes? What actions by and images of China are believed to influence foreigners? In sum, Chinese identifications and images of foreign actors affect Beijing's judgments about their importance, about the challenges and opportunities they pose for China, and about the extent to which shifts in their behavior or attitudes through Chinese manipulation or other factors seem likely or improbable.

Beijing's conception of foreign actors affects its definition of prevailing international and domestic *situations*. Notions about likely changes in the behavior or attitudes of foreign actors or in Chinese capabilities are factors in reconsidering Chinese programs of action. Perceptions of impending developments may even trigger a reassessment of goals and objectives. Domestic resource availability and economic performance, leadership stability and consensus in China, the state of superpower relations, and the severity and nature of foreign threats to China presumably all enter into Beijing's formulation of relevant situations. Yet the recognition of general factors does not fully explain what triggers a change in the definition of policy situations. What, if anything, could convince Chinese officials that the problems and opportunities posed for China by the United States and the Soviet Union have changed? That the hostility between the superpowers will continue without Chinese encouragement? That economic relations with South Korea are compatible with close ties with North Korea? That a chill in relations with Washington need not involve substantial economic costs? That it is useful to frown on rather than bless a Japanese military buildup? The ability to comprehend Beijing's definitions and perceptions of a situation is a prerequisite to identifying what the Chinese will view as desirable and feasible, and what to them are signs to change policy lines and priorities.

It is people, not governments, who hold values, formulate strategies, define situations and problems, and implement policies, and internal differences can therefore be expected on all these scores. There is no reason to believe that China's leaders are somehow uniquely able to achieve consensus on policy perspectives, to eschew bureaucratic aggrandizement, or to suppress personal rivalry. The history of major Chinese initiatives in domestic as well as foreign policy suggests that they are often accompanied by acrimonious debates or struggles, and are influenced by the rising or falling political fortunes of their advocates. This linkage between domestic politics and foreign policy indicates yet another set of research agenda. What kinds of foreign developments are most likely to induce divisive policy debates about resource reallocation, debates that will inevitably affect the domestic status, reputation, and influence of particular *individuals, factions,* or *institutions?* Along what lines are bureaucratic positions on values, strategies, and situational definitions most likely to take shape? What are the domestic stakes and implications of alternative foreign policy programs of action for various officials and bureaus?

We noted earlier the elusiveness of China's chosen program of action. Actual conduct is much more accessible, albeit still imperfectly so. The ability to discern patterns of *actual conduct* can help in weeding out some plausible programs of action in a probabilistic manner. The absence of patterns (e.g., consistency, coherence, continuity, coordination) across instruments, time, or policy issues or arenas implies either the absence of a foreign policy or the inability to execute one. In a sense, the actual conduct of China provides our central dependent variable. Failure to grasp actual conduct will surely result in policy and analytic frustration. If we wish to make more than a contribution to historical knowledge, the identification of patterns for recurring classes of phenomena must be a priority.

The search for patterns may be organized in terms of problems or arenas. Two examples of the former are the management of situations of potential armed conflict and the handling of direct foreign investment in China. How do the Chinese warn, test, and confront adversaries in situations involving the actual or potential use of force?[5] How do they mix enticements and controls in attracting and maintaining foreign investments in China? As examples of arenas, we may note Chinese conduct in bilateral negotiations and international organizations. In bilateral negotiations, how do the Chinese manipulate agenda setting, bargaining postures, and choices of locale, timing, and participants?[6] In the arena of international organizations, how do they try to cope with possible disparities between proclaimed goals and actual conduct?[7]

Our discussion so far has dealt with the substantive aspects of Chinese foreign policy. To comprehend how these elements interact requires a grasp of several sorts of processes. Perhaps the most obvious is that mix of politics and administration we often call the *policy process.* Major institutions, factions, and individuals naturally influence the choice of alternative programs of action, the discrepancy and delay between the selection of a program and actual implementation,[8] and the odds that particular internal coalitions will emerge. Every national policy process has some norms of consent and command that can be violated only at substantial political cost. We have a special need to understand latent veto power and its milder variant, the capacity to impose domestic political costs. We must also be alert to the possibility that particular acts by Chinese foreign affairs personnel are primarily moves in a domestic rather than a foreign policy game.[9]

Cognitive processes, which are at least partially accessible to us, are also important.[10] Given the enormous differences in culture, historical experience, and political ideas between China and many other nations, we need to beware of simply projecting our own cognitive habits on to the Chinese. For example, Beijing's public rhetoric gives considerably more attention to economic matters (and relatively less to military matters) than does Washington's. Does this imply an analogously different view of what the key indicators of national power and prospects are? As another example, many Western texts on Chinese foreign policy are organized on a country or regional basis rather than on a policy or problem basis (e.g., détente, armament, foreign trade, international law). Do the Chinese think about foreign policy in terms of "relations with X," be the X the United States, the USSR, France, or Sub-Saharan Africa? Or is this categorization just a matter of Western academic convenience or proclivity?[11] Our final illustration is the familiar question of the time horizon of Chinese foreign policy. Are we justified in assuming a temporal perspective similar to that of Western foreign policy establishments, or do the Chinese take a more long-term view in some matters?[12]

• When we note the importance of understanding cognitive process, we are not talking about the rather arbitrary and untested use of language fragments. We are instead referring to information processing in the broadest sense, with the necessary sensitivity to all its cultural and psychological aspects. Just to cite one instance, much has been made of the epistemology of the Chinese word for crisis (*weiji*). Yet what is perhaps the only relevant empirical study shows that contemporary native Chinese speakers make no connection at all between the concept of crisis and the notion of opportunity (*ji*), and rather little connection between the former and the notion of danger (*wei*).[13] After all, what would we think of a foreign scholar who proposed that Americans are religious because they refer to a vacation as a *holy*(i)*day*, and to the first meal of the day as *break fast*? The notion would be treated as seriously as a proposal that Americans revere authority figures because they name cities after political notables (Washington, Lincoln, Madison, Houston, Baltimore).

The richness of the Chinese language does not warrant the conclusions drawn from the selective and impressionistic usage of fragments. Nor does the well-known diplomatic sensitivity of the Chinese to particular words and phrases justify the assumption that language is more important to them than to others. Israeli and Lebanese (or U.S. and Soviet) diplomats seem no less nit-picking in drafting international documents.

Perhaps one of the most elusive areas of understanding involves *emotional* or *affective processes*. It strains credulity to imagine that Chinese elites differ from political upper levels elsewhere in always maintaining their cool. Are some situations, actors, or acts especially likely to trigger fear, anger, or hatred? We are not arguing here for the definition of a modal cultural personality. Attempts have been made to translate in- dividual-level observations to inferences about Chinese society as a whole, and their merits are open to discussion.[14] We are more concerned with the emotional reactions of key leaders and policy elites to particular treatments (e.g., Zhou Enlai's encounter with John Foster Dulles in the early 1950s), evoked memories (e.g., the Japanese proposal to build a memorial in China to Manchukuo and its Japanese creators and defenders), and policy shifts (e.g., Western arms sales to Taiwan).

Product

We can ask a variety of questions about any of these elements of Chinese foreign policy. In this respect, the analysis of Chinese foreign policy resembles the analysis of any other state's foreign policy. The intellectual requirements for a well-reasoned answer in terms of evidence and inference are generic to foreign policy analysis, regardless of the particular difficulties posed by information constraints. To the extent that the analysis of Chinese foreign policy does not meet these requirements, the results, or analytic products, are seriously flawed and thus warrant skepticism.

The major types of *analytic product* are descriptive, explanatory, predictive, prescriptive, and evaluative (see Figure 2.1).[15] *Descriptions* of what is or has been going on (who, where, what, when, and how as opposed to why) have played a prominent role in writings about Chinese foreign policy.[16] Descriptions differ in the extent to which the charac- terization of the phenomenon studied will apply to other instances of the same phenomenon that have not been studied. "Generalizability" depends on the nature of sampling from a relevant universe, which in turn requires some clear idea of what the universe consists of. We do not argue that descriptive results must have a formal statistical basis to be generalizable. We do contend that variations in the phenomenon of interest should be covered by the cases studied. Moreover, there must be some notion about classification and representation (e.g., is X a member of a particular class; can X be used as a typical case or representative for the other members of this group?).

Lucian Pye's recent work on the Chinese commercial negotiating style offers an exemplary illustration of generalizable description.[17] It contains rich implications and insights about Chinese calculations and behavior in a variety of mixed-motive games that involve tacit or explicit bargaining and signaling (e.g., truce talks, border negotiations, crisis communication, legislative logrolling in international organizations). It gives a sophisticated treatment of Beijing's approach to multiple-sum games (as opposed to the usual emphasis of sinologists on the zero-sum aspects of military-political confrontations), and of behavioral and motivational patterns that characterize China's lower-level operators (as opposed to the usual focus on Chinese decision making at the highest political level). Moreover, to guard against possible biases or idiosyncrasies in the recall and descriptions of American commercial negotiators, Pye includes Japanese informants to provide a third perspective on the Chinese negotiation style. By examining Chinese, U.S., and Japanese conceptions of and approaches to commercial bargaining, Pye embeds his observations in a cross-national context, at the same time calling attention to broader concerns, such as the difficulties of engaging in effective communication across cultural and linguistic barriers.

Of course, some analysts of Chinese foreign policy may not be interested in generalizability even to China, let alone to international relations knowledge. Such cases-for-themselves ("we climbed it because it was there") are of more general interest only if they demonstrate that some X happened once and thus could happen again. The usefulness of this kind of knowledge depends on considerations external to the individual case study, no matter how thoroughly and creatively it has been performed.

Explanatory products address the why questions of past and present Chinese foreign policy. They deal with causality—always a difficult business, and the Chinese conduct of foreign policy provides a richly barbed set of obstacles. Causal explanation in a reasonably strict sense can be arrived at deductively from a logically closed set of premises or inductively from observable data patterns. The general state of international relations theory and the sometimes strongly held views about China's uniqueness argue against the former. We are therefore left with inductions.

As for accurate description, sound inductive explanation calls for attention to the joint effects of the various foreign policy elements of policy formulation, choice, and conduct. In this respect, Donald Zagoria's work on the "Vietnam Triangle" offers a positive example.[18] This study is a highly skillful attempt to bring together and address in one work concerns pertinent to many cells of our matrix for foreign policy analysis (Figure 2.1). Zagoria shows that foreign events provided an opportunity for some bureaucratic factions in Beijing to reshape the Chinese policy agenda and to press for their favored domestic policy positions. Furthermore, his analysis indicates that the outcome of the policy debate had a substantial effect on China's relations with the United States, the Soviet Union, and North Vietnam, because none of the latter governments shared the winning Chinese coalition's perspective. In short, Zagoria's research deals with the interactions between values (the modernization of the People's Liberation Army, the pursuit of economic growth, the preservation of "ideological purity"), institutions and personalities (dubbed the hawks, doves, and "dawks"), and situations (set by the fall of Khrushchev and the U.S. escalation of the Vietnam War). He links effectively different levels of analysis (individual, faction, nation-state, Communist "camp," East-West relations), and illuminates the policy consequences of divergent perspectives in both the domestic and foreign arenas.

Inductive causal explanation also requires that the analyst recognize that causality is a relationship between at least four items, not two: ". . . that which intervenes, . . . that state of affairs which is interfered with by the intervention, . . . the actual effect of the intervention, and . . . the outcome that would have prevailed but for the intervention."[19] From this philosophical perspective, providing a plausible account of what led up to a particular set of Chinese decisions or actions should not be the sole or even the primary purpose of an explanatory analysis. Instead, it becomes important to deal with the competitive merits of *alternative* plausible interpretations. Researchers should focus on alternative possible histories instead of treating ex post facto analysis of what did happen as the only valid approach. For example, how would the course of Sino-American or Sino-Soviet relations have differed if the Korean War had not occurred with the U.S. drive to the Yalu? If Lo Reqing's policy views had prevailed during the Vietnam War? If Lin Biao's alleged coup attempt had succeeded? Unless such questions are explored, causal possibilities are dismissed out of hand rather than scrutinized.

What we want from explanatory analyses of Chinese foreign policy is no different from what we should aim for in any intellectually satisfying explanation: (1) distinguishing between necessary and sufficient conditions; (2) separating both conditions from background noise (i.e., irrelevant conditions); (3) weighing different possible facilitating conditions for the conduct that took place according to relative importance; and (4) clarifying the leads and lags between cause and effect. We doubt that these objectives can be reached through the use of juxtapository logic, reductive assumptions, or metaphorical treatments—three approaches to explaining Chinese foreign policy that are well represented in the literature.

In juxtapository logic, the researcher amasses a wide array of details about the context of the situation or event to be explained. This might include, for example, information about the domestic political and economic conditions of China during a particular foreign policy episode (e.g., economic hardship, mass campaigns), Chinese media coverage of that episode, and the diplomatic activities undertaken by the Chinese leaders. Alternatively, the researcher might provide a detailed chronology of events leading to the situation or problem of interest (who said what to whom when). Whether an analyst stresses the description of concurrent or serial events (or both), the intent is the same—to insinuate linkages between the diverse events and weave them into a coherent story. The narration more often than not implies or suggests the inevitability of the outcome in question. A good example of this type of research is Richard Wich's recent study,[20] in which he tries to tie together events as geographically and temporally distant as the Soviet invasion of Czechoslovakia, the Vietnam War, the Cultural Revolution, and the Sino-Soviet clash at Chenpao.

The juxtapository logic approach tends to overemphasize the coherence, consistency, and purposiveness of Chinese behavior and to exaggerate the historical inevitability of this behavior on particular occasions. It usually conveys to the reader some rather paradoxical impressions. On the one hand, the Chinese leaders are presented almost as bureaucratic superheroes, who not only have a grand strategy but are also capable of carrying it out consistently, quickly, and decisively. Beijing's officials are portrayed as particularly competent in recognizing emergent policy problems, formulating responses, and implementing their decisions with foresight, dispatch, and efficiency. Yet in trying to demonstrate the plausibility of one account of the events described, the analyst may alternately portray the officials as so "boxed in" by a situation as to leave but one recourse or alternative open to them—the one that actually took place. No longer omnipotent, Chinese leaders appear rather as captives of circumstances beyond their control.

In this type of analysis, concerns about "what might have happened" are cast aside in favor of historically deterministic accounts of "what did happen." Less obviously but no less importantly, scholarly attention is distracted from questions about "what did not happen." Yet (as anyone familiar with the Sherlock Holmes books will recall) it is sometimes vital to explain *nonevents* that appear out of character with a subject's past behavior, to consider the dog that did not bark, or the arms sale to Taiwan that did not cause the PRC to recall its ambassador to the vendor.

Reductive analyses attempt to explain the behavior of a political unit in terms of its more basic components. Yet two problems weaken the validity of reductive explanations of China's or any other state's foreign policy. First, they usually lack clearly stated composition laws that enable the analyst to translate observations about individuals to inferences about entire political systems (e.g., to reason from the characteristics of Mao or Deng to Chinese institutional conduct in foreign affairs). Second, such explanatory analysis rarely deals with the sort of evidence necessary to defuse charges of irrelevance or omitted conditions. For instance, do countries or cultures that share the alleged Chinese traits display similar foreign policy behavior? Alternatively, can "Chinese" manifestations of psychological or cultural orientations be found in non-Chinese countries? Do Taipei and Singapore (whose elites are predominantly of Chinese ancestry) demonstrate foreign policy similarities to Beijing? Does India, with its very different heritage, engage in foreign policy conduct similar to China's (e.g., an emphasis on rectitude, moral persuasion, and public rhetoric without tangible action)?

Analyses that employ a metaphor to illuminate Chinese foreign policy are far more prevalent than far-reaching juxtapositions or elemental reductive treatments. In such explanations, the authors ask the readers to think about China as, for example, the image of Mao, a rational unitary actor, the successor of a long imperial tradition, or a skillful player of the board game of *wei ch'i* (*weiqi*).[21] Metaphors are limited as explanations owing to their inherent resistance to falsification and their lack of specific implications.[22] They are appropriately used as stimulating analogies or as sources for hypotheses. They might begin and enrich analyses, but should not substitute for them. Metaphors tantalize intellectual curiosity, but do not fulfill it.

We have dwelt at some length on descriptive and explanatory products because they provide many of the critical ingredients for *prediction*, *prescription*, and *evaluation*. The conduct of description and explanation lays the foundation for the other three types of endeavors, and determines the chances for their success. This applies to substantive foreign policy matters as well as to inferential quality. We are all condemned—or more positively, privileged—to draw on history. That is not at issue. The choices involve what aspects of history will be exploited in what ways and for what purposes.

For example, the existing research has seemingly concentrated on military-political crises with a significant potential for conflict escalation (such as Chinese crisis management in the Korean, Quemoy, and Sino-Indian conflicts), and on domestic political-economic situations that impinge on foreign policy (e.g., the conduct of foreign policy during periods of high tension among the elite such as the Cultural Revolution or during economic setbacks such as the Great Leap Forward). We are in a relatively good position to predict, prescribe, and evaluate Chinese conduct in situations of substantial threat, duress, or adversity. In contrast, we have a much weaker foundation with respect to Chinese monitoring of the international environment (with the possible exception of superpower relations) as it induces or hinders Beijing's foreign policy choice or conduct, Chinese policy formulation during more "normal" times, or Chinese conduct of "quiet diplomacy" in routine settings.[23]

Similarly, we have a relatively strong knowledge foundation for notable personalities such as Mao Zedong, Lin Biao, Zhou Enlai, and Deng Xiaoping; and for the institutions of the party and the People's Liberation Army. We are on much weaker ground regarding the views and behavior of lower-ranking operatives and institutions at the ministerial and bureau level.[24] The reasons for this situation are perhaps largely beyond the control of analysts of Chinese foreign policy, but the consequences remain.

Also, much more attention has been devoted to China's policy enunciation than to its policy formulation and policy implementation. Yet substantial disparity may exist between proclaimed intentions and justifications on the one hand, and actual choice and conduct on the other hand. Surely this situation must inspire some nagging doubts. We know that policy pronouncements are affected by Beijing's concern with multiple audiences. Chinese leaders are well aware that in addition to their own cadres and citizens, foreign enemies, friends, and potential coalition partners are all listening hard. The regime must fine-tune its public communications carefully to elicit different desired reactions from its numerous audiences. Beijing may, for example, seek to communicate support for an ally while simultaneously signaling restraint to an adversary; to warn the populace of the possibility of war and to mobilize resources for civil defense without encouraging mass panic or resignation or provoking a preemptive strike by an enemy. Beijing may speak in many tongues; moreover, many different voices may be proclaiming different priorities or objectives. Bureaucratic signal distortions may occur between those who formulate and execute foreign policy and those who portray foreign policy through the media.[25]

The unbalanced patterns of attention in the analysis of Chinese foreign policy have some straightforward implications for the discipline's current ability to predict, prescribe, and evaluate Chinese foreign policy. We are better equipped to deal with the subject of public goals and media presentations than to handle actual policy formulation or conduct; we know more about political-military crises and the foreign policy implications of major domestic turmoil than we do about routine management of the bread-and-butter items of foreign affairs.

The situation presents a number of challenges and pitfalls. First, the "missing chapters" in the description and explanation of Chinese foreign policy demand research attention. Second, the situation underlines the need to draw upon studies of other states as a necessary context for illuminating or assessing aspects of Chinese foreign policy that are as yet only dimly understood. An intellectual position that China is unique denies us that possibility. Whether to treat China as a member of a larger and better-known class is not purely an intellectual issue; it has serious import for the possibility of well-informed policy judgments about the People's Republic.

Third, the unevenness of our knowledge can lead us to commit rather fundamental errors in our interpretations. It is quite easy in an intellectual community that shares common limitations to let weaknesses or biases slip below the level of conscious attention. For example, reliance on Chinese public policy rationales and justifications may incline us to overemphasize Beijing's rationality, consistency, and foresighted initiatives and to underestimate the role of inadvertence, miscalculation, and belated adjustment to a changing external environment. Could the Chenpao clash have been a result of accident, negligence, or blunder? Allen Whiting's analysis of possible miscalculation by Mao in the Quemoy confrontation suggests the usefulness of entertaining such less flattering possibilities.[26]

Similarly, Beijing's public stress on superpower relations can lead us to neglect the lessons the Chinese may have learned from the experiences of other industrial latecomers (South Korea's success in foreign construction and engineering) or of other command economies (Poland's efforts to absorb amounts of Western capital, whole plants, and technology in excess of its digestive capacity, and the resulting economic and political woes). Ignoring the impact of such "third country" experiences upon Chinese policy appraisals may unrealistically exaggerate the importance of superpower relations and domestic factors for Chinese foreign policy.

The general research incentives to pursue matters of interest to one's peers and to ask questions one can reasonably hope to answer certainly apply to scholars of Chinese foreign policy. However, our ability to predict Chinese foreign policy can be limited not only by sheer lack of knowledge, but also by missing opportunities to pursue issues for which we already have some sense of what questions to ask and what information to seek. One obvious premise is that factors and relationships that apply to other countries for the topic at issue will also operate for China. This "common variable" perspective, which seems to provide a sensible starting point, is nicely illustrated by Kim Woodard's analysis of Chinese energy matters.[27]

Woodard tries systematically to map the current state and probable future condition of variables that will affect the energy policy of China or of any other developing country with substantial natural resources. What are the present and potential production rates of coal, oil, and hydroelectric power in China? How are these rates likely to be affected by different policies (e.g., introduction of Western technologies, intensified exploration efforts, alternative export or domestic consumption targets)? How soon? At what cost? What are the thresholds of profitability?

Using explicitly stated alternative assumptions, Woodard projects forthcoming Chinese energy supply and demand under different conditions. He examines physical constraints and unavoidable value trade-offs. Just as Mongolia is not in a position to practice gunboat diplomacy, so China is unlikely to become the Saudi Arabia of East Asia. China cannot ignore the relationship between oil production decisions and such other desiderata as increased export revenues, domestic industrialization, and technological self-reliance and national sovereignty and indigenous government control over the exploitation of natural resources. Its energy policies will necessarily be affected by and affect these concerns, with international implications.

Analyses that predict policy consequences provide an important base for policy prescription, especially if they allow for alternative futures. So do descriptive and explanatory studies that illuminate variations in Beijing's behavior and identify its critical decision points. Historical case studies that neglect these tasks are of less value for policy prescription. If China is a constant, then the policy that should be followed toward China must be determined by factors other than Chinese foreign policy. Without a causal understanding of Beijing's foreign policy that allows us to assign different odds to different patterns of future Chinese conduct, we can only provide background information and not policy analysis.

The previous discussion suggests particular value in two sorts of analytic product about Chinese foreign policy. The first is the iconoclastic case study, which analyzes a particular slice of Chinese history in a fashion that challenges a prevailing consensus or defies the conventional wisdom about what China has done and why, what it will do, and how it will respond to others' actions of omission or commission. Such studies help to change our questions and alter our assumptions.

The second product is less dramatic, perhaps more tedious to conduct, and surely less enjoyable to read: the systematic empirical study that creates and exploits a data base appropriate for statistical or logical analysis. In this kind of work, a researcher may treat China as just one case among many national cases in a search for cross-national patterns or deviations. Alternatively, one may examine observations about China during various periods in a search for continuing or changing relationships. In either case, the work would not focus on the production of supportive examples, but would instead emphasize detailed empirical calculation of the relationships between the behaviors and variables of interest. The large number of observations in such studies allows the analyst to introduce explicit controls for the influence of intervening factors, domestic or foreign. Such data also enable him or her to go beyond either-or dichotomies to form conclusions couched in terms of differing degrees of probability, varying magnitude of influence, alternative lead and lag relationships, and limited or general validity across subsets of situations, issues, or arenas. This approach has important advantages for establishing temporal precedence and feedback loops and differentiating the relative influence of multiple simultaneous causal factors. It helps in identifying the scope conditions that distinguish situations in which one or another of several very different expectations may apply.

Many important questions in the research on Chinese foreign policy bring up exactly these analytic issues. For example, to what extent, for what reasons, with what time intervals, and in what situations does domestic instability or vulnerability produce more aggressive Chinese foreign policy? Under what conditions does external threat produce domestic instability or vulnerability? How can one assess the comparative merits of competing propositions—for example, does Beijing exploit foreign crises for domestic political purposes, or does it try to insulate domestic politics from external turbulence?[28] To what extent are steps toward or away from normalization of Sino-Soviet relations a function of increases or decreases in Soviet threat, the U.S. stance toward Taiwan, evolving U.S.-Soviet relations, and political disputes within China?

The challenges posed by puzzles involving rival causal explanations and complex interactions among numerous variables call for a rigorous social science methodology. Without discriminating longitudinal analysis, it is hard to see how we can reliably decipher behavior that is compatible with alternative explanations (e.g., is Beijing pursuing a united front or alliance model in its foreign policy?)[29] or identify and anticipate switches in Chinese policy lines or models. The feasibility of statistical and logical approaches has been amply demonstrated.[30] The barriers to their adoption are largely a matter of taste.

Perspective

We now turn to the third and final dimension of the cube in Figure 2.1: perspective. *Perspective* indicates the extent to which substantive priorities, premises, styles, or issues are generated by official Chinese postures, by official U.S. postures toward China, or by other sources. Because of our own parochial limitations, we shall concentrate on the extent to which Chinese foreign policy analysis is shaped by Chinese or U.S. policy practice and mood. The significant influence of these sources implies that our intellectual agendas are fundamentally reactive rather than anticipatory, and that they tend to lack independent concerns based on scientific or knowledge accumulation grounds.

Of course, analysts who specialize in Chinese foreign policy are as prone to the "ambassadorial problem" as any group whose career commitment centers on a particular foreign culture or group. Anthropologists have long been aware of the problem of slipping into a representational, or at least protective, way of thinking about the subjects of one's life work. Although Chinese leaders are almost universally described by analysts as tough-minded realists and on occasion even as fanatic "ideologues," there is nevertheless evidence of a protective stance. One businessman described his company's experience in hiring a China specialist to aid its trade negotiation with the Chinese in the following terms:

> His advice was all negative. He never gave us a hint as to how we might have cashed in on the negotiations. Instead he was constantly worried about Chinese feelings and sensitivities. You would have thought from the way he advised us that that bunch of tough Communists who had gone through the Cultural Revolution were a group of delicate, thin-skinned Victorian sewing-circle ladies.[31]

Another illustration of the protective stance is the view of some China specialists that U.S. sales of advanced fighter aircraft to Taiwan could actually topple Deng from power. These specialists subsequently fail to draw the full implications that such extraordinary fragility of Chinese leadership or policy would entail for (to give one example) U.S. confidence in Deng's regime as a quasi-military ally.

Of course, ambassadors can go both ways, and others have expressed valid concerns about the undue influence of changes in U.S. or Chinese policy on analysts' research agenda and perspective. Greg O'Leary noted that "a view of the world close to that of the United States government has frequently been accepted as an objective account independent of any value assumptions."[32] Harry Harding has also expressed similar concerns, noting forthrightly that the attitudes of China specialists often seem closely correlated with the state of official Sino-American relations, and have often tended to fall "in line with official Chinese interpretations of their own society."

> When the Chinese said the Cultural Revolution was a good thing and that China had discovered a new path to economic development, most of us readily agreed. Now that they say Mao made mistakes and that the Chinese economy is inefficient, we agree with that judgment too. Where we once idolized Mao for his noble attempt to revolutionize China, now we wish Deng Xiaoping well in his valiant battle to liberalize it.[33]

Even if the ambassadorial problem is avoided, there may well be less obvious but even more fundamental influences on the agendas and perspectives of analysts. One obvious possibility is the catch-up approach of adjusting emphases to fit what China has done recently rather than to discern what it will do next. For example, the increased legitimacy of studies on bureaucratic politics and factions as an alternative to treating the Chinese government as a unitary actor followed the Cultural Revolution. Similar temporal patterns can be discerned with respect to the Sino-Soviet break, the Sino-American rapprochement, and the ebb and flow of Beijing's Four Modernizations program. The shifts from the monolithic to the pluralistic image of the Communist countries, from the portrait of China as an aggressive power to that of China as a cautious status quo power, from China aligned with the Soviet Union to China in the pursuit of an omnidirectional foreign policy, or from bullish to bearish forecasts about China as a market for exports and as an attractive site for direct foreign investment: All seem for many analysts to have followed rather than preceded public reorientations of Beijing's policies. Certainly, analysts need to take changes in Chinese policy into account as fresh evidence. That is far different from arguing that these policy changes warrant frequent alterations in research agendas and perspectives—that is, in key topics and questions, even basic premises. A continuing need to make such basic alterations suggests flaws in selecting topics, questions, and premises.

At one extreme, the tribe can assimilate the anthropologist, and the observed then train the observer. Let us take as a given the prevailing portrait of the Chinese in much of the Western scholarly literature. According to this portrait, the Chinese abhor disorder (*luan*), defer to authority and seek sheltering relationships, and have been taught by Mao to think dialectically and to trust knowledge gained from practice.

The Chinese regime is depicted as prone to make sudden and massive changes in policy lines.

If much Western analysis of Chinese foreign policy is indeed based on this perception, we would expect to find some distinct characteristics. Emphasis would be placed on the consistency, coherence, and purposiveness of Beijing's conduct as opposed to the possibility of behavioral randomness, inconsistency, or fragmentation. Scholarly reliance would be based heavily on authoritative sources such as government statements and senior scholars. Changes in officially approved practices (e.g., the change from Wade-Giles to Pinyin) would meet with quick conformity in scholarly behavior. Knowledge gained from first-hand experience such as on-site field research would be valued above other bases for learning.[34] Positions on major interpretive questions would fall along two polar opposite stands. Fundamental revisions would be made with nary a blush in consensus views on "acceptable" general priorities and conclusions, and the revised positions would be given all the legitimacy of their dismissed predecessors. There can be much debate about the extent to which analyses of Chinese foreign policy show or have shown these traits. If these traits are widespread, however, there is little room for debate about the implications for the merit of the analyses.

CONCLUDING OBSERVATIONS

Our preferences or biases on the various dimensions—substance, product, and perspective—may be clear by now. We stress knowledge about situations, conduct, and programs of action over knowledge about actors (especially about individual decision makers) and values. Like streetcars, situations and policy problems have a tendency to come around again. Conduct is the bottom line. As a corrective for the current overemphasis on political and military security questions, we recommend more attention to economic and technological questions as these play into international politics. For the same reason, we would aim for more explanation, prediction, and prescription than description. When the descriptive base is too thin or fragile to permit this, we would concentrate on descriptions that generate durable and generalizable results. These results should have a statistical or formal logical quality, once unduly limiting mind sets have been opened up by counterconsensus case studies.

We recommend that propositions be stated in a way that permits falsification by empirical testing. In particular, propositions that provide only the starting point for inquiry should not be confounded with the satisfying results of inquiry. To illustrate, the proposition "China's domestic politics affect its foreign policy" introduces an inquiry. The results should answer questions about how much, with what differences in conduct, after what period of time, and subject to what (if any) external manipulations.

High priority should go to trimming rather than adding to the existing set of alternative plausible interpretive schemes. The major goal of researchers should be to anticipate the future, with studies of the past serving purely as instrumental means for that purpose. Finally, agendas and perspectives should be independent from the current vagaries of official policy in Washington or in Beijing, and from the prevailing fashions in the salons of Western policy or intellectual circles. The writers that hold up best over time—in fine literature as in foreign policy analysis—do not confuse a leading paragraph designed to appeal to the readers' preexisting interests with a story line that the readers already agree with.

We began this chapter with a set of apologies. We conclude it by pointing out that our perspective in the previous pages involves far more general issues than the analysis of Chinese foreign policy. The controversies between the partisans of largely intuitive, impressionistic, unique case, and private expertise approaches to analysis and those who favor more public and more mundane approaches range far and wide in the study of individuals and groups. Some thirty years ago, psychologists engaged in a furious debate about the payoffs from two approaches to social science prediction. On one side were the so-called clinicians, who believed in the utility of the clinical or case-study method, and felt confident about the practitioners' ability to reach correct patient diagnosis on the basis of their unarticulated or unarticulable insights. On the other side were those who stressed the need and desirability for systematic observations and data collection, statistical analysis of large samples and explicitly coded variables, and rigorous verification of hypotheses regarding symptom-ailment relationships. They rejected the notion that "every person is unique," or that experts necessarily have a unique source of wisdom just because they say so. One participant in this debate summarized it in the following words:

> Is any clinician infallible? No one claims to be. Hence, sometimes he is wrong. If he is sometimes wrong, why should we pay any attention to him? There is only one possible reply to this "silly" question. It is simply that he *tends* (read: "is likely") to be right. "Tending" to be right means just one thing—"being right in the long run." Can we take the clinician's word for this? Certainly not. As psychologists we do not trust our memories, and have no recourse except to record our predictions at the time, allow them to accumulate, and ultimately tally them up. We do not do this because we have a scientific obsession, but simply because we know there is a difference between veridical knowledge and purported knowledge, between knowledge which brings its credentials with it and that which does not. After we tally our predictions, the question of success (hits) must be decided upon. If we remember that we are psychologists, this must be done, either by some objective criterion, or by some disinterested judge who is not aware of the predictions. When as clinicians we have done all these things,

and thus provided a secure basis for deciding how much trust we *can* put in ourselves, what have we done? We have carried out a validation study of the traditional kind! I am led by this reasoning to the conclusion . . . that the introduction of some special "clinical utility" as a surrogate for validation is inadmissible. If the clinical utility is really established and not merely proclaimed, it will have been established by procedures which have all the earmarks of an acceptable validation study. If not, it is a weasel phrase and we ought not to get by it.[35]

NOTES

1. See, for example, Robert C. North, "Recommendations for Research on China" (Northwestern University, Evanston, Ill., 1969), mimeo.; Howard L. Boorman, "The Study of Contemporary Chinese Politics," *World Politics* 12 (July 1960):585–599; A. M. Halpern, "Contemporary China as a Problem for Political Science," *World Politics* 15 (April 1963):361–376; Chalmers Johnson, "The Role of Social Science in China Scholarship," *World Politics* 17 (January 1965):256–271; John W. Lewis, "The Study of Chinese Political Culture," *World Politics* 18 (April 1966):503–524; Davis B. Bobrow, "Old Dragons in New Models," *World Politics* 19 (January 1967):306–319; and Samuel S. Kim, "China's Place in World Politics," *Problems of Communism* 31 (March-April 1982):63–70.

2. For an almost envious European reaction to Chinese skill in this respect, see the essay by Lawrence Freedman, "The Triangle in Western Europe," in Gerald Segal, ed., *The China Factor* (New York: Holmes & Meier, 1982), pp. 105–125. For some examples of Chinese presentations of their own importance, see the papers by Chinese authors in *China–United States Comprehensive Security* (Stanford, Calif.: Stanford University Northeast Asia–United States Forum on International Policy, 1982). Some recent data indicating an exaggeration of Beijing's importance at least among the "China as a military ally" school in the United States include the treatment of PRC defense spending in the 1981–1985 economic plan, where it is constant in absolute terms and declining as a share of the government budget (*South China Morning Post,* December 27, 1982, p. 4). As Lucian Pye observed some years ago, "Fraud is too strong a word, but contradiction is too bland to describe the peculiar inconsistency between China's policy rationalizations and her actual priorities in defense." See his "Dilemmas for America in China's Modernization," *International Security* 4 (Summer 1979):3. Other useful perspectives are provided by John Franklin Copper, *China's Global Role* (Stanford, Calif.: Hoover Institution Press, 1980); and Jonathan D. Pollack, *China's Potential as a World Power,* P-6524 (Santa Monica, Calif.: Rand Corporation, 1980).

3. Allen S. Whiting, "Chinese Foreign Policy: A Workshop Report," *Items of the Social Science Research Council* 31 (March-June 1977):3.

4. See, for example, Kim, "China's Place in World Politics," p. 64.

5. On this topic, see Allen S. Whiting, *China Crosses the Yalu: The Decision to Enter the Korean War* (New York: Macmillan, 1960), and *The Chinese Calculus of Deterrence* (Ann Arbor: University of Michigan Press, 1975); and Steve Chan, "Chinese Conflict Calculus and Behavior: Assessment from a Perspective of Conflict Management," *World Politics* 30 (April 1978):391–410.

6. Lucian Pye, *Chinese Commercial Negotiating Style,* R-2837-AF (Santa Monica, Calif.: Rand Corporation, 1982).

7. Samuel S. Kim, *China, the United Nations, and World Order* (Princeton, N.J.: Princeton University Press, 1979).

8. A vivid example of bureaucratic foot-dragging or noncompliance was provided by Michel Oksenberg. He reported that agreements reached by the top U.S. and Chinese leaders on the claims-assets issue repeatedly came unglued due to implementation failures at lower levels. Elsewhere, Lucian Pye warned against the common assumption of U.S. business executives that in China "the 'top man's' words would prevail." See Michel Oksenberg, "The Dynamics of the Sino-American Relationship," in Richard H. Solomon, ed., *The China Factor: Sino-American Relations and the Global Scene* (Englewood Cliffs, N.J.: Prentice-Hall, 1981), pp. 58–59; and Pye, *Chinese Commercial Negotiating Style,* p. 17.

9. Roger L. Dial, "Defense of Diplomatic Functions and Ideals During the Cultural Revolution," in Chun-tu Hsüeh, ed., *Dimensions of China's Foreign Relations* (New York: Praeger, 1977), pp. 256–279.

10. For an example of what is possible, see Paul J. Hiniker, *Revolutionary Ideology and Chinese Reality* (Beverly Hills, Calif.: Sage Publications, 1977).

11. One exception to the typical presentation of a series of "PRC relations with X" is the text organization of James C. Hsiung and Samuel S. Kim, eds., *China in the Global Community* (New York: Praeger, 1980).

12. Jonathan D. Pollack, *Security, Strategy and the Logic of Chinese Foreign Policy* (Berkeley: University of California Institute of East Asian Studies, 1981).

13. Davis B. Bobrow, Steve Chan, and John A. Kringen, *Understanding Foreign Policy Decisions: The Chinese Case* (New York: Free Press, 1979), pp. 69–70.

14. Robert Jay Lifton, *Revolutionary Immortality: Mao Tse-tung and the Chinese Cultural Revolution* (New York: Vintage, 1968); Lucian W. Pye, *The Spirit of Chinese Politics: A Psychological Study of the Authority Crisis in Political Development* (Cambridge, Mass.: MIT Press, 1968); Richard H. Solomon, *Mao's Revolution and the Chinese Political Culture* (Berkeley: University of California Press, 1971); and Hiniker, *Revolutionary Ideology.*

15. We do not suggest that U.S. scholars *should* prescribe policies for the Chinese; we merely observe that some *do*. Even a casual reading of the literature (e.g., on modernization, political reforms, détente) will show that there are many self-appointed or invited (e.g., in technology) advisors to the Chinese. Moreover, prescriptive or evaluative overtones abound and are at least implicit in such conventional labels as "extremists," "ideologues," "moderates," and "pragmatists" in describing Chinese leaders or policies.

16. James C. Hsiung, "The Study of Chinese Foreign Policy: An Essay on Methodology," in Hsiung and Kim, *China in the Global Community,* p. 3.

17. Pye, *Chinese Commercial Negotiating Style.*

18. Donald S. Zagoria, *Vietnam Triangle: Moscow/Peking/Hanoi* (New York: Pegasus, 1967).

19. Alasdair Macintyre, "Causality and History," in Juha Manninem and Raimo Tuomela, eds., *Essays on Explanation and Understanding* (Dordrecht, Holland: Reidel, 1976), p. 148.

20. Richard Wich, *Sino-Soviet Crisis Politics: A Study of Political Change and Communication* (Cambridge, Mass.: Harvard University Press, 1980).

21. Scott A. Boorman, *The Protracted Game* (New York: Oxford University Press, 1969).

22. Davis B. Bobrow, "The Relevance Potential of Different Products," in Raymond Tanter and Richard H. Ullman, eds., *Theory and Policy in International Relations* (Princeton, N.J.: Princeton University Press, 1972), pp. 204–228.

23. Samuel Kim's work offers a refreshing exception in this respect. In addition to his *China, the United Nations, and World Order,* see "Whither Post-Mao Chinese Global Policy?" *International Organization* 35 (Summer 1981):433–465.

24. See, for example, Michel Oksenberg, "Economic Policy-Making in China: Summer 1981," *China Quarterly,* No. 90 (June 1982):165–194; and Harlan W. Jencks, "The Chinese 'Military-Industrial Complex' and Defense Modernization," *Asian Survey* 20 (1980):965–989.

25. For examples in the foreign policy context, see Steve Chan, "Rationality, Bureaucratic Politics and Belief System: Explaining the Chinese Policy Debate, 1964–66," *Journal of Peace Research* 16 (1979):333–347; and three Rand reports: Harry Harding and Melvin Gurtov, *The Purge of Lo Jui-ch'ing,* R-548-PR (February 1971); Thomas Gottlieb, *Chinese Foreign Policy Factionalism and the Origins of the Strategic Triangle,* R-1902-NA (November 1977); and Kenneth G. Lieberthal, *Sino-Soviet Conflict in the 1970s,* R-2342-NA (July 1978), all published in Santa Monica, Calif., by the Rand Corporation. For examples in the domestic policy context, see Thomas Fingar and the *Stanford Journal of International Studies,* eds., *China's Quest for Independence: Policy Evolution in the 1970s* (Boulder, Colo.: Westview Press, 1980).

26. Allen S. Whiting, "New Light on Mao; Quemoy 1958: Mao's Miscalculations," *China Quarterly,* No. 62 (June 1975):263–270.

27. Kim Woodard, *The International Energy Relations of China* (Stanford, Calif.: Stanford University Press, 1980).

28. For two examples of the treatment of the substantive questions just raised, see Greg O'Leary, *The Shaping of Chinese Foreign Policy* (New York: St. Martin's Press, 1980); and Melvin Gurtov and Byong-Moo Hwang, *China Under Threat: The Politics of Strategy and Diplomacy* (Baltimore: Johns Hopkins University Press, 1980).

29. For a discussion on the subject of united-front versus alliance models, see J. D. Armstrong, *Revolutionary Diplomacy: Chinese Foreign Policy and the United Front Doctrine* (Berkeley: University of California Press, 1977).

30. Examples are Akihiko Tanaka, "China, China Watching and CHINA WATCHER," in Donald A. Sylvan and Steve Chan, eds., *Foreign Policy Decision Making: Perception, Cognition and Artificial Intelligence* (New York: Praeger, 1984), 310–339; Thomas W. Robinson, *Alternative Regime Typology: The Case of Future Domestic and Foreign Policy Choices for Mainland China,* P-4531 (Santa Monica, Calif.: Rand Corporation, 1971); John A. Kringen, "Allocating Foreign Affairs Resources: Chinese Policy Toward the Third World in the 70's" (Paper presented at the annual meeting of the International Studies Association, Los Angeles, March 19–22, 1980); Seiichiro Takagi, "Perception of Causal Relationships and the Shelving of the '10-Year National Economic Development Plan,'" in Shinkichi Eto and Toru Nakagawa, eds., *The Political Structure of Contemporary China* (Tokyo: Institute for Research on Japan's International Problems, 1982), pp. 238–274; Lowell Dittmer, "The Strategic Triangle: An Elementary Game–Theoretical Analysis," *World Politics* 33 (July 1981):485–515; Andre D. Onate, "The Conflict Interactions of the People's Republic of China," *Journal of Conflict Resolution* 18 (December 1974):578–594; and Davis B. Bobrow, "Ecology of International Games," *Peace Research Society (International) Papers* 11 (1969):67–88.

31. Quoted in Pye, *Chinese Commercial Negotiating Style*, p. 62.

32. O'Leary, *Shaping of Chinese Foreign Policy*, p. 13.

33. Harry Harding, "From China, with Disdain: New Trends in the Study of China," *Asian Survey* 22 (October 1982):955.

34. Harding offered the following instructive anecdote: "I remember vividly the ease with which a young graduate student humiliated a senior sinologist in the early 1970s simply by announcing that he had spent twenty-four hours in the North China city which the professor had spent half a career studying but had never visited." Harding, "From China, with Disdain," p. 953.

35. Paul E. Meehl, *Clinical Versus Statistical Prediction: A Theoretical Analysis and a Review of the Evidence* (Minneapolis: University of Minnesota Press, 1954), pp. 138–139.

CHAPTER 3

THE DOMESTIC POLITICAL DIMENSIONS OF CHINA'S FOREIGN ECONOMIC RELATIONS

Susan Shirk

Since the death of Mao Zedong, China has entered a new era in its economic relations with foreign countries. Foreign trade had been revived in 1972–1973 under Mao's reign, but only after his death and the overthrow of the Gang of Four did trade become a major component of China's economic development strategy. Total imports and exports were expanded almost 300 percent, from about US$15 million in 1977 to over US$43 billion in 1981.[1] The post-Mao leaders took the even more momentous step of opening up China for foreign investment. Foreign companies were invited to enter into joint ventures and other forms of cooperative production in China. At the same time the monopoly of the central foreign trade officials over foreign trade and investment activities was shattered by a policy permitting local officials and factory managers to make foreign business deals on their own.

In the past, especially after the split with the Soviet Union, the goal of Chinese development strategy had been to create "an independent and complete industrial system." Foreign trade had constituted a comparatively small percentage of China's national product and foreigners had been prohibited from investing in China.[2] Economic independence had required, according to the Chinese press, "not only that we should be able to manufacture ourselves every kind of product that we need, but also that within our own country we should be self-sufficient in raw and other materials."[3] To achieve independence, China purchased industrial plants that would produce commodities previously imported from abroad and pursued a policy of import substitution. The import substitution policy and the large size of China's domestic market explain why China's foreign trade constituted only 5 to 8 percent of the national product between 1949 and 1979.[4]

When Deng Xiaoping returned to power in 1977, he began to reevaluate the previous strategy of economic independence. The policy of self-sufficiency had succeeded in creating a large industrial economy that was largely "independent and complete," but by the mid-1970s, economic growth had slowed down, technology was stagnant, and living standards remained low. Beginning in 1979, Deng and his fellow leaders invited foreign businesses to enter into joint ventures and other forms of cooperative production in Chinese factories, in an effort to revive and modernize the Chinese economy. They encouraged Chinese industries to produce for export and allowed them to import foreign equipment. They granted local governments and factories a considerable degree of autonomy in negotiating trade and investment contracts with foreigners, even permitting them to retain and spend a percentage of the foreign exchange they earned in the process. Deng declared that there was no longer any danger of exploitation at the hands of the foreign imperialists because China was now able to control its own "door" and adopt an open-door policy on the basis of safeguarding national interest.[5]

The expansion of China's role in the world economy will undoubtedly have major international ramifications. Although its total trade is still comparatively small (US$43.1 billion in 1981),[6] China could eventually become a major exporter of agricultural products, petroleum, coal, nonferrous metals, textiles, pharmaceuticals, and even electronic equipment and machinery. The potential Chinese market of over a billion people has attracted foreign producers seeking to revive lagging international sales. Even though 80 percent of China's population consists of rural peasants too poor to afford many domestically produced consumer goods—much less imported ones—the nation has an urban consumer market of over 200 million people and an industrial economy badly in need of modern equipment.

Many foreign firms have been willing to undertake coproduction in China largely in the hopes of eventually gaining a share of this huge import market. Foreign banks are eager to lend to China because in contrast to Third World countries already burdened with heavy international debts, China has a healthy balance of payments, substantial gold reserves, a budget that is almost balanced, and modest foreign indebtedness. (The Bank of China is itself becoming active in lending abroad.) China's place in the international economy is potentially very significant, but much depends on what policies the Chinese leaders decide to pursue in the future.

China's foreign economic policy choices, like those of other developing countries, depend in large part on domestic political forces. There has been much political controversy and debate over the new open-door policy since it was initiated. Newspaper articles on foreign trade and investment have a distinctly defensive tone, as they seek to respond to critics of the policy.[7]

Will the new open-door policy be sustained or will the political conflicts sparked by the policy force China to shut the door again and return to the policy of self-sufficiency? This chapter addresses the question by analyzing the political coalitions for and against opening China to foreign trade and investment. I seek to discover which groups have and have not benefited from the policy of opening up China to foreign trade and investment; how these "winners" and "losers" have tried to influence China's foreign trade and investment policies; and how the structure of the Chinese economic and political system shapes this policymaking process. My analysis is based on interviews with Chinese economic officials conducted during visits to China in 1980, 1981, and 1982 and during their visits to the United States in 1982 and 1983; on interviews with foreign executives who have done business in China; and on reports from the Chinese press. Although, as is usually the case with the study of contemporary Chinese politics, the data are insufficient to "prove" the impact of political forces on economic policies, I hope to raise questions that help researchers to decide where to focus their research when access to China becomes easier.

CHINA'S POLITICAL ECONOMY, 1949–1978

Before the shift in economic policies began in 1978, certain regions, industrial sectors, and bureaucratic institutions were favored, protected, and subsidized by Chinese economic policies and structures. This set of groups, which could be called the "Communist coalition," consisted of the inland provinces, heavy producer goods industries (especially iron and steel and machine building), and the planning agencies and industrial ministries in the central government.

Favoritism toward these regions, sectors, and institutions stemmed from the fundamental features of the Chinese economic and political system since 1949. Despite periodic policy shifts, the Chinese system exhibited continuity in certain basic structural characteristics.[8]

1. The Soviet-style *command economy*. Central planners set prices, wages, and output quotas and allocated capital, materials, labor, and products according to a national plan.
2. The centralized *bureaucratic state*. Industrial revenues were accumulated by the central government and reallocated as budgetary grants to the provinces and as investment grants to enterprises throughout the country. Industrial ministries oversaw all economic activity and had, in effect, national industrial monopolies.
3. The *"big push" strategy* of extensive growth. Planners achieved high growth rates by devoting a large proportion of national income to fixed capital investments in industry, particularly in producer goods industries.[9]
4. *Regional redistribution* through the central government. Centralized control over public finance and industrial investment was used, in part, to achieve greater regional equality by developing the inland provinces.[10]

5. The policy of *economic self-reliance*. China was closed to foreign investment; foreign trade was held to low levels and used for import substitution.

The cumulative effect of these structures and policies was to expand heavy industry rather than light industry or agriculture.[11] This expansion drive, which was unconstrained by calculations of the cost of capital, labor, or other inputs, created constant supply shortages. These shortages motivated enterprises to guarantee their supply of inputs through vertical integration and led provinces to strive for local self-sufficiency.[12] As a result, levels of inter-regional trade were low. The Chinese system also created national economic monopolies, each headed by a ministry, as well as local monopolies for large provincial enterprises. Protected from the threat of either domestic or international competition, Chinese industrial enterprises and the ministries that administered them had little incentive to reduce their costs, raise productivity, or improve the quality of their products. Although centralized control over investment and planning was progressively weakened after 1959, and especially after 1966,[13] central finance and investment policies were used to redistribute revenues from the more developed coastal provinces to the less developed provinces in the interior of the country.[14] Another effect was the centralization of power in the hands of the economic planning agencies, industrial ministries, and Communist Party organs in Beijing.

How has the expansion of foreign trade and investment affected the interests of the groups—inland provinces, heavy industry, the central bureaucracies—that were favored prior to the open-door policy? How does the structure of the Chinese political and economic system shape the way these groups attempt to stem the current tide? What kinds of policies are these group pressures likely to produce?

REGIONAL CONFLICTS

The new foreign trade and investment opportunities, combined with the policies allowing local governments and enterprises to negotiate independently and retain a proportion of their foreign exchange earnings, have stimulated economic competition among Chinese cities and provinces. Local political authorities seek to develop their local economies with the profits of trade and foreign investments in a manner reminiscent of the local authorities of the mid-nineteenth century who sought to build local armies with the *likin* taxes collected along domestic trade routes.

In this new competitive environment, the coastal provinces appear to be winning most of the prizes.[15] Foreign investments are concentrated in a few coastal provinces and municipalities, especially Shanghai and the special economic zones (SEZs, areas granted special powers to offer concessionary terms to foreign investors) in Guangdong and Fujian provinces. The four SEZs in Guangdong and Fujian were able to attract 60 percent of direct foreign investment in China in 1981.[16] As centers of light industry, the coastal areas are the source of a large percentage of China's manufactured exports. For example, 1,700 of Shanghai's 8,000 factories are now engaged in producing for export.[17] The coastal ports also ship exports for many inland enterprises; despite increasing competition from inland ports up the Yangze, the port of Shanghai still handles one-fifth of total national exports.[18]

The new open-door policy has created a real bonanza for the coastal provinces, especially Guangdong. During 1981 Guangdong reportedly earned over US$1 billion in foreign exchange.[19] Foreign exchange earnings can be used to import foreign equipment and materials, and despite the formal prohibitions against domestic sales of foreign exchange, local officials sell foreign currency on the black market to obtain Chinese currency for construction projects. Because coastal areas are attractive sites for foreign investment, local officials can also sometimes persuade potential investors to finance local energy projects and road construction.[20]

The government is freeing the coastal regions from central controls in order to take advantage of their natural strengths: port facilities, relatively sophisticated technical personnel and skilled workers, and ties to overseas Chinese capitalists who prefer to invest in their home provinces. At the same time, the central government is purposefully enhancing the superiority of these coastal regions and trying to make them even more attractive to foreign investors by targeting many of its investments in transportation and energy infrastructure on these areas.[21] In theory, building on the stronger international position of the coastal regions will benefit the development of the whole national economy.[22]

The inland provinces, in contrast, have obtained few benefits from the new policy, and local officials see the gap between inland and coastal provinces widening. The inland economies are based on the extraction of minerals and the manufacture of industrial equipment. These industries were thrown into a slump by national economic readjustment policies that diverted investment funds from heavy industry to light industry and agriculture. Officials in the inland provinces are trying to break into the light consumer-goods industries but have a hard time competing with the brand-name products (bicycles, watches, televisions) from Shanghai and Tianjin, which are widely preferred by consumers. The inland provinces need export markets for their raw materials, especially coal and nonferrous metals, but they are short of capital for exploration, production, and marketing.[23] When these provinces have succeeded in attracting foreign funds for large construction projects to extract and transport coal, the joint ventures have been plagued by uncertainties in the international energy market.[24]

Current regional differences in interests echo prior cleavages in China. The outlying coastal areas were traditionally centers of commercial power; the inland areas had access to political power. The inland areas were more culturally conservative than the coast, which was exposed to foreign trends through trade.

Today, the inland provinces in China rely on administrative regulations and conservative cultural appeals to defend themselves against the threat of foreign and domestic competition. They have established local blockades and other forms of what central leaders sometimes condemn as "administrative interference" to protect their infant consumer-goods industries by keeping out high-quality brand-name merchandise from Shanghai and other light-industrial centers.[25] In 1982 Anhui objected to an exhibit of Shanghai products held in their province. Anhui officials argued that because many of the products were now being produced in local factories (because of the readjustment and profit-retention policies favoring the development of light industry), the exhibition ought to be closed down. The dispute had to be resolved by the State Economic Commission, which ruled that Shanghai was entitled to hold the exhibition but not to display products identical to those made in Anhui.

Although Chinese economists recognize that restrictions on domestic trade are economically inefficient, protectionist pressures from inland provinces are difficult for policymakers to resist. As economist Xue Muqiao astutely noted about the contradictions among localities caused by uneven industrial development: "In general, the industrially developed areas wish to acquire greater independence and the underdeveloped ones prefer unified management and unified allocation of products by the central government. . . . For these reasons it has been very difficult for the state organs of economic management to reach an agreement on changing the current system of planning and management."[26]

The inland areas have also publicized the danger of corrosion of Chinese culture by decadent ideas and life-styles from abroad. Many of the scare stories about the infiltration of bourgeois foreign culture come from the inland provinces. Complaints about pornographic pictures and tapes (called "yellow materials") imported from abroad have been heard from areas as deep in the interior and remote from foreign contact as Shanxi.[27]

Meanwhile, the coastal regions have used their economic resources to prevent the central government from restricting their freedom to do business with foreigners. The Special Economic Zone Office, which was established directly under the State Council at the apex of the governmental structure, has been an effective voice for the SEZs.[28] In one instance, the office complained that the efforts of SEZ officials to attract foreign investment were stifled by regulations preventing them from traveling abroad and requiring that they get upper-level permission for every meeting with foreigners. After the director of the SEZ office, Gu Mu, accompanied Party secretary Hu Yaobang on a visit to Fujian in November 1982, he took the case to the Communist Party secretariat.

The secretariat ruled in favor of the zones. The regulations were changed, and the SEZ officials received passports to travel abroad.

Officials from the coastal areas have also launched a counterattack against accusations that their cities have abandoned socialism for capitalism and have become dens of iniquity due to the open-door policy. They began to fight back at the National People's Congress in late 1982. One Guangdong official protested that some inland provinces were discriminating against travelers from Guangdong by searching their luggage and separating them from other travelers in order to prevent smuggling.[29] Ren Zhongyi, first Communist Party secretary of Guangdong, addressed "some people at home and abroad [who] still have various concerns about our open-door policy" and "some comrades [who] are afraid to mix with foreigners" in a speech reminding them that Japan's economic progress was achieved through trade. Ren held up Guangdong as a positive model of what can be accomplished when China "smashes the blockade of imperialism" and opens the door to foreign countries: "The experience of Guangdong Province shows that where the door is kept wide open to the world, economic and cultural development is quicker." Other officials cited statistics showing that the open door had resulted in higher average economic growth rates over the past three years in Guangdong (7.4 percent) than in the rest of the nation (6.7 percent). They also claimed that some of the reports about Guangzhou youth wearing U.S. army jackets, rampant gambling, and other examples of bad life-styles imported from the West were false.[30]

Representatives of the Guangdong and Fujian economic zones presented a vigorous defense of foreign trade and investment and of the zones themselves. They countered critics who argued that SEZs would become colonies by explaining that whereas colonies were regions that had lost their sovereignty to foreign capitalist aggression, SEZs were run by a socialist government as an application of its sovereignty. They responded to critics who claimed that SEZs caused corruption by pointing out that as corruption also occurs in areas and departments that have no foreign dealings, it is not *created* by the special zones.[31]

The interests of the coastal provinces in keeping China's door open to foreign trade have probably been favored by the large number of leaders with ties to the south, especially to Guangdong, in top Communist Party circles.[32] Nevertheless, one perceives a certain apprehension in Beijing about the growing affluence and independence of Guangdong. Party secretary Ren Zhongyi's plan to end his province's energy dependence on coal supplies from Shanxi by building a nuclear power plant in conjunction with Hong Kong was delayed by Beijing officials for many months before final approval was granted. One *Renmin ribao* article discussed the "crime of plotting to split the state" by referring to the example of Lin Biao, who "plotted to flee south to Guangzhou to establish another central regime there."[33]

An even greater potential threat to the political power of Beijing is the economic power of Shanghai. This pre-1949 center of industry, trade, and commerce was until very recently kept on a tight leash by the central government. When Guangdong and Fujian were given the freedom to deal directly with foreign businesses and offer them concessionary terms, Shanghai was not. When the local governments were given the right to retain a share of their domestic and foreign exchange revenues, Shanghai, along with Beijing and Tianjin, was not given similar financial autonomy. These restrictions reflect not only the dependence of the national treasury on the economies of Shanghai and the other two municipalities, but also the central leaders' distrust of Shanghai.[34]

The political problems of regional unity and equity caused by the open-door policies have been addressed by new policies encouraging "interprovincial cooperation."[35] The central leaders want to ease the capital shortages of inland China and disarm its opposition to opening-up policies by urging coastal enterprises to use their capital reserves to invest in inland enterprises. Managers of coastal enterprises naturally see such investments as a good means of guaranteeing their supplies of raw materials, energy, and other inputs. This type of interprovincial cooperation represents the beginning of capital transfers in China. The possibility for capital transfers puts Shanghai "capitalists" in competition with foreign capitalists to develop inland coal and metal deposits. (An intriguing question: Would an inland province prefer to have its natural resources exploited by joint ventures with foreigners or with Chinese from another region?)

The strains on regional relations created by opening up China to foreign business suggest several important questions. First, will the coastal cities continue to control foreign capital and technology, or will inland China win a share by forcing them to channel these resources through the center? Second, to what extent can a modern socialist economy overcome recurring regional cleavages by devising new practices or institutions that cut across old lines? And last, as the economic reformers in the PRC try to decentralize the command economy, do they lose the economic and political tools necessary to maintain regional integration?

SECTORAL CONFLICTS

The expansion of foreign trade and investment has had a differential affect on heavy and light industries in China. Light industries have been better able to take advantage of the new opportunities for exporting than heavy industries, which feel the threat of competition from imports more strongly. Heavy-industrial enterprises and bureaus have also felt threatened by domestic economic policies and reforms. Industrial read-justment policies cut their capital investments from the center and lowered their output quotas.[36] New policies designed to motivate managers to cut costs and raise efficiency by permitting enterprises to retain a portion of their profits worked to the advantage of light-industrial enterprises but not heavy-industrial ones. As a rule, light-industrial products—especially consumer goods like televisions—have been assigned higher prices than raw materials and heavy-industrial products. Regardless of how well the enterprise is managed or how hard the workers work, a tape-recorder factory will always earn—and be able to retain—more profits than a steel mill.

Heavy industries are not inherently opposed to China's participation in international business. Managers of heavy-industrial enterprises would like to attract foreign capital to replace the funds Beijing has diverted to light industry, and would be glad to put their idle capacity to use in producing for export. Some foreign companies have been attracted by China's reserves of coal, petroleum, and nonferrous metals, and have been willing to join in projects to help develop and export them. Iron and steel and machinery plants find, however, that their antiquated equipment, erratic product quality, remoteness from ports, and lack of familiarity with the international market frustrate their trading ambitions. There is little international demand for Chinese heavy-industrial products, which are mostly of relatively low quality and technological sophistication.

All Chinese industries would like to promote their export prospects by upgrading their production processes with imported equipment, but they are continually frustrated by their comrades in the Chinese machine-building industry. The machine-building industry was a major beneficiary of the extensive growth and self-sufficiency policies of the past. It supplied equipment for almost all Chinese factories under monopolistic conditions, expanding at an annual rate of about 20 percent during the 1950s through the 1970s.[37] By 1978, there were over 100,000 machinery manufacturing enterprises in China, nearly one-third of the total number of industrial enterprises.[38] The Ministry of Machine Building administers 11,000 of these enterprises, which employ 5.5 million workers.

The Ministry of Machine Building is an important source of protectionist pressures in the Chinese system. It reacted with alarm when Chinese factories began to modernize through purchases of imported equipment. The machine-building industry's monopoly was being challenged by foreign competition. The ministry flexed its bureaucratic muscles and demanded a policy of "buy Chinese" for factories upgrading their equipment. It revived a 1950s institution, a special equipment approval division empowered to approve all factory imports of equipment, even those in joint foreign-Chinese enterprises.[39] A request for imported equipment is submitted to the State Planning Commission, which in turn sends it to this division in the Ministry of Machine Building. If the ministry determines that one of its factories can produce the same piece of equipment (regardless of cost), it vetoes the import.

This regulation has created conflict between the machine-building ministry and other heavy- and light-industrial ministries that want to modernize with sophisticated foreign equipment. Foreign business executives report instances in which the ministry has even prevented the metallurgical and petroleum industries from sending representatives abroad to shop for equipment.[40] Several disputes over equipment imports between the machinery ministry and the other producer-goods industries have had to be resolved by the State Economic Commission or State Planning Commission.

Chinese heavy industries, especially its machine-building industries, urged further measures to protect local manufacturers. They complained that the "blind importation" of cars and other vehicles cost the country three to four times the total investment for the domestic car industry.[41] They cited examples of products such as the industrial steam turbine engine of the Hangzhou Steam Turbine Plant, which, although of sufficiently high quality to be exported to ten countries, was having difficulty selling to the domestic market because of enterprises' "blind faith in foreign merchandise."[42] Some newspaper articles described the purchase of domestic equipment as "an important test of patriotism."[43]

Protectionist pressures forced the Chinese government to decree in January 1981 that in principle, equipment that could be produced locally should not be purchased abroad. In 1982, import duties on cranes, engines, and other machinery were raised (duties on some scarce raw materials and parts were lowered), and import licenses were required for vehicles, computers, and various types of equipment.[44] The Chinese have subsequently tended to purchase licenses for foreign technologies rather than import equipment outright; the equipment imports that are permitted are justified by the goal of import substitution. Machine industry protectionism has clearly resulted in decreased purchases of foreign equipment: Imports in the first half of 1982 declined 43 percent from the same period in 1981.[45]

Protectionist pressures have also surfaced in China's negotiations with foreign companies about their participation in exploiting offshore petroleum fields. Foreign business representatives report that the Chinese require that oil companies use local equipment whenever possible and contract with local enterprises to supply support services. In several instances, however, while making a political point by insisting on local suppliers, the Chinese have in fact formed joint ventures with more experienced foreign companies for the purpose of supplying the services.

Light-industrial enterprises are also wary of foreign competition in the growing domestic consumer market. Electronics enterprises were successful in raising customs duties on imported tape recorders, radios, and televisions during 1982.[46] The establishment of a two-tier system of exchange rates at about the same time raised the price of imported products.[47]

However, government efforts to protect the domestic market have also impeded the efforts of light-industrial plants to attract foreign investment. Periodic increases in customs duties on imported materials, the control of product prices by the State Planning Commission, and restrictions on domestic sales make it difficult for the foreign partner in a joint venture to make a decent profit. The Hitachi television joint venture in Xiamen (Fujian Province) was told to cut its production volume during 1982 from 300,000 to 130,000 sets and to export at least 50 percent of these sets (despite an original agreement that had left export decisions under the jurisdiction of the Japanese partner).[48] The Camel cigarette factory, also in Xiamen, is being squeezed by the same restrictions. The Camel factory is prohibited from marketing its products outside the special economic zones, and the Hitachi television factory cannot market its products outside of Fujian Province.

Although protectionist pressures emanate from both heavy and light industries in China, light industries are generally better able to attract foreign investment and compete internationally. Although industries in centrally planned economies are notoriously poor at meeting the needs of their customers, consumer-goods industries are somewhat more responsive to customer preferences (because consumers choose their own purchases) than are industries that produce for other factories. Therefore it is not surprising that light-industrial enterprises have moved quickly to come up with products that will sell well abroad. The efforts of other Soviet-style economies to export machinery have usually been unsuccessful because of technological backwardness and erratic quality.

The machinery ministry also produces all of China's cameras, and it has recently used its bureaucratic clout to win a share of the domestic household appliance market. But it will be a long time before these cameras, refrigerators, and washing machines are sufficiently sophisticated and well-made to be able to compete in the world market. Therefore, we may expect continued tension between the machinery industry and light industry over the import of foreign equipment and over incentives for foreign investment and exports. Because the Ministry of Machine Building appears to have more political strength at the level of central governmental policymaking than light industry, light-industrial enterprises may begin to call upon their foreign partners to bolster their influence in foreign economic policymaking. Eventually, they may press for restructuring of the state bureaucracy in order to right the political imbalance between light and heavy industry.

BUREAUCRATIC CONFLICTS

A major obstacle to economic reform in China is resistance from the Communist Party and the People's Liberation Army (PLA). Worried that economic reforms will make their political skills obsolete and diminish their power, party officials often fail to implement the reforms or even attack them for deviating from political orthodoxy. Army officers also are concerned about loss of power and status and about cuts in military spending. Military critics argue that the reforms will destroy the Maoist legacy of "politics in command."

The politics of economic reforms such as the open-door policy, however, involve more than just a struggle between the reformist leaders and the conservative Communist Party and People's Liberation Army. Conflicts within the government bureaucracy—for example, between the trade ministry and other ministries over control of imports and exports—are highly significant in shaping foreign economic policies in China. Now that it is occasionally possible to interview some bureaucrats and policymakers in China, we can move beyond the simple Party and PLA resistance model to study the conflicts between governmental agencies and between center and local levels of government.[49]

In the Chinese socialist command economy all economic sectors (for example, the machinery industry, the electronics industry, the coal industry, the petroleum industry, the iron and steel industry, and the light consumer goods industry) are organized into vertical national bureaucracies headed by ministries in Beijing. Each minister is like a division head in a huge conglomerate "China Incorporated." Sitting in Beijing, ministers are able to articulate the interests of the industry they represent. In this way the structure of the socialist economic and political system gives industrial sectors a powerful voice in policymaking.

Communist policymakers and bureaucrats abhor competition; they try to structure economic activity along a syndicalist line to avoid it. Each ministry has a monopoly in its own products. Conflicts between ministries are frequent, nevertheless, and often require the intervention of higher-level leaders. By creating new opportunities for profit, the post-1978 economic reforms have intensified the conflicts among government bureaucracies. Articles in the press criticize agencies for thinking only of their own interests and for engaging in constant "wrangling in economic work" and "arguing back and forth."[50]

Resolving these interagency disputes takes up much of the time of the State Planning Commission and State Economic Commission. For example, the machine-building ministry was eager to enter the consumer goods market (which under industrial readjustment policies is expanding and offers high profits) with washing machines and refrigerators, but the Ministry of Light Industry saw this as a challenge to its monopoly. The State Planning Commission called a meeting among several ministries to divide up the burgeoning market for ten high-volume consumer products, including washing machines. The Ministry of Machine Building emerged victorious, with a sizable share of the washing-machine business (it was assigned the multicycle and washer-dryer machines; the Ministry of Light Industry kept the simple machines). Other issues such as approvals for machinery imports, customs duties for imported consumer goods and raw and semifinished materials, export licenses, approvals for large joint ventures, tax policies toward foreign investment, and rules about the management of foreign exchange also have a different effect on different ministries and often require higher-level intervention.

There also have been conflicts between industrial ministries and the new superagency headed by Minister Chen Muhua, the Ministry of

Foreign Economic Relations and Trade (MOFERT), over the control of foreign trade and investment. MOFERT has trading companies to handle imports and exports for each industrial sector and prefers to channel all trade through them.[51] This centralized monopoly of trade (a characteristic of all Soviet-style planned economies) facilitates the management of foreign-exchange balances, and from the standpoint of central planners, avoids "chaos" and confusion. The ministries prefer to control their own trade activities and thereby retain a larger percentage of the foreign exchange they earn to use for imports of new equipment. Several ministries, including the powerful machine-building ministry, have won the right to have their own trading company; others, including the Ministry of Light Industry, have not.[52] These bureaucratic conflicts have important implications for China's policy toward foreign business. Ministries without their own trading arm actively seek foreign partners for joint ventures because it is easier for them to acquire foreign currency and equipment this way than by importing equipment through the MOFERT trading company.

The Ministry of Finance often clashes with the industrial ministries, MOFERT, and local governments over foreign trade and investment taxes and customs duties. The Ministry of Finance receives taxes and customs duties but the profits of international business activities are retained by the industrial ministries, the trading companies under MOFERT, and local governments. Finance officials naturally prefer higher taxes and duties; the other officials would rather take a higher share in profits. If the total cost of the export or investment (which includes price, taxes, and customs duties) is too high, foreign business concerns will go elsewhere.

Case studies of how the bureaucracy handles such issues should help clarify the power resources that influence the outcome of interagency battles. How important is the amount of revenue produced by the enterprises under the ministry? The number of enterprises or employees? Having its own trading company? The patronage of a top-level political leader? Does it help to have important foreign investors on your side? How can we explain the continuing strength of the heavy-industrial ministries, especially the machine-building ministry, even in this era of economic reform and readjustment?

There are also conflicts between the central government and local governments over control of foreign trade and investment. MOFERT was upset by the cutthroat competition among provinces and cities for foreign capital and equipment created by policies that decentralized the power to negotiate with foreign firms.[53] Provinces and cities competed to attract foreign investment by offering concessionary terms and promising access to the domestic market. MOFERT efforts to control local dealings with foreign investors appear to have been unsuccessful. The major role of coordinating economic cooperation with foreign companies has been assumed by the China International Trust and Investment

Corporation (CITIC) and by various local international trust and investment corporations, rather than by MOFERT bodies. MOFERT bureaucrats resent these trust and investment corporations, which are independent bodies often headed by Chinese former capitalists.

MOFERT has been more successful in gaining control over exports. The new opportunities for foreign-exchange profits motivate enterprise managers and officials in local bureaus to enter the exporting business even if they have to procure the product from another unit. They are willing to sell at low prices in order to earn foreign exchange. Some enterprises will even sell the coal allocated to them for their own use. This "blind competition" lowered the world price for tungsten and cashmere, products for which China provides a significant proportion of the international supply. Arguing that "foreign merchants are the only ones who stand to gain" from this kind of competition, MOFERT imposed export licenses and taxes on a large number of products in 1980 and again in 1981 and 1982.[54] MOFERT also established a special commissioner to oversee trade in the four main ports of Guangzhou, Shanghai, Tianjin, and Dalian.[55]

The center also contends with the provinces over who should pay for the infrastructural investments needed to attract foreign investment and facilitate trade. Fujian and Beijing clashed over the financing of the new Fuzhou airport, which is vital for tourism as well as foreign business. The center won, and Fujian must pay for the airport itself out of the retained profits of their trade and industry. Guangdong Province must also pay for its new rail line. Both projects would have been financed by the central authorities in the past. Large energy projects have also sparked conflict between the provinces, which seek to guarantee their own energy needs, and the central government, which is concerned about maintaining a balance among regions, energy sources, and foreign and domestic equipment.

STRUCTURAL CONSTRAINTS

In addition to the conflicts between regions, industrial sectors, and bureaucratic organizations that influence China's foreign economic relations, the character of China's economic system also constrains its dealings with foreign firms. The centralized structure of the command economy limits the ability of enterprises, localities, or bureaucratic agencies to engage in international business. The national plan regulates almost all activities related to production. Factory managers cannot freely hire labor, raise wages, choose products, set prices, or invest profits in other enterprises. An enterprise that wants to import, export, or engage in joint production with a foreign firm inevitably comes into competition with the national plan, which is enforced by the central planners and industrial ministers.

Enterprises must compete with the national plan for scarce vital inputs—supplies, power, and skilled manpower. This is the reason Deng and his allies have had to create special institutions and grant them exceptions to the rules of the command economy.

The most striking example of this type of innovation is the creation of the four special economic zones in Fujian and Guangdong and their bureaucratic representative, the SEZ office under the State Council. The zones were placed outside the plan to give them the flexibility to attract foreign investors. They have attracted skilled workers with higher-than-usual wages, and their foreign connections have given them a strong claim on electric power supplies. According to SEZ officials, however, being outside the plan makes it difficult for them to obtain building materials and other supplies for joint-venture operations. The supply problem is so acute that the SEZ office recently demanded a change in policy that in effect reincorporates supplies for SEZ enterprises into the national plan. Enterprises outside the SEZ that want to export or engage in coproduction with foreign firms have similar although lesser difficulties because the plan never specifies their complete sources of supply. Managers must procure 10 to 25 percent of annual supplies on their own initiative.

Energy is also a problem. Factories often purchase new foreign equipment only to find that they cannot obtain the electric power to operate it. Power supplies have been a major source of contention between the managers of new joint ventures, especially in the SEZs, and provincial planning authorities, who tend to give priority to their traditional industrial customers (especially heavy industry, which consumes energy with remarkable inefficiency).[56]

The central authorities face a double-bind situation in the relationship between joint Chinese-foreign enterprises and the national economic plan. They would like to free the joint enterprises from the contraints of the plan to make it easier for them to compete in the international market, but they also want to guarantee that these enterprises suit Chinese development goals, are able to obtain supplies and power, and do not escape the planners' unified management.[57]

The contest for foreign currency brought into the country through foreign trade and investment also strains the planned economy. Enterprises, cities, and provinces that have earned foreign exchange don't always want to use it to import equipment, and sometimes would rather have Chinese renminbi to use for construction, social services, and other needs. Others want to import but are unable to obtain foreign currency through administrative channels. Because the central planners are loath to permit the free exchange of currencies within China, a black market in foreign exchange is growing instead. Guangdong reportedly sold some of the US$1 billion of foreign exchange it earned in 1981 to enterprises in interior provinces at two to three times the official exchange rate.[58] The many issues regarding the management of foreign exchange and the relationship between the foreign exchange game and the production plan game will have an important impact on the future of foreign investment and exports to China.

The advent of foreign trade and investment also puts pressure on administered prices in China. Most Chinese economists acknowledge the irrationality of using prices that have remained unchanged since the early 1950s and that bear no relationship to supply or demand. Nevertheless, policymakers fear a thorough price reform because its redistributive consequences would be so politically divisive. Partial rationalization of prices often does not work. For example, the trading companies of cities trying to attract foreign investment have permission to negotiate export prices freely. But they cannot change shipping prices, which are high by international standards. Managers of exporting enterprises report that they often use a third set of prices—not domestic plan prices or international market prices, but prices based on estimates of real cost—to plan production because the domestic plan prices are so irrational.

The discrepancy between domestic administered prices and international prices distorts the incentives of enterprises and trade companies to import and export. As one journal article put it, "The prices of some commodities, for instance, are high at home and low abroad, resulting in a loss when exported, while the prices of others are low at home and high abroad, producing a profit when exported."[59] In order to encourage the export of certain manufactured goods, the central government must subsidize the manufacturers through the MOFERT trading companies. And in certain product lines, the trading companies make more of a profit from importing than from exporting. China's involvement in international business thus creates pressures for price reform.

Past efforts of Soviet-style command economies to actively participate in international trade have been stymied by the shortages and inflexibilities of their planning system.[60] A partially reformed command economy, like that of China in 1984, can exacerbate these problems. Even Hungary, whose domestic economy is much more decentralized than China's, has not dismantled the trade monopoly of its central trade ministry; enterprises must clear all deals through the trade ministry's trading companies. Only Yugoslavia has granted its enterprises the freedom to trade on their own, and the central government still subsidizes exports.[61] China has gone further in decentralizing foreign investment and trade activities than any communist country but Yugoslavia. Even so, the unreformed features of China's command economy limit its ability to compete in international business. The question for the future is whether international competition will substitute for domestic economic reform in a centralized economy or intensify the pressures for economic reform.

FUTURE RESEARCH ISSUES

The "Communist coalition" of inland provinces, heavy industries (especially machine building), and central planning agencies and industrial ministries, which was favored and protected by prior policies encouraging self-sufficiency, now appears to be the major source of opposition to the new open-door policy in China. A coalition of coastal provinces, light industries, and local governments appears to be the prime beneficiary and supporter of this policy. Also, the structure of the economic planning system itself impedes the policy.

By mid-1982 it appeared that the Communist coalition had used its bureaucratic strength to successfully obstruct the open-door policy. The issue of protection for domestic industry was utilized to cut back on equipment imports and prevent Chinese-foreign joint ventures from selling to the domestic market. Support for foreign trade and investment was undercut by publicizing the smuggling, corruption, and cultural pollution carried in the wake of foreign business contacts, which stirred up fears that these contacts would result in the recolonizing of China. Strong criticism of several high-level public officials who had been duped by slick foreign business operatives (usually Overseas Chinese from Hong Kong) made other officials excessively suspicious of the foreigners with whom they were negotiating.[62] Worried that they might be accused of being "soft on capitalism," these Chinese officials made unrealistic demands of the foreigners and treated their profit expectations as illegitimate. MOFERT officials also tried to recentralize the management of foreign trade and Chinese-foreign enterprises.

Later in 1982, the top-level leaders and the coalition supporting foreign trade and investment moved to liberalize China's policies toward foreign investment. They were worried about the "misgivings of some foreign firms and people from financial circles over investing or setting up factories in China."[63] They realized that their hopes for a huge infusion of direct foreign investment to modernize the Chinese economy would not be fulfilled unless Chinese officials took a more realistic attitude toward the profit requirements of foreign investors and gave these investors more attractive incentives for producing in China. Newspaper articles told people that it was "wrong to haggle over the profits foreigners will make"; that they should understand that "foreign companies want to make money" and that "the marketing of products and the profit rates are matters of great concern" to them.[64] Although profit is a delicate political issue in a Communist system, the press met it head on: "There is a truth which is easy to understand: Capital in the international market always goes after profits. It will not come if it has no prospects of gain or will gain a lower profit rate than the international average."[65]

The authorities also implemented preferential tax cuts for joint ventures and lifted restrictions on the proportion of joint-venture products that can be sold on the domestic market. Joint ventures are no longer required to maintain a foreign-exchange balance by exporting their products; especially if China lacks a product that can substitute for an import, the joint venture can sell it domestically.[66] The move away from protectionism was defended by the argument that "excessively tight protection can turn the national industry into a 'hothouse plant' which loses its competitive capability, unable to face the world and brave the storm."[67] In addition, central planners extended the authority to negotiate joint ventures independently to Shanghai, Chongqing, and Hainan Island and raised Shanghai's retention rate for foreign exchange and domestic revenue.

This analysis leaves many questions unanswered. Our understanding of the politics of Chinese economic policy–making is still so incomplete that we are unable to determine why the Communist coalition could obstruct the open-door policy up to the middle of 1982, or why the coalition supporting foreign trade and investment could force it open again in late 1982 and 1983. Understanding such policy shifts will require much more information than we presently have about the Chinese policymaking process. Even before we have this information, however, we can suggest the key analytical issues that should guide our research on economic policy–making in the future.

1. What is the connection between the economic interests of an industrial sector and the bureaucratic interests of its ministry? Does the ministry articulate the preference of all the enterprises in that sector (including all employees, managers, engineers, and workers?), or only some of them? Which ones? Do enterprises under direct central administration and those under provincial or local administration have different preferences? Is the ministry sometimes more concerned about protecting domestic sales than the enterprises, which have few marketing responsibilities and only a weak profit incentive? How explicitly do ministers express the interests of their particular sector in top-level governmental discussions? When ministry officials deliberate together, do they invariably articulate departmental concerns, or are there factional alignments or consensus pressures that counteract departmentalism?

2. How can regional interests be determined, and what is the connection between regional interests and sectoral and bureaucratic ones? How does a province determine what its economic policy preferences are? What happens to minority economic interests in a province (steel mills in Guangdong or garment manufacturers in Taiyuan)? Industrial sectors are represented by their ministries, but how do regional interests come into play? Every province has representative offices in Beijing, but we do not know what role they play in the policy process. Are certain regions more heavily represented in the personnel of certain ministries? (For example, are a large number of the cadres in the machine-

building ministry from the Northeast, where many of the largest factories are located?) Are regions the basis for the factional ties that seem to pervade Chinese bureaucratic institutions? Do, for example, members of a Shanghai faction promote the open-door policy while members of a Northeast faction argue for protection of local heavy industry? If so, then how can we explain the antimarket, antitrade ideology of the Shanghai "radicals" during the Cultural Revolution decade?

3. What are the power resources that influence the outcome of bureaucratic, sectoral, and regional battles? How important is the amount of revenue generated by the enterprises under a ministry or in a sector or province? The number of enterprises or the number of employees? Whether or not the ministry has its own trading company? The patronage of a top-level leader? Having the support of powerful foreign investors? Only when we determine what the most important power resources are will we begin to understand why the Communist coalition was able to delay and impede the new open-door policy but not prevent it.

4. What is the role of the Communist Party in regional, sectoral, and bureaucratic conflicts over economic policy? Why were the problems of the special economic zones resolved in the Party secretariat in late 1982? The local Party organizations have been given the responsibility for handling the consolidation of local factories; is this because the Party is the only organization able to mediate sectoral and bureaucratic disputes? Is the Party itself an opponent of the open-door policy and a member of the Communist coalition, or is it also divided along regional, sectoral, and center-local lines?

5. Now that China has chosen to enter the world economy, what will be the impact of international factors on the future of the open-door policy? What difference will it make that China opened up foreign trade just when the world economy was sinking into a deep recession and worldwide protectionism was on the rise?[68] As a minor energy exporter instead of an energy importer, China gains nothing from the drop in energy prices. Will the benefits of lower prices for other imports counteract the serious problems of export markets created by the recession and by protectionism? The Chinese seem determined to expand their exports of textiles and machinery, even though raw materials and agricultural commodities would be likely to find markets more easily. Will this export strategy fall victim to the realities of slack international demand and trade restrictions? Will China's new diplomatic offensive in the Third World expand markets for exports there? Will Chinese efforts to strike good bargains with foreign companies that want to invest in China also be frustrated by the international recession? Some companies that have idle productive capacity because of low demand have already decided that given Chinese protectionism and the bureaucratic and other problems of joint production in China, they cannot afford a joint venture in China if the terms are not good. Will other firms pull out as soon as the Chinese make demands on them?

International joint ventures require local governments to share risks with their foreign partners. In the past year, the financial difficulties of their multinational partners have caused serious economic damage to Yugoslavia and South Korea, to name two examples. This could happen in China as well. Cooperation with large multinational firms that may have to cut back or close operations because of financial problems could jeopardize China's development efforts. China may find that in view of the domestic political conflicts sparked by joint ventures, international borrowing and outright purchases of technology might be a good substitute for direct foreign investment.

Involvement in international trade and investment offers opportunities for China to modernize its economy, but it also increases China's dependence on the world economy.[69] The current leadership is gambling heavily on the economic benefits of foreign trade and investment. The Communist coalition will certainly leap on any evidence of Chinese vulnerability or weakness in the international arena as a sign of exploitation at the hands of the capitalists. Yet in the current international economy, only low wages, low taxes, and the promise of the huge China market will attract foreign investors and customers to China. All in all, there is no reason to expect that China will reap the same dramatic successes as countries such as Japan that began exporting in an earlier, more profitable era. The conjunction of the domestic political pressures created by the Communist coalition and the international risks created by the recession may make it difficult for Deng Xiaoping and his successors to keep China's door open in the future.

NOTES

1. The 1977 figure is from the State Statistical Bureau, PRC *Statistical Yearbook of China, 1981* (Hong Kong: Economic Information Agency, 1982), p. 357. The 1981 figure is from *Zhongguo jingji nianjian 1982* [Yearbook of China's economy, 1982] (Beijing: Economic Management Periodical Publishers, 1982), Section VIII, p. 4, and *China Business Review* (*CBR*) 10 (July–August 1983):53.

2. Among foreign economists there is considerable debate about the size of China's trade ratio (total trade as a proportion of gross national product), based on methodological issues. For a discussion of these issues (and a high estimate), see Dwight H. Perkins, "The Central Features of China's Economic Development," in Robert F. Dernberger, ed., *China's Development Experience in Comparative Perspective* (Cambridge, Mass.: Harvard University Press, 1980), pp. 131–133. However, the Chinese themselves now state that this ratio was much too small in the past. For example, economist Zhang Peiji wrote, "Up to 1979, total value of China's exports accounted for only 0.8 percent of the world's exports. Total value of the goods the state procured for export accounted for only 4–5 percent of the country's total industrial and agricultural output value, a ratio far below that of other countries." "Development of China's Foreign Trade," in George C. Wang, ed., *Economic Reform in the PRC* (Boulder, Colo: Westview Press, 1982), p. 177. Press articles also compare the small size of

China's exports (0.9 percent of the world total according to one account, 0.8 percent according to Zhang) with the export share of the United States (10.9 percent), West Germany (10.5 percent), Japan (6.3 percent), France (6 percent), and Great Britain (5.6 percent). Foreign Broadcast Information Service, Daily Report, China [henceforth FBIS-China], September 15, 1981, p. K15.

3. *Renmin ribao* [henceforth *RMRB*], February 10, 1966, quoted in Audrey Donnithorne, *China's Economic System* (New York: Praeger, 1967), p. 331.

4. Chu-yuan Cheng, *China's Economic Development: Growth and Structural Change* (Boulder, Colo.: Westview Press, 1981), p. 447.

5. Deng Xiaoping's speech to the Twelfth Communist Party Congress, *Hongqi*, No. 18 (1982), in FBIS-China, September 16, 1982, p. K7.

6. *CBR* 10 (July-August 1983):53.

7. A good example is the defense of foreign trade by Trade Minister Chen Muhua, *RMRB*, September 20, 1982, p. 5. The absorption of foreign investment through the special economic zones has been defended by referring back to Lenin's policies. *Nanfang ribao* (*NFRB*), Guangzhou, July 5, 1982, in FBIS-China, July 15, 1982, p. P1. See also *Guoji maoyi* [International trade], August 1982, in Joint Publications Research Service (JPRS), 82457, December 14, 1982.

8. Benjamin Ward, "The Chinese Approach to Economic Development," in Dernberger, *China's Development Experience*, pp. 91–119.

9. Average annual rates of accumulation (of which the largest share was devoted to investment in fixed capital in industry) were 24.2 percent in 1953–1957, 30.8 percent in 1958–1962, 22.7 percent in 1963–1965, 26.3 percent in 1966–1970, and 33 percent in 1971–1975. *Beijing Review*, No. 12 (March 23, 1981):25, quoted by Robert F. Dernberger, "The Chinese Search for the Path of Self-Sustained Growth in the 1980's: An Assessment," in U.S. Congress, Joint Economic Committee, *China Under the Four Modernizations* (Washington D.C.: Government Printing Office, 1982), p. 21.

10. Nicholas R. Lardy, *Economic Growth and Distribution in China* (New York: Cambridge University Press, 1979).

11. Whereas in 1952 heavy industry accounted for about one-third of industrial production, by 1977 it accounted for over one-half. During the period 1949–1978, the gross value product of heavy industry multiplied 90.6 times, while agriculture and light industry rose only 240 percent and 1,980 percent respectively. Dong Furen, "Chinese Economy in the Process of Great Transformation," in Wang, *Economic Reform in the PRC*, p. 136.

12. Economist Dong Fureng sees regional self-sufficiency as related to the previous policies of national self-sufficiency: "In the past, we wrongly sought after complete self-sufficiency and even treated external economic relations from an out-of-date moral viewpoint. We looked upon imports of foreign goods and capital as something disgraceful. . . . Affected by this view, regions, departments, and enterprises were soon caught up with the idea of complete self-sufficiency. Pursuing autarky, quite a few regions (provinces, autonomous regions, and even countries) disregarded their respective comparative advantages and disadvantages and set up their own comprehensive systems to reach out for self-sufficiency." Ibid., p. 135. The argument that the drive for local self-sufficiency is caused by the shortages created by the command economy was made by Hungarian economist Janos Kornoi, and has been elegantly applied to China by Christine Wong, "The Economics of Shortage and the Problem of Post-Mao Reforms in China," (unpublished paper, 1982).

13. Wong, "Economics of Shortage," p. 7; Audrey Donnithorne, *The Budget and the Plan in China: Central-Local Economic Relations* (Canberra: Australian

78   *Susan Shirk*

National University, 1972) and *Centre-Provincial Economic Relations in China* (Canberra: Australian National University, 1981).

14. Nicholas R. Lardy, "Economic Planning in the People's Republic of China: Central-Provincial Relations," in U.S. Congress, Joint Economic Committee, *China: A Reassessment of the Economy* (Washington, D.C.: Government Printing Office, 1975), pp. 94–115. For a reassessment of the impact of Chinese policies on regional inequalities see Suzanne Paine, "Spacial Aspects of Chinese Development: Issues, Outcomes and Policies 1949–79," *Journal of Development Studies* 17, 2 (1981):133–195.

15. By coastal provinces, I mean the seven provinces (Liaoning, Hebei, Shandong, Jiangsu, Zhejiang, Fujian, Guangdong, including the municipalities of Beijing, Tianjin, and Shanghai) that constituted the modern industrial sector of the economy before 1949. Charles Robert Roll, Jr., and Kung-chai Yeh, "Balance in Coastal and Inland Industrial Development," in U.S. Congress, *China: A Reassessment*, p. 81.

16. *CBR* 9 (September-October 1982):21.

17. Xinhua News Agency, November 29, 1982, in FBIS-China, December 3, 1982, p. P3.

18. Xinhua News Agency, May 16, 1983, in FBIS-China, May 17, 1983, p. P3.

19. *Ming pao* (Hong Kong), July 6, 1982, in FBIS-China, July 6, 1982, p. W3.

20. During 1980 to 1982, over one-third of the cost of capital construction in the Shenzhen SEZ came from foreign investors. *NFRB*, June 14, 1982, in FBIS-China, June 24, 1982, p. P2.

21. "Coastal cities have good economic foundations, developed transportation and communication systems and a long history of establishing economic and technical contacts with foreign countries. They should have more decision-making power to promote foreign economic relations. We should give full play to their advantages." *RMRB*, December 31, 1982, in FBIS-China, January 4, 1983, p. K22.

22. Zhang Peiji, "Stick to Open Policy and Expand Foreign Trade," *Economic Reporter*, May 1982.

23. On National People's Congress debates over economic reform and readjustment among the representatives of different provinces, see Dorothy J. Solinger, "The Fifth National People's Congress and the Process of Policymaking: Reform, Readjustment, and the Opposition," *Issues and Studies* 18, 8 (August 1982):63–106.

24. For discussions of the problems in the Chinese negotiations with Fluor and Occidental see the *Los Angeles Times*, July 19 and August 23, 1983.

25. For example, Xinhua News Agency, March 3, 1982, in FBIS-China, March 5, 1982, p. K4; Xinhua News Agency, April 20, 1982, in FBIS-China, April 21, 1982, pp. K11–12; *Hongqi*, No. 9 (1982); British Broadcasting Company–Far East (BBC/FE), June 30, 1982; *RMRB*, February 28, 1983, in FBIS-China, March 4, 1983, p. K17.

26. Xue Muqiao, "Economic Management in a Socialist Country," in Wang, *Economic Reform in the PRC*, p. 33. A similar pattern has been found with regard to economic sectors in Japan by T. J. Pempel and Keiichi Tsunekawa, "Corporatism Without Labor? The Japanese Anomaly," in Philippe C. Schmitter and Gerhard Lehmbruch, eds., *Trends Toward Corporatist Intermediation* (Beverly Hills, Calif.: Sage Publications, 1979), p. 269.

27. *Shanxi ribao,* August 2, 1982, in FBIS-China, August 13, 1982, pp. R3–5; Shanxi Provincial Service, December 11, 1982, in FBIS-China, December 15, 1982, pp. R2–3.

28. One of its primary roles is "making the problems existing in the special zones known to the higher levels." *Wen hui pao* (Hong Kong), June 24, 1982, in FBIS-China, June 24, 1982, p. W1.

29. *Wall Street Journal,* March 3, 1983.

30. *RMRB,* December 8, 1982, in FBIS-China, December 15, 1982, pp. P1–5. There are also reports that the campaign to wipe out corruption in Guangdong has inhibited normal business activity. Guangdong is afraid to barter its imported goods for coal from other provinces for fear of being accused of smuggling. Officials are afraid to make contacts with foreigners, and demand that a third party be present in business negotiations so as not to become the targets of suspicion. *Ming pao* (Hong Kong), July 12, 1982, in FBIS-China, August 3, 1982, p. W1.

31. *RMRB,* September 13, 1982, in FBIS-China, September 20, 1982, p. K16; *Wen hui pao* (Hong Kong), June 17, 1982, in FBIS-China, June 25, 1982, p. W2; *NFRB,* July 5, 1982, in FBIS-China, July 15, 1982, pp. P1–3.

32. *South China Morning Post* (Hong Kong), September 14, 1982, in FBIS-China, September 14, 1982, pp. W6–9; *CBR* 9 (September-October 1982):4.

33. *RMRB,* March 16, 1983, in FBIS-China, March 25, 1983, p. K8.

34. In 1983 Shanghai's autonomy was expanded and the terms it could offer foreign companies were improved in order to attract more foreign capital to China. Xinhua News Agency, May 16, 1983, in FBIS-China, May 17, 1983, p. O3.

35. *Shijie jingji daobao* (*SJJJDB*), November 1, 1982, p. 4; *RMRB,* April 27, 1980; *China Daily,* July 22, 1982; *SJJJDB,* June 28, 1982, in FBIS-China, July 23, 1982, p. O3; *Liaowang,* June 20, 1982, in FBIS-China, August 3, 1982, p. K17; *RMRB,* August 2, 1982, in FBIS-China, August 10, 1982, p. K10; *RMRB,* August 16, 1982, in FBIS-China, August 26, 1982, p. K6; *China Daily,* January 22, 1983. There have been recent efforts to regulate interregional cooperation through the center—for example, there is a new office to handle the practice in the State Planning Commission—because of complaints that the practice has interfered with the planned economy. *Guangming ribao,* September 11, 1982, in FBIS-China, September 16, 1982, p. K15.

36. In 1981 the production targets assigned to enterprises under the Ministry of Machine Building were worth only 10 billion yuan, the equivalent of one-quarter of their total production capacity. *Ban yue tan,* July 25, 1982, in FBIS-China, August 13, 1982, p. K9.

37. Jack Craig, Jim Lewek, and Gordon Cole, "A Survey of China's Machine-Building Industry," U.S. Congress, Joint Economic Committee, *China Economy Post Mao* (Washington, D.C.: Government Printing Office, 1978), p. 291.

38. Wong, "Economics of Shortage," p. 4. Also see *Beijing Review,* No. 16 (April 18, 1983):24–25.

39. Donnithorne, *China's Economic System,* p. 324.

40. See *CBR* 8 (May-June 1981):34–35.

41. *RMRB,* February 11, 1981, in BBC/FE, February 16, 1981; *Guangzhou ribao,* May 20, 1982, in JPRS, 81681, September 1, 1982.

42. *RMRB,* March 31, 1982, in JPRS, 80839, May 18, 1982.

43. Ibid.

44. *China Daily,* October 8, 1982, p. 4; Japan External Trade Relations Organization (JETRO), *China Newsletter,* No. 41 (November-December 1982):17.

45. Xinhua News Agency, July 16, 1982, in FBIS-China, July 19, 1982, p. K19; *CBR* 9 (September-October 1982):26.

46. *Hong Kong Standard,* August 28, 1982, in FBIS-China, August 30, 1982, p. W5.

47. *CBR* 8 (November-December 1981):64.

48. Japan Economic Journal, June 22, 1982, p. 4.

49. As Michel Oksenberg, "Economic Policy-Making in China," *China Quarterly,* No. 90 (June 1982), and David M. Lampton, "Water Politics," *CBR* 10 (July-August 1983):10–17, have begun to do.

50. *Jingji ribao (JJRB),* January 3, 1983, in FBIS-China, January 18, 1983, pp. K15–16, K23–24, and Xinhua News Agency, January 12, 1983, in FBIS-China, January 18, 1983, p. K8.

51. See Chen Muhua, *RMRB,* September 20, 1982, p. 5.

52. As of early 1982, there were already nineteen trading corporations under the machine-building ministry, the Shipbuilding Corporation, and the metallurgical ministry, and twenty-eight integrated industry and trade corporations under the machine-building ministry alone. *CBR* 9 (January-February 1982):9.

53. Chen Muhua, *RMRB,* September 20, 1982, p. 5.

54. *Zhongguo xinwen she,* July 23, 1982, in FBIS-China, July 27, 1982, p. P1; JETRO, *China Newsletter,* No. 41 (November-December 1982):18; *Caimao jingji,* No. 6 (June 15, 1982), in JPRS, 81938, November 8, 1982.

55. Xinhua News Agency, February 23, 1983, in FBIS-China, February 25, 1983, p. K15.

56. In 1979 China's heavy industrial enterprises accounted for 28 percent of national income but 60 percent of total energy consumption; light industries accounted for 18 percent of national income and 10 percent of energy consumption. Light industry consumes only one-quarter the energy per unit of output consumed by heavy industry. *CBR* 9 (January-February 1982):13.

57. *Ta kung pao* (Hong Kong), August 9, 1982, in FBIS-China, August 16, 1982, pp. W5–7.

58. *Ming pao* (Hong Kong), July 6, 1982, in FBIS-China, July 6, 1982, p. W3.

59. *Caimao jingji,* No. 4 (August 20, 1981), in JPRS, 80435, March 30, 1982.

60. For numerous examples see the essays in Alan A. Brown and Egon Neuberger, eds., *International Trade and Central Planning* (Berkeley: University of California Press, 1968).

61. David Granick, *Enterprise Guidance in Eastern Europe* (Princeton, N.J.: Princeton University Press, 1975), pp. 274–275.

62. The most-publicized case was that of Vice-Minister of the Chemical Industry Yang Yibang. Xinhua News Agency, July 27, 1982, in FBIS-China, July 27, 1982, p. K4. A Tianjin case was described in inflammatory terms in *Tianjin ribao,* August 6, 1982, in FBIS-China, August 12, 1982, p. R3.

63. *RMRB,* May 14, 1983, in FBIS-China, May 18, 1983, p. K3.

64. *SJJJDB,* no date, and *China Daily,* May 17, 1983, in FBIS-China, May 17, 1983, p. K3.

65. *RMRB,* May 14, 1983, in FBIS-China, May 18, 1983, p. K2.

66. Xinhua News Agency, April 8, 1982, in FBIS-China, April 11, 1983, p. K8.

67. *RMRB,* May 14, 1983, in FBIS-China, May 18, 1983, p. K3.

68. Xue Muqiao argues that China is less vulnerable to world recession than other countries because "Our economic development mainly depends on our own efforts and more than 90 percent of our products are sold within our country. Most of our export commodities are also in great demand in China. If they cannot be exported, they can be sold in China." Xue also points out that world recession, by lowering the prices of foreign technology, can work to China's advantage, just as the 1930s world economic crisis enabled the Soviet Union to import foreign equipment and accelerate its development. "Xue Muqiao on Quadrupling," *SJJJDB*, December 13, 1982, in FBIS-China, January 6, 1983, p. 2.

69. Albert O. Hirschman, *National Power and the Structure of Foreign Trade* (Berkeley: University of California Press, 1980).

CHAPTER 4

INTERNATIONAL
SYSTEMIC CONSTRAINTS
ON CHINESE FOREIGN POLICY

Michael Ng-Quinn

Chinese foreign policy, like any other foreign policy, can be analyzed from various perspectives.[1] No one perspective is sufficient to fully explain Chinese foreign policy. My task in this chapter is to explicate and evaluate the relative importance of international systemic constraints on Chinese foreign policy. I shall examine both the Western literature and Chinese views of the same subject matter.

The Western literature on systemic theories is extensive.[2] Much of the debate seems to center on two issues: theoretical rigor and the composition and boundaries of a system. If we accept that the metaphysical substance of human behavior is not logically homeomorphic to theories in physics, much of the debate on the rigor of systemic theories as if they were theories in physics—as exemplified by the recent dispute between Kenneth Waltz and Morton Kaplan—seems excessively idiosyncratic.[3] As long as there is a discrepancy between "metamethodological homogeneity" and "the heterogeneity of reality and its unamenability to a single model of scientific explanation,"[4] theorists will continue to disagree. However, their disagreement on grounds of rigor or the lack thereof does not nullify the basic analytic usefulness of those elements of the systemic approach on which common agreement is possible. The systemic approach in this sense marks a scientific revolution in the study of international relations.[5]

Although the concept of "system" has been used by different theorists to denote different things, most agree more or less on the following points:

1. As defined by Morton Kaplan, at the highest level of abstraction, "A system of action is a set of variables so related, in contradistinction to its environment, that describable behavioral regularities characterize the internal relationships to each other and the external relationships of the set of individual variables to combinations of external variables."[6] As Ernst Haas puts it, a system is "the network of relationships among

relationships; not merely the relations among nations, but the relations among the abstractions that can be used to summarize the relations among nations."[7]

2. On a more operational level, a system is seen as consisting of two components: structure and processes. A structure is an abstraction denoting units "standing in characteristic relationships to each other."[8] In the words of Kenneth Waltz, "the structure is the systems-level component that makes it possible to think of the units as forming a set as distinct from a mere collection."[9] The component units are interconnected, and thus a change in any part may affect the whole.[10] "Processes" refers to the actual foreign policy behavior of units and their regularized patterns of interaction.

3. The major proposition of the systemic approach is that processes are constrained by the systemic structure. War and peace are seen as primarily shaped by external forces that are above and beyond the immediate control and influence of decision makers and domestic politics. According to Waltz, "Each state arrives at policies and decides on actions according to its own internal processes, but its decisions are shaped by the very presence of other states as well as by interactions with them." Furthermore, "since the variety of actors and the variations in their actions are not matched by the variety of outcomes, we know that systemic causes are in play."[11]

4. Both structure and processes imply regularities. The former denotes regularities that are durable and static enough to be termed "characteristic relationships." The latter involve regularized patterns of behavior that are relatively less durable and more dynamic. A two-term variable, for instance, is more suitably called a process than a structure. The difference between a mere mesh of relations and a structure can be illustrated by the difference between free-floating vapors in the air and various types of clouds: The differentiating criterion is the degree of interrelatedness of the units involved. Structures of clouds are determined by their height, shape, state of vapor content, and so on. Once clouds have been formed, regularized patterns of interaction among the vapors within them are constrained by cloud structures. However, the same clouds are simultaneously affected by irregular-vapor activities in the surrounding air, which are in turn susceptible to irregular influences of the physical environment such as temperature, wind conditions, and landscape. Once clouds have formed, their structures constrain the processes of vapor activities within them, but their original formation and subsequent transformation are also influenced by other irregular and often unpredictable elements in the surrounding or extrasystemic environment.

This summary represents the broadest common denominator among systemic theorists. However theorists disagree about how a structure is determined. What are the characteristic relationships? What is the composition and what are the boundaries of a system? I shall address these questions from the perspectives of three different approaches: a power or state-centric approach, emphasizing competition; a functionalist approach, emphasizing cooperation; and a capitalist world-system approach, emphasizing the role of a capitalist economy. The Chinese view of each approach will be briefly assessed.[12]

THE POWER OR STATE-CENTRIC APPROACH

Empirical international reality is complex and varied, yet any feasible and useful analysis of it must begin and end at some finite point. If everything counts as equally important, no analysis will be necessary. The key to understanding international relations, therefore, lies in *differentiation* and *prioritization*. Although the Olympics and the Miss Universe pageant are indeed aspects of international relations, they are certainly not as significant as the issues of arms proliferation or limitation, for example. In the state-centric approach, the criterion for establishing priorities is the notion that "the starting point of international relations is the existence of states, of independent political communities."[13] The leaders of these independent states can also be assumed to desire—as the Chinese do—an independent foreign policy.[14]

This approach to inter-*national* relations posits that *territoriality*, *sovereignty*, and *security* are the three autonomous and irreducible political points of departure. In this light, the characteristic relationships that make up a structure in systemic theories should be political. They should be strategic relationships based on the distribution of power among states, which in turn is determined by the states' relative capabilities. Because the principles of territoriality, sovereignty, and security preclude any higher supranational authority, the international system is characterized by anarchy and self-help.

Capabilities are relative: What one state is capable of doing depends on what others are capable of undoing. In this context, Chinese capabilities in terms of geography, population, natural resources, economy, military forces, and science and technology are indeed relatively tangible and quantifiable, and thus more susceptible to a cross-national comparison.[15] However, capabilities such as will, persuasion, political strength, diplomacy, deterrence, and strategy are relatively intangible, and thus are harder to compare. This makes it difficult to determine what the distribution of power is, and thus what the international structure is. Under the circumstances, comparisons of capabilities can only be made on the basis of periodic empirical tests of strength. In a nuclear context (assuming that neither side is willing to risk nuclear confrontation), these tests will have to be confined to areas and issues that do not directly threaten either country's territoriality, sovereignty, and security, or limited to shows of strength carried out by proxy.

Although systemic theorists emphasize the system level—i.e., the structure that constrains the processes, structural transformation is nevertheless brought about by changes in relative capabilities. If the sources of change in a state's capabilities come from within the state, can we still emphasize the system level? Stanley Hoffmann reminds us that "changes in those (domestic) regimes and forces affect the structure"[16]; Richard Rosecrance asserts: "Power in any event is largely determined by domestic, and thus unit-level and reductionist, influences"[17]; John Ruggie states that "in any social system, structural change itself ultimately has no source *other than* unit-level processes."[18] To these charges, Waltz replies: "I wrote not of power, but of the distribution of power, as being a defining structural concept . . . system-level and unit-level must be carefully distinguished so that the effect of each on the other can be examined."[19] If we accept the distribution of power as our major criterion, the systemic argument stands.

From this power or state-centric perspective, the Chinese recognize that the Soviet Union and the United States "are stronger than other countries" and "are locked in a wild scramble for power." Militarily, the two are seen as roughly balanced, though U.S. power is seen as having eroded. "In a continued arms race with the United States, an opponent stronger than itself, the Soviet Union would soon exhaust itself financially." Therefore, the possibility of the Soviet Union surpassing the United States in the 1980s "does not seem very likely."[20] The net result of these constraints is a loosening of bipolarity that the Chinese see as "multipolarization." For the superpowers, "the contradiction between their abilities and their wishes will become more prominent," and regional problems will become more difficult to control. Local and regional military conflicts will increase, as will small- and medium-scale wars.[21] Finally, on the hardware of power, the Chinese realistically acknowledge that any thorough disarmament is impossible, but propose that the superpowers stop the testing, improvement, and production of nuclear weapons and reduce their stockpile by 50 percent before others join the disarmament process.[22]

The above examples suggest that the Chinese do hold a power or the state-centric view of the international system. Before elaborating on the relevance of this approach to Chinese foreign policy, let us first consider the other two alternative approaches.

THE FUNCTIONALIST APPROACH

The power or state-centric approach has been challenged by theorists who emphasize other, more cooperative aspects of the international system. The major problem with these alternative approaches is that they merely add to the basic premises of the power approach instead of proposing different premises. They have not provided criteria of differentiation and prioritization that would subsume territoriality, sovereignty, and security under other categories. Let us cite a few examples.

In the field of international law and organization, Chinese participation has indeed been relatively active and positive.[23] The Chinese view the United Nations as playing a positive role in promoting the New International Economic Order and economic development, the Law of the Sea, human rights, decolonization, disarmament, and peacekeeping, and in condemning the actions of South Africa, Israel, and Vietnam. However, as Foreign Minister Wu Xueqian complained in 1983, many "correct" resolutions have not been implemented.[24] Moreover, the Chinese see the veto provisions as being inconsistent with the basic principle of equality, though they also see practical difficulties involved in any revision of the Charter.[25] In terms of constraints on Chinese foreign policy behavior, the Chinese tend to abide by the principles of international law and organization if they are consistent with, if not favorable to, Chinese interests. The Chinese use of international law to defend their claim of sovereignty over Xi Sha and Nan Sha (the Paracel and Spratley island groups) and their position over the railway bond conflict with the United States are cases in point.[26] However, when an appeal to international law yields no results, and when the Chinese feel that their territoriality, sovereignty, and security are threatened, no principles of international law and organization have hindered the Chinese from taking other measures to resolve conflicts, as perhaps demonstrated by the 1979 war with Vietnam.

Within East Asia, the futility of notions of regional integration, let alone a world society, can be demonstrated by the Mongolian tilt toward the Soviet Union, the impasse over Kampuchea, the distrust that some ASEAN members have not only of Japan but also of China (which China seems reluctant to acknowledge),[27] the distrust that China has of potential Japanese expansionism in the Pacific area[28] (especially in light of the textbook controversy[29]), the continued Korean division,[30] and the Taiwan problem.

In the West, there may be functionalist and "eco-inclusionist" promotion of global cooperation; the rise of postindustrial societies is supposed to lead to cross-national concerns over ecology, urbanization, industrialization, technology, and services.[31] The Chinese, however, tend to emphasize ultimate self-reliance and independence, as well as the indigenous conditions of each developing country. For them, there is no universal model.[32] Instead of global cooperation, the Chinese see global differentiation, if not confrontation, between the North and the South. The Chinese are therefore in favor of *partial* (as opposed to global) cooperation within the South, on the basis of "collective self-reliance."[33]

Proponents of transnational and transgovernmental relations have only shown that such relations exist; there is little evidence that nonstate actors have actually replaced states as the *primary* units of the international system. For instance, U.S. oil corporations may have refused to sell oil to the United States Navy in order to maintain good relations with

Arab oil-producing states in the 1973 Middle Eastern crisis, but this utilization of international politics as a tool to enhance business performance should not be confused with the ultimate political loyalty of corporations if and when territoriality, sovereignty, and security are at stake. Ultimate political loyalty is determined by the nationality of the majority of those who control the corporations (stockholders and top management), despite their multinational subordinate components. Moreover, multinational corporations can be subjected to the regulation of national governments.[34]

The Chinese recognize the dangers of dependency and destruction of the national character of one's economy posed by transnational corporations. The Chinese therefore advocate ultimate self-reliance and independence, and the exertion of control over foreign investments through such mechanisms as governmental regulation, nationalization, and joint ventures.[35] To the Chinese, transnational actors are manageable: They are not considered the primary units of the international system.

Some argue that unlike money, power is not fungible but situation-specific. Power assets in one area may be liabilities in another.[36] In some cases, security may not be an issue, or military power may not be usable or effective. In other cases, "complex interdependence" or "mutual vulnerability" make disruption of the relationship costly to both sides.[37] A systemic structure cannot be defined only in terms of a singular "distribution of power"; many modes of power may have to be taken into consideration, depending on the specific issues involved. The international system is best characterized as one based on multiple issues.[38]

Whether power is fungible is debatable. Although the mighty United States seemed unable to "force" Iran to release the hostages during the hostage crisis, it is nevertheless unclear what would have happened had the hostages been harmed. Arab oil-producing countries were able to use oil as a weapon during the Middle East crisis of the early 1970s, yet it is unclear whether the affected industrialized states would have exercised their power and forcefully seized the oil fields had oil production totally ceased, thus suffocating their economies.

The Chinese seem to understand that there is a limit to what a weaker state can do. They support the formation of cartels as well as the establishment of a New International Economic Order,[39] but they have not joined the Group of 77. Instead, they have joined such establishments of the "old" international economic order as the World Bank and the International Monetary Fund (IMF).[40] The Chinese also realize that the developed countries can cope with an oil crisis through conservation, coordination, and manipulation of other market mechanisms, diminishing the effectiveness of oil as a weapon.[41] Despite an emphasis on South-South cooperation, Chinese trade with the Third World only amounted to 23 percent in 1981. Moreover, the Chinese realize that unilateral aid to the Third World cannot be sustained.[42] Finally, the Chinese have no illusions about how the power of the South is limited by its uneven development, its dependency on the North, and the various historical and political differences and conflicts among its members.[43]

The problem with the multiple issue–based system is that it lacks differentiation and prioritization. Although international relations consist of many aspects, some are more important than others. Even proponents of "complex interdependence" concede that "military power dominates economic power in the sense that economic means alone are likely to be ineffective against the serious use of military force."[44] The basic universal concerns over territoriality, sovereignty, and security differentiate international relations into strategic and nonstrategic aspects, and assign a higher priority to the former. Under normal circumstances, strategic and nonstrategic power may not seem to be interchangeable. However, when territoriality, sovereignty, and security are at stake, different kinds of power resources can be converted into one. Force is ultimately usable if the costs incurred by its use are seen to be necessary and worthwhile in order to preserve or protect something of a higher and irreducible value. Even Keohane and Nye concur that "survival is the primary goal of all states, and in the worst situations, force is ultimately necessary to guarantee survival."[45]

As far as the Chinese are concerned, their experience in the past hundred years should make it doubly clear that the strategic aspects of international relations count more. Due to China's relative isolation from the world economy until recent times, "complex interdependence" does not seem to be applicable.

Without disputing the centrality of states, some analysts nevertheless argue that the international system is not anarchic, and that there are social rules based on common interests that govern interaction among states.[46] Some of these rules have become institutionalized; they are sometimes called "international regimes."[47] According to Stephen Krasner, "Regimes can be defined as sets of implicit or explicit principles, norms, rules, and decision-making procedures around which actors' expectations converge in a given area of international relations. Principles are beliefs of fact, causation, and rectitude. Norms are standards of behavior defined in terms of rights and obligations. Rules are specific prescriptions or proscriptions for action. Decision-making procedures are prevailing practices for making and implementing collective choice."[48]

The basic function of regimes, according to Krasner and others, is to coordinate state behavior. Regimes are needed when "Pareto-optimal outcomes" cannot be achieved through uncoordinated individual calculations of self-interest (the game of prisoners' dilemma), or when the decision of one actor is contingent upon another's decision in avoiding mutually undesirable and disastrous outcomes (the game of chicken).[49]

The problem with the socialization or regimes approach is its dependence on prior agreement on security issues; regimes and institutions supplement but do not replace the basic premises of the state-centric approach. As Krasner concedes, "Pure power motivations preclude regimes."[50] Susan Strange captures the problem concisely: "All those international arrangements dignified by the label regime are only too easily upset when either the balance of bargaining power or the perception of national interest (or both together) change among those states who negotiate them."[51]

Changes in the balance of bargaining power or the perception of national interest affect regimes but not the international structure, which can only be transformed by changes in the general balance or distribution of power (not just specific bargaining power). In this sense, regimes are neither autonomous nor durable enough to generate any structural constraint on states. Regimes are merely tools or processes, constrained by the more durable international structure. As Robert Jervis has suggested, there are at least four conditions for the formation and maintenance of a security regime: (1) the great powers must desire it; (2) the states involved must believe that others share the value they place on mutual security and cooperation; (3) the states must agree that security is not enhanced by expansion; and (4) war and unilateral pursuit of security must be seen as costly.[52] These conditions are seldom met in an anarchic, state-centric international system.

In summary, the functionalist, eco-inclusionist, interdependent, and multiple issue–based models do not seem to fit the international system. If they do apply, it is to a subsystem operating under the anarchic, state-centric and power-oriented international system, where territoriality, sovereignty, and security are the criteria that differentiate and prioritize international relations.

THE CAPITALIST WORLD-SYSTEM APPROACH

A third wave of literature tries to characterize the international system primarily in economic rather than political-strategic terms. According to Immanuel Wallerstein and Christopher Chase-Dunn,[53] the contemporary world-system consists of an interstate system plus an integrated capitalist world economy built on a hierarchy of exchange relations between the more-developed core and the less-developed periphery. States and the interstate system are but the political side of the capitalist mode of production; they are instruments to reorganize production relations on a world scale when the accumulation process outgrows its existing political framework. States are utilized by the classes that control them to expropriate their share of world surplus value.

The world proletariat consists of wageworkers in the core and politically coerced workers and small commodity producers in the periphery. The world bourgeoisie is engaged in both interclass and intraclass conflict, forming both interstate and intraclass or transnational alliances. Capital may flow from one area to another, across national boundaries. While the uneven development of capitalism maintains the division of sovereignty in the core through interimperial rivalry, the political and military power of states is used to supplement and alter the economic competitive advantages of different groups with different interests. Market forces are manipulated to enhance the world market position of the classes and factions controlling the state.

Meanwhile, the competitive nature of the interstate system prevents any state from gaining a monopoly and subjects producers to the necessity of increasing productivity. Successful extraction of world surplus value thus hinges on the effective use of state power and the ability to produce efficiently for the competitive world market.

The capitalist world-system incorporates even socialist states. Capital accumulation can be carried out socialistically. A relatively more self-sufficient position and concentration of state power may enable socialist states to respond to world market changes more readily and give them a competitive edge. But the capitalist nature of the world-system is not altered by the existence of socialist national subsystems.

The world-system approach as summarized above has several problems. In the first instance, it reduces the irreducible: Politics cannot be reduced to economics. There are political conflicts of a noneconomic nature, and political relations may still exist even in the absence of economic exchange relations. Moreover, states and the competitive interstate system predate the rise of capitalism.[54] From a global perspective, the balance-of-power system did not evolve out of sixteenth century Europe alone; it also characterized, for instance, premodern China's relations with various Central Asian states (such as the Hsiung-nu, Turks, and Mongols) as well as with Japan. This had nothing to do with capitalism and did not produce a world empire incorporating all of the states involved.[55] There may be a correlation between the competitive interstate system and the capitalist world economy, but neither one has created the other.

The role of the state in determining its degree of participation in the capitalist world economy is likewise underestimated. Unless capitalism is forcefully imposed, local elites will favor participation in the world economy only when they believe it to be in the interest of their domestic rule.[56] A relatively self-sufficient state can choose to abstain from joining or to withdraw from the capitalist world economy; this may even encourage greater egalitarianism and socialism within the state, as the oppressive elements, including the bureaucracy, will be deprived of international allies.[57] A relatively self-sufficient state can also choose to abstain from participating in noncapitalist, socialist world economy, as China refused to join the Council for Mutual Economic Assistance (COMECON) in order to undermine Soviet hegemony.[58] Here even Marxism proved to be constrained by nationalism rather than being truly transnational.[59] By the same token, depending on the orientations of the local elites and their perceptions of their state's position in the competitive interstate system, a state can choose to join or rejoin the capitalist world economy, or the socialist one, or both. A state can also choose to alternate between participation and withdrawal.[60] For a relatively self-sufficient state such as China, it is a matter of choice—to be made on the basis of both economics and politics. Politics, like economics, is autonomous and irreducible, though the two may be interrelated. Since 1949, the Chinese state, state building, and participation in the competitive interstate system have been independent of capitalism, and they predate China's increased participation in the capitalist world economy.

The conception of a single capitalist world-system that incorporates even socialist states has been disputed by those who argue that the Soviet Union and other COMECON members constitute a separate socialist world economy.[61] The characterization of the capitalist world-system in terms of exchange relations has also been critiqued from a Marxian perspective. It is argued that trading with capitalist states does not make one a member of a capitalist system; nor does it necessarily make one internally capitalist, which is determined by whether the class controlling the means of production is the bourgeoisie or the proletariat. Capitalism is a mode of production that presupposes certain relations of production leading to class formation and class struggle. Class struggle presupposes not only a commercial class extracting surplus through exchange, but also a working class; class struggle also means seizure of state power, which is not only economic but also ideological and political. Thus, a worldwide transnational class struggle presupposes not only a worldwide transnational bourgeoisie, but also a worldwide transnational proletariat engaged in class struggle within a universal state. In the absence of the latter two criteria, there can be no integrated capitalist world-system, but only individual capitalist and other states engaged in exchange relations without leading to a worldwide class struggle for control over a universal state that does not exist.[62] Such exchange relations do not necessarily constitute a hierarchy or dependency.[63]

Whether the Chinese fully understand the theoretical implications of the capitalist world-system approach is unclear. At least one prominent Chinese economist has remarked that the core-periphery dichotomy is invalid.[64] There is, however, evidence showing that the Chinese do share some of the views of the world-system theorists. For instance, the Chinese describe the world economy as a product of capitalism, international division of labor, increase in the export of capital, state intervention, and the development of state monopoly capitalism. The net result is the internationalization of capital.[65] Moreover, through merger, diversification, and internationalization, monopoly capitalism is seen as being capable of penetrating different societies with different political systems.[66] Nevertheless, within the world economy the Chinese see possibilities for a variety of models, as Romania, Korea, and Yugoslavia have developed their own.[67]

The Chinese, like the world-system theorists, see a hierarchy of exchange relations between the developed and the developing states. As the Chinese put it: "Today, foreign capital and international trade constitute the main forms of exploitation," which "takes place through exchanges of unequal value." However, unlike the world-system theorists, the Chinese do not accept a static core-periphery dichotomy, but see the relationship between the developed and the developing states as interdependent and dynamic. To the Chinese, "without the developing nations, the economics of the developed nations might well crumble." Although the Chinese concede that "the developing countries are still dependent on the advanced countries in such areas as investment, technology, and trade," they nevertheless see the developing countries as "already beginning to challenge the developed nations in certain economic areas." Because the developing countries together constitute three-quarters of the world's population, occupy three-fifths of the world's land, possess oil and twenty major strategic metals, and offer numerous markets, "the future development of the world economy depends to a large degree on the economic development of the developing countries."[68] In the words of Foreign Minister Wu Xueqian, if the economic difficulties of the developing countries "are not resolved or are aggravated, the entire world economy is bound to suffer."[69]

Instead of accepting the status quo, the Chinese see a need for both international and internal structural reforms.[70] In their view, basic differences between capitalist and socialist systems remain, and reforms cannot be transplanted but must respond to local needs.[71] The negative Chinese views of capitalism can be summarized as follows. Capitalism has still not collapsed only because production forces have turned out to be more primary than production relations. Production in capitalist societies has been spurred by advancement in science and technology and by state monopoly; new industries, new credit systems, and new markets have been created. Crises of capitalism can also be transferred from the developed to the developing countries through the help of transnational corporations. But an imbalance has also developed between the overinvested military industry and other industries and agriculture in capitalist and developed countries. The result is an increase in inflation, debt, consumption, and waste. The parasitic nature of capitalism is thus intensified, and other moral and social problems also arise.[72] Compromises by capitalists may have improved the material conditions of workers in capitalist countries, but their social status has actually deteriorated as they continue to be exploited.[73] Structurally, the proportion of units engaged in material production has decreased as the number of non-production units has increased.[74] Contradictions between production and consumption will persist as long as production is motivated by a fear of failure and competition, and consumption by exploited workers is precluded by subsistence wages.[75] The combination of overproduction and underconsumption (or the relative diminishing of markets) leads to a new chronic phenomenon of "stagnation-inflation" (*tingzhi pengzhang*), and state policies can cope with only one problem at a time with only temporary results.[76] As banks and industries join forces, capitalism becomes more diversified and internationalized, but its nature remains the same.[77] The aim of capitalists is to exert control over politics.[78]

Like world-system theorists, the Chinese also try to link economics to politics at the international level.[79] The Chinese see economic problems in both the United States and the Soviet Union and their respective blocs. Contradictions within each bloc have intensified, and the loosening of both blocs hinders both the United States' reassertion of hegemony and the Soviet Union's quest for it.[80] Moreover, the establishment of a New International Economic Order is not just an economic issue but also a political one.[81] The relationship between the North and the South is closely tied to the issues of whether hegemonism can be contained and world stability maintained. Economic problems in the developing countries may lead to political turmoil, which in turn may provide an opportunity for the Soviet Union to intervene, sometimes using "aid" as a way in.[82]

Given the Chinese views of the world economy portrayed above, how should the Chinese respond? Here the role of the state matters most: Depending on the orientation of the Chinese elites at any given time, China has alternated between relative withdrawal from and relative participation in the capitalist world economy. Both withdrawal and participation are *relative* because self-reliance and foreign trade are not mutually exclusive. In the 1973–1976 period, for instance, when the Gang of Four had the upper hand and "slavish comprador philosophy" (*yang nu zhe xue*), "crawlingism" (*pa xing zhu yi*), and "worshipping foreign things and fawning on foreign powers" (*chong yang mei wai*) were denounced, no closed-door policy was advocated. Instead, in addition to self-reliance, it was argued that foreign things should be made to serve China (*yang wei zhong yong*) and useful foreign technology and equipment should be imported. What should be avoided, according to the Gang, was to become dependent on imports and to let foreign monopoly capitalists exploit China by exchanging their capital and equipment for Chinese labor and natural resources.[83] Likewise, in the era after the Gang of Four was removed from power, advocates of foreign trade also prefaced their policy statements by emphasizing the importance of self-reliance, equality, mutual benefit, and centralized state planning. Exports were needed, it was argued, to pay for the necessary imports and to give aid to the Third World. The Gang's policy was said to have played into the policy of imperialists who aimed at isolating and containing China. One 1977 article, although emphasizing foreign trade, stated that collaboration with capitalist countries to extract Chinese natural resources, joint ventures, and the lease of territories or territorial water to foreign countries had never been and would never be allowed.[84] On this cautious note, the Chinese elites began to increase China's participation in the capitalist world economy.

The caution of Chinese leaders is understandable in the context of China's historical experience with foreigners and imperialism. Politically, the management of foreign trade is indeed a highly sensitive task. However, as the Chinese elites have also come to realize: "In the world today, production, commodity circulation and science and technology are so highly developed that no single country has all the resources and technology needed for developing its economy." To maintain a balance, "China relies mainly on its own efforts and makes external assistance supplementary." Between 1979 and 1982, for instance, foreign capital only amounted to 37.5 percent of total investments.[85]

The forces of the capitalist world economy have thus made the Chinese elites realize that economic construction is essential[86] and that despite its population, resources, and history, China is but a "small and weak" country in terms of material production, science and technology, and the people's livelihood. The task is to transform a socialist economy into "socialist big production." This requires the destruction of the habitual forces of small production and the transformation of the relations of production and the superstructure.[87]

Socialist production does not preclude the recognition of the historical contribution the capitalist class has made in building a world economy. The material foundation created by capitalism for the new world should in fact be fully utilized. Science and technology are the wealth and product of humankind's prolonged struggle, and are thus common to all people. They have no class nor national boundaries; they are inheritable regardless of social system and synthetic in terms of dialectic theory. To the economically and technologically backward countries, exchange with foreign countries and imports of technology are a short cut to surpassing advanced countries, as demonstrated by the experiences of Romania, Czechoslovakia, and China itself during its first five-year plan. What one acquires for oneself (*zi ji na lai*) is not the same as what is given by foreigners (*yang ren song lai*). What one can produce, even of a worse quality, should not be imported, and one should try hard to improve the quality. If a country needs technology but can produce the equipment, then only the technology should be imported and not the equipment. If only turnkey equipment is needed, there is no need to import a whole plant.[88] Finally, despite China's disadvantages—backwardness, lack of capital, huge population, and unexploited natural resources, the Chinese elites nevertheless see advantages in China's centralized system of socialism, thought preparation, security and political prestige, and they see a favorable external environment. China is ready for a greater degree of participation in the world economy.[89]

What the Gang of Four feared was a revival of capitalism as a result of foreign trade and the import of nonproletarian ideas along with the import of foreign technology and equipment. For foreign trade to work, its economic benefits must in some way be translated into political chips for its advocates. The current Chinese elites (who overthrew the Gang of Four) believe that greater participation in the capitalist world economy is not only in the interest of their domestic rule but also in the national interest (though it is difficult to differentiate between the two). Whether the current policy will succeed will depend on how its effects on self-reliance and independence are perceived by those who are politically opposed to foreign trade but economically susceptible to its benefits. If Chinese self-reliance and independence can be maintained within a framework of participation, then the static hierarchy between the core and the periphery, as postulated by world-system theorists, may also be challenged. Finally, the ability of the Chinese elites to choose between participation and withdrawal shows that the world economy—capitalist or otherwise—does not constrain the behavior of states as much as the international structure does.

SYSTEMIC CONSTRAINTS: BIPOLARITY

Though all three views of the international system—the power approach, the functionalist approach, and the world-system approach—have some impact on Chinese foreign policy, the power or state-centric approach seems to be of primary importance owing its emphasis on territoriality, sovereignty, and security. The Chinese recognize that the Soviet Union and the United States "are stronger than other countries." This Chinese perception is objectively valid if we take into consideration the following three military criteria: (1) at the nuclear level, both have the second-strike or retaliatory capability to strike effectively at the core territories of their actual and potential adversaries should nuclear confrontation occur; (2) at the conventional level, both maintain numerous troops at home and abroad, giving them the capacity to project power at any given time; and (3) both have a considerable number of formal military and semimilitary alliances with other states (including, in the Soviet case, a score of treaties of "friendship and assistance"). I call these two states *poles*; A "pole" is a state possessing such superior capabilities that other states are drawn to it for protection and other benefits.

Using different sets of criteria, analysts can conceptualize different modes of polarization. Unipolarity, bipolarity, tripolarity, multipolarity, and even "bi-multipolarity" may all be a matter of definition.[90] However, to the extent that polarity can be defined in terms of a specific set of empirical criteria, it does serve a useful analytic purpose in delineating the distribution of power and thus the systemic structure. Although the goals of decision makers certainly influence decision making, the actualization of goals and the implementation of decisions (a state's external actions) are nevertheless constrained by the state's own capabilities in relation to those of other states, i.e., the distribution of power. In this sense, systemic stability depends on the actions of states, which are in turn constrained by the distribution of power. Because polarity entails a certain distribution of power, both the actions of states and stability are constrained by polarity.[91]

It is also useful to draw a distinction between *polarity*, which is the actual distribution of power based on relative capabilities, and *polarization*, which is the tendency to cluster around powerful states. Some suggest that polarity does not necessarily imply polarization.[92] I disagree. Polarity does imply polarization, but not necessarily *tight* polarization. In this sense, depolarization does not necessarily mean the diminishing of polarity, only a loosening of it. The loosening of a bipolar system, for instance, does not necessarily mean the diminishing of bipolarity or the formation of multipolarity. Particular forms of polarity and polarization can be either tight or loose.

Based on these criteria, China is not a pole, but the United States and the Soviet Union are.[93] Under bipolarity, competition, if not enmity, between the two poles is inevitable, for only they can threaten each other with a strike at the other's core. In the absence of a third pole or common threat, it is unlikely that the two poles will form an alliance. The idea of establishing a world empire through collusion would probably be unattractive to either pole, because of mutual distrust; and because the "overhead costs" of a world empire would be too high.[94] A world empire would also eliminate external insecurity and competition, which might encourage internal laxity and disintegration.

Under bipolarity, whether tight or loose, any state perceived by the two poles as a potential asset usually has to "lean" to either one side or the other; it usually cannot remain either neutral or equally friendly with both poles. Under highly competitive conditions, neutrality may be interpreted by each pole as negative and potentially favorable to the other pole, and thus unfriendly. The attempt to be equally friendly with both poles at the same time is likely to arouse equal suspicion from both. (Anomalies do exist. Due to historical development or other special circumstances, the two poles may mutually prefer neutrality over certain areas in order to maintain a balance of power or general stability, or to lessen competition.)

In order to survive bipolar competition, a state being courted by both poles usually must choose sides. Choosing sides does not preclude the possibility of subsequently shifting and reshifting sides, although higher costs may result owing to a relative loss of trust. Nor does choosing sides necessarily mean a total loss of freedom: Within a coalition (tight or loose) centered around a pole, variety or polycentricity may still be permissible in areas not directly related to central strategic concerns (especially under loose bipolarity).

Defiance against bipolarity is always a temptation for second-level states, yet unless they have already achieved the capabilities and status of a "pole," their attempts inevitably fail. As the Chinese experience in the 1960s has demonstrated, it is costly, if not dangerous, to defy or confront both poles at the same time.

Although many secondary powers may aspire to be poles themselves, they may nevertheless find good reasons to accept bipolarity in the meantime. There is at least one element of certainty under bipolarity, namely, competition (if not enmity) between the two poles, which imposes certain constraints on the behavior of other states. The other states can at least build and plan their policies around this structural certainty. Structural constraints and coalitions may decrease the freedom of states and diminish their opportunities, but they also minimize costly uncertainties and surprises. Interaction among states is likely to be relatively stable.

Second, under bipolarity an initial conflict among members of the two coalitions, if left uncontrolled, might escalate and ultimately involve the two poles. Fear of that ultimate confrontation, at the nuclear level or otherwise, will motivate members of both coalitions to exercise moderation and restraint in resolving their initial conflicts. The two poles themselves will also have enough incentives to confine their own conflicts to the peripheries. If the cores of both coalitions are left relatively undisturbed, the bipolar international structure is likely to remain stable.[95]

There is a third reason that bipolarity is acceptable, if not preferable, to many second-level states. With only two poles, each coalition is bound to be large. As one coalition expands, the other will have to follow suit, resulting in a competitive spiral. Riker's "size principle"—that a coalition should be just large enough to allow maximization of spoils[96]—does not apply here, as the stakes go beyond specific "shares of spoils" to general stability and survival. As the size of a coalition increases, its aggregate capabilities will also increase. Eventually, the collective weight of the coalition will be overwhelming enough to cover any irregular or isolated individual weakness or, for that matter, breach of obligation on the part of individual members. Precisely because of this insurance, coalition members, especially secondary powers, can afford to be lax in fulfilling their commitments; they may occasionally be tempted to delegate their responsibilities to others or to defer to the pole's leadership whenever high costs are incurred. The pole, in order to maintain the coalition, will have no choice but to assume whatever extra responsibilities its own capabilities allow, thus benefiting the other members of the coalition.

Constrained by bipolar international structure, Chinese foreign policy falls within a narrow range of possibilities. At any given time, China may lean toward either the United States (as in the mid-1940s and the 1970s) or the Soviet Union (the late 1940s and the 1950s). It may also alternate between the two poles, and it is precisely this availability of alternatives that gives China bargaining leverage. The ability to shift sides also prevents the two poles from considering China as a permanent part of the enemy's camp.[97]

China is unlikely to be neutral or equally friendly with both poles. Defiance against both poles is a possibility (as in the mid-1960s and possibly in the 1980s), but this attempt at independence is likely to fail so long as China remains a secondary power. Within a coalition (tight or loose) centered around a pole, China will be able to maintain a certain degree of independence (as in the 1950s within the socialist camp, and in the 1970s within the loose coalition dominated by Western capitalists). It may also delegate responsibilities or defer to the pole whenever high costs are incurred (for example, the Chinese have called for cooperation against Soviet hegemonism while spending too little on national defense themselves).

Space limits preclude the presentation of detailed empirical evidence to show how Chinese foreign policy behavior has been constrained by bipolarity since the 1940s.[98] In the 1970s, the Chinese consistently portrayed the Soviet Union as the more dangerous of the two super-powers,[99] using support for national liberation movements, economic cooperation, military aid, and international division of labor as pretexts to extend its hegemony.[100] According to the Chinese, the Soviets charged high interest rates and required aid recipients to buy Soviet products, pay back their loans with low-priced products and raw materials, and pay high salaries to Soviet experts. The Chinese also accused the Soviets of intervening in the domestic affairs of aid recipients.[101] In the economic realm (assuming a Soviet-dominated socialist world economy), "con-sultative-regulative planning" (*xie tiao jihua*) meant producing what the Soviets needed.[102] The Chinese argued that the Soviet notions of "limited sovereignty," "socialist big family," and "export of revolution" were inconsistent with proletarian internationalism, which emphasized in-dependence and equality of different nationalities. Treating themselves as "guardians" (*jia zhang*), the Soviets advocated an unacceptable "for-mulism" (*fang shi fang fa*) to regulate interparty relations.[103] Finally, the Chinese saw the United States as being on the decline, which created an imbalance and thus increased the danger of war.[104] Soviet proposals regarding arms limitations and reduction and détente were said to be false and unreliable. Because the Soviet system was more centralized, the Chinese predicted that Soviet expansion would be more adventurous and frantic.[105] (Even the radicals concurred with this prevailing view of Soviet hegemony, though they were more inclined to emphasize the domestic sources of Soviet external behavior.)[106] Realizing that between the two superpowers, "in essence, rivalry is primary," and "the Soviet Union's chief rival is the United States,"[107] the Chinese decided to lean toward the United States.

In the 1980s, two forces seem to have pushed the Chinese toward rapprochement with the Soviets. First, the forging of a global anti-Soviet coalition has been hindered by economic problems and divisions within the West as well as within the Third World.[108] Since the 1970s, the Chinese have noted the tendency of some Western elements to "divert the Soviet peril to the East, to China."[109] The Chinese feel compelled to remind the West that the focal point of superpower contention is still Europe; it has not moved to the East.[110] They also warn that although the détente policy of the Soviets may have brought some benefits to Western Europe, it is only a smoke screen.[111] While mutual suspicion persists between China and the West, the Chinese may consider it unsafe to continue assuming an anti-Soviet stand alone. Second, recurrent tensions in Sino-American relations, especially over the Taiwan question,[112] may also have prompted the Chinese to keep the Soviet option open.

The current Chinese view is that militarily, the two superpowers are roughly balanced. The United States is seen as being on the defensive, though recently it has attempted to rebound.[113] U.S. isolationism is seen as a mere tactic to gain some freedom of action for internal consolidation, not as a mainstream shift.[114] The Soviet Union is also perceived as unlikely to surpass the United States militarily because of economic constraints.[115] The expected net result is continued contention between the two superpowers (bipolarity), although regional problems will become more difficult to control, loosening this bipolarity. Failing to draw a distinction between "polarity" and "polarization," the Chinese take the loosening of bipolarity to mean multipolarization, leading to multipolarity.[116]

This new interpretation gives the Chinese a certain degree of flexibility, as well as an opportunity for internal debate. On the one hand, they realize that there is no escape from bipolarity (despite its loosening) and that even some members of the nonaligned movement lean toward one or the other superpower.[117] On the other hand, the Chinese also believe that it is dangerous to rely on a superpower for protection against a third actor.[118] A more "independent" Chinese foreign policy is called for; rapprochement with the Soviets can thus be justified even though mutual suspicion continues.[119] As proposed in the *Beijing Review*, "the situation of opposing mainly one hegemonic power in a period while opposing another in other period is likely to appear."[120]

Given this ambivalence, it is unclear whether China will continue to lean toward the West, attempt to establish neutrality, defy bipolarity, or shift sides more frequently. What is clear is that as long as China has not acquired the requisite capabilities to become a pole, its external behavior will remain constrained by bipolarity.

SYSTEMIC CONSTRAINTS: TRIPOLARITY

Using a different set of criteria, one might see China, the United States, and the Soviet Union as forming a tripolar international structure. Theoretically, the three poles could compete with each other on an independent basis; they could be mutually positive, negative, or neutral toward each other. However, if one party decides to operate independently, there is no guarantee that the other two will act likewise. Maintaining one's independence unilaterally entails the risk of being isolated by an alignment between the other two. This fear will encourage all three poles to seek alignment, or it will insure that each pole will impede any alignment between the remaining two.

The basic characteristic of tripolarity is fluidity. Unlike bipolarity, under which at least one competitive relationship is certain, tripolarity entails no necessary enmity nor amity. Today's friend can be tomorrow's enemy. Under such ambiguous circumstances, it would seem that the safest course for each pole would be to establish and maintain positive relationships with both of the other two poles. There are two possible outcomes.

First, if the other two poles also have a positive relationship, there will be mutually positive relationships among all three. However, as in the case of all three acting independently, each will fear being sold out by a closer relationship between the other two. As a result, none will be satisfied with the status quo, and the same uncertainty and instability will result from even more intensified competition among the three.

Second, if the other two have a negative relationship, the third can act as a pivot by pursuing positive relationships with both and then playing the other two against each other. The problem with the scenario is that the advantages of a pivotal role will be clear to all three, and thus all three will compete for that position, restoring the game to its original form—uncertainty and instability.

Alternatively, instead of trying to establish positive relationships with both of the other two, one can try to align with only one of them at the expense of the third. There is a chance of one being rebuked if the other two are already aligned. However, one's chances of success are good if the other two already have a negative relationship. If one pole is considered a common adversary by two, an alignment between the two and the exclusion of the third is likely. In the absence of trust, relative stability under tripolarity hinges on whether there are clear incentives for two poles to align against the third.[121]

Under tripolarity, the exact distribution of power at any given time is complicated by the greater number of possible alignments among the three poles, as well as between the poles and their proxies. As there are more opportunities for everyone, the uncertainty is also proportionally greater. Unlike a bipolar situation, where restraint is necessary to avoid ultimate confrontation, under tripolarity restraint in dealing with one pole may send a wrong signal of weakness to the third. Yet collision with one pole will only benefit the third. Fear of a two-front confrontation not only increases the cost of defense, but also heightens the temptation to preempt.

In a tripolar international structure, Chinese foreign policy behavior may fall within a broader range. Unlike a bipolar distribution power, which requires China to lean toward one of the two poles at any given time (defiance against both being only a temporary anomaly), under tripolarity, China *is* a pole and does not have to lean toward anyone.

Depending on what the incentives are in a given situation, China can be in competition with the other two poles on an independent basis; in competition for the position of pivot; isolated by an alignment between the other two; or aligned with one vis-à-vis the third. Interaction will be more dynamic and less regularized than in a bipolar situation.

Several authors have examined Chinese foreign policy behavior from this perspective of tripolarity or "strategic triangle."[122] None, however, have provided a clear definition of a pole. One author, for instance, describes interaction under tripolarity as consisting of "transactions" or "exchanges" of benefits and sanctions, that are reciprocal but not necessarily symmetrical. Moreover, "there may be symmetrical relationships between players of unequal power."[123] In other words, interaction among the three poles is not any different from interaction between a "pole" and a "nonpole" as long as the latter is also capable of providing reciprocal but not necessarily symmetrical benefits and sanctions. How, then, can a pole be differentiated from a nonpole if not by their asymmetrical capabilities? If it is just a matter of exchanges, without counting symmetry, then either every state is a pole (multipolarity), or else every state is a nonpole; there can be no "tripolarity" or "strategic triangle."

As defined earlier, polarity must be based on superior capabilities that distinguish the poles from the nonpoles and cause the nonpoles to be drawn to the poles. Using such criteria as effective second-strike nuclear capabilities, sizable troop placements at home and abroad, and military alliances, one can only distinguish two states from the rest, namely the United States and the Soviet Union. Any claim of tripolarity or multipolarity[124] must be substantiated by explicating criteria that can consistently differentiate between poles and nonpoles.

Empirically, there is little evidence that China possesses the same capabilities as the United States and the Soviet Union. I therefore see no evidence of tripolarity, although the possibility is still open. Any argument based on tripolarity hinges on whether one can come up with a clearer, yet "operationalizable" definition of a pole in that context.

CONCLUSIONS

The systemic argument presented above suggests that Chinese foreign policy behavior can best be understood in terms of the constraints imposed upon it by the structure of the international system. According to this approach, all other variables—including decisionmakers and domestic politics as well as accidents, unintended consequences, coincidences, confusion, and stupidity—are relevant only if they cause changes in Chinese capabilities, leading to changes in the distribution of power or structural transformation. This approach allows for variables that are particularistic, uncertain, and in flux, thus not susceptible to systematic observation and analysis (especially when pertinent information is lacking), but these variables will not affect general and strategic aspects of foreign policy behavior until they have been translated into capabilities, which are more readily observable.

The strength of the systemic approach is its ability to provide a general or strategic outline of a state's foreign policy. Under bipolarity, we know that China has to lean toward one pole, and we also know that despite polemics, China's options are limited and its ability to pursue an independent posture vis-à-vis the superpowers is constrained. The only uncertainties are China's choices of which pole to align with and what the extent of an alignment will be. Given this premise, we should be able to distinguish "significant sounds" from a background of "noise" in analyzing specific policies and events.

Once patterns of strategic interactions involving China and the superpowers are identified, other aspects of Chinese foreign policy behavior usually fall within narrow expected ranges. For instance, much of China's policy during the 1970s toward regions such as Europe, the Middle East, Latin America, and Africa can be seen as efforts to forge a broad "united front" vis-à-vis the Soviet pole. Even within the East Asian region, where Chinese leadership would be a logical goal of Chinese foreign policy, China's freedom of action is constrained by bipolar competition. In order to contain Soviet expansion, the Chinese favor the continued presence of U.S. forces in the region and an increase in Japanese defense expenditures and capabilities, although both the United States and Japan are capable of undermining, if not competing for, regional leadership. China's improved relations with members of the Association of Southeast Asian Nations (ASEAN) can also be seen as consistent with China's leaning toward the United States. China's competition with the Soviet Union is also reflected in its relations with Vietnam and North Korea.[125] In this sense, there is no independent "regional foreign policy"; most aspects of China's behavior in the East Asian region can be seen as related to bipolar competition.

Leaning toward a pole does not necessarily mean total loss of freedom: Within a coalition (tight or loose), variety or polycentricity may still be permissible in areas not directly related to central strategic concerns. The weakness of the systemic approach is its inability to account for these variations and details within a given pattern. Moreover, under bipolarity, all one knows is that China will have to lean toward one pole at any given time. In order to tell which side China will lean to at any given point, one must bring in nonsystemic variables relating to the decision makers and domestic politics. On this point, even Waltz concurs: "A theory of international politics bears on the foreign policies of nations while claiming to explain only certain aspects of them."[126]

It is thus futile for any analytic study of Chinese foreign policy to emphasize a single cluster of variables. Equally useless is a "laundry list" of variables without prioritization. In the absence of pertinent empirical information about internal processes, one must begin with the most readily observable variables—China's relative capabilities and external behavior. Having taken this first step, one should then consider variables relating to Chinese decision makers and domestic politics, provided that empirical information is available. In examining those variables, at least two major questions should be raised: Do they increase or decrease Chinese capabilities, and do they help explain variations and details within a pattern not covered by the systemic approach? Beyond this, we can only put the systemic approach in the perspective of Chairman Hu Yaobang's remark at the Twelfth National Congress of the Chinese Communist Party: "China's future is closely bound up with that of the world as a whole."[127]

NOTES

1. Michael Ng-Quinn, "The Analytic Study of Chinese Foreign Policy," *International Studies Quarterly* 27 (June 1983):203–224.

2. Jerome Stephens, "An Appraisal of Some System Approaches in the Study of International Systems," *International Studies Quarterly* 16 (September 1972):321–349; and John J. Weltman, *Systems Theory in International Relations* (Lexington, Mass.: D. C. Heath, 1973).

3. See Roger D. Spegele, "Deconstructing Methodological Falsificationism in International Relations," *American Political Science Review* 74 (March 1980):104–122; Kenneth N. Waltz, *Theory of International Politics* (Reading, Mass.: Addison-Wesley, 1979); and Morton A. Kaplan, *Towards Professionalism in International Theory* (New York: Free Press, 1979).

4. Gabriel A. Almond and Stephen J. Genco, "Clouds, Clocks, and the Study of Politics," *World Politics* 29 (July 1977):489.

5. The "systemic approach" was implicit in the writings of Lasswell, Schuman, Polanyi, and others in the 1930s and 1940s; see William T. R. Fox, *The American Study of International Relations* (Columbia: University of South Carolina Press, 1968), p. 107. For a discussion of the systemic approach in relation to other approaches, see Arend Lijphart, "The Structure of the Theoretical Revolution in International Relations," *International Studies Quarterly* 18 (March 1974):41–74.

6. Morton A. Kaplan, *System and Process of International Politics* (New York: John Wiley & Sons, 1957), p. 4.

7. Ernst B. Haas, *Beyond the Nation-State* (Stanford, Calif.: Stanford University Press, 1964), p. 53.

8. Oran R. Young, *A Systemic Approach to International Politics*, Center of International Studies Research Monograph No. 33, Princeton University, Princeton, N.J., 1968, p. 6.

9. Waltz, *Theory of International Politics*, p. 40.

10. Robert Jervis, "Systems Theories and Diplomatic History," in Paul G. Lauren, ed., *Diplomacy* (New York: Free Press, 1979), pp. 212–216; also Young, *A Systemic Approach*, pp. 6–7.

11. Waltz, *Theory of International Politics*, pp. 65–69.

12. For a Chinese survey of various Western approaches, see Chen Lemin, "Introduction to 'Analysis of Contemporary International Relations' in Western

Countries," *Guoji wenti yanjiu* [Journal of international studies], No. 2 (1981):55–64.

13. Hedley Bull, *The Anarchical Society: A Study of Order in World Politics* (New York: Columbia University Press, 1977), p. 8.

14. Qi Wen, "Correctly Understand Our Independent Foreign Policy," *Hongqi* [Red flag], No. 21 (1982):24–28; Li Dai, "Independence and Our Foreign Relations," *Shijie zhishi* [World knowledge] No. 19 (1981):2–4.

15. John F. Copper, *China's Global Role* (Stanford, Calif.: Hoover Institution Press, 1980); and S. Rhee, "China's Co-operation, Conflict, and Interaction Behavior: Viewed from Rummel's Field Theoretic Perspective," in Roger L. Dial, ed., *Advancing and Contending Approaches to the Study of Chinese Foreign Policy* (Halifax, Nova Scotia: Centre for Foreign Policy Studies, Dalhousie University, 1974), pp. 111–196.

16. Stanley Hoffmann, *Primacy or World Order* (New York: McGraw-Hill, 1978), p. 146, n9.

17. Richard Rosecrance, "International Theory Revisited," *International Organization* 35 (Autumn 1981):693, n7.

18. John G. Ruggie, "Continuity and Transformation in the World Polity: Toward a Neorealist Synthesis," *World Politics* 35 (January 1983):285. Italics in original.

19. Kenneth N. Waltz, "Letter to the Editor," *International Organization* 36 (Summer 1982):680.

20. Xing Shugang, Li Yunhua, and Liu Yingna, "Changing Balance of Soviet-US Power," *Beijing Review*, No. 19 (May 9, 1983):14–19.

21. Zong He, "Changes and Developing Trends in the International Situation," *Beijing Review*, No. 21 (August 8, 1983):14–27.

22. Si Chu, "International Disarmament Struggle and Our Country's Stand," *Hongqi*, No. 9 (1983):37–40; see also Yan Fa, "On Disarmament," *Hongqi*, No. 11 (1980):45–48; and *Guoji xingshi nianjian 1983* [Yearbook of International Affairs] (Shanghai: Zhongguo dabaike quanshu chubanshe, 1983), pp. 18-52.

23. Samuel S. Kim, *China, the United Nations, and World Order* (Princeton, N.J.: Princeton University Press, 1979); Gerd Kaminski, "A New Chinese Approach Towards an International Order?" *Vierteljahresberichte*, No. 92 (June 1983):167–176; and William R. Feeney, "Chinese Global Politics in the United Nations General Assembly," in James C. Hsiung and Samuel S. Kim, eds., *China in the Global Community* (New York: Praeger, 1980), pp. 140–163.

24. See Wu Xueqian's speech at the United Nations General Assembly on September 27, 1983, in *Beijing Review*, No. 41 (October 10, 1983):25. See also Qi Yan, "The United Nations and the Third World," *Shijie zhishi*, No. 20 (1981): 2–5.

25. Sun Lin, "On the Revision of the United Nations Charter: Development and Problems," *Guoji wenti yanjiu*, No. 2 (1982):12–17.

26. Zhang Hongjeng, "Chinese Sovereignty over Xi Sha and Nan Sha from the Perspective of International Law," *Hongqi*, No. 4 (1980):19–24; Chen Tiqiang, "The Case of Hubei-Guangdong Railway Bond and the Problem of the Immunity of Sovereign States," *Shijie zhishi*, No. 6 (1983):2–4.

27. Lin Xiaocheng, "Security Strategy of the ASEAN," *Guoji wenti yanjiu*, No. 1 (1983):50–55.

28. Jin Fuyiao, "Pacific Economic Community: An Exploratory Survey," *Guoji wenti yanjiu*, No. 2 (1983):52–56; Zhang Biqing, "The Conception and Future of the Pacific Community," *Shijie zhishi*, No. 8 (1983):8–9.

29. Commentator, "Be Alert to the Danger of the Revival of Japanese Militarism," *Hongqi*, No. 16 (1982):37–40; *Guoji xingshi nianjian 1983*, pp. 168–183.

30. Tao Bingwei, "A Look at the Korean Question," *Guoji wenti yanjiu*, No. 2 (1982):18–21.

31. David Mitrany, *A Working Peace System* (Chicago: Quadrangle Books, 1966); Dennis Pirages, *The New Context for International Relations: Global Ecopolitics* (North Scituate, Mass.: Duxbury Press, 1978); and Dennis Pirages, "The Ecological Perspective and the Social Sciences," *International Studies Quarterly* 27 (September 1983):243–255.

32. Li Cong, "Socio-Economic Development Strategies of Developing Countries," *Hongqi*, No. 14 (1982):44–47.

33. Xia Zhenxing, "North-South Economic Relations and the North-South Dialogue," *Guoji wenti yanjiu*, No. 2 (1981):15–20; *Guoji xingshi nianjian 1983*, pp. 195–208.

34. Jeffrey Leonard, "Multinational Corporations and Politics in Developing Countries," *World Politics* 32 (April 1980):454–483.

35. Chen Zhaoxing, "Direct Investment of Developed Countries in the Developing Countries: A Preliminary Analysis," *Guoji wenti yanjiu*, No. 2 (1983):10–17; Teng Weizao and Jiang Zheshi, "The Development of Transnational Corporations and Their Function in the World Economy," *Hongqi*, No. 2 (1981):43–48; Lu Wei, "New Development in the Post-War Export of Capital of Imperialism," *Hongqi*, No. 18 (1980):43–48; and Guo Zhenyuan, "Contemporary International Monopoly Organization: The Transnational Corporation," *Shijie zhishi*, No. 13 (1982):15–17.

36. David A. Baldwin, "Power Analysis and World Politics: New Trends Versus Old Tendencies," *World Politics* 31 (January 1979):161–194.

37. David A. Baldwin, "Interdependence and Power: A Conceptual Analysis," *International Organization* 34 (Autumn 1980):471–506; and Robert O. Keohane and Joseph S. Nye, *Power and Interdependence* (Boston: Little, Brown and Co., 1977).

38. Donald E. Lampert et al., "Is There an International System?" *International Studies Quarterly* 22 (March 1978):143–166.

39. See note 33 above; and Vice-Premier Yao Yilin's speech at the Sixth UNCTAD Session in *Beijing Review*, No. 26 (June 27, 1983):17–18.

40. Samuel S. Kim, "Chinese Global Policy: An Assessment," in Hsiung and Kim, *China in the Global Community*, pp. 216–249.

41. Qian Jinxi, "On the Impact of Energy Problems on Developed Capitalist Countries," *Hongqi*, No. 2 (1982):46–48; Zhang Shie and Xu Mei, "Economy of Developing Countries Under the Impact of World Economic Crisis," *Guoji wenti yanjiu*, No. 1 (1983):19–24; Yang Wei, "The Fluctuation of Oil Price and Its Prospect," *Guoji wenti yanjiu*, No. 3 (1983):3–8; Xie Yao, "Some Views on the Present Situation and Prospects of the Oil Market of the Western World," *Guoji wenti yanjiu*, No. 1 (1981):40–47; and Tang Di, "Oil Price in Retrospect and in the Future," *Shijie zhishi*, No. 7 (1983):6–7.

42. Commentator, "The Firm Foundation and Strategic Meaning of South-South Cooperation," *Hongqi*, No. 10 (1983):6–9.

43. Xu Mei, "A Precis of South-South Cooperation," *Guoji wenti yanjiu*, No. 2 (1982):45–49.

44. Keohane and Nye, *Power and Interdependence*, p. 16.

45. Ibid., p. 27.

46. Richard Rosecrance, "The Political Socialization of Nations," *International Studies Quarterly* 20 (September 1976):441–460; Alex Inkeles, "The Emerging Social Structure of the World," *World Politics* 27 (July 1975):467–495.

47. See essays in *International Organization* 36 (Spring 1982):185–510.

48. Stephen D. Krasner, "Structural Causes and Regime Consequences: Regimes as Intervening Variables," in ibid., p. 186.

49. In *International Organization* 36 (Spring 1982), see Arthur A. Stein, "Coordination and Collaboration: Regimes in an Anarchic World," pp. 299–324; Robert O. Keohane, "The Demand for International Regimes," pp. 325–356; and Ernst B. Haas, "Words Can Hurt You: Or, Who Said What to Whom About Regimes," pp. 207–244.

50. Krasner, "Structural Causes," p. 192.

51. Susan Strange, "Cave! Hic Dragones: A Critique of Regime Analysis," *International Organization* 36 (Spring 1982):479–496.

52. Robert Jervis, "Security Regimes," *International Organization* 36 (Spring 1982):360–362.

53. Immanuel Wallerstein, *The Modern World-System* (New York: Academic Press, 1974); Christopher Chase-Dunn, "Interstate System and Capitalist World-Economy: One Logic or Two?" *International Studies Quarterly* 25 (March 1981):19–42; and Christopher Chase-Dunn, ed., *Socialist States in the World-System* (Beverly Hills, Calif.: Sage Publications, 1982), pp. 21–56. Compare this conception of capitalism as a transnational force with Eberhard's "gentry-layer" in medieval China: Wolfram Eberhard, *Conquerors and Rulers: Social Forces in Medieval China*, 2d rev. ed. (Leiden, Netherlands: E. J. Brill, 1965).

54. William R. Thompson, "Uneven Economic Growth, Systemic Challenges, and Global Wars," *International Studies Quarterly* 27 (September 1983):346; Aristide R. Zolberg, "Origins of the Modern World System: A Missing Link," *World Politics* 33 (January 1981):253–281; George Modelski, "The Long Cycle of Global Politics and the Nation-State," *Comparative Studies in Society and History* 20 (April 1978):214–235; Edwin A. Winckler, "China's World-System: Social Theory and Political Practice in the 1970's," in Walter L. Goldrank, ed., *The World-System of Capitalism: Past and Present* (Beverly Hills, Calif.: Sage Publications, 1979), pp. 53–72.

55. Michael Ng-Quinn, "External Factors, Optimal Size, and the Perpetual Survival of an Empire: The Chinese Experience," (forthcoming).

56. Tony Smith, "The Underdevelopment of Development Literature: The Case of Dependency Theory," *World Politics* 31 (January 1979):247–288. On the role of the state, see also Jack A. Goldstone, "Theories of Revolution: The Third Generation," *World Politics* 32 (April 1980):425–453.

57. Richard C. Kraus, "Withdrawing from the World-System: Self-Reliance and Class Structure of China," in Goldrank, *World-System of Capitalism*, pp. 237–259.

58. Edward Friedman, "On Maoist Conceptualizations of the Capitalist World System," *China Quarterly*, No. 80 (December 1979):806–837.

59. R. N. Berki, "On Marxian Thought and the Problem of International Relations," *World Politics* 24 (October 1971):80–105.

60. Bruce Cumings, "The Political Economy of Chinese Foreign Policy," *Modern China* 5 (October 1979):411–462; and Friedrich W. Y. Wu, "From Self-Reliance to Interdependence?" *Modern China* 7 (October 1981):445–482.

61. Albert Szymanski, "The Socialist World-System," in Chase-Dunn, *Socialist States*, pp. 57–84; and Cal Clark and Donna Bahry, "Dependent Devel-

opment: A Socialist Variant," *International Studies Quarterly* 27 (September 1983):271–293.

62. Vincente Navarro, "The Limits of World-System Theory," in Chase-Dunn, *Socialist States*, pp. 85–96; and Bruce Andrews, "The Political Economy of World Capitalism: Theory and Practice," *International Organization* 36 (Winter 1982):135–163.

63. For various interpretations of exchange relations and the global political economy, see R. Dan Walleri, "The Political Economy Literature on North-South Relations," *International Studies Quarterly* 22 (December 1978):587–624.

64. Qian Junrui, "Seriously Study the Economics of Developing Countries," *Hongqi*, No. 11 (1982):18–22.

65. Shi Jin, "Capitalism Has Eventually Entered Old Age," *Hongqi*, No. 3 (1981):45–48; and Qian Junrui, "Seriously Study World Economics and Promote the Four Modernizations in Our Country," *Hongqi*, No. 9 (1980):31–35.

66. Teng Weizao and Xiong Xingmei, "New Development of Post-War Centralization and Monopoly of Capitalist Production," *Hongqi*, No. 16 (1980):43–48.

67. Qian Junrui, "Seriously Study World Economics"; Xiong Fu, "From Stone to Jade," *Hongqi*, No. 1 (1980):29–31; Xiong Fu, "Yugoslavian People Advancing on the Socialist Road," *Hongqi*, No. 18 (1981):19–24; and *Guoji xingshi nianjian 1983*, pp. 247–271.

68. Chen Licheng and Tan Shizhong, "Developing Countries' Role in World Economy," *Beijing Review*, No. 13 (March 28, 1983):13–16, 25.

69. See note 24 above.

70. Zhang Shie, "Some Problems Concerning the Economic Development of Developing Countries," *Guoji wenti yanjiu*, No. 2 (1982):55–60.

71. Zhou Shulian, "What Can Be Learned from the Western Experience in Business Administration?" *Hongqi*, No. 16 (1982):43–45.

72. Xiong Xingmei, "Peculiarities of the Reproductive Cycle and Economic Crises of Post-War Capitalism," *Hongqi*, No. 1 (1982):45-48; and Zhou Qihua, "On the Erosion of Contemporary Capitalism," *Hongqi*, No. 20 (1980):36–41.

73. Wu Jian and Wang Dachao, "Correctly Recognize the Living Conditions of the Working Class in Capitalist Countries," *Hongqi*, No. 4 (1981):45–48.

74. Jie Deyuan, "On the Transformation of the Organizational Structure of the National Economy in Post-War Developed Capitalist Countries," *Hongqi*, No. 9 (1981):45–48.

75. Wang Huaining, "Inflation in Post-War Imperialist Countries," *Hongqi*, No. 11 (1981):44–48.

76. Guan Mengjue, "A New Chronic Illness of Imperialist Economics—'Stagnation-Inflation,' " *Hongqi*, No. 4 (1982):45–48.

77. Tao Dayong, "The Expansion and Transformation of Finance and Capital of Post-War Imperialist Countries," *Hongqi*, No. 19 (1981):44–48.

78. Ibid. It is unclear whether this exertion of control over politics is an end in itself or merely a means to furthering economic ends.

79. Huang Suan, "Economic Situations of the Western World in the 80's and Its Political Repercussions," *Guoji wenti yanjiu*, No. 4 (1982):3–9, and "How to Observe International Politics from International Economics," *Shijie zhishi*, No. 11 (1981):15–17.

80. Li Dai, "The Impact of Economic Crisis on International Relations," *Beijing Review*, No. 22 (May 30, 1983):14–18; original Chinese version in *Hongqi*, No. 7 (1983):31–34. See also *Guoji xingshi nianjian 1983*, pp. 209–246.

81. Dai Lunzhang, "The Struggle by Developing Countries to Establish a New International Economic Order," *Hongqi*, No. 22 (1981):37–40.

82. Chen Xiuying, "A Brief Survey on the Problem of Global Negotiations," *Guoji wenti yanjiu*, No. 1 (1982):58–62. See also sources cited in notes 32, 33, and 79 above.

83. Wei Bingkui, "Insist on Self-Reliance," *Hongqi*, No. 1 (1974):85–88; Li Xin, "Self-Reliance Is a Question of Line," *Hongqi*, No. 4 (1975):82–86; Jiang Jinghong, "Get Rid of the Emphasis on External Factors and Self-Consciously Resist Corruption," *Hongqi*, No. 8 (1975):59–61; Fang Hai, "Criticize Slavish Comprador Philosophy," *Hongqi*, No. 4 (1976):21–26; and Gao Lu and Chang Ge, "Criticism of Deng Xiaoping's Comprador-Capitalist-Bourgeois Economic Thought," *Hongqi*, No. 7 (1976):25–30.

84. Guo Maoyan, "Expose the Gang of Four's Plot in Attacking Foreign Trade," *Hongqi*, No. 4 (1977):57–61; and Li Qiang, "Recognize the Correct Line and Actively Develop Socialist Foreign Trade," *Hongqi*, No. 10 (1977):31–38.

85. Zheng Hongqing, "Opening to the Outside World and Self-Reliance," *Beijing Review*, No. 11 (March 14, 1983):15–20.

86. Joint editorial of *Renmin ribao* [People's daily], *Hongqi* and *Jiefangjun bao* [Liberation Army daily], "Bright China," in *Hongqi*, No. 1 (1978):6–10.

87. Editorial, "Emancipate the Mind and Speed Up Advancement," *Hongqi*, No. 10 (1978):11–16.

88. Xu Ke and Liu Furong, "A Few Questions Relating to Imports," *Hongqi*, No. 2 (1979):26–30; Dai Yi, "Historical Lessons on Closed-Door Policy," *Renmin ribao*, March 13, 1979, p. 3; Commentator, "Develop Foreign Trade and Improve the Four Modernizations," *Renmin ribao*, February 21, 1980, p. 2; and *Renmin ribao* editorial, "Foreign Trade Must Serve the Adjustment of the National Economy," February 25, 1981, p. 1.

89. Editorial, "On Our Country's Foreign Economic Relations," *Hongqi*, No. 8 (1982):2–10.

90. Richard N. Rosecrance, "Bipolarity, Multipolarity, and the Future," *Journal of Conflict Resolution* 10 (September 1966):314–327.

91. This is a response to Joseph L. Nogee, "Polarity: An Ambiguous Concept," *Orbis* 18 (Winter 1975):1193–1224.

92. David P. Rapkin and William R. Thompson (with Jon A. Christopherson), "Bipolarity and Bipolarization in the Cold War Era: Conceptualization, Measurement, and Validation," *Journal of Conflict Resolution* 23 (June 1979):261–295.

93. The following discussion draws heavily on Ng-Quinn, "Analytic Study of Chinese Foreign Policy."

94. Chase-Dunn, "Interstate System," p. 39.

95. Kenneth N. Waltz, "The Stability of a Bipolar World," *Daedalus* 93 (Summer 1964):881–909.

96. William H. Riker, *The Theory of Political Coalitions* (New Haven, Conn.: Yale University Press, 1962).

97. Jervis, "Systems Theories," p. 224.

98. For a detailed presentation, see Michael Ng-Quinn, "Effects of Bipolarity on Chinese Foreign Policy," *Survey* 26 (Spring 1982):102–130.

99. Joint editorial of *Renmin ribao, Hongqi*, and *Jiefangjun bao*, "Strive for New Victory," in *Hongqi*, No. 10 (1972):5–9; and Deng Xiaoping, "Speech at the United Nations," *Hongqi*, No. 5 (1974):45–52.

100. Wu Qun, "Hegemonism Cannot Decide the Fate of World History," *Hongqi*, No. 10 (1973):17–20.

101. Nan Jing, "International Commentary: The Most Greedy International Exploiter," *Hongqi*, No. 9 (1974):82–86.

102. Xing Hua, "The Real Face of Soviet Social Colonialism," *Hongqi*, No. 11 (1977):69–76.

103. Commentator, "Proletarian Internationalism and Soviet Hegemonism," *Hongqi*, No. 4 (1980):14–18; and Yang Hui and Zhan Xihuang, "Is It Internationalism or Hegemonism?" *Hongqi*, No. 23 (1980):44–48.

104. Commentator, "The Immediate Danger of War and the Defense of World Peace," *Hongqi*, No. 11 (1979):53–58.

105. Institute of World Economy, Chinese Academy of Social Sciences, "Soviet Social Imperialism Is the Most Dangerous Source of World War," *Hongqi*, No. 7 (1977):73–80.

106. Liang Xiao, "International Commentary: The Economic Sources of Soviet Revisionist Hegemonism," *Hongqi*, No. 10 (1975):81–86.

107. "Chairman Mao's Theory of the Differentiation of the Three Worlds Is a Major Contribution to Marxism-Leninism," *Peking Review*, No. 45 (November 4, 1977):34; and "Soviet Military Strategy for World Domination," *Beijing Review*, No. 4 (January 28, 1980):15.

108. Wu Ren, "Has the United Front Against the Soviet Union Been Realized?" *Shijie zhishi*, No. 2 (1981):2–3, 15.

109. Jen Ku-ping, "The Munich Tragedy and Contemporary Appeasement," *Peking Review*, No. 50 (December 9, 1977):6–11.

110. Chen Xiong, "The Hot Spot Is Not the Focal Point," *Shijie zhishi*, No. 10 (1981):2–3; and Qi Ya, Zhou Jirong, and He Linfa, "The Focal Point Has Not Been Moved Eastward from Europe," ibid. pp. 3–6.

111. Zhang Zhen and Rong Zhi, "Some Reflections on the 'Policy of Detente' of the Soviet Union," *Guoji wenti yanjiu*, No. 4 (1982):18–22; Huang Tingwei, Ha Mei, and Li Zhongcheng, "New Tune of Soviet 'Detente' Offensive," *Shijie zhishi*, No. 7 (1981):2–3, 8; and *Guoji xingshi nianjian 1982*, pp. 25–33.

112. Special commentator, "Where Lies the Crux of Sino-American Relations?" *Guoji wenti yanjiu*, No. 2 (1982):3–7; Zi Zhongyun, "Test of History— U.S. Policy Towards Taiwan at the Time of the Birth of New China," *Guoji wenti yanjiu*, No. 3 (1982):34–42; and Zhuang Qubing, Zhang Hongzeng, and Pan Tongwen, "On the Taiwan Relations Act of the United States," *Guoji wenti yanjiu*, No. 1 (1981):21–27.

113. Xie Xiaochuan, "New Characteristics of Soviet-U.S. Contention," *Shijie zhishi*, No. 3 (1983):10–12.

114. Zhao Jihua, "On American Neo-Isolationism," *Guoji wenti yanjiu*, No. 1 (1983):32–38.

115. Lu Nanquan and Zhou Rongkun, "Principal Problems Confronting the Soviet Economy at Present," *Guoji wenti yanjiu*, No. 2 (1981):35–43, 48; Yang Qingfa, "The Soviet Union Is Faced with Economic Problems," *Shijie zhishi*, No. 8 (1981):2–5; see also note 24 above.

116. See note 21 above; and Li Ning, "A Year with Greater Tension and Tumult," *Guoji wenti yanjiu*, No. 1 (1983):3–11.

117. Yin Chengde, "Surging Tide of the Times—the Non-Alignment Movement," *Guoji wenti yanjiu*, No. 2 (1983):3–9; and Zhou Jirong, Wang Yulin, and Sun Kun, "On the Non-Aligned Movement," *Shijie zhishi*, No. 5 (1983):4–6.

118. Liu Yili and Li Shuqiao, "The Important Meaning of Strengthening the Unity and Cooperation of Third World Countries," *Hongqi*, No. 13 (1982):44–47.

119. An example of mutual suspicion is an exchange on the border issue. See Commentator, "Response to the 'Observer' of the *New Times*," *Shijie zhishi*, No. 3 (1983):2; and Li Huichuan, "Where Lies the Root of Deadlock in the Sino-Soviet Frontier Talks?" *Guoji wenti yanjiu*, No. 1 (1981):11–20.

120. See note 21 above, p. 17.

121. B. Lieberman, "Coalitions and Conflict Resolution (Russia, China, U.S.)," *American Behavioral Scientist* 18 (1975):557–581.

122. Lowell Dittmer, "The Strategic Triangle: An Elementary Game–Theoretical Analysis," *World Politics* 33 (July 1981):485–515; G. Segal, "China and the Great Power Triangle," *China Quarterly*, No. 83 (September 1980):490–509; and Michel Tatu, *The Great Power Triangle: Washington-Moscow-Peking* (Paris: Atlantic Institute, 1970).

123. Dittmer, "Strategic Triangle," pp. 486–488.

124. J. M. Saniel, "The Erosion of the Bipolar Power Structure in the 1960's: Its Impact upon East Asian International Relations," *Asian Studies* 11 (August 1973):6–40; Robert L. Pfaltzgraff, "Multipolarity, Alliances, and U.S.-Soviet-Chinese Relations," *Orbis* 17 (Fall 1973):720–736; and Karl W. Deutsch and J. David Singer, "Multipolar Power Systems and International Stability," *World Politics* 16 (April 1964):390–406.

125. Pei Monong, "China's Future Position in Asia," *Shijie zhishi*, No. 10 (1983):2–4.

126. Waltz, *Theory of International Politics*, p. 72.

127. *Beijing Review*, No. 37 (September 13, 1982):29.

Part 2
Interactions

CHAPTER 5

CHINA AND THE UNITED STATES: THE LIMITS OF INTERACTION

Steven I. Levine

INTRODUCTION

According to its chief U.S. architects, the Sino-American reconciliation of the 1970s was brought about by sober-minded Chinese and U.S. practitioners of realpolitik who discerned the advantage of forming a de facto strategic partnership in their parallel competition against the Soviet Union.[1] President Jimmy Carter and National Security Advisor Zbigniew Brzezinski expressed that thought in the guidelines for the latter's pivotal May 1978 trip to the PRC: "We see our relations with China as a central facet of U.S. global policy. The United States and China share certain common interests and we have parallel, long-term strategic concerns. The most important of these is our common opposition to global or regional hegemony by any single power."[2] In both the Shanghai Communiqué of February 1972 and the December 1978 agreement to establish diplomatic relations, opposition to hegemonism (the code name for Soviet global expansionism) was the foundation on which the edifice of Sino-American relations was erected. Washington's purported advantage in the Washington-Moscow-Beijing strategic triangle was that the United States enjoyed better relations with the USSR and PRC than each of them did with the other.[3] During the 1970s Sino-Soviet hostility was usually assumed to be a virtually permanent structural feature of the international system, ensuring the perpetuation of this U.S. advantage.

Washington believed that as Sino-American reconciliation matured into entente, enhanced stability in Asia would ensue as the PRC abandoned the politics of revolutionary transformation in favor of its new role as a "responsible partner" in defending the status quo against the bullyboys in Moscow and Hanoi.[4] Additional benefits in the fields of trade, cultural exchange, and so forth were also anticipated. From a Chinese perspective, reconciliation and de facto strategic alignment with the United States reduced China's vulnerability to Soviet coercive pressures. In the post-Mao period, it also provided China with enhanced access to the international capitalist economy from which technology, financial credits, and investments flowed, thereby facilitating economic development.

From a more critical perspective, however, the Sino-American relationship of the 1970s appears rooted in the soil of mutual obsession with the growth of Soviet power. In this sense, Moscow played the role of an unwitting go-between in bringing Washington and Beijing together. An exploration of the origins and significance of this obsession in postwar U.S. history would take us too far afield, but a comment on the function of anti-Sovietism in PRC foreign policy may provide a context for our examination of Sino-American relations.

For more than a decade (1969–1981), the notion of building an anti-Soviet united front was much more than a policy designed to protect the PRC from a perceived Soviet threat.[5] It defined the central political-strategic role that China sought to play in contemporary Asia and throughout the world. It provided the rationale, the integrating mechanism, and a measure of consistency to the disparate elements of China's foreign policy, and it served as the means for China to transcend its relative weakness and play a key role on the stage of world (as well as Asian) politics. Anti-Sovietism also provided a sense of direction and identity to a Chinese leadership that appeared to require an overarching negative national purpose in facing the outside world. Moreover, anti-Sovietism was the key that opened the door to the United States. From Washington's perspective. Beijing's anti-Sovietism neatly dovetailed with its own world view, and PRC willingness to forge a U.S. connection provided a vital psychological boost at a time of flagging U.S. self-confidence. Unfortunately, by definition, anti-Sovietism precluded the pursuit of a rational PRC policy vis-à-vis the USSR. Throughout the 1970s Sino-Soviet relations remained hostile but not confrontational.

Beijing's decision in 1982 to resume its suspended dialogue with Moscow and improve relations through increased trade and cultural exchanges lacked the drama of the opening act of Sino-American rapprochement in 1971–1972, but points clearly enough to the changing Chinese foreign policy environment in which relations between China and the United States take place. Because they already enjoy the framework of diplomatic relations and because they do not need to play to domestic public opinion, the USSR and China can ameliorate their relations incrementally.[6] This slow improvement in Sino-Soviet relations is a sign that the PRC is entering a new era in its relations with the superpowers, neither aligning with one against the other (with the USSR against the United States in the 1950s; with the United States against the USSR in the 1970s) nor confronting both as in the 1960s. Over the next decade, China's relations with both countries may contain mixed elements of cooperation and competition—the norm in international relations. This will enhance Beijing's flexibility and its autonomy, and will prevent Washington and Moscow from attempting to use China as a pawn ("the China card") in their relations with each other. As has been true since the end of World War II, China's relations with the United States and with the Soviet Union can be properly understood only if we transcend the limitations of a bilateral framework of analysis.

THE INSTITUTIONALIZATION
OF SINO-AMERICAN RELATIONS, 1979–1981

In terms of both accomplishments and expectations, the two and a half years following the establishment of formal diplomatic relations between Washington and Beijing on January 1, 1979, are likely to be viewed as a high-water mark in U.S.-PRC relations at the governmental level. During this time, the relationship was transformed through the establishment of multiple institutional ties at both official and unofficial levels.

Bilateral trade increased from US$1.14 billion in 1978 to US$5.2 billion in 1981, and a large number of U.S. companies established relations with their Chinese counterparts in anticipation of substantial further growth in trade. By mid-1981 some two dozen U.S. corporations had established resident offices in Beijing; U.S. oil companies were participating actively in the search for oil in China's offshore waters, and Americans had begun to impart their management skills to Chinese cadres.[7] The extension of most-favored nation (MFN) status to the PRC in February 1980 boosted PRC exports to the United States.

In 1978 and 1979 a framework for scientific and technological exchanges was established with the signing of seventeen protocols in a wide variety of fields. The Committee for Scholarly Communication with the PRC in Washington linked the National Academy of Sciences with the Chinese Academy of Sciences and the Chinese Academy of Social Sciences. Beijing's decision in 1978 to send students abroad for advanced study resulted in some 6,000 PRC students on U.S. campuses by mid-1981. (This number had reached approximately 9,000 by late 1982.)[8] Several dozen U.S. colleges and universities established formal agreements of their own with Chinese institutions, and several hundred Americans, ranging from undergraduates to senior scholars, were studying in the PRC by the early 1980s.

An expanded program of cultural exchanges brought major exhibits of Chinese art, archaeological finds, music and dance troupes, and sports teams to the United States, and a reciprocal flow of U.S. films, symphony orchestras, and exhibits to the PRC.[9] The number of China-bound U.S. tourists increased exponentially, and an average of 100 Chinese delegations visited the United States monthly.

At the time of normalization, government officials believed that the promotion of economic, cultural, scientific, educational, and other links would create multiple constituencies in each society with a vested interest in the future well-being of the overall U.S.-PRC relationship.[10] Rather than let the bridge of Sino-American friendship hang by the single strands of high-level official discussions, as had been the case under the Nixon and Ford presidencies, the Carter administration wanted to braid a thick cable of contacts between the two countries. The alacrity with which U.S. and Chinese organizations, institutions, and individuals responded to the opportunity to establish contacts with each other is striking. It was almost enough to revive the hoary myth of a "special relationship" between the United States and China based on a presumed natural affinity of the two peoples.[11] American attitudes toward the PRC underwent a dramatic change during these years as positive images replaced the negative stereotypes of the Cold War years.[12]

During this high tide of Sino-American relations, the Carter administration sent a stream of cabinet-level officials to the PRC, including the secretaries of treasury, commerce, agriculture, defense, and energy and the special trade representative.[13] A long list of agreements was signed with the Chinese concerning such areas as cultural and scientific exchange, trade, maritime transport, civil air transport, grain sales, and consular offices.[14] As the administration moved away from a policy of evenhandedness between Moscow and Beijing toward a pronounced tilt in favor of the Chinese, its view of China was neatly summed up by Vice-President Mondale in his August 1979 speech at Beijing University: "We are committed to joining with you to advance our many parallel strategic and bilateral interests. Thus any nation which seeks to weaken or isolate you in world affairs assumes a stance counter to American interests." Mondale further expressed a maximalist vision of the bright future of Sino-American relations and the benefits it would confer on both sides.[15]

Even as the relationship between China and the United States was expanding rapidly, its underlying geostrategic rationale continued to be shared opposition to Soviet expansionism. Therefore, at first cautiously, but then with increasing momentum, the administration moved toward consummating its relationship with the PRC by strengthening military-security ties in such areas as intelligence cooperation. The Chinese agreed to the establishment of a joint missile monitoring station in Xinjiang (run by Chinese technicians) to replace U.S. facilities in Iran. Secretary of Defense Harold Brown's trip to the PRC in January 1980, shortly after the Kremlin's invasion of Afghanistan, found the Chinese leaders in a receptive mood. Washington soon announced its willingness to sell nonlethal military equipment to the PRC and further expanded the list of military-related items that could be sold to China in March 1980. Delegations were exchanged in the areas of military education, logistics, and science and technology.[16] Amidst considerable loose talk in Congress and the press about using "the China card" against the USSR, it seemed only a matter of time before the remaining barriers to weapons sales to the PRC would be swept aside.[17] In fact, only five months into the new administration of President Reagan, these barriers did fall when Secretary of State Alexander Haig announced during a June 1981 visit to the PRC that the United States was now prepared to consider defensive weapons sales to the PRC on a case-by-case basis.[18]

By this time, the relationship had developed an enormous momentum despite the unresolved Taiwan issue. This momentum was by no means an unalloyed achievement, for like a car outdriving its headlights, the ever-accelerating pace of developments in the Sino-American relationship had carried Washington and Beijing beyond the limits illuminated by a well-thought-out policy. A sense of the direction and ultimate destination of Sino-American relations was lacking. In its understandable enthusiasm to consolidate the new relationship with the PRC and create a network of bonds that could not easily be destroyed, the Carter administration inadequately addressed the fundamental question of the limits of congruent Chinese and U.S. interests. In particular, insufficient attention was given to the serious consequences of moving toward a full-fledged military-security partnership with the PRC. The Carter administration's closed style in making China policy, bypassing Congress and the public, was largely responsible for this neglect.[19]

During this period, Chinese leader Deng Xiaoping and his associates encouraged rising U.S. expectations by repeatedly stressing the importance of forming an anti-Soviet united front as the essence of China's foreign policy.[20] Yet one need not probe too deeply to discover that even at this time of apparent convergence in U.S. and Chinese world views and policies, a fundamental divergence in Washington's and Beijing's conceptions of security cooperation prevailed. Despite verbal disclaimers, it is reasonably clear that officials in the Carter White House were thinking in terms of a protoalliance between the United States and the PRC. Nothing else explains the intensity of high-level visits, the strategic intelligence briefings for the Chinese, and the steadily lowering barriers to trade in high-technology goods with military applications during the second half of the Carter term. Only the Taiwan issue remained to roil the waters of Sino-American amity.[21]

In contrast, the concept underlying PRC relations with the United States was the united front, implying a lesser degree of cooperation and above all, the preservation of China's autonomy in the field of foreign policy, with only partial and occasional coordination on specific questions. Because subsequent difficulties between Washington and Beijing are often ascribed to disagreements about the Taiwan issue, it is important to note this conceptual divergence, which transcends the single, albeit complex, issue of Taiwan. While Washington appeared buoyed by the prospect of gaining a new if informal ally, China maintained its fundamental foreign policy characteristic—an allergy toward alliances that has been evident since the break with the Soviets in the 1950s. As Washington pressed toward crossing the Rubicon of arms sales to the PRC, Chinese leaders apparently had second thoughts about the prospect of a protoalliance with the United States.

From an historical viewpoint, foreign involvement in Chinese military affairs, including military modernization and the defense of China's national security, has been one of the most sensitive and contentious issues in Chinese politics. Such involvement is often perceived as a threat to China's independence of action or as creating an unacceptable degree of dependence. This psychological dimension of Chinese military politics was perhaps less well understood in Washington than it might have been. In any case, beginning in the summer of 1981 the momentum of Sino-American relations sharply diminished, and problems emerging from the decade of rapid progress began to demand attention. Most importantly, having reached a certain point in their relations with Washington, the Beijing leadership now began to address the most important item remaining on their current foreign policy agenda—achieving a less hostile relationship with the Soviet Union.[22]

DARK CLOUDS OVER THE
SINO-AMERICAN RELATIONSHIP

In the early 1980s the amicable atmosphere of official U.S.-PRC relations was fouled by prolonged wrangling over a series of bilateral issues. A new era of discord seemed to threaten the short-lived entente. As the Chinese put it, dark clouds hung over the relationship. Beijing placed responsibility on Washington for dispelling these dark clouds, which it blamed U.S. actions for creating.

The focal point of contention was and remains U.S. policy toward Taiwan, particularly the issue of arms sales. When it was passed on April 10, 1979, PRC leaders expressed dissatisfaction with the Taiwan Relations Act, which established the American Institute in Taiwan as the "unofficial" instrumentality for conducting the "cultural, commercial and other unofficial relations with the people of Taiwan" referred to in the Sino-American joint communiqué establishing diplomatic relations. Nevertheless, apparently convinced that the Carter administration viewed U.S. relations with Taiwan as little more than an unfortunate historical vestige, Beijing moved forward vigorously to develop its links with Washington.

Ronald Reagan's 1980 campaign criticism of Carter's China policy, his suggestion that relations with Taiwan be reestablished at an official level, and his evident long-standing personal sympathy for the Chinese Nationalists angered Beijing. Chinese leaders responded with a series of warnings against backsliding in Sino-American relations. Although President Reagan quickly reaffirmed his commitment to the previous administration's China policy, particularly concerning the principle of one China, these first discordant notes were not forgotten by the Chinese, who proceeded to probe Reagan's intentions on a series of issues.

The first was the thorny issue of the FX—an advanced fighter aircraft designed for the export market, which the Nationalist government on

Taiwan wanted to purchase.[23] Subjected to crosswinds of pressure from Taiwan and its supporters on the one side and from Beijing and its supporters on the other, the administration delayed making a decision until January 1982, when it finally denied the FX to Taiwan on the grounds that no military necessity justified the sale.[24] However, it did agree to a license for Taiwan to produce sixty F5Gs—a fighter aircraft similar to that already in Taiwan's air force—under an earlier coproduction arrangement. Beijing was understandably perturbed by this compromise.

Meanwhile, in pursuit of its goal of national reunification, the PRC launched a new campaign directed at Taiwan. Its centerpiece was a nine-point plan announced by elder statesman Ye Jianying on September 30, 1981, ostensibly guaranteeing Taiwan stability, security, and prosperity in return for recognition of PRC sovereignty over the island.[25] In this connection, Beijing began pressing Washington first to reduce and then to eliminate U.S. arms sales to Taiwan, claiming that this unwelcome interference in Chinese internal affairs was a major obstacle to the peaceful reunification of Taiwan. Protracted negotiations in search of a formula that would satisfy Beijing while stopping short of U.S. capitulation to Chinese terms were concluded in August 1982. A tortuously worded communiqué conveyed Washington's pledge that "it does not seek to carry out a long-term policy of arms sales to Taiwan, that its arms sales to Taiwan will not exceed, either in qualitative or quantitative terms, the level of those supplied in recent years. . . . and that it intends to reduce gradually its sales of arms to Taiwan, leading over time to a final resolution."[26] In return, the PRC stated that its striving for peaceful reunification of Taiwan was "a fundamental policy." The United States formally expressed its understanding and appreciation of this Chinese policy.

Despite the ambiguities in this agreement, it is reasonably clear that Beijing had again succeeded in extracting further concessions from Washington without giving up very much in return. Moreover, the Chinese immediately expressed their view that this agreement was merely an interim measure along the road to a complete termination of any security relationship between Washington and Taipei.[27] PRC media and leaders initiated a barrage of criticism aimed at the Taiwan Relations Act, which they condemned as contravening the principles jointly subscribed to by the U.S. and China at the time of normalization.[28]

In a June 1983 interview with Professor Winston L. Y. Yang of Seton Hall University, Deng Xiaoping reiterated the earlier PRC offers on Taiwan and added the significant point that in a reunified China, Taiwan could continue foreign arms purchases as long as its armed forces posed no threat to the mainland.[29] In this vein, the PRC passed up the opportunity to condemn the latest U.S. arms sales package to Taiwan (worth US$530 million) in July of that year. Yet on a visit to the United States in September, Foreign Minister Wu Xueqian reiterated the centrality of the Taiwan issue in U.S.-PRC relations, and Beijing continued to take umbrage at signs of congressional support for Taiwan interests.[30]

Many other dark clouds—some rather oddly shaped—obscured the horizon of Sino-American relations in the early 1980s. Let us look briefly at some of these.

The Bilateral Trade Issue

In order to offset a chronic trade deficit with the United States, the Chinese pressed for an upward revision of the quota in textiles—a major PRC export commodity to the U.S. (about US$800 million in 1982). When negotiations to amend the 1980 agreements failed to produce accord by January 1983, the United States unilaterally imposed limits on Chinese imports, and China retaliated by curtailing purchases of U.S. agricultural goods.[31] Further negotiations produced a compromise agreement by midyear, but failed to satisfy U.S. textile producers (or their conservative congressional supporters), who sought other means to restrict Chinese textile exports.[32]

The Hu Na Case and Political Asylum

Chinese tennis star Hu Na's request for political asylum in July 1982 (granted in April 1983) produced a symbolic confrontation between the United States as the "land of liberty" and the PRC as an "oppressive totalitarian" state. China canceled a nineteen-item official sports and cultural exchange program for 1983 with the United States to protest the decision.[33] Meanwhile, a substantial number of Chinese exchange students sought to remain in the United States.

Academic Exchanges: Reciprocity, Access, Espionage

In addition to the enormous disparity between the number of Chinese studying in the United States and the number of Americans studying in China (at least 20 to 1), many U.S. scholars complained of inadequate access both to documentary collections and to Chinese society. The opportunity for Americans to engage in field research in China was sharply curtailed following revelations of harsh and repressive conditions in the Chinese countryside by a U.S. researcher whom the Chinese accused of improper activities. In the summer of 1982, another U.S. student was expelled from China for unauthorized collection of state secrets—agricultural statistics from internal documents. The implication was that many U.S. students were engaged in espionage activities. U.S.

public security officials entertained similar suspicions about Chinese students in the United States.

The Huguang Bond Case

The September 1982 award by a federal district court in Alabama of some US$40 million to nine U.S. holders of 1911 Manchu dynasty era railroad bonds (to be paid by the PRC as a successor government) unleashed a Sino-American legal imbroglio amidst PRC charges that its sovereignty had been violated.[34]

Commercial Air Transport

Pan American's resumption of service to Taiwan in June 1983 led to PRC protest and a demand that Washington transfer the U.S.-PRC air route to another commercial carrier. Washington refused and hinted at the revocation of CAAC's (the Civil Aviation Administration of China, China's state airline) rights in the United States if Pan American was penalized by Beijing.

These and other cases contributed to a gradual deterioration in the atmosphere of U.S.-PRC relations, which was mirrored in a new wave of mutual disenchantment on the part of at least some Americans and some Chinese with each other's societies and systems of values. The official guardians of public morality in the PRC condemned the decadent life-styles and bourgeois morality that emanated from the capitalistic United States and touted the superiority of the socialist system. Meanwhile, books by "new China hand" journalists Fox Butterfield and Richard Bernstein presented the U.S. public with a harsher view of a repressive, puritanical, and police-ridden Chinese society than had been customary during the years immediately preceding.[35] Even Ross Terrill, a previously sympathetic observer, expressed his new view of China as an authoritarian state with a disillusioned population and uncertain prospects.[36] Clearly, the idea that more knowledge produces better understanding and enhances international amity had not been validated by this experience.

By the second half of 1983 the atmosphere of U.S.-Chinese relations had been improved somewhat by efforts on both sides. Following Defense Secretary Caspar Weinberger's visit to Beijing in September 1983, it was announced that Premier Zhao Ziyang would visit Washington early in 1984 and that President Reagan would journey to Beijing soon after that. Summit diplomacy—a diplomacy richer in symbols than in substance—would sustain the relationship that had been conceived in similar circumstances in 1972.

PERSPECTIVES ON SINO-AMERICAN
RELATIONS IN THE 1980s

What is the explanation for the apparent deterioration of Sino-American relations? Focusing on the governmental level, let us consider in turn several mutually reinforcing theses concerning the most recent phase of U.S.-PRC relations. These may be called: (1) the strategic reservoir thesis; (2) the U.S. mismanagement thesis; (3) the normal conflict thesis; (4) the high politics–low politics interaction thesis; and (5) the strategic realignment thesis.

The Strategic Reservoir Thesis

On the eve of Secretary of State George Shultz's visit to the PRC in February 1983, several of the architects of China policy in preceding administrations—Henry Kissinger, Zbigniew Brzezinski, Michel Oksenberg—lamented the serious state of disrepair into which Sino-American relations had fallen. They argued that the lofty vision of global strategic cooperation that had underlain Sino-American rapprochement during the Nixon-Kissinger era had faded. The spirit of U.S. generosity, high expectations, and mutual understanding that had informed relations during the Carter administration had yielded to narrow calculations of interest, revived ideological enmity, and mutual suspicion. Recalling the wild mood swings of the historic U.S. love-hate relationship with China, they feared the substantial erosion of relations unless a major effort was launched to repair the damage wrought by the Reagan administration.[37]

The central notion in their critique was the issue of strategic cooperation. In this view the Sino-American relationship may be compared to a reservoir filled by a series of policy initiatives centering on the strategic dimension of the relationship. Once the water level in the reservoir drops because of neglect of global strategic issues, the noisome objects at the bottom of the reservoir—the bilateral issues of Taiwan arms sales, trade, political asylum, and so forth—are revealed and demand primary attention. Thus, the only way to keep these bilateral issues submerged is to replenish the reservoir by reemphasizing strategic cooperation. This was their prescription for restoring a healthy Sino-American relationship.

Interestingly, the official PRC diagnosis of what had gone wrong in Sino-American relations was a variation of this strategic reservoir thesis, although the conclusions the Chinese drew were somewhat different from those of U.S. critics. Beijing asserted that normalization and the subsequent flowering of relations had been based upon Washington's acceptance of certain fundamental political principles and promises, the most important being recognition of the principle of one China and the promise to phase out the U.S. security relationship with Taiwan. However, as an editorial in the *Journal of International Studies* (sponsored by the Foreign Ministry) put it:

> To make promises and pledges is not the same as actually to carry them out in practice. The development of Sino-American relations faces an ever-increasing threat precisely because, after establishing diplomatic relations, the United States violated these promises and pledges in practice, encroached upon China's sovereignty, and interfered in China's internal affairs.[38]

Washington's purported failure to honor its solemn commitments, then, was deemed the cause of the difficulties that had arisen. If the United States would stick to its promises, then the bilateral problems (above all the Taiwan arms sales issue) could easily be resolved, presumably on China's terms. This became the leitmotiv of official Chinese comments about Sino-American relations at the highest level.[39]

Washington's reluctance to honor its commitments was explained by reference to the imperialist character of the United States—a feature the Chinese had overlooked in the preceding period. A scholarly article detailing the schemes of the Truman administration to separate Taiwan from China was reprinted in *Renmin ribao* in order to demonstrate the long-standing character of U.S. interference in Chinese internal affairs.[40] In the latter half of 1981 Chinese leaders and the media resumed their criticism of U.S. foreign policy in the Middle East and Central America, and spurned Washington's invitation to join in sanctions against the USSR and Poland.

Reflecting on the strategic reservoir thesis, it is clear that the resignation of Secretary of State Haig in June 1982 removed the Reagan administration's major advocate of emphasizing the strategic dimension of Sino-American relations. Although flattering references to the importance of China in world politics remained in the official U.S. vocabulary, in actuality the Reagan administration tended to view the PRC primarily as a regional power in Asia rather than a global actor and was no longer inclined to accommodate Chinese sensibilities and desires. As Beijing had stopped stressing the urgency of an anti-Soviet united front, however, it was doubtful that a U.S. initiative to reemphasize strategic cooperation would produce much more than a mildly positive change of atmosphere in Sino-American relations. This conclusion was borne out by Secretary of Defense Caspar Weinberger's trip to the PRC in September 1983.

The American Mismanagement Thesis

A second and related explanation for the unsatisfactory state of U.S.-PRC relations is that Reagan has needlessly angered the Chinese by his inept handling of the relationship and by his indulgence in loose and provocative language on the Taiwan issue in particular. Democrats are particularly fond of this line of argument. For example, the chairman of the House Subcommittee on Asian and Pacific Affairs, Rep. Stephen Solarz (D–N.Y.), wrote: "The deterioration of Washington-Peking relations has almost nothing to do with any change in direction of U.S. policy and almost everything to do with the Administration's political insensitivity and diplomatic bungling."[41] He laid the blame for the administration's poor performance directly upon President Reagan himself.

It is no doubt true that candidate Reagan's criticism of Carter's China policy, his campaign talk about restoring official relations between Washington and Taipei, and the presence of pro-Taiwan conservatives in his personal entourage made for a poor beginning to his administration's relations with the PRC. It is true that Reagan's initial and perhaps continuing instincts with respect to China policy reflected his belief that the Carter administration had treated the government on Taiwan shabbily. Reagan saw Taiwan as a loyal U.S. ally whose interests had been sacrificed to propitiate Beijing. An additional irritant to the PRC was the Reagan administration's slowness in resolving important issues. It took a full year to make the FX decision, and nine months to make the decision in the Hu Na case. In the long gestation period of decision making, the PRC had ample time to develop its case and the administration earned no credit from the PRC for its negative decision on the FX.

Nevertheless, the U.S. mismanagement thesis implies an exaggerated estimate of the change in U.S. China policy under Reagan. To be sure, there were some significant changes. The Carter administration had eased PRC entry into the World Bank and the IMF in May 1980, but the Reagan administration blocked China's entry into the Asian Development Bank (ADB) by insisting that Taiwan, a charter member of the ADB, be allowed to retain its membership—a "two-China policy" that Beijing adamantly rejects as a violation of the 1978 U.S.-PRC normalization agreement. The strategic emphasis of U.S. foreign policy on Japan and South Korea, traditional U.S. partners, implied the demotion of the PRC in U.S. global policy. Yet notwithstanding its ideological affinity for the Nationalist government on Taiwan, the Reagan administration continued and in some respects furthered the China policy of the preceding administrations, to the dismay of its own conservative supporters. Talk about upgrading relations with Taiwan largely disappeared from Reagan's vocabulary as soon as he took office, and the pro-Taiwan conservatives on the White House staff were leashed if not muzzled. China policy was placed in the hands of mainstream foreign service professionals.

The administration's faulty start on China policy may not only have engendered genuine doubts in Beijing concerning U.S. commitment; more importantly, it gave the Chinese the important diplomatic advantage of being an aggrieved party. Beijing adroitly exploited this extremely useful posture in order to press for U.S. concessions on a variety of bilateral issues, particularly that of arms sales to Taiwan and technology transfer.

In short, to the extent that Washington managed the relationship—as it certainly did—it was less in matters of substance than of style, although it is doubtless true that *how* policy is managed may be no less significant than *what* the policy actually is. Moreover, the cost of mismanagement is often figured in the coin of substantive concessions—a price that the United States has in fact paid in its relations with the PRC under President Reagan.

The Normal Conflict Thesis

A third perspective on Sino-American relations is that the surfacing of bilateral problems in recent years is neither unexpected nor cause for alarm, but rather both normal and manageable. On the whole, so the argument goes, the Washington-Beijing link has remained strong, and the prospects for further improving relations are good. Not surprisingly, this was the position taken in public by officials of the Reagan administration. In a speech to the National Committee on U.S.-China Relations, Assistant Secretary of State for East Asian and Pacific Affairs John Holdridge said in December 1982: "I am upbeat on the future of U.S.-China relations. . . . The momentum is now building for renewed progress."[42] In a statement to the House Subcommittee on Asian and Pacific Affairs, his successor Paul Wolfowitz asserted: "It is inevitable as relations mature and develop, and as trade and exchanges advance and multiply, that the attendant bilateral problems grow progressively more complex." Nevertheless, Wolfowitz claimed that "the prospects for further progress are encouraging."[43]

In this perspective, the consolidation of the framework of U.S.-PRC relations via normalization and the institutionalization of relations through the creation of multiple linkages create many areas of contact within which certain problems will inevitably arise. These problems can be discussed on their own merits and necessary compromises can be achieved without threatening the basic relationship between the two countries. Within any international relationship—especially one in which the two parties have such different social systems—the emergence of bilateral problems is a sign of normal growth, not a warning signal of malignancy. The overall political diplomatic framework defines certain parameters within which the relationship fluctuates over time.

A logical policy prescription may be deduced from this perspective. As it is in neither the Chinese nor the U.S. national interest to jeopardize the overall relationship, the two sides should deal with bilateral problems at the working level of government as they arise, rather than magnify the problems by linking the resolution of specific issues to the health of the total relationship or by issuing threats and warnings. Such a low-key, pragmatic approach to conflict resolution would redound to the longer-term benefit of both sides, for their underlying shared interests outweigh the divisive, short-term bilateral issues, including even the Taiwan question.

The appeal of this approach to U.S. officials is self-evident. The Chinese perspective is somewhat different, however. Deeply ingrained in the Chinese diplomatic tradition is a pronounced proclivity to deal with all manner of foreign policy issues, at the rhetorical/normative if not the operational level, as matters of principle in the first instance.[44] A corollary is hypersensitivity to real and imagined slights and a propensity toward engaging in linkage politics at the international level as a means of maintaining ideological consistency. (The Chinese can be very flexible in practice, however, when it suits them.) By freely exercising these natural reflexes, PRC officials gain a tactical advantage vis-à-vis their U.S. counterparts by suggesting that unless a particular issue is resolved in line with Chinese preferences the overall relationship may suffer. In specific instances these suggestions may be little more than diplomatic ploys, yet the cumulative effect of discounting Chinese warnings may be serious. Thus the normal conflict thesis, although not without merit, is too sanguine a perspective on Sino-American relations.

The High Politics–Low Politics
Interaction Thesis

As previously noted, the United States and the PRC sought both before and after diplomatic normalization to strengthen the official relationship by promoting linkages through trade and other economic activity and through cultural exchanges. Institutional pluralism was seen as both a bridge and if need be, a buffer. Both the United States and the PRC had long used people-to-people diplomacy in their separate foreign policies. Now they were agreeing to transform it into a joint instrument for the common good of both countries.

Unfortunately, not everything has worked out this way. As Sino-American relations burgeoned within and outside the framework of official and semiofficial protocols governing the exchanges, it proved impossible and undesirable to maintain strict central control over every sphere of activity. Within each area of interaction a separate dynamic developed, and problems emerged that could not have been fully anticipated. These problems challenged the assumption of harmony that underlay the rationale for the network of relations. Given the Chinese tendency to treat every issue as a matter of principle within a linkage framework, the result was that the "low politics" of cultural exchanges, trade disputes, and political asylum not infrequently produced a negative impact on the "high politics" of global strategy, military-security cooperation, and foreign policy coordination. This was precisely the reverse of what the expanded network of relationships was intended to achieve. Let us briefly examine a couple of specific issues to clarify this point.

After the process of Sino-American reconciliation had been publicly initiated in April 1971 with the visit of a U.S. table tennis team to China ("ping-pong diplomacy"), sports continued to play a definite role in Sino-American cultural exchanges. When Chinese tennis star Hu Na sought political asylum in the United States in July 1982, a minor crisis in U.S.-PRC relations ensued. After enormous bureaucratic infighting within the U.S. government, Hu Na was finally granted asylum in April 1983. At this point, charging that President Reagan personally had participated in a plot to lure Hu Na away from her family and her country, the Chinese leadership and media let loose a volley of angry words at the United States and peremptorily canceled the entire schedule of officially arranged cultural exchanges for the remainder of 1983. Through a combination of official ineptness on Washington's part and Beijing's apparent determination to make an issue of the case, an extremely minor matter—which should have been resolved quickly and quietly at a low level—grew into a symbolic confrontation between the United States and the PRC involving principal political figures on both sides.

The question of high-technology transfer and PRC scientists' access to classified U.S. research is obviously more complicated. Technological modernization and scientific progress are important components of China's current development strategy, and PRC leaders look to the United States, among other developed countries, as a key supplier of advanced technology and as a training ground for scientists, engineers, and other technical specialists. Many U.S. high-tech corporations are naturally eager to sell goods to China, and unimpeded access to research and information is the norm in the U.S. academic world. However, within the U.S. government, particularly the Department of Defense, security considerations have been invoked to impede or block the flow to the PRC of certain kinds of advanced technology that can be used for military purposes. Similarly, the State Department established procedures to review access of PRC scholars to technical information concerning military as well as certain other sensitive fields.[45] The Chinese have complained that with respect to export licensing procedures they were being treated as a potential enemy rather than as a friendly country.

In essence, the dynamic of developments in the spheres of high-technology trade and science-technology exchanges posed problems that required decisions at the top levels of government. Specifically, the White House had to determine what category the PRC should be placed into for high-technology exports, and this in turn involved a judgment as to the kind of relationship the United States expected to have with the PRC in the future. In response to pressures both from U.S. companies and the Chinese themselves, Washington gradually relaxed barriers to high-technology transfer to the PRC and by mid-1983 had placed China in the category of friendly nations for which all but a very few types of sensitive technology would henceforth be routinely approved.[46] As this example shows, there is a continuing interaction between "low" and "high" politics in Sino-American relations, and complex coalitions of domestic and foreign actors may influence the decision process on these issues.

The Strategic Realignment Thesis

The final perspective emphasizes that the governments of both the United States and the PRC view their bilateral relationship within the context of their overall foreign policies. As previously noted, over the past two or three years Beijing has moved away from its apparent "pro-Western" orientation and adopted a more self-assertive foreign policy emphasizing China's independence from both superpowers and its identification with the Third World. Beijing has also gradually improved its relations with Moscow. Chinese disavowals of any connection between Sino-Soviet and Sino-American relations must be treated skeptically in view of the historical interconnectedness of these relations over several decades.

It appears that sometime in 1981 Beijing decided to adjust its stance toward Washington by de-emphasizing the cooperative aspects of the relationship and drawing attention to continuing areas of disagreement and unresolved problems. PRC leaders emphasized that their open-door policy of advancing Chinese modernization via expanded participation in the international capitalist economy would continue, and in this connection, the Sino-American economic relationship would retain its significance. However, with respect to the strategic relationship that had set the tone for Sino-American relations in the 1970s, Deng Xiaoping and his associates decided to pursue a more self-consciously independent path.

From this perspective, the main (although not the sole) responsibility for the exacerbation of U.S.-PRC relations lies with Beijing rather than Washington. Beijing's handling of the seemingly endless series of irritating minor incidents that have pockmarked Sino-American relations since 1981 is seen as more important than their actual substance. As a presidential candidate in 1980, Reagan set in motion the downward spiral of U.S.-PRC relations, and his administration handled many of the incidents in an unfelicitous manner. Yet it was Beijing that time and again took the initiative to inflate the significance of these intrinsically petty incidents. Meanwhile, it has served Beijing's tactical purposes to blame Washington for the deterioration of relations, calculating (correctly in many instances) that U.S. anxiety about the future of the relationship will reap a harvest of concessions on those issues (Taiwan arms sales and technology transfer) that most concern the Chinese. However, if the cooling of Sino-American relations really is the result of a decision for strategic realignment in Beijing, even additional major U.S. concessions on the Taiwan issue are unlikely to restore the lost momentum of Sino-American relations.

THE FUTURE OF SINO-AMERICAN RELATIONS

Let us now consider several probable characteristics of U.S.-PRC relations over the next several years. Our discussion is based on the assumption that a regime similar to that now in power in Beijing will continue in office and the government in Washington will also remain essentially stable.

First of all, Sino-American relations will likely be characterized by *selective engagement* rather than *comprehensive engagement* as was the case during the apogee of the relationship during the late 1970s. The Chinese leadership has realized that its interests may best be served by emphasizing only those aspects of the U.S. connection that promise a concrete payoff for their modernization program while incurring minimal internal and external political costs. This means monitoring educational and cultural exchanges to limit interaction in China between Americans and Chinese. It also means keeping a weather eye on urban Chinese youth, particularly students and the children of cadres, for signs of untoward interest in U.S. culture and consumerism. Reiteration of the need for ideological conformity is a hallmark of postrevolutionary Communist society. In foreign affairs, selective engagement means reemphasizing the distinction between the United States as an imperialist "First World" power and the PRC as a developing socialist Third World country. It also means carefully limiting the security-strategic component of U.S.-PRC relations and pursuing an omnidirectional foreign policy with renewed attention to the Asian periphery of China, including the USSR.

Secondly, there may be an increasing divergence between the official and the unofficial components of the overall Sino-American relationship. Further progress in official relations will be slowed by the Taiwan arms sales issue and other disputes likely to crop up from time to time, but unofficial relations may develop more smoothly, especially in noncontroversial areas such as tourism and essential areas such as economic exchanges. In this respect, the institutional linkages established over the past decade may after all play the role of a buffer in times of political difficulty. There is less likelihood of a positive spillover effect into the arena of high politics. Rather, both Chinese and U.S. organizations that derive some benefit from mutual contact (access to foreign travel, funding, prestige, knowledge) will pursue their organization's advantages within certain limits defined by the overall state of U.S.-PRC relations, even if official relations between Beijing and Washington are stagnating or declining.

Third, economics is likely to prove the most significant dimension of Sino-American relations over the coming decade, supplanting the strategic-security nexus. Even here, the engagement will be selective rather than comprehensive. Having refined their development priorities during the period of economic readjustment, the Chinese have targeted certain areas of their economy in which the investment of U.S. capital and the application of U.S. technology should prove most efficacious. These areas include transport, energy, computers, and other high technology industries.[47]

Another attraction of the economic dimension is that it is *relatively*—although by no means completely—insulated from political complications. The Chinese have had considerable experience in divorcing international economic from political considerations when it suits their interest to do so. In the United States a growing consciousness of the importance of foreign trade will likely overbalance protectionist sentiment. Moreover, U.S. business executives and their Chinese counterparts are relatively less ideological or value-oriented in their approach to each other than, say, academics, educators, and politicians. Bilateral interest-based disputes such as the textile quota issue of the early 1980s are more readily subject to compromise solutions than are symbolic value-based issues such as political asylum.

Finally, the Taiwan arms sales issue will probably remain a contentious one in Sino-American relations for numerous interconnected reasons. U.S. flexibility is limited by the provision of the Taiwan Relations Act that the U.S. "provide Taiwan with arms of a defensive character [Sec. 2b(5)]" and that "the President and the Congress shall determine the nature and quantity of such defense articles and services based solely upon their judgment of the needs of Taiwan [Sec. 3-(b)]." PRC attempts to secure repeal of this act are more likely to antagonize U.S. legislators than achieve success, and the executive branch will probably remain more inclined to pacify the Chinese (if that is possible) with economic concessions than by further weakening the residual U.S. defense commitment to Taiwan.

The PRC will probably continue to focus considerable attention on the Taiwan arms sales issue for several reasons besides the usual principled objections that Beijing often presents. In general terms, a manageable level of discord with the United States serves several positive functions for the current regime of Deng Xiaoping and his associates, and it is presumably for this reason that they chose to rekindle an issue that had been carefully set to one side in the earlier phase of Sino-American relations.

First, it helps to enhance their political legitimacy by demonstrating to domestic audiences that China retains its independence from both superpowers and is unafraid of antagonizing the United States. Second, it signals Moscow that China is serious about repositioning itself between the United States and the USSR as an autonomous actor, interested in good relations with both countries but neither beholden to nor formally constrained by either. Third, raising the Taiwan arms sales issue puts pressure on the United States to yield further concessions either on that issue or in other areas of Sino-American contention. By playing the role of an aggrieved party, Beijing is in a position to exercise greater control within the relationship than it could otherwise. Finally, if the United States does agree to further concessions on the Taiwan arms sales issue (either via a new agreement or by accepting Beijing's reading of the August 1982 agreement), this may enhance apprehension on Taiwan concerning the island's future security and improve the prospects for PRC-Taiwanese discussions focusing on the island's future. It remains to be noted that a skillful PRC diplomacy would press its case with particular vigor during presidential election years, and also that a clumsy diplomacy could backfire.

CONCLUSIONS

The Sino-Soviet alliance of the 1950s collapsed under the weight of the unrealistic expectations that both sides harbored during its initiation and early flowering. The idea of a U.S.-PRC alliance (even an informal one) was never a realistic prospect, and the impetus of strategic cooperation against the USSR that may have been necessary to reverse the Cold War between Washington and Beijing can probably no longer serve as a solid foundation for Sino-American relations. To reach a point of equilibrium—dynamic rather than static—in U.S.-PRC relations will require an understanding, particularly in Washington, of the limits as well as the possibilities of the relationship, and the wisdom not to attempt to restore the strategic momentum of 1979–1981.

For the Chinese it will require a modification of their zero-sum Leninist style of conflict resolution, with its stress on immutable principles, confrontation to achieve capitulation, and insistence on linking minor and major issues. Restraint in handling problems that emerge within separate areas of interaction is the best way to avoid the escalatory spiral of action and retaliation that can unravel even the best-knit of relationships. Should an unraveling occur, however, the very considerable advantages that both Chinese and Americans have derived from their relations during the past decade would be jeopardized, and the security of East Asia and ultimately the world would be placed at risk. Thus a sober and realistic understanding of the parameters within which the PRC-U.S. relationship functions is an indispensable requisite for the task of managing that relationship successfully in the future.

NOTES

I would like to acknowledge the valuable research assistance of Peggy Spitzer Christoff and Alice Kelly Ho in preparing this chapter.

1. Henry A. Kissinger, *The White House Years* (Boston: Little, Brown and Co., 1979), pp. 684–787; Zbigniew Brzezinski, *Power and Principle* (New York: Farrar, Strauss, Giroux, 1983).

2. Brzezinski, *Power and Principle*, Annex 1, p. 1.

3. Ibid., p. 204; see also Richard H. Solomon, "The China Factor in American Foreign Relations," in Richard H. Solomon, ed., *The China Factor: Sino-American Relations and the Global Scene* (Englewood Cliffs, N.J.: Prentice-Hall, 1981), pp. 1–47.

4. Harry Harding describes this as a transformation from China's status as a radical aligned state in the early 1950s to a conservative aligned state in the 1970s. "Change and Continuity in Chinese Foreign Policy," *Problems of Communism* 32 (March–April 1983):1–19.

5. The analysis in this paragraph is based on the author's "China in Asia: The PRC as a Regional Power," in Harry Harding, ed., *Chinese Foreign Relations in the 1980s* (New Haven, Conn.: Yale University Press, forthcoming).

6. For analyses of Sino-Soviet limited détente see, in addition to Chi Su's chapter in this book (Ch. 6), Donald S. Zagoria, "The Moscow-Beijing Detente," *Foreign Affairs* 61 (Spring 1983):853–873; William E. Griffith, "Sino-Soviet Rapprochement?" *Problems of Communism* 32 (March–April 1983):20–29.

7. John L. Scherer, ed., *China Facts and Figures Annual* (Gulf Breeze, Fla.: Academic International Press, 1980, 1982), 3:163; 5:179. *China Business Review* 8 (July–August 1981):54–57.

8. Thomas Fingar and Linda A. Reed, *Students and Scholars from the People's Republic of China in the United States, August 1981* (Committee on Scholarly Communication with the People's Republic of China and National Association for Foreign Student Affairs, Washington, D.C., September 1981), p. 1; *China Exchange News* 10 (December 1982):16.

9. See National Committee on U.S.-China Relations, *U.S.-China Relations: Notes from the National Committee*, Vol. 11, No. 1-2 (Spring-Summer 1981); Vol. 11, No. 3 (Fall 1981); and Vol. 11, No. 4–Vol. 12, No. 1 (Winter 1981–Spring 1982); and Center for U.S.-China Arts Exchange, *U.S.-China Arts Exchange Newsletter*, Vol. 3, No. 1 (Spring 1982).

10. Brzezinski, *Power and Principle*, p. 417; for the rationale of this decision see Michel Oksenberg, "The Dynamics of the Sino-American Relationship," in Solomon, *The China Factor*, pp. 55–66.

11. Michael Hunt, *The Making of a Special Relationship: The United States and China to 1914* (New York: Columbia University Press, 1983).

12. William Watt, *The United States and Asia* (Lexington, Mass.: D. C. Heath, 1982).

13. Brzezinski, *Power and Principle*, p. 417; "Two Years of U.S.-China Relations," *Department of State Bulletin* 81, 2047 (February 1981):33–36.

14. "Two Years of U.S.-China Relations," pp. 33–36.

15. *Department of State Bulletin* 79, 2031 (October 1979):10–13; quote at p. 10.

16. See (Colonel) Monte R. Bullard, "The US-China Defense Relationship," *Parameters* 13, 1 (March 1983):43.

17. For a thoughtful presentation of conflicting views on this subject, see *The Implications of U.S.-China Military Cooperation*, A workshop sponsored by the Committee on Foreign Relations, United States Senate, and the Congressional Research Service (Library of Congress) (Washington, D.C.: Government Printing Office, 1981).

18. *Department of State Bulletin* 81, 2053 (August 1981):36.

19. Robert Sutter, *Executive-Legislative Consultations on China Policy, 1978–1979*, prepared for the House Committee on Foreign Affairs (Washington, D.C.: Government Printing Office, June 1980).

20. See, for example, Deng Xiaoping's interview with *Christian Science Monitor* Chief Editor Earl Foell, *Christian Science Monitor*, November 15, 1980, p. 1.

21. To be sure, the State Department, an unequal and somewhat reluctant partner in the White House–directed drive for a strategic relationship with the PRC, pointedly described the United States and China as friends rather than allies, and Assistant Secretary of State Richard Holbrooke asserted that henceforth the U.S.-PRC relationship would be conceptually decoupled from the Soviet-U.S.-Chinese strategic triangle. *Department of State Bulletin* 80, 2041 (August 1980):50. But since the chief proponent of this view—Secretary of State Cyrus Vance—had already resigned by this time, the advocate of treating Sino-American relations primarily in the context of Soviet-American strategic competition—National Security Council advisor Brzezinski—prevailed easily. Brzezinski, *Power and Principle*, pp. 403–404, 416–419.

22. Steven I. Levine, "The Soviet Factor," in John Bryan Starr, ed., *The Future of US-China Relations* (New York: NYU Press, 1981), pp. 78–93.

23. For a thorough discussion of this issue in the context of Sino-American relations in the early stages of the Reagan administration, see A. Doak Barnett, *The FX Decision: "Another Crucial Moment" in U.S.-China-Taiwan Relations* (Washington, D.C.: Brookings Institution, 1981).

24. *Washington Post*, January 12, 1982, p. All.

25. See *Beijing Review*, No. 40 (October 5, 1981):10–11.

26. *Department of State Bulletin* 82, 2067 (October 1982):20.

27. See Chinese Foreign Ministry Statement of August 17, 1982, in *Beijing Review*, No. 34 (August 23, 1982):15–16.

28. For a thorough and perceptive discussion of the Taiwan issue in U.S.-China relations see Allen S. Whiting, "Sino-American Relations: The Decade Ahead," *Orbis* 26, 3 (Fall 1982):697–719. See also the interesting observations by Charles T. Cross, the first head of the American Institute in Taiwan, who suggests that by endorsing Beijing's nine-point plan for the reunification of Taiwan, the United States had allowed itself to become vulnerable to additional Chinese pressure on Washington to achieve forward movement on the Taiwan arms sales issue. Charles T. Cross, "Taipei's Identity Crisis," *Foreign Policy*, No. 51 (Summer 1983):55.

29. See Allen S. Whiting's commentary on this point in the *New York Times*, August 23, 1983, p. 27; the *Beijing Review* article on Deng's interview omitted any mention of this offer, however. *Beijing Review*, No. 32 (August 8, 1983): 5–6.

30. *New York Times*, July 20, 1983, p. 6; September 27, 1983, p. 3; *Christian Science Monitor*, December 1, 1983, pp. 1, 72.

31. For a skeptical view of China's case see John F. Copper, "U.S.-China Trade: China's Unconvincing Case," *Christian Science Monitor*, February 8, 1983, p. 23.

32. *New York Times*, July 31, 1983, pp. 1, 12; August 1, 1983, pp. 1, 25.

33. *New York Times*, April 8, 1983, pp. 1, 6.

34. See *Beijing Review*, No. 11 (March 14, 1983):24–27, 30; also *Christian Science Monitor*, March 3, 1983, p. 10.

35. Fox Butterfield, *China: Alive in the Bitter Sea* (New York: Times Books, 1982); Richard Bernstein, *From the Center of the Earth* (Boston: Little, Brown and Co., 1982).

36. Ross Terrill, "Trying to Make China Work," *Atlantic* 252, 1 (July 1983):20–29.

37. Henry Kissinger in the *Washington Post*, January 30, 1983, p. C8; Zbigniew Brzezinski in the *New York Times*, January 31, 1983, p. 19; Michel Oksenberg in the *New York Times*, January 27, 1983, p. 23.

38. "Where Lies the Crux of Sino-American Relations?" *Guoji wenti yanjiu* [Journal of international studies], No. 2 (1982):2.

39. See, for example, Hu Yaobang, "Report to the 12th National Congress of the Communist Party of China," *Beijing Review*, No. 37 (September 13, 1982):30.

40. Zi Zhongyun, "Test of History—US Policy Towards Taiwan at the Time of the Birth of New China," *Guoji wenti yanjiu*, No. 3 (1982):34–42; *Renmin ribao* [People's daily], July 13, 1982, p. 6.

41. *New York Times*, June 17, 1983, p. 27.

42. U.S. Department of State, "Current Policy," No. 444, December 13, 1982, p. 3.

43. U.S. Department of State, "Current Policy," No. 460, February 28, 1983, p. 3.

44. For a succinct overview of traditional China's foreign policy system see Samuel S. Kim, *China, the United Nations and World Order* (Princeton, N.J.: Princeton University Press, 1979), pp. 19–48; see also Harry Harding, "Change and Continuity in Chinese Foreign Policy."

45. *The Chronicle of Higher Education*, September 15, 1982, p. 12.

46. *Far Eastern Economic Review* 120 (June 16, 1983):16, 18; *New York Times*, June 17, 1983, p. 3.

47. See, for example, the report of the joint production venture between the American Motors Corporation and Peking Auto Works in the *New York Times*, May 3, 1983, pp. 1, 44.

CHAPTER 6

CHINA AND THE SOVIET UNION: "PRINCIPLED, SALUTARY, AND TEMPERED" MANAGEMENT OF CONFLICT

Chi Su

Just a few years ago, the relationship between the Soviet Union and the People's Republic of China was marked by a degree of conflict so severe, so persistent, and so pervasive that there appeared to be little or no cooperation between them. Yet only four months after consummating the tortuous process of normalizing relations with the United States and only two months after concluding its "punitive" campaign against Vietnam, Beijing proposed a talk with Moscow "to settle the outstanding issues between the two countries and improve bilateral relations."[1] Subsequently, more concrete signs of a thaw appeared. Without altering the structure of the "competitive containment" of the 1970s, these two Communist giants, under the leadership of Deng Xiaoping, Leonid I. Brezhnev, and Brezhnev's successor, Yuri V. Andropov, seemed to be slowly exploring the possibilities as well as the limits of rapprochement.

Are the new developments of the early 1980s merely the tip of an iceberg, signifying a more fundamental shift in Beijing's and Moscow's policies? Or are they merely adaptations to changed circumstances? What are the reasons behind the changes so far? And what possibilities may lie ahead in the evolution of Sino-Soviet relations during the rest of the 1980s?

This chapter attempts to answer these questions. It begins by examining some of the recent developments in Sino-Soviet relations. Then, Soviet views of the changes in post-Mao China's domestic and foreign policies are discussed, along with their implications for the "new" Soviet policy. The second half of the chapter presents a more detailed exposition of changing Chinese perspectives and desires, followed by some concluding remarks on the future prospects of Sino-Soviet rivalry.

RECENT DEVELOPMENTS

Contrary to popular belief, the first breeze across the icy area of Sino-Soviet relations blew westward from Beijing, not eastward from Moscow. On April 3, 1979, a Foreign Ministry note to the Soviet embassy in Beijing informed the latter of China's formal decision not to renew the 1950 treaty and offered normalization talks. Soviet Foreign Minister Andrei A. Gromyko accepted the offer on April 17, 1979. Between September 27 and November 30 of that year, delegations from both sides met in Moscow for five preliminary sessions and six plenary sessions.

According to both Chinese and Soviet sources, the Chinese side raised three demands during these sessions: (1) a reduction of Soviet armed forces in the Sino-Soviet border areas; (2) the withdrawal of Soviet troops from the Mongolian People's Republic; and (3) discontinuation of Soviet support for Vietnam's invasion of Kampuchea. The Soviet delegation resubmitted its 1978 proposal for a draft declaration on the principles of mutual relations. Both sides claimed in their later accounts to have proposed an expansion of economic, cultural, scientific, technological, and other exchanges between the two countries.[2] At the end of this round of talks, both agreed only to resume further discussions in early 1980.

In the meantime, however, the Chinese leadership under Deng, who had just emerged victorious from the Third Plenum of the Eleventh Chinese Communist Party (CCP) Congress (December 1978), took its first step toward "de-Maoization" of the PRC's domestic policy and "de-ideologization" of its foreign policy. In his speech commemorating the thirtieth anniversary of the founding of the PRC, Marshal Ye Jianying openly and for the first time blamed Mao Zedong for some of the leftist mistakes committed during the late 1950s and 1960s. In Ye's opinion, it was Mao's erroneous tendencies, rather than the precipitous withdrawal of Soviet aid in 1960 or any natural disasters, that were more responsible for China's economic difficulties of the early 1960s. Ye also carefully avoided mention of Soviet revisionism.[3] During 1979 there was a parallel upsurge in China of highly favorable references to the "golden years" of the 1949–1957 period as well as to the "great significance of the Eighth CCP Congress (1956)"—themes that Soviet writers had trumpeted for years.[4]

The year 1980, as Deng stated in a major speech, "started off unpropitiously."[5] In response to the Soviet invasion of Afghanistan at the turn of the year, China suspended the Sino-Soviet talks previously scheduled for early 1980. More interestingly, though, was that as with the U.S. incursion into Cambodia in 1970, Beijing made the announcement only after a lapse of three weeks, and the statement left the door open for future resumption of the talks.[6] Partly because of the inherent differences in these two cases and partly because of the momentum of improved Sino-American ties, the relations between Beijing and Moscow remained frozen throughout 1980.

Despite this turn of events, China appointed a new ambassador to Moscow in late January, filling a six-month vacancy. Furthermore, in continuation of the trend set in 1979, the name of Anti-Revisionist Street, where the Soviet embassy is located, reverted to its previous name, "Dongnei Da Jie" (East Inner-Gate Boulevard). Press articles admitted that the famous "nine commentaries" of the early 1960s were incorrect on the nature of the Soviet "revisionist system."[7]

Beginning in 1981, Moscow showed distinctly greater interest in reaching out to its eastern foe than it had previously. Soviet advisor Mikhail Kapitsa, an expert on China, visited Beijing twice in early 1981 as "a guest of the Soviet Embassy." On March 7, 1981, Moscow suggested that the two countries discuss the implementation of "confidence-building measures" along the border.[8] On September 25, a proposal to resume border negotiations was introduced, and on December 16, Moscow offered to resume contacts between the two countries in the area of scientific and technological cooperation. However, despite its predictably adverse impact on future Sino-Soviet border talks, a treaty involving Pamir borders was signed on June 16, 1981, between the USSR and Afghanistan, thus formally legalizing Soviet possession of territory claimed by the Chinese.[9]

China's behavior was subdued by contrast. Beijing evaded a public reply to Moscow's March 1981 proposal, and suggested "indefinite postponement" of border talks. It protested the Soviet-Afghan treaty, but signed a railroad transport protocol with the Soviets. In the meantime, Beijing allowed a team of Chinese gymnasts to compete in Moscow for the world gymnastics championship and attend a reception hosted by the Soviet-Chinese Friendship Society on November 20, 1981. There were even indications that the term "social imperialism" was quietly being dropped from Chinese publications, to be replaced by a single codeword: "hegemonism."[10]

In 1982, the movement toward rapprochement appeared to quicken. The Soviet Union continued to play the eager suitor, with Brezhnev personally pitching in. On March 24, 1982, he declared in a widely publicized speech in Tashkent that "we have never denied and do not deny the existence of a socialist social system in China . . . have never supported in any form and do not support the so-called 'concept of two Chinas' . . . [and] have never regarded as normal the state of animosity and alienation between our countries." He proclaimed that "there has never been . . . nor is there any threat to the People's Republic of China from the Soviet Union."[11] In a September 26 speech at Baku and an October 27 speech to a group of high-ranking military officers, Brezhnev again stated his desire for Sino-Soviet normalization.[12] China reacted cautiously, publicly acknowledging Brezhnev's statements but at the same time stressing the importance of "deeds" over "words," and hinting at its awareness of possible Soviet attempts to exploit the difficulties in Sino-American relations.[13]

On February 3, 1982, a Soviet Foreign Ministry note reaffirming its interest in reopening border talks was sent to the Chinese embassy in Moscow. Six days later, the Soviet Ministry of Higher and Secondary Special Education followed up with the suggestion that the annual exchange of students and teachers for language training be resumed. In the same period, a Soviet diplomat and top expert on the border question, Sergei L. Tikhvinskii, made a "private" visit to Beijing in January. This was followed by another visit by Kapitsa in May.

Compared with 1981, the Chinese were more forthcoming in 1982, sending a stream of visitors to the Soviet capital: a small group of economists in February, another athletic team in March, a trade delegation in May, and finally a "private" visit by the Chinese expert on Soviet affairs, Yu Hongliang, in August. Both China and the Soviet Union agreed in April to increase their trade by 45 percent for the following year. In September, an agreement on exchange of publications was signed. Finally, between October 5 and 21, Soviet and Chinese delegations met in Beijing for the first post-Afghanistan talks. During the six plenary sessions, China reportedly added a demand for Soviet troop withdrawal from Afghanistan to the 1979 list. The Chinese also insisted on using the term "consultations" to describe the talks.

Brezhnev's death in early November 1982 provided an opportunity for Sino-Soviet contacts at the highest level thus far. After praising Brezhnev as "an outstanding statesman" at the airport in Beijing, Chinese Foreign Minister Huang Hua proceeded to Moscow and conferred with Andropov, the new general secretary of the Communist Party of the Soviet Union (CPSU). Upon returning to Beijing, Huang expressed "optimism" about the prospects of future Sino-Soviet talks.[14] *Pravda*'s editor in chief, Viktor G. Afanasyev, suggested that the talks could lead to an agreement on troop reduction along the borders.[15] At the more authoritative level, Andropov himself reaffirmed in a speech to a central committee the Soviet desire for better relations between the two countries.[16]

Developments in 1983 were equally methodical, indicating careful management of their complex relations by both sides. The year began with an unusual article by an "Observer" of the popular Soviet magazine, *New Times*, assailing China for its "patently unfounded territorial claims on the USSR."[17] Judging from its contents (which specifically cited recently published Chinese maps, journals, and dictionaries), it appears that Moscow used this article to publicly question China's sincerity in "normalization" rather than to dispute China's stand on the border question per se. China quickly rose to defend its "historical research" with a much shorter "Commentator's" article in its own popular magazine *Shijie zhishi* (World knowledge),[18] but publication of this type of this research seems to have diminished substantially for the rest of 1983.

The second round of post-Afghanistan talks took place in Moscow between March 1 and 15, 1983, shortly after U.S. Secretary of State George Shultz's visit to Beijing in February. The negotiations produced no breakthroughs. However, on March 8, the Chinese delegation reportedly raised the issue of Soviet SS-20 missiles for the first time, stating its objection to their possible transfer from Europe to Asia.[19] According to Western diplomatic sources, the Soviets took a curious step in July 1983, mobilizing all Soviet bloc nations to send identical notes to Beijing, urging China to declare itself in the socialist camp and to condemn U.S. policy. Beijing responded by repeating its opposition to "hegemonism," capitalist or socialist.[20] On August 27, Andropov called for an improvement in Sino-Soviet relations and promised to dismantle Soviet SS-20 missiles in Europe after the successful conclusion of Geneva talks on intermediate nuclear forces, rather than transfer them to Asia.[21]

On September 1, 1983, the Soviet Union shocked the world by shooting down Korean Airlines (KAL) Flight 007, killing all 269 passengers aboard. Amid world outcry against this action, China reacted cautiously, allowing itself only to express "regret," but not to join any protests or sanctions against Moscow.[22] On September 2, China's state chairman, Li Xiannian, expressed pleasure over Andropov's assurances.[23] On September 8, Kapitsa was again welcomed into Beijing to pave the way for the forthcoming October talks. Yet, barely a few hours after Kapitsa left Beijing, the Chinese Foreign Ministry issued a statement calling on Moscow to compensate "the bereaved families" of the KAL passengers.[24] On the following day, an editorial in *Renmin ribao* asked the Soviet Union to "considerably reduce" the Soviet SS-20 missiles already deployed in Asia.[25]

Immediately following the departure of U.S. Secretary of Defense Caspar W. Weinberger from China in late September, the PRC announced that the third round of Sino-Soviet talks would be held in Beijing on October 6, 1983.[26] The talks, lasting through October 28, again failed to achieve major breakthroughs. However, both sides agreed to double trade for the following year, and increase the number of exchange students from 10 to 100. The Soviet Union agreed to assist in renovating four textile plants in Haerbin that had been built in the 1950s with Soviet aid.[27]

Several features of the recent developments in Sino-Soviet relations seem to stand out. First, it was China, not the Soviet Union, that first initiated the process of rapprochement. Even with the interruption of the Afghanistan invasion, the Deng leadership has carefully maintained the momentum since 1979 and has generally synchronized its Soviet policy with domestic policy readjustments. The Soviet approach on the other hand was neither innovative nor imaginative in 1979–1980. It was only in early 1981 that Moscow began to play its cards with a vengeance, initiating visits, making highly publicized calls, and putting forward a series of proposals.

Second, in both substance and style of diplomacy, the policies of China and the Soviet Union show distinct differences. As was the case with the 1969–1978 talks, the Soviet Union has preferred to settle first on a broad set of principles governing their mutual relations, while China has insisted on the removal of specific "obstacles" to normalization. Hence the failure of repeated rounds of talks so far.[28]

More revealing, though, the Soviet style of shaking hands with its negotiating partner contrasts sharply with the Chinese approach. The Soviet style is at once more manifest and more assertive. The Soviets made no proposal to the Chinese in 1980, but then made five in a span of eleven months (March 1981 to February 1982). None were kept secret from the outside world for long. Similarly, at the start of 1981 Soviet officials suddenly grew fond of visiting Beijing, with Kapitsa making three trips and Tikhvinskii one trip before Yu Hongliang ventured out to the Soviet capital in August 1982. Brezhnev made three personal but public appeals to the Chinese. Finally, Moscow made an awkward attempt in July 1983 to have China declare itself in the socialist camp.

By contrast, Chinese hand shaking appeared lukewarm, halfhearted, yet ever steady. China removed the pejorative tags for the Soviet Union— "revisionism" and "social imperialism"—without fanfare. It responded to the Soviet overtures of 1981–1982 slowly, preferring instead to start with athletic visits, book exchanges, and trade expansion. Beijing has played down the importance of the bilateral talks by describing them as "consultations" rather than "negotiations." The Chinese wrote a retort to the *New Times* article, but the tone was not as sharp, and Beijing has henceforth implicitly honored the Soviet wish. And in contrast to its pre-1979 practices, China has never rejected a proposal from the Soviet side since it initiated the normalization process in that year.

However, China stood fast on certain "principles" throughout the 1979–1983 period. Beijing vigorously protested the signing of the Soviet-Afghan border treaty in 1981. It held its ground on antihegemonism when the Soviet Union beckoned it to return to the fold of the socialist camp in 1983. It demanded compensation—but nothing more—for the KAL passengers, some of whom were citizens of Taiwan and Hong Kong. And Beijing has always balanced its calls for normalization with a recitation of China's demands on Soviet troop withdrawal.

Third, initial signs began to appear in 1981 of the Chinese tendency to balance between—and extract concessions from—the two superpowers. Under the slogans of "antihegemonism" and "independence," China reaffirmed its identification with the Third World. It carefully scheduled the two rounds of Sino-Soviet talks in 1983 to follow closely the visits of the two U.S. secretaries. Beginning in 1981, when the Soviets were seen as actively pursuing the Chinese, the Taiwan Relations Act, which had received only a mild and private protest from Beijing in 1979, was blown up as one of the major issues threatening Sino-American relations.[29] Subsequently, when Sino-American relations were partially stabilized in 1983, pressure began to build up on Moscow on the issue of the SS-20 in Siberia.

Fourth, as several Western observers have pointed out, the Sino-Soviet normalization process of the past few years has not gone beyond the improvement of atmospherics.[30] So far, advances have been made only in the realm of economic, scientific, and cultural exchanges. Underneath the steady flow of proposals, appeals and gestures, the Soviet leadership has appeared unwilling to alter its geopolitical posture to allay Chinese fears. In fact, as the treaty with Afghanistan indicates, primacy has always been given to cementing "socialist gains" rather than untying the Gordian knot of Sino-Soviet relations.

The Chinese seem unprepared to give the Soviets a free ride on any and all issues concerning China's security. Both keep a keen eye on the moves in Washington. And both are reluctant to go beyond the appearance of a rapprochement by compromising on their larger interests: for Beijing, security; for Moscow, its newly acquired role in world politics.

SOVIET VIEWS AND POLICIES

As discussed earlier, Soviet policy toward China during the 1979–1983 period was characterized first by a continued resistance to Chinese demands on the one hand, and then since 1981, a sudden resurge of outward interest in reconciliation.[31] From the data available, it appears that Soviet policy before 1981 was determined by the Soviet Union's profound distrust of the systemic roots of China's policies and the intentions of the post-Mao Chinese leadership, as well as by an acute awareness of the extent to which China could complicate Soviet efforts at "restructuring international relations." The shift was inspired by growing discord in the relationship between China and the United States, which presented an opportunity to loosen the "international anti-Soviet united front."

Soviet perceptions of China's systemic roots and intentions first took shape in the late 1960s. Under Khrushchev, the most prevalent characterization of China was one of "petit-bourgeois nationalist deviation," with clear emphasis on the petit-bourgeois nature of the regime.[32] At the height of the Cultural Revolution (1966–1968), Moscow began a serious reconsideration of the great China puzzle. The intensive search under way within the newly streamlined Soviet sinology (especially at the Institute of the Far East, established in 1967) resulted in a decisive shift in the Soviet view of the Chinese threat. Instead of treating Maoism as a "petit-bourgeois," "dogmatic-sectarian," "leftist" deviation of Marxism-Leninism, the new Soviet perspective cast Maoism as based solely on nationalism, and thus outside the Marxist-Leninist framework and antipodal to "internationalism." In June 1969, Brezhnev formally proclaimed before the gathering at the international Communist conference China's "departure from Marxism-Leninism and a break with internationalism."[33] Ten days after the conclusion of this conference, the Soviets even blatantly tampered with the final document of the conference to make their point. The document adopted by the conference exhorted the Marxist-Leninists of the world to fight against "revisionism, dogmatism and left sectarian adventurism." But in the CPSU Central Committee resolution passed on June 26, 1969, the formula was changed to read: "revisionism, dogmatism and *nationalism*."[34]

During the 1970s, the theme of "Chinese nationalism"—or variations such as "chauvinism," "social chauvinism," "reactionary nationalism," or "great-Han chauvinism"—loomed even larger as the central organizational concept of the entire Soviet conception of China. As the series of *Kommunist* editorials (Nos. 12 of 1973, 1974, 1975, and 1977) and numerous other Soviet scholarly works testified, Chinese nationalism remained the predominant prism through which Chinese policies with or without the overarching presence of Mao were viewed.[35] As late as 1979, one *Kommunist* editorial still insisted that "at the present time some of Mao's more untenable premises are being abandoned and Maoism itself is being adapted to the objectives of building a strong militarist state. But the principal hallmark of Maoism—reactionary nationalism—remains."[36]

This line of analysis continued undiminished into the early 1980s. To be sure, Soviet China watchers duly noted the major changes implemented by the Deng leadership, as did their Western counterparts. It was thus acknowledged in Moscow that "class struggle" had been removed as the main element of the PRC's domestic policy. The Chinese leadership has accelerated the pace of rehabilitation of the "rightists," strengthened the role of the Party, and streamlined the state machinery to carry out the Four Modernizations. At the same time, the Chinese have nurtured growth in the economic private sector and introduced more efficient management systems. They have displayed a greater willingness to utilize foreign capital and technology to serve China's development interests. Although noting the difficulties involved in these changes for the Chinese, the general assessment seems to be that the trend in China has been positive, compared with "the naked arbitrary rule and voluntarism" of the earlier times.[37]

The crucial question for the Soviets, however, is not whether the Chinese political-economic system has changed for the better. Rather, it involves an assessment of the systemic roots of these internal changes in China and their implications for the Soviet Union. For a great majority of Soviet officials and scholars, the answer seems ready at hand: China's current policies are merely manifestations of a deep, prevalent Chinese nationalism that has propelled Mao and the post-Mao leadership onto a "special Chinese road," with anti-Sovietism as one of its main premises.

In this view, the root cause for China's "departure from internationalism" is not China's semifeudal and semicolonial historical background, because similar backgrounds in other countries have led them to eagerly embrace "scientific socialism." Nor is it due to the predominantly peasant composition of the populace: The peasantry could still be led onto the socialist path if the proletariat provided correct leadership and heeded the advice of the developed socialist country. China's political degeneration cannot be blamed on its backward economic base, for China's economic growth would otherwise have led to a strengthening of socialism in that country. Instead, industrialization and improvement of living standards in China in the 1950s—achieved with the help of the Soviet Union—only prompted the Chinese leaders into nonsocialist experiments of their own. The ongoing process of change during the 1980s, though positive, will not in and of itself render China more socialist than before.

For the Soviets, therefore, the root cause of the China problem still lies in the host of subjective, uniquely Chinese factors best captured by the term, "Chinese nationalism." If the core of these subjective factors is not changed, improvements in the objective conditions of that country will only provide "a more dependable material and political base for Beijing's hegemonic, anti-Soviet foreign policy."[38] Or, as two Soviet authors have warned, "the consolidation of the CCP within the Maoist regime which is something the Beijing leadership is striving for may lead to a worse confrontation between China and the Soviet Union and its allies, and to Beijing's closer military and political alliance with world imperialism."[39]

Based on this perception, the Soviets have used a different yardstick than that implicitly adopted by Western scholars in analyzing post-Mao Chinese affairs. Whereas Westerners have often measured "de-Maoization" by contrasting the policy practices of Mao and his successors, thereby labeling Deng and others "authoritative reformers," Soviet scholars, equating Maoism with Chinese nationalism, have analyzed post-Mao policy by gauging the degree of "de-nationalism" and "pro-internationalism."[40] Thus, while Western analysts attached much significance to the rehabilitation of Liu Shaoqi, Peng Dehuai and others, the Soviets condemned China's continued blacklisting of Wang Ming, Gao Gang and other "internationalists."[41] Whereas many in the West hailed the revival of Mao's "theory of new democracy" as reflecting a desire to attenuate class struggle in the country, the Soviets viewed it as another Chinese attempt to "raise Chinese specifics to an absolute and ignore the common principles governing socialist construction."[42] The West noted with apprehension China's abandonment of the charges of Soviet revisionism. The Soviets saw a renewed, though subdued, Chinese effort to build a "Chinese form of socialism" via the Four Modernizations. In Moscow's view, for all practical purposes, Mao's shadow lingers on.

This pessimistic view seems to be reinforced by Soviet analysis of the factional struggle in China. As in the past, Soviet specialists seem convinced of the Chinese factions' joint hostility toward the Soviet

Union. As O. B. Rakhmanin (first deputy chief of the CPSU Liaison Department) stated in 1981:

> An acute power struggle continues within the ruling group itself. . . .
> However, the strife at the Beijing upper level does not affect the strategic
> goals proclaimed by Mao Zedong. All the Chinese leaders are united
> by the desire to turn the PRC into a strong military-industrial power.
> They all support the platform of the "sinicization of Marxism" and
> positions of great-power chauvinism, hegemonism and anti-Sovietism.
> The differences between them concern mainly the methods and pace
> of the accomplishment of the set tasks.[43]

Not surprisingly, Deng Xiaoping has emerged as the archvillain in the Soviet mind, rivaling Mao's status in previous decades. In a rebuttal to the Western portrayal of Deng as a "progressive reformer," a *Kommunist* article noted, "In fact, Deng Xiaoping is a typical mouthpiece of the right-wing nationalist and pro-imperialist trends in Maoism which emerged a long time ago and are now dominant in the country's politics."[44]

More to the consternation of Moscow's top leadership was perhaps the assessment by Soviet China watchers of the PRC's future political leaders, which appeared in *Problemy Dalnego Vostoka* (*PDV*) in mid-1982. Curiously, it was also published in the journal's English-language version, *Far Eastern Affairs*. After studying the CCP Communist Youth League (CYL), which has supplied many talents to the current Chinese leadership (CCP General Secretary Hu Yaobang and Foreign Minister Wu Xueqian among them), the author of this article concluded that in the course of the 1960s and 1970s the ranks of the CYL had been filled with people thoroughly imbued with Maoist ideas, and that the post-Mao CYL had reaffirmed (through its new charter) its adherence to Mao's foreign-policy line, including a "struggle against the world's first socialist country."[45] If the promotion of Hu and a host of others to top CCP positions foreshadows more recruitment from the CYL's ranks, one may infer from the analysis of the *PDV* article that the next generation of leaders in China will be at least as nationalist and anti-Soviet as the present one. This prospect is undoubtedly being taken very seriously in Moscow.

Against this background of deep-seated and long-standing Soviet distrust of Chinese nationalism and the distinct unwillingness on the part of Soviet leadership to accommodate "national Communism" on a more or less equal basis, arguments for reconciliation based on a positive assessment of internal Chinese development would indeed be quite unappealing to the Kremlin.[46] Arguments that take Chinese nationalism as their starting point but seek instead to neutralize its threat to the Soviet Union or, better yet, to divert it toward "imperialism" might win a more favorable audience inside the Kremlin. Such an opportunity, in the Soviet view, has been provided by the increasingly evident "contradictions" between China and the United States since 1981.

Soviet discussion of these "contradictions" has covered quite a few areas. Some observers noted domestic U.S. opposition to arms sales to China and to playing the "China card." Others dwelt on the limits of Sino-American cooperation and the suspicions that each side still harbors toward the other. The Taiwan question, of course, has been acknowledged by the Soviets as the most serious problem between Beijing and Washington.[47] Even Rakhmanin, the most consistent and vehement Soviet spokesperson, and the most hostile toward China, noted in April 1981: "At the same time it is impossible not to see that there are divergences and contradictions in the positions of the Chinese leadership and the imperialists, even though they are united by anti-Sovietism and anti-socialism. Each side is endeavoring to bind the partner, but is unwilling to forfeit a free hand to bind itself with far-reaching commitments."[48]

The statement that came closest to suggesting the possibility of inducing the Chinese away from the United States appeared in Kapitsa's report to the 1982 Conference of Soviet Sinologists. Although carefully toeing the "orthodox" Soviet line on China, his message nevertheless came through clearly:

> As far as the PRC situation is concerned, the situation is as follows: quite a few Maoist leaders who imposed ethnocentrism on China are buried at the Babaoshan cemetery. But many of them are still alive, hold high posts, and continue to poison the atmosphere with national chauvinism. However, an increasing number of people realize that the present-day world is not the "Celestial Empire" of the time of the Tang or Qing Dynasties, that China is lagging behind some "barbarian" nations by dozens and even hundreds of years, that China must work hard for 50-70 years to carry out the necessary modernizations and pursue a correct policy instead of brainwashing their own people, and that finally, the imperialists will not help China modernize. *As China acquires experience in international discourse, the following conviction is becoming widespread: the role of junior partner to imperialism runs counter to the interest and dignity of the Chinese people.*[49]

Soviet analysts of the 1980s thus share a "least common multiple"— their perception of Chinese nationalism—and, from 1981, a "least common denominator"—their perception of an opportunity to undermine the Sino-American relationship. The latter may from time to time prompt Moscow into solicitous gestures toward China, as the Soviet behavior of 1981–1983 has shown. But the former has placed severe limits on what the Soviets will do to advance rapprochement further, and probably will continue to do so in the near future, for the perception of Chinese nationalism has two implications that cut deep into Soviet consciousness.

On the bilateral level, this Soviet perception entails a very disturbing understanding that the Soviet Union must, now and in the future, deal with a large, united, fiercely independent and possibly increasingly strong power on its eastern front. More importantly, on the international level Chinese nationalism threatens the core Soviet conception of its own role and status in the world today. As the Soviets see it, they have overcome centuries-old backwardness, the hostile encirclement of "imperialism," and enormous human loss and suffering to attain the ability to restructure the liberal world order in a direction more favorable to the pursuit of their ideals and interests. Chinese nationalism threatens this Soviet design, and its policies may even reverse the "linear progression of history." Although each Chinese demand (regarding Vietnam, Afghanistan, Mongolia, and Sino-Soviet borders) is difficult for Moscow to meet, the underlying factor seems to be a profound fear that any Soviet concession will seriously erode "socialist gains" of the past decades. Soviet leaders fear that the ripple effect may undermine both Soviet ideology (e.g., how to treat other instances of "national Communism") and policy (e.g., the territorial dispute with Japan).

For Sino-Soviet rapprochement to move ahead, it will probably take very bold leadership in the Kremlin to overcome the nervous fear of Chinese nationalism and face the risks involved in accommodating nationalism. This step would have to be aided by a willingness on the part of Chinese leaders to match Soviet concessions.

CHINESE VIEWS AND POLICIES

Compared with the changes in Moscow's China policy, the softening of China's attitude toward the Soviet Union during the 1979–1983 period appeared to be less opportunistic or reactive in nature. China's attempt at normalizing the relationship with its bitter foe has proceeded hand in hand with an endeavor to normalize political and economic life at home. Hence, just as the Chinese leadership strove to impart greater "pragmatism" and less "ideology" into China's body politic, it sought to take the bitter edge off its confrontation with the USSR—all to provide China with greater breathing space for its modernization drive.

In all probability, this new policy has a broad base among the Chinese leadership, reflecting a collective yearning for a break with China's turbulent past, and a reinvigorated quest for peace with itself and with its international environment. To be sure, differences in opinion have occurred on certain potentially important issues.[50] But the underlying trend has been toward a stable management of its relationship with the Soviet Union in a way less dangerous to China's modernization task.

Four common threads have crisscrossed official and unofficial Chinese writings of this period to form the basis of the new policy. The first concerns China's view of the Soviet political-economic system; the second, its assessment of the intention and capability of "Soviet hegemonism"; the third, its perception of the current state and consequences of Soviet-American competition; and the fourth, its goal to "safeguard world peace."

The Soviet Political-Economic System

Chinese writings on the Soviet system have been unusually scarce and inarticulate in the early 1980s. Two factors may be responsible. First, it may reflect the confusing state of Soviet studies in the PRC. As is now widely known, between 1966 and 1976, "the social sciences workers had been brutally persecuted; scientific organizations had been disbanded; and all research works had been discontinued."[51] In view of its political sensitivity, Soviet studies in China must have been among the hardest hit. For example, the study of the history of Sino-Soviet relations—an area highly important to their polemical duel in the 1960s—was criticized by the director of the Institute of Modern Chinese History of the Chinese Academy of Social Sciences (CASS), Liu Danian, for its "narrow concerns" and "lack of theoretical research."[52] Wang Youping, the Chinese ambassador to the Soviet Union for much of the 1970s, even apologetically admitted his embassy staff's "departure from the principle of seeking truth from practice" in their line of work. "For various reasons," he said, "we have reported what the home audience liked to hear. When the Soviet Union had a bad year, we would have an easy time making our reports. Anyway, we always reported that the Soviet Union was caught in the double bind of domestic and international difficulties, and had no way out."[53]

Amid calls for "urgently strengthening the Soviet studies," the Institute of Soviet and East European Studies was created under the auspices of CASS in 1980.[54] Other research institutes were established in Shanghai, Haerbin, Changchun, and other cities. Conferences and seminars were held, and researchers were sent abroad to familiarize themselves with the state of the art in the West.[55] The Chinese are preparing a handbook on Soviet sinology, *E su zhongguoxue gaikuang* (Survey of Russian/Soviet sinology),[56] and a bimonthly called *Sulian dongou wenti* (Problems of the Soviet Union and Eastern Europe) is being published.[57] Another bimonthy, *Xueshu qingbao* (Scholarly information), that began circulation internally in 1981 is devoted entirely to foreign studies of Soviet politics, economy, and society.[58] Finally, *Sulian wenti ziliao* (Materials on Soviet questions) has been distributed selectively by the Institute of Soviet and East European Studies of the Chinese People's University in Beijing.[59] According to Kapitsa, China had bought nearly 500,000 books from the Soviet Union by early 1982.[60]

The revival of Soviet studies in China undoubtedly entailed much organizational and personnel confusion. People began to drift back from different work units all over the country. Working relationships had yet to be forged within and between institutes, and tension may have persisted among those who had different fates during the Cultural Revolution.

Different opinions have surfaced among those studying the Soviet Union. For instance, in a conference on contemporary Soviet literature held in Haerbin in 1979, it was reported that "the majority of the comrades" regarded the Soviet system to be socialist, but others held it to be "an imperfect, flawed, and petrified socialism" or simply "revisionism."[61] In 1981, two authors exchanged fire between Wuhan and Beijing over the extent to which tsarist Russia was a "military feudal imperialism."[62] Similar debates with policy implications have doubtless been going on in various conferences and internal documents. But given the political mood in Zhongnanhai (to be discussed below), the leadership probably deliberately allowed the researchers much latitude and time in their exploration of new perspectives. As Wang Youping put it: "As for the nature of Soviet social system, many researchers now hold different opinions. I think it is not necessary to make a hasty conclusion in this regard. We should proceed from reality, lay out all the facts, reason, explore, refer to the principles of Marxism-Leninism and Mao Zedong Thought, study the new situation, look at the facts, and reach a consensus only step by step."[63]

This confusion and contention of thoughts in Soviet studies was made possible only by the prevailing political reality in China. In this new context, as Donald Zagoria has written in a recent article, "it would be patently hypocritical for them [the Chinese] to continue their ideological critique of the Russians: they can hardly accuse the Russians of 'heresies' that they themselves are practicing."[64] Considering their pressing need at the time to draft all sorts of landmark documents (e.g., verdicts on Mao Zedong, Liu Shaoqi, and the new constitution), the Chinese leaders probably had neither the time nor the appetite to thoroughly reevaluate their views on the Soviet system. Furthermore, there seems to have been a conscious decision made in Beijing in early 1980 to refrain from criticizing others' domestic systems and policies. "We should respect every party's and people's ways of handling their own affairs," Deng said in a speech in 1980. "They will find their own path, and seek ways to solve problems. No other Party should play the Father Party by bossing others around. We opposed others making orders to us. So we ourselves should never make orders to others."[65] Hence, since 1979 the Chinese practice with regard to the Soviet system has been to continue the internal search for facts and analyses on the Soviet Union, suspend a conclusion on this question, and settle only on its own least common denominator, "hegemonism." This concentrates on the features of Soviet foreign policy while leaving open the question of its domestic sources.

"Soviet Hegemonism"

Since its debut in the Shanghai Communiqué in 1972, "hegemonism" has been one of the most popular terms used by the Chinese to describe the Soviet Union. From 1979 on, it even began to replace "revisionism" and "social imperialism" as *the* major codeword in the Chinese vocabulary. Generally speaking, "Soviet hegemonism" depicts a superpower that has the capability to project its power worldwide, has the intention to do so, and is carrying out this policy, resorting if necessary to outright invasion.

According to the lead article in the inaugural issue of *Xiandai guoji guanxi* (Contemporary international relations), published by a hitherto secretive organization, the Institute of Contemporary International Relations, the basic goals of Soviet hegemonism are to: "Treat the U.S. as the main adversary, and Europe as the strategic center of gravity. Flank Europe with advances from the Middle East and Africa, thus rendering the NATO countries completely impotent as a fighting force. Treat Asia and the Pacific as an important strategic region, seeking to link this front with the western front. In the meantime, accelerate Soviet expansion into the important or weak links in the Third World." To achieve these goals, Soviet hegemonism seeks to "rely on its military power, resorting even to nuclear blackmail; use 'detente' to play out its political tricks; strengthen its economic power and supplement it with 'economic bait'; and strive to 'attain victory in the entire world with means short of total war.'"[66]

This line of analysis continued to set the tone for almost all Chinese writings on the Soviet Union through 1983, but beginning in 1981, some discordant notes began to creep in, undermining the orthodox view of both Soviet capabilities and intentions. The organ journal of the CASS Institute of World Economics and World Politics, *Shijie jingji* (World economy), for instance, has published article after article portraying the Soviet Union's economic difficulties and attributing the basic cause of Moscow's problems, as in Western analyses, to the Soviet economic structure. These problems are thus seen as fundamental and chronic.[67] Other Chinese articles have described how Moscow's ambitions are outstretching its resources. Furthermore, the disturbances in Poland were seen as seriously threatening the Soviet Union's position in its own backyard.[68]

One author, Li Ni, even cited approvingly Brezhnev's report to the Twenty-Sixth CPSU Congress (February 1981) to illustrate his point on the extent of Soviet discomfiture. In his report, Brezhnev urged the socialist countries to study each other's experiences in building socialism and not to "obliterate specific national features or the historical distinctions of the socialist countries."[69] Beginning in late 1982, scholars made meek suggestions on the possibility of changed Soviet intentions toward China. For example, Li Ni wrote in early 1983 that the new Kremlin leadership under Andropov would be forced to devote most of its energy to domestic problems; hence, it might also desire a more stable external environment.[70]

It is important to note, however, that throughout the 1979–1983 period the overwhelming emphasis in China's official and scholarly writings was placed firmly and squarely on the danger of Soviet hegemonism. With the exception of articles devoted strictly to economic analysis, all discussions on Soviet woes have been more than balanced by warnings of the continuing Soviet threat. The Soviet occupation of Afghanistan has been roundly condemned from time to time as "a key link in Soviet global design."[71] The largest known peacetime Chinese maneuvers took place near the Sino-Mongolian border in 1981, with Deng proclaiming to the gathering troops that "Soviet hegemonism is accelerating its global strategic deployment, posing a grave threat to world peace and our country's security."[72]

Meanwhile, Chinese scholars have repeatedly warned against overestimating the difficulties faced by the Soviet Union. Denying the validity of the "paper bear" theme, quite a few writers (including CASS economists) have insisted that the pace of Soviet military spending continues to outstrip U.S. spending; that Soviet economic growth, despite its downward trend, still surpasses the growth of most Westen nations; that overall Soviet military force, though weaker than the combined forces of the West, still enjoys superiority in the areas most hotly contested by both sides (Europe, the Middle East, and the Gulf) due to the Soviet Union's geographical proximity.[73] As to Soviet intentions, two authors bluntly ridiculed Moscow's favorite thesis on world transition "from capitalism to socialism" as nothing but a transition "from American predominance to Soviet predominance."[74]

In short, these authors maintained that despite its difficulties Soviet hegemonism has lost neither its capabilities nor its expansionist ambitions. Hence, high vigilance is still required to safeguard world peace. In this connection, even Li Ni, who seems otherwise inclined to highlight Soviet woes, has joined two other renowned Chinese specialists in calling the proposal of "no first use" (of NATO nuclear weapons) made by four distinguished former U.S. policymakers in 1982 as "unrealistic." For Li and others, this proposal is simply premised on a mistaken assessment of Soviet hegemonism: "It presumes all the difficulties faced by Moscow will induce restraint and moderation in its behavior."[75] For the Chinese, this presumption is extremely premature.

Soviet-American Competition

Like the Soviets, the Chinese have rarely, if ever, viewed Sino-Soviet relations strictly in a bilateral context. The starting point for any policy analysis has always been the larger international environment (or as the Soviets prefer, the "correlation of world forces"). This seems to hold true particularly for China, the weakest among the major powers. As the world rotates, the Chinese have in turn identified the major sources of war as "American imperialist aggression" (the 1950s), "collusion between U.S. imperialism and Soviet revisionism" (the 1960s and early 1970s), "collusion and contention between the U.S. and the USSR" (the mid 1970s), and "Soviet hegemonism" (the late 1970s). Since 1981, the emphasis seems to be shifting steadily toward a new factor: "Soviet-American competition."

In the Chinese view, this shift is largely the result of a fundamental change in U.S. global policy in general and U.S. Soviet policy in particular. The shift began during the last year of the Carter administration when Washington, shocked by the Soviet invasion of Afghanistan, started to take a much harder line toward Moscow. With the inauguration of Ronald Reagan into the White House, backed by a Republican majority in the Senate, anti-Sovietism quickly became the central foreign policy guideline. As Chinese analysts have noted, Reagan has sought to meet the Soviet challenge and reverse Soviet gains of the past decade.[76] He has sharply increased the U.S. defense budget, vigorously pursuing both nuclear and conventional buildup programs. He has strenuously resisted Soviet advances into the Middle East and elsewhere in the Third World. He has firmly rejected détente, seeking instead to "negotiate from strength." Reagan has also striven for better coordination with his allies in Europe and Japan, better understanding with some anti-Communist countries previously alienated by Carter's human rights policy, and finally, continued cooperation with the PRC.

To be sure, this new policy is fraught with difficulties and paradoxes.[77] The Chinese have raised several questions. Can the U.S. economy sustain the massive military buildup favored by Reagan and his conservative supporters? Can relations between the United States and Europe be managed successfully, given their divergent security needs and sharper-than-ever economic competition? How can Washington continue to support Israel and South Africa and neglect the quest of the Third World for a more just economic order? Last but not least, how can the U.S. retain China's cooperation if it insists on interfering in China's internal affairs through arms sales to Taiwan and the Taiwan Relations Act? Despite their expressed doubts and complaints, the Chinese believe that U.S. policy under Reagan has taken a qualitative turn toward a reassertion of U.S. power.

If the pattern of competition is set by Soviet ambition and U.S. reassertion, its outcome is and will be determined by the balance of forces between the two superpowers. According to the Chinese, this was (in 1981) and will remain throughout the 1980s a state of "coexistence in stalemate" (*jianchi gongchu*).[78] Several factors are at work here. Economically, both will grow at approximately the same pace (the Soviet Union, between 2 and 3 percent, and the United States at 2.5 percent per annum) in the 1980s.[79] Militarily, both sides have achieved "essential equivalence" in nuclear and conventional forces and will probably maintain a general balance for the rest of the decade. Both sides will continue to be constrained by enormous domestic problems. Furthermore, both will be increasingly subject to pressures arising from within their own camp, and both, because of the relative decline in their strength, will increasingly lose their influence over allies and friends. Finally, both are keenly aware of the danger of direct superpower collision, and will thus only seek gains short of a total war. Therefore, though the need for survival may compel Moscow and Washington to seek temporary compromises, the logic of their competition will not only preclude a return to détente à la the 1970s, but ensure a tense stalemate in their uneasy coexistence.[80]

Not surprisingly, the Chinese see both opportunities and dangers in this situation. For all their proclaimed aversion to Reagan's Taiwan policy, this U.S. president has probably been regarded by some in Beijing as a blessing in disguise. He has essentially relieved the People's Republic of the burden of "antihegemonism" by spearheading the effort of his own accord. Moreover, with tensions between the United States and the USSR, China has come to occupy the most advantageous corner of the big-power triangle. This position, which is similar to that held by the United States in the early 1970s, enables Beijing to enjoy a much greater degree of operational flexibility within the triangle.

This role reversal was pointed out rather bluntly by Prince Norodom Sihanouk to his host Deng Xiaoping in early 1982: "Today the U.S. needs China, not China the U.S." (to which Deng replied diplomatically, "We have said this often").[81] Perhaps to enhance the consciousness of the average Chinese reader, the deputy editor in chief of Xinhua News Agency, Mu Guangren, wrote:

> This [Reagan's strategy] means that the U.S. will continue to need China to tie down the million Soviet soldiers on the north, and the several hundred thousand Vietnamese soldiers on the south. And it will need to coordinate with China on Afghanistan and Kampuchea in support of these peoples' resistance and of ASEAN's effort against Soviet and Vietnamese threat. The U.S. will also need to coordinate with China on any and all steps that may bear on global strategic situations.[82]

Unfortunately, opportunities usually come hand in hand with risks. From the Chinese viewpoint, the "coexistence in stalemate" entails a very different danger than before, i.e., local wars.[83] Paradoxically, this danger is rooted at once in the superpowers' competition (which the Chinese openly condemn) and in their declining control over world affairs (which China openly applauds). From the former, the Chinese sense a Soviet penchant for aggression and a U.S. willingness to project anew its power into the trouble spots of the world. From the latter, the Chinese see greater possibilities for local powers, aided by massive infusions of modern weapons from the superpowers, to resort to violence to settle their own differences. From the interaction of both, the Chinese fear the escalation of local conflicts into larger-scale wars that China can neither ignore nor afford. The strategic task for the Chinese leadership is thus more complicated in the 1980s than its single-minded opposition to hegemonism in the 1970s. If antihegemonism was but a euphemism for China's quest for security, then the name of the game in the 1980s is not independence (as is so often claimed aloud), but peace.[84]

A Long-Term Peaceful Environment

It should surprise no one that peace is the centerpiece of China's foreign policy concerns in the 1980s. Peace is a necessary condition for the success of China's modernization program, on which the Deng leadership has implicitly, if not explicitly, based its claim of legitimacy. In typical fashion, the theme of peace crept into the public domain by a circuitous route. As early as January 1979, the *Hongqi* (Red flag) "Commentator," in hailing the U.S.-PRC normalization as "an important event beneficial to world peace," noted in passing: "Our country has affirmed that in order to fulfill our great goal of Four Modernizations within this century, we need a long-term peaceful international environment."[85] Subsequently, "peace" has slowly acquired greater salience in China's declaratory policy, and in all likelihood, it has become *the* central principle governing China's foreign policy behavior.

In speeches made in 1980 and 1982, Deng identified the Four Modernizations as the core of the three major tasks facing China in the 1980s,[86] and stated: "Our strategy in foreign affairs is to seek a peaceful environment for carrying out the four modernizations. This is not a lie; it is the truth."[87] Translated into operational terms by Hu Yaobang: "The principles that guide China's relations with other countries have always been (the Five Principles of Peaceful Coexistence). These principles apply to our relationships with all the countries, *including the socialist countries.*"[88]

As part of the Chinese "peace program," China has sought to expand ties worldwide. It offered India "unconditional talks" on restoring good relations in April 1981, followed by Huang Hua's visit to New Delhi in June 1981 (the first in twenty-one years). Beijing restored ties with all major Western European Communist parties through the exchange of high-level visits (Italy, April 1980; Spain, November 1980; France, March 1982; and Holland, March 1982). It encouraged Pakistan to pursue the UN-sponsored negotiations on Afghanistan. China renewed its pledge of identity with the Third World. It joined some international organizations previously regarded as ideologically repugnant (the World Bank, IMF) or inimical to national security (the International Atomic

Energy Agency). With more mixed motives, Beijing has launched a series of peace offensives since 1979 to its "dear compatriots" in Taiwan.

China's new strategy can also be seen in its management of Sino-American relations in recent years.[89] Following thunderous threats over U.S. arms sales to Taiwan, for example, China apparently contented itself with the ambiguous wording of the communiqué of August 17, 1982. Retaliation for the U.S. decision on the Hu Na case was carefully limited to government-sponsored cultural exchanges (which numbered less than the non-government-sponsored ones) and 1983 sports visits (thus sparing the 1984 Olympics). Its reaction to the U.S. refusal to buy more Chinese textile products was to curtail "proposed" but not "realized" purchases of U.S. soybeans and grain. Its prescribed punishment on the Pan American case was aimed only at Pan Am, not at the U.S.-PRC air link; and even for Pan Am the effect was more apparent than real. Finally, on the Huguang bond case, Beijing retained counsel despite China's invocation of sovereign immunity, and even submitted a deposition to the Alabama court. The "dark clouds" so far seem to have only cast shadows, but not rains, on the Sino-American relationship.

China's initiation of rapprochement with the USSR in 1979 was apparently motivated by the same desire to foster "a long-term peaceful environment," to expand contacts while attenuating conflicts as much as possible. By 1981, the thaw was not only encouraged by Soviet overtures; in the Chinese view, it was made possible by a hardened U.S. policy toward the Soviet Union. It was only in this year that China began to feel more relaxed about the "Soviet threat." Articles began to appear expressing confidence in the strength of the forces of antihegemonism,[90] articulating the belief that "the existence of an anti-Soviet united front has become an objective reality,"[91] or even claiming, in global structural terms, the isolation of the Soviet "pole" by five other "poles": the United States, Western Europe, Japan, China, and the Third World.[92] Since 1982, a limited Sino-Soviet rapprochement had probably become even more desirable to Beijing in view of the sharpening of Soviet-American competition and the increasing danger of local wars that could escalate. China's most rational course of action to maintain peace was to strike a more "independent" posture, simultaneously distancing itself from the United States (which needed no more coaxing on antihegemonism) and appearing conciliatory to the Soviet Union.

The desire for peace with the Soviet Union, however, has been and will continue to be tempered by China's fear of Soviet hegemonism—a fear conditioned by their recent history and by the wide gap in their capabilities. Therefore, Moscow's words and gestures toward Beijing will always be measured in a global as well as a Sino-Soviet context. China's behavior toward the USSR will also be influenced considerably by U.S. policy toward Moscow and by the worldwide rivalry of the two superpowers. In the meantime, Beijing's approach to Sino-Soviet rapprochement is likely to remain more subdued than the Soviet Union's, lest it damage China's Western connection with its perceived benefits in defense, technology transfer, and trade.

At the height of China's war against the Japanese in the early 1940s, Mao Zedong laid down three principles to guide the feeble Chinese Communist Party in maneuvering against its two powerful but rival enemies—Japan and the Nationalist government of China. For the sake of the CCP's survival and development, he said, the confrontation with enemies should be handled dialectically, in a "principled (*youli*), salutary (*youli*), and tempered (*youjie*)" manner.[93] These three principles seem to have been consciously applied by the post-Mao Chinese leadership in managing its relations with the Soviet Union since 1979. The approach is "principled" in the fundamentals of conflict, "salutary" to China's quest for peace, and "tempered" in the treatment of their differences.

CONCLUSIONS

The pendulum of Sino-Soviet relations has swung from alliance to near-total confrontation in the past three decades. Now it seems to be inching back toward the center. For Moscow, the new movement seems mainly inspired by the tactical need to reduce its two-front threat. For Beijing, the shift appears to be part and parcel of a general reorientation of domestic and foreign policies, reflecting a deep yearning among China's populace and leadership to advance the nation into the top ranks of the family of nations by the end of this century. Ironically, the policy changes in both countries have been inspired by the successes, not the failures, of the Sino-American strategic cooperation fashioned in the late 1970s. Despite outward appearance, however, the Beijing-Moscow thaw has not been accompanied by a corresponding change in the basic, negative view each country's leaders have of each other. Nor has either side taken steps to alter the structure of "competitive containment" emplaced during the last decade.

In the near future, barring a fundamental (and improbable) change in the Soviet attitude toward "national Communism," the Soviets will probably insist on a substantial reduction of Sino-American security ties as an unspoken precondition to any Soviet concession. The Chinese will continue to repeat their now time-honored demands—for Soviet troop withdrawal from the Sino-Soviet borders, Mongolia, and Afghanistan and the cessation of Soviet support for Vietnam in Indochina as a litmus test of the intentions of Soviet hegemonism. However, because these demands are divisible (unlike the three Chinese conditions to normalization with the United States a decade earlier), it seems entirely possible that progress could be made incrementally on one demand or another, leading to an even further relaxation of relations, *if* the Chinese perceive a lessening of Soviet threat (through internal weaknesses or a sharper escalation of Soviet-American rivalry) *and if* the Soviets are satisfied with the nature and degree of the Sino-American relationship.

The outcome of this zigzag process will undoubtedly depend in part upon other actors. A successful settlement of the Afghanistan issue coupled with complete Soviet troop withdrawal would add impetus to rapprochement. Vietnam might play the role of "spoiler" before it finally decided to play along, if ever. But most important of all, both Moscow and Beijing will watch any moves by Washington extremely closely. Should the United States be perceived by Moscow and Beijing as bent on restoring its pre-Afghanistan or even pre-Vietnam position in the world, *and* as successfully harnessing the support of its allies in liberal democracies, then both China and the Soviet Union would have a greater incentive to resolve their differences. They could begin by tackling a strictly bilateral issue: thinning out border troops on both sides, perhaps. If Washington skillfully mixes competition with cooperation in its relationship with Moscow and appears ever ready to respond to China's aspiration for peace and modernization, the factors that have thus far inhibited a Sino-Soviet rapprochement will continue to work on both sides. As usual, this game of two is really not played by two actors, but by three or more.

History is replete with instances of shifting alliances among nations. In the flow of Sino-Soviet relations, both the mutual courtship of the 1950s and the single-minded confrontation of the 1970s may prove to be aberrations. It seems unlikely that China and the Soviet Union will return to a mode of alliance in the 1980s, but the future is far from certain. In all probability, the rapprochement between China and the Soviet Union will proceed at a steady but tortoise-like pace—if not given a "big push" by the West. However, if China is now seeking "peace" under the slogan of "independence," it may just as well seek true "independence" in the glittering name of "peace," under the general condition of heightened Soviet-American competition.

NOTES

1. Tong Yixin, "China and the Soviet Union Start Negotiations on Mutual Relations," *Zhongguo baike nianjian 1980* [Chinese encyclopedic yearbook, 1980] (Beijing: Zhongguo dabaikequanshu, 1980), p. 268.

2. For the Chinese sources, see ibid. and "The Soviet Union," in *Shijie zhishi nianjian 1982* [World knowledge yearbook, 1982] (Beijing: Shijie zhishi, 1982), pp. 545–546. For the Soviet source, see M. S. Ukraintsev [pseudonym of M. S. Kapitsa], "Soviet-Chinese Relations: Problems and Prospects," *Problemy dalnego vostoka* [Problems of the Far East, hereafter *PDV*], No. 2 (1982):17–18.

3. Ye Jianying, "A Speech on the 30th Anniversary of the People's Republic of China," *Renmin ribao*, September 30, 1979, pp. 1–4.

4. See, for example, the lead article by Li Hong, "On the Great Historical Significance of Our Party's Eighth Congress," in *Lishi yanjiu* [Historical research], No. 4 (1979):3–12.

5. Deng Xiaoping, "The Current Situation and Tasks (January 16, 1980)," in *Deng Xiaoping wenxuan, 1975–1982* [The selected works of Deng Xiaoping, 1975–1982] (Beijing: Renmin chubanshe, 1983), p. 204.

6. *Renmin ribao*, January 21, 1980, p. 1.

7. For example, Special Commentator, "Marxism and Revisionism Can Not Be Confused," *Renmin ribao*, April 3, 1980, p. 5.

8. This and other Soviet proposals are discussed in Ukraintsev, "Soviet-Chinese Relations," pp. 21–23.

9. David Rees, "Soviet Border Problems: China and Japan," *Conflict Studies* (London), No. 139 (1982):12–13.

10. For example, in *Zhongguo baike nianjian 1980,* a passage on "a brief history" of the USSR reads: "After Khrushchev and Brezhnev clique usurped the power of leadership, the Soviet Union gradually degenerated into a social imperialist country" (p. 188). This passage was dropped in the 1981 edition of *Zhongguo baike nianjian.*

11. *Pravda*, March 25, 1982, p. 2.

12. *Pravda*, September 27, 1982, p. 2; October 28, 1982, p. 1.

13. *Renmin ribao*, March 27, 1982, p. 6.

14. *Renmin ribao*, November 15, 1982, p. 1; November 19, 1982, p. 6.

15. Donald S. Zagoria, "The Moscow-Beijing Detente," *Foreign Affairs* 61 (Spring 1983):858.

16. *Pravda*, November 23, 1982, p. 1.

17. Observer, "What Is the Purpose?" *New Times*, No. 3 (1983):12–14.

18. Commentator, "Response to the 'Observer,' of the *New Times*," *Shijie zhishi* [World knowledge], No. 3 (1983):2.

19. *Washington Post*, March 17, 1983, p. A31.

20. *Washington Post*, September 9, 1983, p. A9.

21. *Pravda*, August 27, 1983, p. 1.

22. To the surprise of many in the West, the Chinese abstained on a UN Security Council draft resolution "deploring" Soviet behavior.

23. *Renmin ribao*, September 3, 1983, p. 1.

24. *Washington Post*, September 17, 1983, p. A11.

25. *Renmin ribao*, September 17, 1983, p. 7.

26. *Renmin ribao*, September 29, 1983, pp. 1, 4.

27. *New York Times*, October 30, 1983, p. 6.

28. For details, see Chi Su, "Soviet Image of and Policy Toward China, 1969–1979," (Ph.D. diss., Columbia University, New York, 1983).

29. This point is discussed in greater detail in Lyushun Shen, "The Washington-Peking Controversy over U.S. Arms Sales to Taiwan: Diplomacy of Ambiguity and Escalation," *Chinese Yearbook of International Law and Affairs* 2 (1982):301–323.

30. This assessment concurs with Zagoria, "The Moscow-Beijing Detente," and William E. Griffith, "Sino-Soviet Rapprochement?" *Problems of Communism* 32 (March-April 1983), as well as with the views expressed by Seweryn Bialer, Harry Gelman, and Kenneth Lieberthal before the U.S. House Subcommittee on Asian and Pacific Affairs on August 2, 1983.

31. Portions of this section are based on my dissertation (see note 28) and my "U.S.-China Relations: Soviet Views and Policies," *Asian Survey* 23 (May 1983):555–579.

32. See, for example, the secret report of Suslov to the plenary meeting of the CPSU Central Committee on February 14, 1964, in M. A. Suslov, *Marxism-*

Leninism: The International Teaching of the Working Class (Moscow: Progress, 1975), pp. 136–197.

33. L. I. Brezhnev, *Following Lenin's Course (Speeches and Articles)* (Moscow: Progress, 1972), pp. 180, 182.

34. *Pravda*, June 27, 1969, p. 1. Emphasis added.

35. For Soviet scholarly works on this theme, see for example S. L. Tikhvinskii, ed., *Novaia istoria Kitaia* [Modern history of China] (Moscow: Nauka 1972); and V. A. Krivtsov, "Maoism and the Great Han Chauvinism of the Chinese Bourgeoisie," *PDV*, No. 1 (1974).

36. Editorial, "Beijing: Yesterday Imperialism's Reserve, Today Its Ally," *Kommunist*, No. 4 (1979):81.

37. For samples of Soviet analysis of the changes taking place in China in the early 1980s, see R. M. Neronov and G. A. Stepanova, "The CCP: Certain Tendencies of Development," *PDV*, No. 1 (1982); V. F. Feoktistov, "The Present-Day Modification of Maoism," *PDV*, No. 1 (1982); and F. M. Burlatskii, "The Interregnum or a Chronicle of the Times of Deng Xiaoping," *Novy mir* [New world], No. 4 (1982).

38. O. B. Borisov [pseudonym of O. B. Rakhmanin], "The Situation in the PRC and Some of the Tasks of Soviet Sinology," *PDV*, No. 2 (1982):12.

39. Neronov and Stepanova, "The CCP," p. 46.

40. For a typical Western analysis of China that compares the policies of Mao and his successors, see Michel Oksenberg and Richard Bush, "China's Political Evolution: 1972–1982," *Problems of Communism* 31 (September-October 1982).

41. O. B. Borisov [pseud.], "The 26th CPSU Congress and Some Problems of Studying the History of China," *PDV*, No. 3 (1981):11.

42. Borisov, "The Situation," p. 9.

43. O. B. Borisov [pseud.], "Certain Aspects of Chinese Policy," *Kommunist*, No. 6 (1981):120–121.

44. O. Vladimirov, "The CCP Central Committee Sixth Plenum and Beijing's Current Policy," *Kommunist*, No. 12 (1981):83–84.

45. V. N. Urov, "The Historical Fate of the Chinese Komsomol," *PDV*, No. 2 (1982).

46. For a Western analysis of the more "optimistic" Soviet view of a changing China, see Gilbert Rozman, "Moscow's China-Watchers in the Post-Mao Era: The Response to a Changing China," *China Quarterly*, No. 94 (June 1983):231–236.

47. See, for example, V. Petukhov, "Taiwan in U.S. and Chinese Policy," *PDV*, No. 1 (1981).

48. Borisov, "Certain Aspects," p. 115.

49. Ukraintsev, "Soviet-Chinese Relations," p. 23.

50. See, for example, Carol Hamrin, "Chinese Reassess the Superpowers," *Pacific Affairs* 56 (Summer 1983); and Gerald Segal, "China and Afghanistan," *Asian Survey* (November 1981).

51. Huan Xiang, "Social Sciences in China," *Zhongguo baike nianjian 1980*, p. 432.

52. Liu Danian, "The Current State of Research on Chinese Modern History," *Jindaishi yanjiu* [Modern history research], No. 2 (1980):34.

53. Wang Youping, "A Talk at the Meeting of Chinese Ambassadors," *Guang jiaojing* [Wide-angle lens] (Hong Kong), No. 91 (April 1980):30.

54. Liu Cunkuan, "On the Soviet Union's Study of China and the Urgency to Strengthen Our Soviet Studies," in *Zhonge guanxi lunwenji* [A collection of articles on Sino-Soviet relations] (Lanzhou, Gansu: Gansu renmin, 1979).

55. For example, the deputy director of CASS Institute of Soviet and East European Studies, Xu Kui, was in the United States in 1982 doing research on the Soviet studies in this country. See his "Soviet Studies in the People's Republic of China," *AAASS Newsletter* 23 (Summer 1983):1.

56. A private source.

57. Most likely a publication for internal use only; an advertisement for this journal is found on the back cover of *Shijie jingji* [World economy] No. 12 (1981).

58. See the advertisement for this journal on the back cover of *Xuexi yu tansuo* [Learning and exploration] No. 3 (1981). The ad identifies it as an "internal-use publication."

59. Harry Harding, "Social Sciences," in Leo A. Orleans, ed., *Sciences in Contemporary China* (Stanford, Calif.: Stanford University Press, 1980), p. 488.

60. Ukraintsev, "Soviet-Chinese Relations," p. 23.

61. "An Outline on the Second All-China Conference on Contemporary Soviet Literature," *Wenyi baijia* [Hundred schools of arts and literature] No. 2 (1979):254–255.

62. Xiao Fan, "A Study of the Characteristics of Russian Imperialism," *Wuhan daxue xuebao* [Wuhan University journal] No. 2 (1981); Fan Daren, "On Tsarist Russia's Military Feudal Imperialism," *Beijing daxue xuebao* [Beijing University journal] No. 5 (1981).

63. Wang Youping, "A Talk," p. 31.

64. Zagoria, "The Moscow-Beijing Detente," p. 854.

65. Deng, *Deng Xiaoping wenxuan*, p. 279.

66. Qi Ya and Zhou Jirong, "Some Conspicuous Problems in the Struggle against Hegemonism," *Xiandai guoji guanxi* [Contemporary international relations] No. 1 (1981):2.

67. See, for example, Lu Nanquan et al., "Why the Continuing Decline of Soviet Economic Growth Rate," *Shijie jingji*, No. 12 (1981); and Chen Konglun, "On the Reasons for the Possible Failure of the USSR's 11th Five-Year Plan," *Shijie jingji*, No. 4 (1982).

68. Chen Qimao and Liu Guangqing, "Soviet Diplomacy Since the 26th CPSU Congress," in *Guoji xingshi nianjian 1982* [Yearbook of international affairs, 1982] (Shanghai: Zhongguo dabaikequanshu, 1982); and Xie Xiaochuan, "The Soviet Union and the U.S.: New Characteristics of Competition," *Shijie zhishi*, No. 3 (1983).

69. Li Ni, "A Retrospect of the International Situation of the Past Year," in *Guoji xingshi nianjian 1982*, p. 6.

70. Li Ni, "A More Tense and Turbulent Year," *Guoji wenti yanjiu* [Journal of international studies], No. 1 (1983):10. See also Xie Xiaochuan, "The Soviet Union and the U.S.," p. 12.

71. For example, Yi Li, "He Who Goes against the Historical Tide Is Doomed to Failure," *Hongqi* [Red flag], No. 24 (1981); and *Renmin ribao* editorial, "Afghanistan People Will Win," December 27, 1982, p. 1.

72. Deng, *Deng Xiaoping wenxuan*, p. 350.

73. For example, Li Cong, "Some Problems in the World Economic Development of the 1980s," *Shijie jingji*, No. 11 (1982):4; and Chen and Liu, "Soviet Diplomacy," p. 33. Li, the deputy director of the CASS Institute of

World Economy and World Politics, notes (p. 1) that his article was based on collective research of the institute staff.

74. Zhang Zhen and Rong Zhi, "A Brief Discourse on Soviet 'Détente Policy,'" *Guoji wenti yanjiu*, No. 4 (1982):19.

75. Zhuan Qubing, Jin Junhui, and Li Ni, "A Few Thoughts on the Article, 'Nuclear Weapons and Atlantic Alliance,'" *Guoji wenti yanjiu*, No. 3 (1983):48. The authors of the cited U.S. article, published in *Foreign Affairs*, are McGeorge Bundy, George Kennan, Robert McNamara, and Gerald Smith.

76. On Reagan's policy, see Jin Junhui, "Reagan's Foreign Policy," *Guoji wenti yanjiu*, No. 1 (1982) and Li Ni's articles cited earlier.

77. Jin, "Reagan's Foreign Policy."

78. The term *"jiangchi gongchu"* was first coined in Qi Ya and Zhou Jirong, "Struggle Against Hegemonism" (1981), p. 10.

79. Xing Shugang, Li Yunhua and Liu Yingna, "Soviet-American Balance of Power and Its Impact on the World Situation in the 1980s," *Guoji wenti yanjiu*, No. 1 (1983):27–29.

80. On these points, see the articles by Xing Shugang et al., Li Ni, and Xie Xiaochuan. See also "Retrospect and Prospect" (a round table), in *Shijie zhishi*, No. 1 (1982) and He Fang, "Retrospect and Prospect of the International Situation," *Shijie zhishi*, No. 1 (1983).

81. *Liaowang* [Outlook], No. 3 (1982):3.

82. Mu Guangren, "The Current U.S. Policy Toward China," *Ban yue tan* [Tab biweekly], No. 16 (1981):53.

83. Xing Shugang et al., "Balance of Power," pp. 30–31.

84. "Independence" emerged in 1981 and particularly in 1982 as a major slogan in China's policy pronouncements. Deng Xiaoping's remark made at the Twelfth CCP Congress (September 1, 1982)—"Independence and self-reliance have always been and will forever be our basic stand. . . . No foreign country can expect China to be its vassal or expect to swallow any bitter fruit detrimental to its own interests"—suddenly became the most quotable quote in all Chinese writings. For Western exposition, see Allen S. Whiting, "Assertive Nationalism in Chinese Foreign Policy," *Asian Survey* 23 (August 1983), and Harry Harding, "Change and Continuity in Chinese Foreign Policy," *Problems of Communism* 32 (March-April 1983).

85. Commentator, "An Event Beneficial to World Peace," *Hongqi*, No. 1 (1979):78.

86. Deng, *Deng Xiaoping wenxuan*, pp. 203–205, 372.

87. Ibid., p. 205.

88. *Renmin ribao*, September 5, 1982, p. 1. Emphasis added.

89. For a more detailed discussion of the following issues, see Steven I. Levine, Chapter 5 in this volume.

90. Pei Monong, "The International Situation and Prospects in East Asia," *Renmin ribao*, March 27, 1981, p. 7.

91. Wu Ren, "Has the Anti-Soviet United Front Been Formed?" *Shijie zhishi*, No. 2 (1981):2–3.

92. Si Mu, "The Current International Situation and Our Socialist Modernization," *Sixiang zhanxian* [Ideological front], No. 4 (1981):13.

93. Mao Zedong, "On the Question of Strategy in the Present-Day Anti-Japanese United Front (March 11, 1940)," *Mao Zedong xuanji* [Selected works of Mao Zedong], Vol. 2 (Beijing: Renmin chubanshe, 1961), p. 744.

CHAPTER 7

CHINA AND THE SECOND WORLD

Donald W. Klein

INTRODUCTION

China has used the term "Second World" for many years as a shorthand description for the developed countries, mainly Japan and Western Europe.[1] The Chinese theory is that in cooperation with the Third World, the Second World could become a force to counter the alleged hegemonism of the two superpowers that constitute the First World.[2] In practice, as usual, reality has been far more complex than this simple formulation. The purpose of this chapter is to explore Beijing's relations with the Second World to test whether superpower hegemonism has been reduced and to see if these Second World ties have benefited China alone or both China and the Third World.

For the analyst, the expression "Second World" requires some clarification and preliminary observations. First, most Second World nations do share some fundamental values, but their foreign policies vis-à-vis China are often only marginally congruent. For example, consider Australia and Denmark. Massive wheat sales to China over two decades have created special Australian-Chinese ties, but nothing even remotely comparable links Denmark and China. To put this a bit differently: China may indeed have a well-defined view of a Second World, but there is surely no unified Second World view of China.

Another crucial preliminary observation is the centrality of Second World ties to the United States. After all, a simple list of Second World countries is also a list of Washington's key allies throughout the world. As a consequence, an analytical framework that ignored this U.S.– Second World link would inevitably lead to muddled thinking and faulty conclusions. On one point, however, the Chinese distinction between the United States and the Second World is useful: No Second World nation's ties with Taiwan are as complex and as important as those of the United States.

THE EARLY YEARS

This chapter focuses on the post-Mao era, but some space must be given to the period before Mao's death. In the bipolar 1950s, when China was Moscow's most important ally, the Second World was perceived as a contemptible lackey of the United States. This shouldn't surprise us. Washington was then the undisputed master of the so-called free world, and the Second World nations were all linked with the United States in pacts directed against Communist nations. By the early 1950s, Washington was militarily tied by the North Atlantic Treaty Organization (NATO) to Western Europe, plus Canada; across the Pacific, the United States was linked by a defense pact to Japan and by the Australia–New Zealand–United States (ANZUS) Treaty to Australia and New Zealand. NATO was of course directed mainly against Moscow, but seven NATO nations also fought against China in Korea (Belgium, Canada, France, Greece, Luxembourg, the Netherlands, and Great Britain)—although most of these countries made only very small or symbolic contributions to the UN forces in Korea. Moreover, four Second World nations (Britain, France, Australia, and New Zealand) allied in 1954 with the United States and three Asian nations (Pakistan, the Philippines, and Thailand) to form the Southeast Asian Treaty Organization (SEATO), clearly an "anti-China" pact.

China's very legitimacy was challenged by most Second World nations in the 1950s; they recognized Taiwan but not the People's Republic. During the PRC's infancy, it was recognized only by Britain, Sweden, Denmark, and Switzerland. Norway and the Netherlands were added to the list in 1954, but a full decade passed before another nation, France, recognized the PRC. This lack of recognition by many Second World nations also meant that the PRC was denied the China seat in the United Nations. With a few exceptions, most Second World nations continued to support the U.S. position that kept the PRC out of the UN until 1971.

What was true about legitimacy also applied roughly to trade. By dollar value or percentages, China's trade with the Second World during the 1950s ranged from totally insignificant to marginal. From the viewpoint of the Second World nations, most of them great trading countries, the China trade was virtually nil. For a brief period coinciding with the Bandung era (roughly 1955–1957), it appeared that PRC–Second World trade might improve markedly, but this was quickly dampened (especially with Japan) when China undertook its Great Leap Forward (1958–1961)—a period of marked hostility toward both the United States and the Second World.

THE 1960s

When China emerged from the Great Leap disaster (c. 1962), it found, and in part helped shape, a very different world. Its relations with Moscow and Washington were almost totally hostile. Not only had it lost the Soviet defense connection; trade with the USSR was also careening downhill, and Soviet technology transfer to China was declining rapidly.

The 1960s are usually seen as the highpoint of China's sponsorship of Third World radicalism. It was during this period, after all, that Beijing enthusiastically supported Indonesia's efforts to form a "revolutionary United Nations." The Chinese gave equally active support to the emerging Palestine Liberation Organization (PLO), and tried to engineer a second Bandung Conference (which ultimately aborted). But most of all, Lin Biao's famous "Long Live the Victory of People's War" (September 1965) was seen as the ultimate clarion call of an increasingly radical foreign policy. (U.S. Secretary of State Dean Rusk, with his penchant for misleading historical parallels, referred to Lin's tract as "China's *Mein Kampf*.") Yet virtually all these steps were verbal; relatively little action matched the fiery prose. For example, Chinese foreign aid in the 1960s was modest, and most of their military aid went to the government of Pakistan (not to a leftist guerrilla force trying to overthrow the Pakistani government) and to Vietnam. Beijing's verbal radicalism abroad was paralleled at home by the extreme turbulence of the Cultural Revolution during the late 1960s. The Chinese, now portraying themselves as the sole defenders of Marxist purity, renewed their ardor for the doctrine of "self-reliance."

The decade of the 1960s did not, in short, seem like a propitious time for improving China–Second World ties. Yet other imperatives forced a change in the Chinese foreign policy agenda during the stormy 1960s. Setting aside revolutionary rhetoric, this was in fact the time when China moved into high gear in its relations with the Second World. Important needs dictated this change, which in other ways may have been repugnant to Mao. First, the need for large-scale food imports sent China into the international grain market. This was (and still is) dominated by the United States, Canada, and Australia. U.S. grain was out of the question in the 1960s, so a simple supply-and-demand situation led China to make huge purchases from both Canada and Australia, a trade that has prospered from 1961 to the present.

Apart from grain, China needed to establish trade with nations that could sell medium- and high-level technology and provide affluent markets for China's products. This profile fit the Second World exactly. By the mid-1960s, Second World nations emerged as the PRC's chief trading partners, and they have remained to this day. The disparity between revolutionary rhetoric and the imperatives of an industrializing state is neatly illustrated by China's foreign trade in 1966, a year of tremendous turbulence caused by the Cultural Revolution. In that year seven of China's ten leading trade partners were Second World countries. We also find that in stormy 1966 no less than 44 percent of China's trade was already with the Second World; fifteen years later, in the calm days of 1981, it was still 44 percent.

Aside from the trade imperatives, for a brief period in the 1960s it appeared that one Second World nation, France, might play a significant role in China's global geopolitical maneuverings. This was the France of Charles de Gaulle, who shared with Mao the desire (but not the strength) to lessen the domination of the superpowers. France formally recognized China in early 1964 (the only Second World nation to do so in the 1960s), and it began to vote for the PRC on the Chinese representation question in the United Nations. But China was soon in the throes of the Cultural Revolution, so little came from this Beijing-Paris link.

In short, beneath the outward and highly visible layer of revolutionary rhetoric was the layer more familiar to political scientists—realpolitik. It seems fair to assume that Mao approved of these concrete actions vis-à-vis the Second World. It is also noteworthy that they came a full decade before Mao's death, and also well before the 1969 border clash with the Soviet Union, which seemingly convinced Mao that some gesture toward the United States was necessary to balance the "more dangerous" superpower, the USSR.

THE NIXON VISIT AND SECOND WORLD TIES

The Kissinger and Nixon trips to China in 1971–1972 were epochal events, and their impact on China–Second World relations was of great importance, especially vis-à-vis Japan. It is easy to forget that Sino-Japanese relations in the late 1960s and early 1970s were still quite strained, notwithstanding Japan's rank as China's leading trade partner.[3] For example, Zhou Enlai made some blistering comments about Japan in his much-publicized interview with journalist James Reston in mid-1971.[4] Then, in the Shanghai Communiqué signed during Nixon's February 1972 visit to China, the Chinese bluntly asserted their opposition to the "revival and outward expansion of Japanese militarism." Yet Beijing soon set aside its tough talk toward Japan, and by the early fall of 1972 the two nations had established formal diplomatic relations (Japan simultaneously breaking its formal—but not its informal—ties with Taiwan).

In the meantime, China moved swiftly on the diplomatic front to establish diplomatic relations with a flock of other Second World nations. In almost all cases, this meant breaking ties with Taiwan. In 1970–1971, Canada, Italy, Austria, Belgium, and Iceland established relations with

Beijing; in 1972–1973, Greece, Japan, West Germany, Luxembourg, Australia, New Zealand, and Spain followed suit. Moreover, formal relations were established with the Common Market in 1975. Because much focus has been placed on a greater orientation toward the West since Mao's death in 1976, it is worth noting that all of these events happened before he died—and they certainly had his approval.

More concrete developments in trade with Second World countries also predated Mao's death. From 1971 to 1975 (the last full year before Mao's death), PRC–Common Market trade tripled and Sino-Japanese trade quadrupled. Moreover, such important and costly ventures as the import of whole plants from Japan and Western Europe reached substantial proportions as early as 1973, when China spent well over US$1 billion on importing plants.[5]

Another China–Second World link that predated Mao's death concerns military relations.[6] The Chinese moved quite gingerly on this issue, apparently trying to strike a balance between reminding the Soviets that such military ties were possible, and yet moving carefully so as not to inflame Moscow. By the early 1980s it seemed evident that most of Beijing's military contacts with the Second World contained an element of bluff. Little has come of the many rumors about Beijing buying this or that airplane, ship, or tank. Indeed, in March 1983 China's defense minister stated bluntly that China would not be buying Western arms, that "such purchases would lead to foreign control of China's defenses," and in any event, China had not been able to buy the "most advanced equipment."[7]

Enough has been said to show that substantial PRC–Second World contacts were in place by Mao's death in September 1976. In particular, there is a clear line of continuity during the Mao and post-Mao periods in China's geopolitical posture toward Japan and the Common Market–NATO countries, and this is equally true for foreign trade patterns.

CHINA AND THE SECOND WORLD AFTER MAO

In addition to PRC–Second World ties established before Mao's death, there have been key changes since his death. In broad categories, the most important changes involve China's willingness to accept economic aid and direct foreign investments (mostly from the Second World) and a spectacular leap forward in what Western political scientists call transnational relations. Most notable are the dispatch of Chinese students for advanced study abroad and the dramatic rise of tourism in China. In all cases, this has meant a sharp rejection or modification of Mao's coveted self-reliance.

Allowing for gross exaggeration by China's current leadership, the extent and quality of contacts with the Second World (and the United States) was apparently a bitterly disputed issue prior to Mao's death.

In the mid-1970s, the famed Gang of Four did discourage foreign involvement, and Mao seems to have acquiesced, but by 1978, China had taken a dramatic new tact. A 1981 study concluded that since 1978 a massive US$25 billion in credit had been extended to China, although Beijing has drawn but a small percentage of this amount.[8] A PRC economist referred in early 1983 to "promised or signed" agreements to provide China with US$5.7 billion since 1979, plus Bank of China "buyer-credit" agreements for US$13 billion with commercial banks in various countries.[9]

Another stark departure from Mao-era policy concerns direct foreign investments that have come, overwhelmingly, from the Second World. The same PRC economist wrote in 1983 that China was engaged in about thirty joint enterprises (such as offshore oil exploration) and had already "absorbed" about US$3 billion in foreign investments in these joint ventures.[10] In a closely related development, since 1980 China has set up special economic zones along the South China coast. Much of the capital in the twenty SEZ factories now in operation comes from Overseas Chinese, but some is Second World money. Through foreign trade, aid, and the economic zones, China has imported US$10 billion of advanced technology and equipment "in the past few years."[11]

By the early 1980s, Chinese students (overwhelmingly in the natural sciences) were a common sight in the United States, Japan, and Western Europe. There is some ambiguity about numbers: Some students are on Chinese government scholarships, but about an equal number are privately sponsored. In any case, over 10,000 are studying in the United States and another 5,000 or so are in Japan or Western Europe. The Sixth Five-Year Plan (1981–1985) calls for thousands more to study abroad.[12] By any standard, this is a massive investment, and a link that far transcends the exact cost of keeping a student abroad for one year. The international scientific community is dominated by the United States, Western Europe, and Japan, so to the degree that Chinese students are part of this community, then ties to the Second World are virtually automatic links to the United States as well.

Anyone who has visited China both before and after Mao's death would have noticed a vivid difference. In the earlier period, one participated in people-to-people diplomacy, like it or not. Visits were inexpensive, and China probably lost money on these ventures. In the post-Mao period, people-to-people diplomacy has given way to an unblushing tourism, with the unmistakable goal of earning foreign currency. China is rapidly opening more tourist sites, and has spent huge sums to improve its facilities, which are slated to accommodate 2 million tourists a year by 1985.

Clearly, these expenditures are paying off. In the short period from 1978 to 1982, tourism rose from 229,000 visitors a year to 1.5 million, earning for China a foreign exchange income of approximately US$800 million.[13] Not surprisingly, the peripatetic Japanese led all Second World visitors, and by 1981 well over 100,000 of them were visiting China each year. In contrast, a decade earlier fewer than 10,000 Japanese went to China. It is also clear that this flood of foreigners, especially those from the West and Japan, are a mixed blessing for Chinese officialdom, and hence the on-and-off warnings to Chinese citizens about the corruptive elements involved in hosting foreigners.

SECOND WORLD CONTACTS: MEASURING THE COSTS AND BENEFITS

China–Second World ties are obviously a very substantial part of China's overall foreign policy, especially in the economic sector. The remaining task is to evaluate these ties from China's viewpoint, and to suggest areas of continuity and change in the future. We have already noted the great disparity between different areas of the Second World. Our analysis will emphasize these distinctions because we can be certain that Beijing emphasizes them as well.

Western Europe

At the purely political level, China now enjoys formal diplomatic relations with all Western European governments. Strategically, China benefits from a strong NATO, and thus it now fosters the link between the United States and Western Europe. As quickly as any conservative European or U.S. politician, the Chinese will remind Europeans of the folly of a Munich-type attitude toward Moscow. Beijing's military planners obviously understand that Soviet troops not confronting NATO might confront them. This explains why China has actively wooed such anti-Soviet European leaders as Margaret Thatcher, who visited China in 1977 as an opposition leader and in 1982 as the British prime minister.

PRC–Western European links have been regularly buttressed in the 1970s and 1980s by visits of senior Chinese leaders to Europe, including China's premier and foreign minister. On the European side, virtually all Western European countries have sent a president, premier, or foreign minister to China in the 1970s or 1980s. Far more senior officials have visited China since Mao's death than before. Clearly, senior Western European and Chinese officials have had ample opportunity to exchange views in recent years. During Zhou Enlai's twenty-six years as premier he never visited a Second World nation, despite a score of trips abroad,[14] yet his successors, Hua Guofeng and Zhao Ziyang, have traveled to Japan (Hua and Zhao), Western Europe (Hua and Zhao), and Australia and New Zealand (Zhao). Mao, of course, visited only the Soviet Union, but Deng Xiaoping has visited both Japan and Western Europe as well as the United States.

Notwithstanding China's decision to forego foreign weapons purchases, it is important to realize that Western Europe is the best place
for China to buy weapons if the need arises. Buying U.S. weapons
would be more complex (in part because of U.S. arms sales to Taiwan),
and Japan simply refuses to sell weapons to anyone. Western Europe
is an extremely fertile area for top-level technology of a quasi-military
nature, such as computers. In Western Europe China can shop around
for the best goods and the best prices, and it can send its students to
Europe's great universities and research institutes.

In terms of economic links, Western Europe is an excellent partner
for China. About 15 to 20 percent of China's total trade has been with
Western Europe over the past two decades, and there is little reason to
expect this to change. Europe is almost a perfect alternative to Japan
or the United States, putting Beijing in a fine position to get good
trading terms or long-term loans, which are virtually a form of foreign
aid. For the most part, China's economy and Europe's economy are
complementary, so there is little likelihood of future trade disputes such
as those that currently darken the trade horizon between Japan and the
Common Market.

The disadvantages in China's dealings with Western Europe seem
very few indeed. In theory, there is a normative problem—the charge
that European nations engage in neocolonial ventures damaging to the
Third World. But except for a tiny number of Third World countries on
the far left, most Third World nations themselves have active links to
Western Europe. The Lomé Convention linking Western Europe and
Africa in economic ventures is a prime example. This disadvantage thus
seems very marginal for China's interests.

Looking to the future, what developments might cause China to
reverse its present rather solid ties to Western Europe? However unlikely
it may seem, a "Finlandization" of Western Europe by the Soviets would
probably cause China to rethink its policies toward Europe. Yet in
concrete terms, it is difficult to imagine what China might do.[15] At the
strategic level, a more likely cause of worsening PRC–Western European
relations would be if Sino-American ties underwent some extremely
negative change—a change so severe that Washington would pressure
Europeans to lessen their ties to China. What, if anything, could cause
such a situation? One must imagine an exceptionally provocative action
by the PRC—an invasion of Taiwan or a bloody attack on the offshore
islands (Quemoy and Matsu), where the Chinese Nationalists still have
major military forces.

Attacks on Taiwan or the offshore islands seem most unlikely, for
China would risk scuttling much that it has gained in the past decade.
Yet the Chinese have demonstrated with Washington that they are
capable of putting on pressure to establish their claim to Taiwan. The
same might be true for Western Europe. By 1983 no fewer than ten
Western European countries had set up ostensibly unofficial trade offices

in Taiwan.[16] No one is fooled by these euphemisms, and the day may come when Beijing puts strong pressure on Europeans to close these offices.

To date, however, only one significant case involving Taiwan-European links has caused Beijing to react with vigor. This was the 1981 approval by the Dutch government for the construction of two submarines for sale to Taiwan. China responded by forcing the Dutch to lower their representation in Beijing from ambassadorial level to chargé d'affaires. This sharp and concrete PRC reaction raises the question as to why Beijing has confined itself to verbal reactions in the face of U.S. sales of military equipment to Taiwan that far surpass the Dutch action. The answer seems to be that concrete moves against the United States could have enormously negative consequences for China, so Beijing merely fulminates. But China can be both "tough" and "principled" against the Dutch, in the hope that other relatively small or medium powers will take heed.

There can obviously be no border disputes between China and any Western European nation, but Hong Kong is a territorial problem. Most of this British colony will automatically revert to the People's Republic in 1997, but in theory, the island part of Hong Kong will remain British "in perpetuity." China ignores this, and flatly asserts that the entire possession will return to China in due course (undefined). For the moment, China profits enormously from the current situation, so precipitous action seems most unlikely. Again, it is useful to recall that despite many ugly provocations directed against Hong Kong during the xenophobic peak of the Cultural Revolution, Hong Kong did remain a British colony.

In brief, virtually all signs point to a continuing good relationship with the countries of Western Europe. This relationship is so profitable that even if China moved toward a more radical, nationalistic posture in world affairs, a dramatic change seems unlikely. We should also remember that China does not really have much leverage on the Western Europeans. By way of a rough comparison, Japan's 1981 trade with the Common Market was over five times greater than China's, and U.S.– Common Market trade was twenty times greater.

Australia and Canada

Although the two countries are an ocean apart, Australian and Canadian ties to China are sufficiently similar to warrant joint treatment. It is only a small exaggeration to say that China's advantage is summed up in one word: grain. China clearly prefers alternatives to U.S. grain, and Australia and Canada fulfill that desire. All signs point to a continuation of large-scale grain purchases (10 to 15 million metric tons a year), so these ties should continue to flourish. The case for continuity is strong, for grain sales flourished even through the worst years of the Cultural

Revolution, the Vietnam War, and the peak years of the Gang of Four in the mid-1970s.

At the strategic level, Beijing fully endorses Canada's NATO membership. Australia's military role is even more pertinent. Apart from Australia's membership in the ANZUS pact (now viewed as part of the Pacific bastion against Moscow's naval buildup in Asian waters), the ever-increasing involvement of Australia in bolstering ASEAN is warmly welcomed in Beijing. In the 1980s, "ASEAN" is a code word in Beijing for containing Vietnam, China's mortal enemy since the 1979 Sino-Vietnamese War.

What, if anything, might sour PRC relations with Australia and Canada? As with the Western European relationship, it would probably take some substantial decline in Sino-American relations, an exceptionally precipitous military action by the PRC (against Taiwan or the offshore islands), or great pressure from Beijing to dissolve Australian and Canadian "informal" ties to Taiwan. None of these actions seem likely.

Japan

In considering Sino-Japanese ties, we should momentarily set aside the Second World category, for Japan belongs in a class by itself. Japan is vastly more important to China than any other Second World nation. Indeed, except for the superpowers, China's most important bilateral relationship is with Japan. For well over a century, East Asian interstate relations have hinged largely on Sino-Japanese affairs, and this relationship was generally very bad indeed from China's viewpoint.

The positive relations of the past decade are only skin deep, for the Chinese are easily reminded of Japan's earlier misdeeds. China's sensitivity was forcefully demonstrated in 1982 during the "textbook controversy." The problem involved changes in Japanese school history texts that whitewashed Japan's invasion and predatory occupation of China during the 1930s and 1940s. The Japanese seemed shockingly obtuse when the issue first arose, and they promised to rectify the situation only when Beijing made it clear that Sino-Japanese relations would be gravely damaged if Tokyo did not make amends.

In economic matters, one is hard pressed to uncover two more complementary economies than those of China and Japan. China has the natural resources Japan needs, and Japan has the technology and the money to assist China in a score of ways. And, of course, their proximity holds down transportation costs—a very real issue in China's links to other Second World nations.

Japan dethroned the Soviets as China's top trading partner in 1965, and it has never budged from this number one position. Japan's trade with China is usually much greater than trade with the number two nation, and in recent years it has usually exceeded trade with all the Common Market nations combined by 50 percent. Similarly, Japan's trade with China is also much greater than Sino-American trade. Despite a few problems, this trade relationship has been highly profitable for both China and Japan, so there is no reason to anticipate significant negative changes.

China has another special reason to foster high levels of trade with Japan—it wants to outbid the USSR. In the early 1970s, Soviet and Chinese trade with Japan was virtually identical in value. But with the sole exception of 1976, when Soviet trade was slightly greater, China has kept ahead. By the early 1980s its trade with Japan was nearly double the Soviet figure.

Other crucial aspects of the Sino-Japanese connection include the technical skills that Japan can supply to improve China's transportation and communication systems. Japan and China are already involved in joint oil drilling operations in waters off China's northern coast, and other such schemes are planned for the future. Aid in various forms and guises pours into China from Japan. More aid is likely in the future, and it will probably surpass the collective aid to China from all other sources.

In terms of indirect aid, about 1,000 Chinese students and trainees are in Japanese universities and institutes, and scores of technical groups conduct inspection missions in both nations. The annual flood of Japanese tourists also adds millions to the Chinese treasury.

Sino-Japanese ties are regularly reinforced by visits between the two nations' cabinet-level ministers. Virtually all senior Japanese political leaders, including the staunchly conservative Liberal Democratic Party chiefs, have visited China. Beginning with Prime Minster Tanaka Kakuei in 1972, four prime ministers have visited China while in office (Tanaka, Ōhira Masayoshi, Suzuki Zenkō, and Nakasone Yasuhiro). On the Chinese side, de facto leader Deng Xiaoping visited Japan in 1978 and 1979, followed by visits in 1980 and 1982 by premiers Hua Guofeng and Zhao Ziyang, and by General Secretary Hu Yaobang in 1983. The United States has roughly matched this high level of exchange, but no other Second World nation comes remotely close to Japanese official contacts with China. The point made earlier about Western European ties can be made with far greater force about Japan: The most senior Chinese and Japanese officials have had ample opportunity to exchange views in recent years.

At the economic and governmental levels, Sino-Japanese ties are the best they have been for a century. China also sees Japan as one more counter on the Asian chessboard to deploy against the Soviet Union. On this point, China has totally reversed its earlier position. Until the early 1970s, Beijing constantly warned against Japan's allegedly growing militarism and attacked its military bonds with the United States. Now, in effect, Beijing actively fosters increased Japanese military strength, in the hope that this would be directed against the Soviets. Beijing also asserts flatly that Japan's most important link is to the United States, with the clear understanding that this reaffirms the United States–Japan Security Treaty. Can Beijing claim that its affirmation of the U.S.-Japanese treaty is part of its larger scheme of cooperating with a Second World country (Japan) to oppose the hegemonism of a superpower (the United States)? Obviously, this is a contradiction in terms, demonstrating that in practice, the real superpower enemy is the Soviet Union, not the United States. The Japanese are somewhat uneasy about Beijing's proclivity to charge the Soviets with hostile behavior toward Japan, but as long as China does not push the matter too far, the Japanese are pleased that Beijing supports their quite modest military structure and no longer seeks to weaken Japan, as it clearly did until the early 1970s.

Finally, we need to explore the range of possibilities that might damage Sino-Japanese relations. Obviously, major changes in Sino-Soviet or Sino-American relations might affect Sino-Japanese ties. In the Sino-Soviet sector, it is hard to imagine an improvement so extreme as to offend Japan. On the contrary, Japan would welcome more cordial Sino-Soviet relations so that it could more easily do business with both.

In Sino-American relations, Taiwan could be a catalyst for severe change. Unlike any other Second World nation, Japan has a very significant interest in Taiwan's future. Many senior members of Japan's ruling Liberal Democratic Party hold very pro-Taiwan views. Public opinion polls reveal that the Japanese public hopes that Taiwan can remain independent. And in business circles, Taiwan is rightly considered one of Japan's best trading partners. Throughout the 1970s, for example, Japan actually had more trade with Taiwan than with the PRC, although trade with the latter moved ahead in the early 1980s.

In any event, a PRC invasion of Taiwan or an assault on the offshore islands would almost certainly gravely damage Sino-Japanese relations. The use of force in Korea might be even more damaging. If this seems very unlikely, we should remember that China and North Korea are linked by a defense pact (China's only military alliance). Finally, China and Japan could have a jurisdictional dispute over the continental shelf, involving important fishery questions or the issue of oil drilling rights in waters not far north of Taiwan. Yet given the many levels of cooperation already in place and working quite well, it seems more likely that Beijing and Tokyo will cooperate in developing fishing areas and in oil exploration. The importance of cooperation and the broad identity of interests in worldwide political issues was the major theme of a Chinese article in late 1982 that reviewed Sino-Japanese relations a decade after diplomatic normalization.[17]

Eastern Europe

All grand theories have untidy elements that never seem to fit very well. In China's "Three Worlds" scheme, Eastern Europe is at best a partial fit. In the first place, as originally formulated by Mao Zedong and unveiled by Deng Xiaoping in his famous 1974 speech at the UN, the Second World was described only by the brief comment that it consisted of the "developed countries" between the First and Third Worlds.[18] Countries such as Canada or France quickly leap to mind, but what about Albania or Bulgaria? An obviously authoritative elaboration of the Three-Worlds Theory in 1977 did include Eastern Europe.[19]

An effective case can be made that since the early 1970s, the PRC *has* used Western Europe, Japan, Australia, and Canada to oppose the hegemonism of one superpower—the USSR. Can a similar case be made for Eastern Europe? By any measurement, it appears that Beijing has made virtually no inroads on Moscow's hold over its staunchest allies— East Germany, Poland, Czechoslovakia, Hungary, and Bulgaria. Beijing's intimate ties with Albania date back to the early 1960s, and are totally unrelated to the Three Worlds scheme. Ironically, Chinese-Albanian relations virtually ended in 1978 owing to Beijing's much-improved ties to the United States, an act of treachery in Albanian eyes. This leaves only Romania and Yugoslavia.

It is true that Romania and China have had quite positive relations, but as with Albania, these ties date back to the early 1960s, when China sought an Eastern European foothold in the wake of the Sino-Soviet split. In any case, the two countries have an impressive level of trade—throughout the 1970s and early 1980s, Romania was among China's top ten trading partners. There has also been a steady exchange of top-level political leaders between Beijing and Bucharest. In recent years, for example, Romanian Party leader Nicolae Ceausescu visited Beijing in May 1978; Party Chairman Hua Guofeng visited Bucharest in August 1978 and Party General Secretary Hu Yaobang traveled to Romania in May 1983. In a crisis, however, neither Romania nor the PRC could offer serious military assistance to counter the Soviet Union. At best, the Chinese and Romanians can support each other with marginal normative and financial assistance.

Much the same must be said for Yugoslavia, with the further comment that Chinese-Yugoslavian trade has never amounted to much. It is true that both countries have courted each other, especially since Tito's 1977 visit to China. The Chinese sent Hua Guofeng to Yugoslavia in August 1978, and he returned in May 1980 for Tito's funeral. More recently, Hu Yaobang visited Belgrade (May 1983).

The striking differences in China's relations with the "Western" Second World (Western Europe, Japan, Australia, and Canada) and the "Eastern" Second World (Eastern Europe) are perhaps captured in Table 7.1. Beyond the more-or-less measurable categories presented in Table 7.1, two more points can be made. First, there is a bedrock political stability about the Western Second World. Second, China's leaders know full well (propaganda aside) that the Western Second World is vastly more independent of the dictates of Washington than the Eastern Second World is of the commands from Moscow. In 1971 Zhou Enlai told

TABLE 7.1
Prospects for Second World Assistance to China

Actual or Potential Benefit to China	Japan	West Europe	Canada/ Australia	East Europe
Technology Transfer	much	much	marginal	nil
Finance Capital	much	much	marginal	nil
Education/Training	much	much	much	nil
Military Equipment	nil	much	marginal	nil
Food	nil	marginal	much	nil
Fertilizer	much	much	marginal	nil

Australian political leader Gough Whitlam that the "minds of East Europeans are not their own, they're not independent, they're controlled by Russia."[20] This view surely prevails in Beijing today, with slight modifications for the Romanians and Yugoslavs. In any event, China's ability to manipulate Eastern Europe to oppose hegemonism is at best very, very slight.

CONCLUDING REMARKS

What lessons, if any, about Chinese foreign policy can be drawn from this analysis of China's relations with the Second World? An important one is that China is not really a captive of its own dogma. If the PRC originally intended to counter the alleged hegemonism of *both* super-powers, it has taken in stride the perhaps unintended effect of bolstering U.S. power. Many analysts would argue, of course, that U.S. power has diminished, but it almost certainly would have diminished more had China, for example, pushed Japan to loosen its military ties with the United States.

Another lesson seems to be China's willingness to sidestep its own alleged determination to help fellow Third World nations when it comes to economic assistance. China's assistance to the Third World has diminished substantially in recent years. Possibly more important, the PRC now competes with the Third World for bilateral economic aid from the Second World, as well as for aid from international organizations such as the World Bank. Beijing's intent to continue seeking this aid has been codified in the Sixth Five-Year Plan (1981–1985).

A third lesson is the familiar one that characterizes China and most nations: opportunism. When the chance arose to cultivate extremely useful Second World relations, Beijing did not hesitate, even if it enshrouded these moves under a rubric of its Three-Worlds Theory. For example, in the 1970s China dealt with the right-wing colonels who then ruled Greece, and with the living symbol of 1930s fascism, Spain under Franco. All this was done, of course, in the name of uniting the Second and Third Worlds to oppose superpower hegemonism.

Our analysis of Sino–Second World relations (setting aside Eastern Europe) plainly has an optimistic tone. From Beijing's viewpoint, this is a well-founded optimism. The 1970s were spectacularly successful: China emerged from partial isolation to a fully acknowledged place in the sun, and its links with Second World nations were certainly important to this emergence. Even if China's Second World links have only a marginal strategic-military usefulness vis-à-vis the Soviet Union, there is no denying the extraordinary utility for the PRC's economic development.

Still, it is useful to recall that the most striking and pervasive element of Chinese foreign policy is change. In its three and a half decades of history, the People's Republic of China has had extreme changes of policies with *every* important nation with which it has dealt. Consider, for instance, that in some period from 1949 to 1984 China has had cordial relations with the Soviet Union, the United States, India, and Vietnam, yet in this same span of years it has fought all four on the battlefield! This cannot simply be attributed to Mao—witness Vietnam. Nor is a distinction between Communist and non-Communist countries an adequate explanation: Two of the above-mentioned nations are Communist and two are not. Whatever the reasons for these extreme changes, it is clear that no analyst can ignore the volatility of Chinese foreign policy.

We should also remember the fundamental point of China's claim to sovereignty over Taiwan. All Second World nations pay lip service to the "fact" of China's sovereignty, yet all of them—and especially Japan—have extensive dealings with Taiwan. To date, the PRC has let this sleeping dog lie. For how long will this continue?

Setting aside these issues, what other domestic or foreign considerations should command our attention? In domestic politics, the 1980s seem destined to be the decade of the Four Modernizations—the policy to modernize agriculture, industry, national defense, and science and technology. By China's definition, the Four Modernizations are intended to guide policy to the year 2000. No one can say that these efforts will fail without Second World cooperation, yet a severing of Second World links would undoubtedly slow China's modernization. It is worth repeating that currently the lion's share of direct and indirect bilateral aid to China is from the Second World, most notably Japan.

Could China's relations with the Second World withstand the turbulence of another Cultural Revolution? First, recall that China's economic ties with the Second World remained largely intact not only through the Cultural Revolution, but also through the Vietnam War and the heyday of the Gang of Four. (Of course, the volume of trade today is vastly larger than during the 1960s and 1970s.) Second, for the short or medium run, most signs seem to point to a victory by Deng Xiaoping's "moderates" over the "radicals." We would be foolish not to expect occasional flurries of strident nationalism or "puritan Communism" that might do limited damage to Second World relations. But the Second World contains some of the world's most experienced business executives, who are accustomed to such excesses from governments of the left or right around the world.

Are there likely to be ideological clashes between the Communism of China and the capitalism of Second World countries? One of the far-reaching lessons of the twentieth century is the power of nationalism. Nationalism destroyed the great Western colonial empires, and we have also seen the power of nationalism in what amounts to the dismemberment of the "worldwide Communist movement." Both the major Communist and capitalist nations have adjusted to this development, so it seems unlikely that ideology will significantly damage Sino–Second World ties in future years.

At the most basic strategic level, does any Second World nation threaten China? The answer is clear if we think of Western Europe, Australia, Canada, or Eastern Europe. The only conceivable Second World threat would be Japan, but this seems no more likely than a renewal of Franco-German hostilities in Europe. In short, the threats to China seem virtually nil. The very mention of a military threat to China brings us back to China's perception of its one real threat—the Soviet Union. After all, the whole idea of the Second World was largely created to counter China's archenemy. In the final analysis, a drastic change involving the Second World and China would most probably come from a reversal of Moscow's quest for global power and influence as a superpower. And that, as Khrushchev once remarked, will happen when shrimps learn to whistle.

NOTES

1. The issue of Eastern Europe as part of the Second World is dealt with toward the end of this chapter.

2. "Chairman Mao's Theory of the Differentiation of the Three Worlds Is a Major Contribution to Marxism-Leninism," *Peking Review*, No. 45 (November 4, 1977):10–41, especially pp. 29–33.

3. On China's hostility to Japan at this juncture, see Chae-Jin Lee, *Japan Faces China* (Baltimore: Johns Hopkins University Press, 1976), pp. 86–91.

4. *New York Times, Report from Red China* (New York: Avon Books, 1971), pp. 81–106.

5. Shannon R. Brown, "China's Program of Technology Acquisition," in Richard Baum, ed., *China's Four Modernizations: The New Technological Revolution* (Boulder, Colo.: Westview Press, 1980), pp. 153–173.

6. For a convenient summary of China's military contacts with Second World countries, see Research Institute for Peace and Security, *Asian Security 1980* (Tokyo, 1980), p. 95.

7. *Boston Globe,* March 4, 1983, quoting a *Los Angeles Times* dispatch from Beijing.

8. Lynn Feintech, *China's Modernization Strategy and the United States* (Washington, D.C.: Overseas Development Council, 1981), p. 41.

9. Zheng Hongqing, "Opening to the Outside World and Self-Reliance," *Beijing Review,* No. 11 (March 14, 1983):15–20.

10. Ibid.

11. Ibid. The "past few years" was not spelled out, but from the context it seems to date from about 1978. For further details on foreign loans and investments, see *Beijing Review,* No. 15 (April 11, 1983):7; No. 23 (June 6, 1983):4; and No. 24 (June 13, 1983):10.

12. In late 1980 a top Chinese official provided some details about students abroad: of the 5,100 students sent abroad in the "last two years," about 4,600 were in natural sciences, 110 were in the social sciences, and 380 in foreign languages. *Beijing Review,* No. 50 (December 15, 1980):7. Exactly two years later, Beijing reported that 12,000 students had studied abroad at state expense, and that 3,500 of them had completed their courses and returned to China. *Beijing Review,* No. 49 (December 6, 1982):25.

13. *Beijing Review,* No. 29 (July 19, 1982):20; No. 13 (March 28, 1983): 6–7.

14. Zhou Enlai did go to Geneva, but for the 1954 Geneva Conference— not on a state visit to Switzerland.

15. A deputy-director of Beijing's Institute of International Studies speculated in early 1982 on the prospect of "Finlandization": "Generally speaking, various strata in Western Europe maintain vigilance against the Soviet Union. In addition, the United States would not allow Western Europe to pledge allegiance to the Soviet Union. Therefore, the possibility of 'Finlandization' in the mid-80s is very remote." Guo Fengmin, "Basic Ideas Behind the Foreign Policies of West European Countries," *Beijing Review,* No. 5 (February 1, 1982):9–12.

16. The ten West European nations are West Germany, Great Britain, France, the Netherlands, Belgium, Greece, Austria, Spain, Sweden, and Switzerland. Denmark is preparing to open a trade office. *Free China Weekly* (Taipei), March 13, 1983, p. 4.

17. *Beijing Review,* No. 40 (October 4, 1982):12–13.

18. *Peking Review,* No. 16 (April 19, 1974):6–11.

19. See note 2.

20. Ross Terrill, "Peking: Trying to Make China Work," *Atlantic* 252, 1 (July 1983):22.

CHAPTER 8

CHINA AND THE THIRD WORLD: IN SEARCH OF A NEOREALIST WORLD POLICY

Samuel S. Kim

INTRODUCTION

Like a true believer suddenly caught exposed in a red-light district, the post-Mao Chinese leadership seems once again compelled to repent and revise its deviating political posture. If China's policy pronouncements and protestations are taken at face value, another reorientation in Chinese world policy has been under way since mid-1981—a shift from a strategic collaboration with the United States verging on a de facto alliance to a more detached and independent foreign policy. In bilateral relations, an independent, nonaligned, and self-reliant policy based on the Five Principles of Peaceful Coexistence (first enunciated in the Sino-Indian Trade Agreement of April 29, 1954) is asserted as the centerpiece of Chinese foreign policy. In the global context, Chinese policy is declared to be firmly anchored upon the principle of Third World solidarity in a common struggle against both superpowers to maintain world peace.

The new posture of independence and nonalignment from both superpowers and solidarity with the Third World poses a variety of intriguing questions. Could this shift be simply (or even necessarily) another exercise in ideological gymnastics designed to cope with a "crisis of faith" at home? The de-Maoification process, pursued without a credible alternative ideology; the Western "pollutants" that began to creep in and expand like the camel's nose in the tent of the open-door policy; and the growing international reputation of China as a conservative status quo power aligned with the capitalist/imperialist superpower have all confronted the post-Mao leadership with a legitimacy crisis that could no longer be ignored. Or could this new bent be but a rhetorical ploy to arrest China's eroding influence and growing credibility problem in Third World politics without making any meaningful foreign policy commitments? In Richard Nixon's tolerant interpretation, "the Chinese feel they have to kick us around a bit to keep their own credentials as a third world nation." Might the new look be a bargaining gambit to exact greater payoffs from the United States during succeeding rounds in a restructured collaborative relationship? Or is it a genuine departure from previous policy, one that if sustained may mark one of the most significant turning points in the history of Chinese foreign policy?

In responding to these questions, this chapter proceeds on the assumption that the dialectics of China's changing world policy are embedded in its policies toward the First World (the United States and the Soviet Union) and the Third World, with the Second World representing the stable middle ground. China's policy toward the Third World and the superpowers is seen as the bellwether of the changes and continuities in the values, norms, and interests guiding China's world policy. Specifically, this chapter addresses the following issues: (1) the relative importance of the Third World in China's world policy; (2) change and continuity in the theoretical assumptions of Chinese world policy; (3) change and continuity in the behavioral manifestations of Chinese world policy, especially in the world political, military, economic, and development domains; and (4) motives for the changes and shifts in Chinese world policy. By way of conclusion, a brief assessment will be ventured on the future prospects of post-Mao Chinese world policy.

The scope of this analysis is limited largely to the Chinese Third World policy of the post-Mao era, especially the latest "readjustment" period (mid-1981 to 1983). For analytical brevity and convenience, however, the post-Mao development of Chinese foreign policy is divided into three periods: (1) the "continuity" period (September 1976 to May 1978), when Mao's Three-Worlds Theory remained largely intact; (2) the "entente" period (May 1978 to mid-1981), when the Three-Worlds Theory lost symbolic and substantive significance as China and the United States moved on a parallel anti-Soviet track; and (3) the "readjustment" period (mid-1981 to the present), during which Mao Zedong Thought and his Three-Worlds Theory have made a partial recovery.

THE THIRD WORLD: A PIVOT OR A PAWN?

China's Third World policy has often shown a Janus face in response to changing domestic conditions and external constraints. Beijing's relations with New Delhi, for example, moved from the cozying-up process initiated by the Five Principles of Peaceful Coexistence in the mid-1950s (the Bandung period) to the Sino-Indian Border War of 1962. In the mid-1960s, Sino-Indonesian relations shifted from near alliance to extreme hostility. And in the late 1970s, Sino-Vietnamese relations rather suddenly and unexpectedly deteriorated from "boundless affection and assistance" (some US$20 billion from 1950 to 1978) to war.

In general, it is during periods of great concern for China's ideological purity—when egalitarianism at home and revolutionary transformation abroad are paramount—that good relations with the Third World play a pivotal role in shaping Chinese foreign policy. But the Third World tends to be relegated to a peripheral role and benign neglect in times of rightist pragmatism in domestic policy and system maintenance in foreign policy. When the united front strategy is applied to both super-powers (a dual-adversary strategy), solidarity with the Third World is pivotal; when the united front strategy is applied to one superpower (an all-against-one strategy), the Third World plays a secondary role. During the present period of readjustment, these competing pressures have complicated China's relations with the Third World.

Positive and Essential Factors

There are several positive, essential factors facilitating the linkage between China and the Third World in contemporary global politics. First and most important, there is the need for mutual help and mutual legitimation. Because of the PRC's long exclusion and isolation from the postwar international system and the still unsettled nature of the two Chinas issue, its quest for full legitimacy has become the most sensitive part of Beijing's foreign policy. Given the Third World's dominance in the global politics of collective legitimation and delegitimation of the United Nations—the U.S. notice of withdrawal from UNESCO is the latest reminder—the Chinese search for foreign policy legitimation cannot succeed without Third World support. China's quest for foreign policy legitimation thus has been an integral part of its Third World policy. For both psychological and symbolic reasons, the Third World also needs China's moral and political support in its pursuit of a more equitable international order.

Second, as a poor developing nation, China cannot escape the status of a Third World country for some time to come. With China's emerging integration into the capitalist world system, the Chinese political economy will become increasingly sensitive to the same pressures and penalties of asymmetrical interdependence that have traditionally plagued much of the Third World. This sharing of economic weaknesses and vulner-abilities may provide a firmer foundation for cooperation between China and the South on world development issues.

Third, the Maoist egalitarian impulse for the underdogs at home and abroad continues to influence the thinking and policymaking of the Chinese political leadership. During much of the Maoist era, this impulse was translated into global ethical concern and care for the world's worst-off and formed a strong symbolic link between Chinese and Third World global politics. By shifting from the conventional mode of politics as power-seeking and power-wielding to a new style of politics as value-realizing and structure-transforming, Maoist China showed great potential for filling a leadership deficiency in Third World politics. At least, this was how many Third World countries interpreted Chinese global policy in the mid-1970s.

Finally, there is the continuing legacy of the Maoist struggle theory of system transformation from below. This theory sees the poor and the weak gradually becoming richer and stronger and rising up in rebellion to destroy the hegemonic structure of the global dominance system in favor of a new social order. Dengist realism has made it more difficult to follow this line of reasoning in post-Mao China, yet superpower hegemonic rivalry serves as a great teacher to the reality principle, pulling the post-Mao leadership back to some of Mao's guiding principles.

Negative and Elusive Factors

On the other side of the dialectics of China's Third World policy lie some serious difficulties and problems. China's repeated self-identification with the Third World as an *equal* member and its continual denial of any leadership role in Third World politics strike a discordant note. China's "status crisis" lies in its dual and inconsistent position in the international pecking order: an inferior Third World status in per capita income and a superior status in aggregate demographic, military, and production terms.[1] According to a 1980 ranking of 142 countries, China placed 120 in per capita GNP.[2] Yet China clearly enjoys the status of a great power when more important aggregate indices are used: it is first in size of population and armed forces; second in grain output; third in strategic nuclear forces, space satellites, cotton, raw coal, and steel output; fourth in total commercial (primary) energy output; and sixth in crude oil and GNP.

In global politics, China enjoys a status that is clearly disproportionate to its economic and financial capability. It is the only "Third World" member of the Big Five on the United Nations Security Council. It is also a "privileged" member of practically all select-membership councils or governing bodies of international organizations, including the World Bank. In joining the International Labour Organization (ILO) in mid-1983, for example, China filled one of the ten seats reserved for "chief industrial states." Only two other Third World states—Brazil and India—have ever done so.

During the entente period, China's status crisis was expressed in contradictory forms along two separate tracks of world politics. In world developmental politics, China shifted from overstating its strengths and virtues as a donor of foreign aid to understating its economic and scientific strength in order to solicit the maximum amount of concessionary multilateral aid. This shift has suddenly placed China in an unaccustomed rivalry with the Third World in the global politics of multilateral financial resource allocation. In world geopolitics, however, the post-Mao leadership took the opposite approach, cultivating expectations that China is both able and willing to play a decisive role as a positive "balancer" in the global strategic equilibrium in favor of the capitalist superpower against the socialist superpower.[3] Afghanistan and Kampuchea, far from being local or regional conflicts, were depicted as front-line battlegrounds against the spread of Soviet hegemonism. The tensions between these approaches have been eased during the readjustment period, placing China in a less awkward and untenable position in Third World politics.

If asserted collectively, national independence, state sovereignty, and economic self-reliance can be congenial principles and powerful weapons in the Third World struggle against great power intervention and penetration. But because of the recent drift toward nationalism and fragmentation among its members, the Third World has wasted much of its economic and political capital on intramural infighting. In spite of its repeated self-definition as a developing socialist country *belonging* to the Third World and its repeated pleas for Third World unity, China too has assumed a posture of independence from, and noninvolvement in, Third World politics. To date, China has refused to join the Third World's economic and political caucuses in global politics—the Group of 77 (125 member states as of the Sixth Session of the United Nations Conference on Trade and Development or UNCTAD-VI in 1983) and the Non-Aligned Movement (101 member states as of the Seventh Summit Conference of the Non-Aligned Movement or NAM-VII in 1983). Indeed, China is the only member of UNCTAD—the most prominent Third World platform for world development politics—that has insisted on, and succeeded in, playing an independent role as a "Group of 1." This isolationism is further reaffirmed by the post-Mao Four Modernizations program—a drive on a grand scale to speed up China's upward mobility from Third World to great-power status in the competitive world system.

From the inception of Third World politics at the Bandung Conference in 1955 (later expanded and formalized at NAM-I in Belgrade in 1961), nonalignment has been the irreducible core principle of Third World politics and the normative foundation of the movement itself. Nonalignment has never implied equidistance or neutrality between East and West on global security and economic issues, but it clearly proscribes any entangling alliance with one bloc against the other. In principle, if not always in practice, nonalignment suggested an alternative normative approach to power (bloc) politics and later an alternative system-reforming path (the New International Economic Order) to the postwar world economic order established and maintained by U.S. hegemony.

China is on target in vehemently attacking the Soviet and Cuban notion of "natural allies" in the Non-Aligned Movement. Both in theory and practice, the notion of "natural alliance" is fundamentally alien to the concept of nonalignment. Despite its repeated, ritualized attack on bloc power, however, it is China's own recurring, almost cyclical, pattern of deviation from the professed norm of nonalignment that makes the Sino-NAM linkage both elusive and problematic. This deviating tendency also makes China susceptible to the charge of being a mercurial and manipulative actor concerned more with its national self-interest and status drive than with the Third World struggle.[4]

In the course of postwar geopolitics, China has attained the dubious distinction of being the only nation that has participated in both an alliance and a war with both superpowers. China is also the only nation to have been threatened at different times with nuclear attack by both the United States and the Soviet Union. China belonged to an alliance (1949–1960) and fought a war (1969) with the socialist superpower, and fought a war (1950–1953) and belonged to a de facto alliance (1978 to mid-1981) with the capitalist superpower. Both alliances and both wars proved inconclusive. This recurring proclivity for alliance realpolitik in the grand Machiavellian tradition has captured the imagination of such U.S. global geostrategists as Henry Kissinger, Zbigniew Brzezinski, and Alexander Haig, but it has also prevented China from assuming a leadership role in the Non-Aligned Movement.

REDEFINING THE LIMITS AND POSSIBILITIES

The rapid post-Mao shift from the ideological superstructure (the "politics in command" model) to the economic base (the "modernization in command" model) inevitably caused a general decline in Chinese normative politics, especially during the entente period. The return of the pragmatists—and yesterday's villains—to power meant putting the Maoist quest for ideological purity on the back burner. As a result, the zone of ideological confusion widened to the point that the post-Mao leadership was compelled to develop a better fit between theory and practice. This renewed attempt to strike a balance between the "leftist deviationist errors" of the continuity period and the "rightist deviationist errors" of the entente period brought about a partial restoration of Mao Zedong Thought and Mao's Three-Worlds Theory. An official reassessment and reformulation of Mao Zedong Thought has been considered necessary both to ease ideological confusion and to restore a measure of legitimacy and stability to Chinese domestic politics.

Mao's Three-Worlds Theory

The Three-Worlds Theory is a simplified model for defining and assessing the main contradictions in the international system. It functions as a geopolitical compass for seeking China's proper place in world politics. Like the Wallersteinian world-system model, which divides the global political economy into core, semiperiphery, and periphery, this theory also makes a tripartite division of the globe; into the First World of two superpowers in predatory competition or collusion; the Third World of developing countries in Asia, Africa, and Latin America; and the Second World of Northern developed countries in between.

Stripped to its core, Mao's Three-Worlds Theory is a theory of antihegemonism designed to strengthen the weak and the poor (including China) and to overcome the strong and the rich. It envisions a united front strategy, derived from China's own revolutionary experience, that has been extrapolated to the global setting to pit the nations of the Third World against those of the First in an unfolding struggle to transform the postwar international system. Although the theory calls for a dual-adversary approach directed against both superpowers, in practice the Soviet Union has often been singled out as the greater threat to world peace.

The Three-Worlds Theory was Mao's response to the increasing untenability of the lean-to-one-side policy that Mao himself had proclaimed a few months before the formal establishment of the People's Republic of China on October 1, 1949. Responding to what he perceived to be irresistible external constraints, Mao declared that all Chinese, without exception, "must lean either to the side of imperialism or to the side of socialism. Sitting on the fence will not do, *nor is there a third road.*"[5] This policy was premised on a two-worlds theory.

During the 1950s, Mao's two-worlds theory was tempered by the notion of intermediate zones, comprising what later were referred to as the Second and Third Worlds. His attempts during the 1960s to define and redefine the theory of intermediate zones in the face of a rapidly changing domestic and international situation only deepened China's identity crisis. By the early 1970s, however, Mao finally resolved this crisis by casting China's lot with that of the Third World, now characterized as "a great motive force pushing forward the wheel of history." Mao's image of China and of a new world order was finally crystallized in his Three-Worlds Theory, unveiled by Deng Xiaoping in a major plenary speech at the Sixth Special Session of the General Assembly in April 1974.[6] Although first formulated by Mao himself in his interview with Zambian president Dr. K. D. Kaunda on February 22, 1974, the theory was officially pronounced before the world audience at the epochal special session blessing the Third World's call for the NIEO.

The essence, credibility, and symbolic appeal of the Three-Worlds Theory remained generally intact during the continuity period. In 1977, the Chinese press was inundated with articles extolling Mao's Three-Worlds Theory. In the most elaborate and comprehensive foreign policy statement issued in the post-Mao era to date, the editorial department of *Renmin ribao* (People's daily), under the aegis of what is now called the leftist "whateverism" faction, devoted the entire six-page issue of November 1, 1977, to a programmatic foreign policy essay entitled "Chairman Mao's Theory of the Differentiation of the Three Worlds Is a Major Contribution to Marxism-Leninism."[7] In a major policy speech before the plenary session of the General Assembly in September 1977—an annual exercise that comes close to being the Chinese "state-of-the-world report"—Foreign Minister Huang Hua reaffirmed post-Mao China's commitment to the theory.[8] It seemed at that time that the theory had been canonized as the cardinal strategic principle to guide Chinese world policy in the post-Mao era.

During the entente period, however, as the gap between Mao's Three-Worlds Theory and China's actual policy widened, the Chinese press began quietly to de-emphasize references to the theory. The 1979 state-of-the-world report conspicuously omitted any reference to the theory. Instead, China's modernization drive was described as in accord "with the behests of Chairman Mao Zedong *and* Premier Zhou Enlai."[9] Even more significant, in 1980 the Chinese state-of-the-world report made no mention either of Mao Zedong or his Three-Worlds Theory.[10]

The official reassessment of Mao Zedong at the Sixth Plenum of the Eleventh Central Committee of the Chinese Communist Party in late June 1981 marked the transition to the present period of readjustment. The "Resolution on Certain Questions in the History of Our Party Since the Founding of the People's Republic of China" (adopted on June 27, 1981) acknowledges that Mao "outlined the correct strategy of the three worlds and advanced the important principle that China would never seek hegemony" and thus "made major contributions to the liberation of the oppressed nations of the world and to the progress of mankind."[11]

This partial endorsement suggests that China is now engaged in a renewed quest for a more ideologically balanced and politically viable compromise between the practical requirements of de-Maoification and the normative requirements of re-Maoification. To sustain progress in the Four Modernizations (industry, agriculture, science and technology, and national defense) without appearing to weaken its national independence and self-reliance, China has resorted to a selective invocation of Maoism. Because Mao is criticized for his "grave mistakes" in his later years (1966–1976) and because the post-Mao canonization of the Three-Worlds Theory in 1977 had the official imprimatur of the now purged "whateverism" faction of Hua Guofeng (i.e., "We must resolutely support *whatever* policy decisions Chairman Mao made and consistently follow *whatever* directives Chairman Mao issued"—italics added), one must not overplay Mao's Three-Worlds Theory.

During the readjustment period, Mao Zedong Thought has been resurrected again in a flexible and ambiguous manner as "the valuable spiritual asset" and "our guide to action for a long time to come."[12] True to form, the Chinese repeatedly claim that there is no de-Maoification (*feimaohua*) in post-Mao China, only demystification (*feishenhua*). Deng Xiaoping offers a more blunt and explicit exposition of what is happening to Mao Zedong Thought during the readjustment period: "In many respects, what we are doing is what Comrade Mao Zedong suggested we should do but have failed to do; setting right what he mistakenly opposed and doing a good job in what he failed to do properly. We will continue to do so for a long time to come. Of course, we have developed and continue   to develop Mao Zedong Thought."[13]

Thus it is independence, self-reliance, and the Five Principles of Peaceful Coexistence, not the struggle theory of system transformation, that have been restored as the valuable legacy of Mao Zedong (and Zhou Enlai). Mao's Three-Worlds Theory remains neither officially emphasized nor officially repudiated during the readjustment period. Between mid-1981 and the end of 1983, there were only a few references to the theory in the Chinese press,[14] and there has been no specific mention or endorsement of Mao's Three-Worlds Theory in any major foreign policy pronouncement during the readjustment period.

China and the NIEO

As a collective consensual package, the NIEO defies simple generalization. From the mainstream Third World perspective, the central demands of the NIEO—improving the terms of trade for the primary commodities, increasing the transfer of resources and technology, reforming international financial and monetary institutions, and enhancing greater participatory democracy in managing the global political economy—are all designed to transform the postwar world economic order and thus to reduce interstate inequities in all key sectors of the global political economy. At the strategic and operational level, the NIEO as conceived by the Third World represents a strange mixture of dependencia theory in its diagnosis and postwar international liberalism in its prescription. The logic of dependencia theory calls for a delinkage strategy of self-reliance as a first step to the long-term structural transformation of the capitalist world economy. Conversely, the logic of international liberalism calls for a linkage strategy of integration into the world economy, based on the principle of the international division of labor and comparative advantage.[15]

Despite China's refusal to join the Group of 77, the NIEO established a strong symbolic and normative bond between Maoist China and the Third World in global developmental politics. Some Chinese principles—resource sovereignty, antihegemony, and self-reliance—found their way, in varying degrees and expressions, into the NIEO Declaration, the NIEO Programme of Action, and the Charter of Economic Rights and Duties of States, resulting in enhanced mutual legitimation between China and NIEO. During much of the 1974–1977 period, these three resolutions practically replaced the UN Charter as China's formal norms for global developmental politics. Even the authoritative *Renmin ribao* began to report world development issues in terms of the NIEO (*Xin guoji jingji zhixu*) conceptual framework.

During the entente period, China's support for the NIEO has continued, though in a drastically revised and muted tone. Several conceptual changes are noticeable. Maoist China's unique style of expounding its principled stand on world developmental issues in support of the general interests of the Third World has been replaced by a more "realistic" redefinition of NIEO politics. This redefinition of "national interests" is a logical corollary of the modernization drive. Beijing also explicitly advocated the linkage approach to coordinate global geopolitical and geoeconomic struggles.

The Chinese image of the NIEO shifted from the dependencia model to the Trilateral model of "interdependence." The two bêtes noires of the Maoist era—global interdependence and the division of labor and specialization—were no longer feared or attacked. Instead, they were functionally redefined as integral parts of the modernization drive. Self-reliance was drastically diluted as the division of labor and specialization in production took precedence over a more balanced and self-reliant approach to development. The trend toward international interdependence in world economic development deepened, and China's role in the transformation of the capitalist world economy was downgraded.[16]

In the process of rectifying the rightist deviationist errors made during the entente period, the pendulum has shifted from the right to the center. The normative components of Chinese developmental politics, especially the principle of self-reliance, have been restored. China conveys the impression of having discovered a new truth and value in the self-reliance model that it had put aside earlier, or at least this seems to be the message for the home audience. The new slogan is "socialist modernization with Chinese characteristics." Following and extending this line of reasoning, the notion that there is or can be a single socialist model of development for all Third World countries is now rejected, both in theory and in practice, by Hu Yaobang, the CCP general secretary. Although the open-door and open-outward policy supposedly remains unchanged, "it is imperative to adhere to the fundamental principle of relying mainly on the planned economy and supplementing it with regulation by the market."[17] China now wants to have its cake and eat it too.

In addition, external events—more specifically the Cancun Summit Conference in 1981, the New Delhi South-South Cooperation Conference in 1982, and the Beijing South-South Symposium, NAM-VII, and UNCTAD-VI in 1983—have forced China to reassess its principled stand on North-South issues. During the readjustment period, Beijing has sought a more legitimate and viable open-door/self-reliance linkage. The NIEO has returned once again to the center of Chinese Third World policy in the global context.

Both proponents and opponents generally agree today that the NIEO is in serious disarray, if not already dead. The postwar world economic order remains unreformed, and North-South negotiations are deadlocked. Responding to this global reality,[18] China has redefined its support of the NIEO in terms of South-South cooperation (collective self-reliance). This redefinition is the most significant shift in the Chinese conceptualization of North-South dialogue in the readjustment period.

This latest Chinese conceptualization follows a dialectical line of reasoning. The world economic crisis is both structural and periodic, requiring mutually complementary interaction between the long-term objective of system transformation and the short-term solution of immediate urgent problems. South-South cooperation and North-South dialogue are two interrelated aspects of the same process of transforming the old economic order and establishing a new one. South-South cooperation is not an alternative to the NIEO. It is a more effective and realistic path toward building independent national economies, reducing external dependency, strengthening Third World solidarity, increasing the South's bargaining power, and generating new momentum for the stalled global negotiations. By tapping and developing its own unlimited potentials, the Third World can also minimize the vulnerabilities of asymmetrical North-South interdependence.[19]

Closely related to the Chinese reformulation of the NIEO in terms of collective self-reliance is a shift in Chinese Third World policy from foreign aid to mutual economic and technological cooperation. As late as September 1981, China claimed it was adhering to the Eight Principles for China's Aid to Foreign Countries first put forth by Premier Zhou Enlai during his African tour in 1964.[20] Most of the Eight Principles express China's egalitarian norms in foreign economic relations—respect for recipients' sovereignty, united aid, and denial of any special amenities for China's foreign aid personnel abroad. During Premier Zhao Ziyang's eleven-nation African tour in January 1983, however, the Eight Principles were reduced and revised as the Four Principles of Sino-African Economic and Technological Cooperation: equality and mutual benefit; emphasis on practical results; diversity in form; and common development. This papered over the growing disjuncture between theory and practice that resulted from China's sudden and dramatic U-turn from an aid-giving to an aid-seeking state in 1978.

To sum up, during the readjustment period post-Mao China attempted to clarify normative incoherence and to seek a more balanced, integrated, and realistic world policy. Judging from policy pronouncements, China has become politically more independent, strategically less aligned, economically more self-reliant, and diplomatically more conciliatory. There has also been a subtle but significant movement toward a more balanced and differentiated posture toward both superpowers, a mixture of a dual-adversary policy (criticizing each superpower based on the intrinsic merit of each case or situation) and a dual-peaceful coexistence policy (promoting functional cooperation with both in spite of conflicts in other areas). World peace and world development are still dialectically linked. Nonetheless, China has begun to show some leaning toward the functionalist, incremental approach to world peace. Increasingly, world development is conceptualized as the foundation of world peace, not the other way around. Above all, China has returned to the Third World again to redefine the permissible and the possible.

BALANCING THEORY WITH PRACTICE

To what extent are these shifts in China's official ideology reflected in its foreign policy? Two politically sensitive weather vanes—China's stand on world political security issues and its stand on world economic and development issues—demonstrate the nature of the post-Mao quest for a neorealist world policy.

World Political and Security Issues

Taking Chinese world policy activities as a whole, there has indeed been a significant shift from a posture of conflict and contention (antihegemony) to one of conciliation and cooperation (peaceful coexistence). According to the 1983 Chinese state-of-the-world report, the Five Principles of Peaceful Coexistence have become not only the basic norm of international relations but also the essential means of ensuring international peace and security.[21]

The number of states having formal diplomatic relations with Beijing increased from 117 in 1979 to 129 in 1983, with most new ties occurring during the readjustment period. In 1983 alone, Beijing established diplomatic relations with four Third World countries: Antigua-Barbuda, Angola, Ivory Coast, and Lesotho. Taiwan is now left with ties only with South Africa and its client states in southern Africa. Even Sino-Albanian relations, ruptured by Tirana's open ideological split with Beijing over Mao's Three-Worlds Theory in 1977 and the latter's cessation of all economic and military assistance in 1978, were restored to the full ambassadorial level in September 1983. After a decision by the Dutch government not to allow any further arms exports to Taiwan, Sino-Dutch relations were restored to the ambassadorial level on February 1, 1984.

One dramatic indicator of the shift in China's global posture is China's delayed recognition of Angola. After the Popular Movement for the Liberation of Angola (MPLA) prevailed in the Angolan civil war in 1975, China refused to extend diplomatic recognition to the new regime because of its close ties with the Soviet Union. A more critical test of China's resolve came on March 31, 1976, when the Security Council voted on a Third World draft resolution. "We absolutely cannot agree to it," declared Ambassador Huang Hua. The draft resolution barely passed by a vote of 9 : 0 : 5. With France, Japan, Italy, the United Kingdom, and the United States abstaining, and with China "not participating in the vote," Security Council Resolution 387 became a dramatic test of the aligned-nonaligned and North-South polarization of the Council.

This showdown resolution appeared ideally suited to reflect China's "principled stand." It condemned South Africa's aggression against Angola, demanded that South Africa stop using the international territory of Namibia (South-West Africa) to mount provocative attacks against Angola, and called upon South Africa to meet the just claims of Angola for full compensation for the damage and destruction inflicted on its territory and for the restoration of the equipment and materials seized by the invading forces. In short, the resolution was clearly anti–South African and correctly distinguished between the aggressor and the victim of the aggression.

China's obsessive anti-Soviet (and anti-Cuban) posture also underlay its nonparticipation on the issue of Angolan membership in the United Nations. On December 1, 1976, immediately following the adoption of a resolution admitting Angola into the United Nations, Foreign Minister Jose Eduardo dos Santos, now president of Angola, attacked both the United States and China for their opposition. There had been an "unnatural alliance" between China, imperialism, and South Africa, he charged, adding that mercenaries recruited by South Africa had been paid in U.S. dollars and had killed Angolans with weapons "made by the Chinese proletariat."[22]

During the readjustment period, the realignment of China's global posture became increasingly evident. By 1982 China openly declared its willingness to establish diplomatic relations with Angola, and pledged not to support antigovernment forces in the future. More significantly, China has assumed a differentiated global posture toward the superpowers, rejecting the U.S. coupling of the Namibian issue with the withdrawal of Cuban troops from Angola.

The essence of this new global posture is that China, departing from its past alignment with one superpower against the other, now claims that it opposes hegemony, no matter *who* seeks it or *where:*

> On the Afghan and Kampuchean issues, both China *and* the United States oppose the Soviet Union and Vietnam. . . . In another case, both China *and* the Soviet Union oppose the United States in supporting Israeli aggression and the South African apartheid rule. This does not mean that China "allies" with the United States under some circumstances or becomes a Soviet partner under other circumstances. [Instead] this precisely proves that . . . China is independent of all the superpowers.[23]

By the end of 1983, China's differentiated opposition to both superpowers had brought its global posture more or less in line with that of the Third World. China now opposes U.S. hegemony in Central America and the Caribbean (especially the Grenada invasion, now characterized as a "political and moral disaster for the United States"), Africa (Namibia, Angola, and South Africa), and the Middle East, and criticizes the U.S. position on a host of global issues involving the NIEO, the UN Law of the Sea Convention, the United Nations Educational,

Scientific, and Cultural Organization (UNESCO), and the IMF. It opposes Soviet hegemony in Vietnam and Afghanistan. And it condemns the external interference in Chad in 1983. In Beijing's view, the conflict in Chad was purely an internal matter of no concern to the United States, France, or the Soviet Union.

China's voting behavior in the United Nations has reflected its growing independence of the two superpowers and its symbolic rapprochement with the Third World. In 1983, for example, China voted for the anti-U.S. draft resolution condemning the invasion of Grenada and abstained on the U.S.-sponsored anti-Soviet draft resolution on the Korean Air Lines incident. In late 1981, after considering "the demands of her friends and wishing to avoid confrontation"—that is, under pressure from Third World countries—China abandoned its long-standing "nonparticipation" in the authorization process of UN peacekeeping operations and agreed to pay its share of the assessed expenses as of January 1, 1982. Through these and other measures China has recovered some of its lost political ground with the Third World.

In 1983, China made several more precedent-breaking moves to establish closer ties with the Third World. These moves were ignored in the U.S. press but received prominent attention from the Chinese media. In March China attended NAM-VII in New Delhi as a special invitee—one of the ten major events of 1983, according to Beijing's retrospective. In April the Beijing South-South Conference, held in China's capital, was attended by some sixty-eight diplomats and scholars from twenty-six Asian, African, and Latin American countries. Although this was an unofficial (nongovernmental) conference, cosponsored by the Chinese Academy of Social Sciences and the Third World Foundation for Social and Economic Studies, it received the official imprimatur of Premier Zhao Ziyang's keynote speech. The conference concluded with "expressed support for a continuing process of consultation between third world scholars, with Beijing 1983 becoming South-South I—the first in a series of regular consultations linked by programmes of work at a variety of levels."[24]

To enhance the credibility of closer Sino–Third World cooperation, on the last day of the thirty-seventh session of the General Assembly in 1982, China publicly expressed its agreement with the basic principles espoused by the Group of 77 to deal with the world economic crisis. For the first time, China sent a nonvoting delegation to the fifth ministerial conference of the Group of 77, held in Buenos Aires in April 1983. In August 1983 a three-member delegation from the Group of 77—Ambassador Faruq Sobhan of Bangladesh, chairman of the Group of 77; Ambassador Kenneth Dadzie of Ghana; and Ambassador Manuel Perez Querrero of Venezuela—paid a week-long visit to China at the invitation of the Chinese Foreign Ministry. The visits were for high-level, behind-the-scenes consultations as well as for mutual public assurance to the Chinese home audience that the Group of 77 and China "have entered into closer relations."

On disarmament issues, the post-Mao readjustment has been less conclusive. China's global posture on disarmament issues has always been fraught with numerous ambiguities and contradictions inherent in the need to balance ideological and security concerns. Caught in the cross-pressures of its own perceived requisite for nuclear deterrence and the growing denuclearization demands of nonaligned countries, China has advanced a twofold "principled stand," calling for a no-first-use pledge by all nuclear powers, particularly by the superpowers, and the withdrawal of all superpower armed forces, including nuclear missiles, from abroad. In practice, however, these two preconditions were considerably muted during the entente period as China unabashedly sided with the hawks in the United States. Détente was viewed then as no more than a contemporary variation on the Munich appeasement theme and was considered a sure catalyst for a world war.[25]

The transition from the entente to the readjustment period has not produced any major turning point in China's global policy on nuclear weapons issues, only adjustments and shifts. China has adopted the principle of differentiated and proportionate responsibilities in nuclear disarmament. Because the two superpowers account for 97 percent of all nuclear warheads in the world,[26] they bear the greatest brunt of the responsibility, and they must lead the way to global nuclear disarmament. In order to justify its own nuclear weapons development as purely defensive, China has reminded the world that it has not a single soldier abroad, not a single military base abroad, and not a single military alliance treaty directed against third-party states.

At home the defense component of the Four Modernizations still remains the lowest priority. China cannot afford to buy all the weapons it needs from abroad, which affects the Chinese debate on national defense in the context of the modernization drive. China has made good the pledge that it cannot be bought off in the Taiwan issue by U.S. arms sales or military technology transfer. Beijing charges that the two-edged approach was nothing but a superpower scheme to split China. As a follow-up, China denied all foreign military hardware to its armed forces, even canceling a big British deal in 1982 and stressing the need to develop its own new weapons. Moreover, the principle of combining military industry with civilian uses has now become the norm. Since 1979, the Chinese army is reported to have contributed 100 million workdays to assisting socialist construction in various places and has also provided disaster relief on more than 5,000 occasions.[27]

As in the past, China still self-consciously avoids using the term "arms control" (*wuqi kongzhi* or *wuqi guanzhi*). Yet the neorealism of its readjustment period has led China to commit itself within the last year to a number of multilateral arms control treaties: the 1959 Antarctic Treaty; the 1967 Treaty on Principles Governing the Activities of States in the Exploration and Use of Outer Space, including the Moon and Other Celestial Bodies; and the two additional protocols (1977) of the

1949 Geneva Conventions. In joining the International Atomic Energy Agency in October 1983, China accepted the IAEA Statute and its legal obligations as a member. But it remains critical of the nonproliferation regime, especially the two-tier discriminatory structure between "nuclear haves" and "nuclear have-nots." For the first time, China has publicly stated before the international community that it neither stands for nor encourages the proliferation of nuclear weapons.[28]

China's "equidistant" posture between both superpowers in the domain of global disarmament politics cannot paper over one crucial geostrategic fact: The United States no longer poses any military threat to China, but many of the Soviet Union's 144 SS-20s are aimed at Chinese targets. The erosion of Sino-American strategic collaboration has not hampered the operations of the electronic intelligence facility at Xinjiang, which was established during the Carter administration for joint Sino-American monitoring of Soviet missile tests.[29] Nevertheless, the tenacious refusal of the United States to pledge itself to the no-first-use principle, in contrast to the Soviet Union's unilateral declaration of no first use, made at the Second Special Session on Disarmament in 1982, has placed China in an awkward position in UN disarmament politics.

"In essence," Harry Harding could write in 1981,"the United States now enjoys the *end of Chinese opposition* to most of its initiatives in the Third World."[30] By the end of 1983, China's list of U.S. hegemonic acts in the Third World had lengthened, and that of Soviet hegemonic acts shortened, a clear reversal of Harding's assessment. China has come a long way during the readjustment period toward realigning its global posture with the Third World's position on most political and security issues.

Nonetheless, it is important to note that Soviet hegemony is being pursued within the parameters of China's security zone, directly threatening China's national *interests*, whereas U.S. hegemony is being pursued outside of China's security zone, merely offending Chinese *norms*. Despite some progress in the improvement of the atmospherics and scholarly exchange and trade (from US$300 million in 1982 to US$700 million in 1983, and projected to increase to US$1.18 billion in 1984) there has been no discernible movement on what the Chinese regard as the three major obstacles to Sino-Soviet normalization: the Soviet occupation of Afghanistan; the Soviet support for Vietnam's occupation of Kampuchea; and the Soviet deployment of heavy military forces along the Sino-Soviet border and in Mongolia.

World Economic and Development Issues

In contrast to the clear shifts in China's policy on world political and security issues during the readjustment period, the changes in Beijing's world economic and development policy are ambiguous. China has attempted to strike a better balance between theory and practice, norms and interests on world economic issues, pursuing, in effect, a dual-track policy. Beijing seeks to renew its development ties with the Third World through South-South cooperation on one (normative) track, while maximizing external inputs of capitalist credits and loans, investment, entrepreneurship, joint ventures, and science and technology on the other (pragmatic) track. The renewed salience of self-reliance, designed to minimize the normative costs of China's world policy, has not made any significant impact on actual policy. There is still a big discrepancy between policy pronouncements and policy performance, between normative pretensions and substantive activities. In Sino–Third World relations, mutual cooperation may still be the professed or idealized norm, but in actual practice the relationship is competitive. In substantive terms, then, the transition from the entente to the readjustment period is more rhetorical than real in most sectors of the global political economy.

What used to be regarded as an "exchange of unequal values" in official policy is now accepted as a legitimate part of "international trade practices and norms." The "objective reality" of a global political economy dominated by core capitalist powers is now said to oblige all countries to engage in commodity exchange. It is considered impossible for any economically backward country to realize modernization with a closed-door policy.[31] Exports have thus been made "the foundation of China's foreign trade." Included in its stated goals for the year 2000 is a plan for China to more than quadruple its exports, to US$80 billion.

As of September 1983, China had trade agreements with 57 Third World countries (48 in Asia and Africa and 9 in Latin America). Although the total volume of Third World trade has increased from US$1.3 billion in 1970 to US$9.3 billion in 1982, its percentage of China's total trade has fluctuated from an all-time high of 27.9 percent in 1970 to an all-time low of 20.7 percent in 1981. In 1982, the proportion rose to 24.0 percent. In short, the Third World, representing 76 percent of the world's 164 countries (by Chinese definition and computation), accounts for only about one-fifth of China's total trade (see Table 8.1). In contrast, China's trade with the Second World remained stable at about 44 percent of the total volume from 1966 through 1981.

Thanks to the progressive deterioration of the terms of trade for commodities in relation to manufactures in the global political economy, China enjoys a comparative advantage in Sino–Third World trade. Although the bulk of its Third World imports are primary commodities (copper, cobalt, zinc, phosphates, cotton, rubber, timber, cocoa, cashew nuts, and tobacco), most of its Third World exports are light-industrial products and textiles. As a result, China has maintained a favorable trade balance with the Third World on the order of US$2.5 billion a year.[32] In contrast, China's trade deficit with the United States was almost US$2.7 billion in 1980, although the gap between imports and exports in Sino-American trade is steadily narrowing.[33]

TABLE 8.1
Proportion of Trade With Third World Countries in China's Total Value of Imports and Exports, 1950–1982

Year	China's Total Value of Import/Export Trade (US$1 million)	Value of Import and Export Trade with Third World Countries (US$1 million)	Proportion of Trade with Third World Countries (Percentage)
1950	1,135.14	151.68	13.4
1960	3,809.20	860.78	22.6
1970	4,585.86	1,280.77	27.9
1980	37,230.58	8,193.04	22.0
1981	40,375.21	8,381.86	20.7
1982	38,983.23	9,307.00	24.0

Source: Chen Muhua, "Developing Trade with Other Third World Countries," *Beijing Review*, No. 38 (September 19, 1983): 16.

The shift from the self-reliance model to the export-oriented development model of the newly industrializing countries has placed post-Mao China in direct competition with the Asian "Gang of Four"— South Korea, Taiwan, Hong Kong, and Singapore, which now account for almost twice the export totals of the entire remainder of the Third World for the U.S. market in textiles and other low-cost manufactured products. After Hong Kong and South Korea, China is the third largest exporter of textiles and garments to the United States, a market worth about US$800 million to China in 1982. China's textiles trade is already a major irritant in Sino-American relations. China's late entry into the U.S. market, at a time when nontariff barriers and quotas had already increased, has fueled domestic conflicts in the United States between free-trade and protectionist interests, particularly between U.S. farmers interested in continuing grain sales to China and U.S. textiles and clothing manufacturers interested in protecting their market against cheaper Chinese imports. By casting its lot with the U.S. farm lobby in opposition to U.S. textile and clothing manufacturers, China has used its "grain card" to ensure that Chinese textile exports will be allowed to compete fairly in the U.S. market.

Against this backdrop, China made another significant move in late 1983 by joining the 50-nation Multi-Fibre Arrangement (MFA). Working under the auspices of the 90-nation General Agreement on Tariffs and Trade (GATT), this multilateral regime is made up of the world's major exporters and importers, accounting for more than 80 percent of the world's trade in cotton, wool, and synthetic fibers. Its principal aim is to secure market stability and a greater share of textiles in world trade, and it prevents importing countries from lowering their export growth rates in textile and clothing below the quotas specified under the MFA. China stopped short of joining GATT, which is blamed by the Third World for the current crisis in world trade. After Taiwan was denied observer status in November 1971, China was invited to participate in GATT but ignored this invitation. China sees GATT as a major instrument of U.S. foreign economic policy to open up more markets in the Third World in those fields (services and high technology) where it still enjoys a comparative advantage and thus to solve the problem of its stagnating export trade.

In trying to improve its terms of trade by shifting from exports of raw materials to exports of finished or semifinished goods, post-Mao China has established four special economic zones (SEZs) in the coastal cities of Shenzhen, Zhuhai, Shantou, and Xiamen. This innovation is modeled after the "free trade zones" (FTZs)—also called "free export zones" (FEZs)—in many Third World countries. It creates an artificial socioeconomic environment characterized by an exceptionally favorable infrastructure, special tax exemptions, low wages, export subsidies, and a prohibition on strikes.

China's initial expectations of the SEZs were far-reaching: to make better use of foreign funds, to import high technology, to increase exports and employment, to raise foreign exchange earnings, to assimilate useful foreign entrepreneurship, and to accelerate the Four Modernizations. The Third World's FTZs (along with its export processing zones, investment-promotion zones, and in-bound industries) have had only limited success in generating employment, either direct or indirect. That is the conclusion of an International Labour Organization study on the employment effects of the multinational corporations in the Third World.[34] To date, China's SEZs have failed to act as a "rainmaker," falling far short of the original expectations, especially in attracting high-tech industries. As an additional inducement to foreign investment, China enacted new regulations on joint ventures in September 1983 to allow SEZ products to be sold within China.

In 1983, the push for modernization further prodded China to participate in the capitalist world economy with yet another unprecedented venture: state-sponsored overseas investment. The China International Trust and Investment Corporation has already taken a 19 percent interest in Santec, a U.S. personal computer company based in Amherst, New Hampshire. The China National Metals and Minerals Import and Export Corporation has also joined the Wheeling-Pittsburgh Steel Corporation in an international joint venture to trade metals and minerals. The total value of China's overseas investment in 1983 (including Hong Kong) was estimated at US$1 billion. U.S. investments in China, by way of comparison, total $500 million.[35] The Bank of China has also become a significant player in the Japanese securities market. In its single-minded drive toward modernization, China has allowed the open door to swing both ways.

Although it is widely assumed that overpopulation is China's greatest problem, the size of the Chinese labor force is also an asset. In keeping with the widespread commodification of labor, post-Mao China has joined the race to outbid Third World countries in exporting cheap labor. China now promotes the business of "international labor cooperation" (*guoji laowu hezuo*) to capitalize on its human resources.[36] The China Construction Engineering Corporation, originally set up in 1957 to oversee government foreign aid projects abroad and major construction projects at home, was transformed in 1979 for this new task. By early 1984, China had established 42 companies to undertake diverse projects in more than 40 foreign countries and regions.[37] Between 1979 and 1981, the number of Chinese workers sent abroad totaled 18,000, worth a signed contract value of US$790 million. By the end of 1982, China had dispatched 31,000 workers and signed 903 contracts worth US$1.3 billion, and in the first half of 1983, it signed 130 contracts worth US$460 million (compared to the 1982 total of US$510 million).[38] China's new aggressive approach to exporting cheap labor puts it into direct competition with the Third World.

In another dramatic departure from the self-reliance model, the post-Mao leadership in 1978 plunged into the race for aid from Trilateral countries, corporations, commercial banks, and United Nations economic and technical assistance agencies. At the same time, China continued to cut its own foreign economic aid, from an annual average of US$638 million during 1970–1973, to US$324 million during 1974–1975, to US$172 million during 1976–1978.[39] In mid-1978, China cut off all assistance to its largest recipients (Albania and Vietnam), in a manner reminiscent of the abrupt Soviet cessation of aid to China in mid-1960.

China's foreign economic aid has not ceased altogether, but it has apparently been redefined and merged with other forms of cooperation, such as "labor service, establishment of joint ventures, coproduction and joint development of natural resources."[40] This is part of a continuing effort to redefine Sino–Third World relations in terms of mutual benefit and cooperation. Contemporary post-Mao China seems to be seeking a more realistic fit between the economic strength of the Third World and the limited capacity of China to supplement it. As Minister of Foreign Economic Relations and Trade Chen Muhua put it, there is a need for "different forms of cooperation, and that is why China has to diversify the form of cooperation with these countries."[41]

By 1981, China's shift from an aid-giving to an aid-seeking country was complete. In a span of three years, China had renounced its unique status as the only developing country to decline multilateral aid and had instead acquired the largest number of multilateral technical aid projects (200). Between 1979 and February 1983, China received some US$230 million in grants from the United Nations Development Program (UNDP), the United Nations Fund for Population Activities, and the United Nations Children's Fund (UNICEF). From UNDP alone, China received US$15 million for 1979–1981 and is expected to receive US$142 million for 1982–1986. In contrast, China's contributions to the UNDP amounted to only US$5.8 million for the period 1973–1983.

Both symbolically and substantively, China's entry into the International Monetary Fund on April 17, 1980, and the World Bank and its affiliates (the International Development Association, or IDA, and the International Finance Corporation, or IFC) on May 15, 1980, marked another turning point. China's strategy of seeking the cheapest possible loans and credits from foreign governments and international monetary and financial institutions while also accepting loans from foreign commercial banks if their conditions are "fair and reasonable" has remained unchanged during the readjustment period. Between 1980 and 1983, China received over $1 billion in loans and credits from the World Bank and the IDA. By the second half of the 1980s, World Bank loans to China are expected to rise to $2 billion a year.

China's grand entry into the world capitalist financial and monetary regime has forced it to reconcile its own economic interests with its ideological support of Third World needs and demands. Throughout the 1970s, China often singled out the World Bank and the IMF for criticism, particularly on the question of Taiwan's vestigial representation as well as on NIEO-related issues. But instead of joining the Group of 24, the Third World caucus in the World Bank, China immediately began to lobby for its own status and interests.[42]

In the process, China succeeded in bending existing rules and procedures to accommodate its own "special status." Instead of opening the contentious issue of status reordering, a simpler decision was made to grant China an exclusive seat on the World Bank's Board of Governors, by increasing the number of seats from 20 to 21, and on the IMF's Board of Executive Directors, by expanding the board from 21 to 22. Less than six months after its official entry, China also managed to double its own quotas (which determine borrowing rights and voting power in both institutions). Its special status within the framework of the weighted voting system not only reversed China's traditional advocacy of international egalitarianism but also lent greater legitimacy to the capitalist international and monetary regime.

By releasing its complete national income statistics to the Committee on Contributions of the General Assembly in 1979 and to the World Bank in 1980, China managed profitably to both reduce its contribution and improve its eligibility for multilateral concessionary aid. In the General Assembly, China reduced its assessment rate—and thus the amount of its required contribution to the United Nations—from 5.5 percent to 1.62 percent between 1980 and 1982, and finally to 0.88

percent in 1983. These reductions were based on what many Third World countries believed to be a grossly understated per capita GNP of only US$152. Like the General Assembly, the World Bank accepted the Chinese data, even though its own estimates placed China's 1978 per capita GNP at US$460. The Third World's complaints fell on deaf ears.

Despite its growing competition with the Third World for aid, China has once again renewed its public support of, and identification with, the Third World, especially since the 1982 joint annual meetings of the World Bank and the IMF. China's rising criticism of the World Bank Group on such issues as the IMF's "unreasonable loan" to South Africa and its "unjust treatment" of Zambia, though obviously intended to establish closer ties with the Third World, amount to more than this. China is increasingly anxious that the promised increase in its loan/credit package for 1984–1985 and beyond can easily be reduced, or even discontinued, by a U.S. veto in the World Bank, even though during World Bank president A. W. Clausen's visit to China in May 1983 both parties publicly characterized the relationship between China and the World Bank as solid and strong.

What beclouds this relationship is a U.S. wild card. At the 1982 joint annual meeting in Toronto, Finance Minister Wang Bingqian singled out the United States for blame for the current financial crisis. "Because the United States has fallen behind on its contributions and will not complete its 1981–1983 contributions until 1984," IDA programs were reduced by 35 percent from US$4.1 billion to US$2.7 billion in fiscal year 1982.[43] Since then, the aid picture has deteriorated even further. In January 1984, thirty-one developed countries finally succumbed to U.S. pressure to reduce the seventh IDA replenishment (IDA-VII) in 1984–1986 to US$9 billion, down from US$12 billion in IDA-VI. In effect, the committed resources of IDA-VII were cut in half in real terms, seriously upsetting World Bank plans to reduce India's share of IDA loans from 33 percent to 20 percent to make room for China. To justify this reduction, the U.S. Department of the Treasury has argued that neither India nor China should receive much IDA help because they both now have access to world capital markets.[44] The shrinking IDA pie and the increasing demands of some forty of the poorest Third World countries will no doubt sharpen the competitive edge of Sino–Third World relations.

In summary, China's dramatic entry into the capitalist world financial and monetary regime, its special status as a board member of both the World Bank and the IMF, the promise of an increased loan/credit package to China for 1984–1985 and beyond, the shrinking IDA pie, and the continuing U.S. hegemony without bearing corresponding costs and responsibilities have all placed China in the increasingly untenable position of balancing its support of the Third World and its pursuit of national economic interests. More than any other factor, China's participation in the last anti-NIEO stronghold has underscored the growing disjuncture between its espousal of Third World solidarity and its commitment to its own modernization drive.

THE MOTIVES FOR A NEOREALIST WORLD POLICY

Despite all the twists and turns in the post-Mao era, Chinese foreign policy remains dialectical on the central issues of theory and practice. The challenge at home is to harmonize the competing claims of socialist values and national interests. With the extensive and deepening engagement in the vortex of the world political and economic arena, the challenge abroad is to balance the normative requirements of independence and self-reliance with the practical need to maximize external capitalist inputs. In both substance and style, the entente period may have been an exception rather than the norm, as the empirical conservatism of "seeking truth from facts"—a new variation on Deng's oft-quoted statement about cats being good, whether black or white, so long as they caught mice—decisively upset the dialectical equilibrium of Chinese foreign policy. During the readjustment period Beijing has attempted to restore a balance between Maoist radical utopianism and Dengist conservative realism.

Beijing has been groping for a more "legitimate" path in the conduct of Chinese foreign policy. Conceptually and theoretically, the neorealist foreign policy is marked by shifts from a linkage, united-front strategy of all against one (the Soviet Union) to a delinkage, differentiated strategy of opposing hegemony regardless of the source; from an aligned to a nonaligned global posture; from a struggle model of system transformation to a coexistent and cooperative model of system adaptation and reform; and from a realist conception of security anchored in balance-of-power geopolitics to a neorealist functionalist conception of security based upon an incremental cooperative process.

As shown in the preceding analysis, however, practice does not always measure up to theory in Chinese world policy, especially in the domain of economic and development issues. Despite the dialectical balancing, the gap between the professed norm of self-reliance and the actual conduct of the open-door policy is still wide. The independent and nonaligned global posture of neorealism has made Chinese foreign policy more flexible (opportunistic), adaptable, and unpredictable. In light of the changing international situation, neorealism calls for a periodic redefinition of the permissible and the possible for Chinese world policy. Neorealism also requires a dual-track policy. On the one hand, it seeks to minimize systemic constraints as well as normative costs. On the other hand, it seeks to exploit systemic opportunities to maximize practical benefits and payoffs.

China's new global posture of independence, nonentanglement, and self-reliance, *if sustained*, may represent the most significant turning point in the history of PRC foreign policy—a low-profile dual peaceful coexistence and cooperation policy vis-à-vis both superpowers. Both domestic and external factors are clearly involved in shaping this reorientation, but the domestic factors appear to be more important and immediate. Revealingly, only 3 of the 374 pages of the *Selected Works of Deng Xiaoping, 1975–1982* (published in 1983) are concerned with foreign affairs. Foreign policy reorientation *followed* domestic policy reorientation. Hence, Chinese policymakers and scholars have had to look at the forces and trends in the international system through a new neorealist prism and come up with a more congruent definition of the international situation.

Domestic/Societal Factors

Any shift in Chinese foreign policy must be viewed against the backdrop of the Sinocentric tradition of cultural and intellectual self-sufficiency and of China's traumatic experience of dependency under Western semicolonialism (1841–1943) and Soviet semi-imperialism (1949–1960). No semantic magic wand can entirely lift the curse of the Open Door, which the Chinese remember as a U.S. "me-too colonialism" at the turn of the century, disguised and legitimized as the protection of China's political and territorial integrity. To the Chinese, the Open Door is what "U.S. imperialism once foisted on China to secure the same privileges as the other imperialist powers."[45]

By unabashedly declaring the inauguration of the open-door policy and the identity of global perspectives and interests with the capitalist superpower, the successor regime has forced open a Pandora's box containing the unresolved legitimacy crisis. To justify the policies of open-door economics and geopolitical alignment, the Deng regime exaggerated what the United States could do for China's economic and security needs, raising Chinese expectations well beyond what the United States was able or willing to offer. Conversely, the open-door policy also increased U.S. expectations well above what post-Mao China was prepared to give. A downward adjustment of unrealistic expectations was both necessary and inevitable.[46]

Post-Mao China's open-door policy had another, unintended impact. With the open door came not only rising commercialism and consumerism (including luxury contraband, pornography, and a variety of other Western "pollutants") but also rising criticism. At home and abroad, the Chinese leadership was virtually barraged by a cacophony of demands to clarify the status of Maoism and the direction of modernization. A poster on the now defunct Democracy Wall in Beijing captured the dilemma Chinese leaders faced: "What kind of modernization does China hope to realize? The Soviet type, the American type, the Japanese type, the Yugoslavian type . . . on these issues the masses know nothing!"

The official reassessment of Mao Zedong Thought in mid-1981 was the first round of neorealist fine tuning designed to clarify ideological confusion in post-Mao Chinese politics. In correcting the leftist deviationist policy of the "two whatevers" of the continuity period, China tilted too far in the rightist deviationist direction during the entente period, doubting and even denying Mao's historical (revolutionary) role and the scientific value of Mao Zedong Thought. In a state of ideological blindness post-Mao China was throwing out the pragmatic baby (all the great contributions made by Mao) with the utopian bath water (Mao's errors in his later years).

What has emerged during the readjustment period is a "Dengification" of Mao Zedong Thought. The quintessence of Maoism has been redefined in terms of three principles: seeking truth from facts; following the mass line; and maintaining independence. What is most notable here is Deng's selective emphasis and codification of a few principles in the Thought of Mao Zedong. Total de-Maoification was recognized as posing an unnecessary threat to the unity and stability of the successor regime. Post-Mao China, it was reasoned, simply could not survive without the symbolism of Maoism or the imperative of the modernization drive. The post-Mao leadership discovered a middle road between the absolute purity of God (Mao) and the absolute necessity of the Philistine (Deng).

As a result, the latest twist in the dialectics of the modernization drive is a call for a new form of class struggle. The new class struggle is needed to build "socialist spiritual civilization" and to feed the development of material civilization. It is supposed to prevent the imperialists *and* hegemonists from "making every attempt to infiltrate, disrupt and subvert our country politically, economically, ideologically and culturally."[47]

Might contemporary socialist China suffer from the same sort of Marxist "alienation"? Marx conceptualized alienation as economic commodification, which fostered social order and the political pacification of the working class in nineteenth-century capitalist society. The acrimonious debate on "socialist alienation" in contemporary China suggests that the legitimacy crisis has not yet been solved. Of some 600 articles and essays on the contending theories of humanitarianism, human nature, and alienation published between 1978 and 1983,[48] a lengthy theoretical essay entitled "An Inquiry into Some Theoretical Problems of Marxism" by Zhou Yang, Chairman of the China Federation of Literary and Art Circles, was most revealing and controversial. Zhou jolted a sensitive ideological nerve center by arguing that the symptoms of "socialist alienation" (*shehuizhuyi de yihua*) are manifest in all fronts—ideological, political, and economic.[49]

Zhou's article stirred new waves in the Party's rectification campaign against "spiritual pollution." The official challenge to Zhou's socialist alienation thesis has become part and parcel of the attempt to strike a balance between leftist and rightist deviational errors. As a *historical* concept and phenomenon, it is suggested, alienation cannot apply to contemporary socialist China, because three major sources of alienation— private ownership, the system of employed labor, and the antagonistic division of labor—have all been abolished. The socialist alienation thesis mistakenly blurs the fundamental difference between socialism and capitalism.[50]

In the end Zhou had to profess self-criticism: "I was preoccupied with opposing 'Left' errors without giving much thought to the grave influence of bourgeois ideology, which has been seeping into China since the policy of opening to the outside world was implemented."[51] To prevent rectification from moving too fast or too far the campaign has been limited to the "ideological sphere," exempting science, economics, and the rural areas.

In foreign policy, the partial revival of Maoism has been linked with the reassertion of independence and self-reliance. Behind the new campaign for ideological decontamination at home and foreign policy readjustment abroad is the failure of the Dengist reform coalition to fully legitimate and institutionalize the geopolitical alignment policy of the entente period. Writing in *Foreign Policy* under a pseudonym, one PRC scholar reminds readers that powerful domestic forces are pushing Beijing toward an independent foreign policy, neither pro-Washington nor pro-Moscow, and that this is the general foreign policy course that post-Mao China is likely to follow in the years ahead.[52]

External/Systemic Factors

Is there a new global reality that is conditioning and shaping the reorientation of Chinese foreign policy? Or is China simply rediscovering the global reality through a new prism? The latter seems closer to the truth. By changing lenses, the Chinese have redefined global reality. People (and nations) usually define first and perceive second, a cognitive process that tends to be self-fulfilling and self-legitimating.

During the readjustment period, the dominant Chinese "world outlook" (*shijieguan*) was reformulated. From a neorealist world outlook, the international situation takes different colors and shapes.[53] The postwar, U.S.-dominated world order is dying, if not already dead, and a new order is struggling to take its place. The First World is declining and the Third World (and China) is rising, in conformity with the long wave of the world historical process.

Whether there is a united-front antihegemonic struggle or not, the world is already on the trajectory of system transformation from bipolarity to multipolarity owing to the steady and irreversible decline in the hegemonic strength of the superpowers. In support of this transformational view, the Chinese have recently advanced three closely related arguments. First, the balance of economic power in the world political economy began to shift from the First World to the Second and Third

TABLE 8.2

A Chinese View of Hegemonic Decline and Multipolarization Based on Changing Proportions of World GNP, 1970–1990 (percentage)

	1970	1980	1990
United States	26.7	24.4	22.0
Soviet Union	13.2	9.8	8.0
First World Total	*39.9*	*34.2*	*30.0*
Western Europe	25.7	28.2	28.0
Japan	7.4	10.6	13.0
Third World	14.2	14.7	16.0
Second and Third World Total[a]	*47.3*	*53.5*	*57.0*

[a]China and the East European countries are excluded from this total.

Source: Adapted from Xing Shugang, Li Yunhua, and Liu Yingna, "Soviet-American Balance of Power and Its Impact on the International Situation in the 1980s," *Guoji wenti yanjiu* [Journal of International Affairs], No. 1 (1983): 31. The authors base their figures on an unidentified "Western source."

Worlds in the 1970s. As shown in Table 8.2, the combined GNP of the superpowers as a percentage of world GNP declined from 39.9 percent in 1970 to 34.2 percent in 1980, and is projected to further decline to 30.0 percent by 1990. The combined GNP of Western Europe, Japan, and the Third World as a percentage of world GNP rose from 47.3 percent in 1970 to 53.5 percent in 1980, and is projected to rise to 57 percent by 1990. The aggregate economic strength of the Third World alone is still marginal; even after two decades of comparatively rapid growth, the Third World still accounts for less than 15 percent of world GNP.

Second, the U.S.-dominated postwar world economic order, consisting of the production system, the trade system, and the monetary and financial system, is believed to have collapsed. In China's view, three competing economic centers are now emerging in the global political economy: the United States, Western Europe, and Japan.[54] In this analysis, the Third World still remains at the periphery.

Third, the U.S.-Soviet arms race has merely made it easier for Second and Third World countries to resist one superpower with the aid of the other. As the superpowers continue to expand the arms race to maintain their dominance, they merely deepen the contradictions between wishes and abilities, between overseas commitments and economic capabilities. The widening gap between their increasing hegemonic requirements and their decreasing hegemonic responsibilities (e.g., foreign aid) has encouraged separatist tendencies among their allies. As a result, bipolarity and bipolarization, which depend on both intrabloc solidarity and interbloc hostility, are giving way to multipolarity and multipolarization. The multipolarization tendency in the last two decades of this century is projected to establish five or more poles in global geopolitics: the United States, the Soviet Union, Western Europe, Japan, and China and regional powers.[55] The Third World is subsumed under "regional powers," unless, of course, China is regarded as the Third World pole.

Thus, the superpowers remain central to China's assessment of the external/systemic constraints and opportunities impinging on its foreign policy. In this connection, the transition from the entente to the readjustment period coincides with a subtle but significant change in the Chinese image of both superpowers. The image of the Soviet Union as the more irrational, adventurous, and aggressive power no longer prevails in the current Chinese perception. Instead, the global influence of the Soviet Union is seen as having peaked in the mid-to-late 1970s, with a decline in the early 1980s. China has finally awakened from its anti-Soviet obsession to find that in many ways the Soviet entanglement in Afghanistan may have actually enhanced its own security. Moreover, China has become more aware of the growing difficulties the Soviet Union faces at home and abroad: rising domestic consumer expectations and pressures; the lengthening shadow of another succession crisis; increasing ideological isolation in the Non-Aligned Movement; an erosion of economic and political control in Eastern Europe; growing geopolitical losses and frustrations in the Third World (Egypt, Somalia, Ghana, and the Sudan); a crushing annual foreign aid burden of US$10 billion to Cuba, Vietnam, and Afghanistan; a persistent foreign exchange drain of some US$7–8 billion a year for grain imports; and deepening nationalist tendencies in Communist parties around the world.

To top it all, the Soviet Union is now trapped in an expensive and open-ended arms race with an opponent that is much stronger than itself economically and technologically. To China, the Soviet Union increasingly appears as a swollen military superstate, gradually exhausting itself financially and morally on the path to overall decline. As if to confirm this image, the Soviet Union, to the dismay of Western financial lenders, recently confirmed that it was unable and unwilling to back the debt of Cuba, a client state. China does not suggest that the Soviet military threat has dissipated, but it is not as obsessively concerned by that threat as it used to be.

The Chinese perception of U.S. global policy is contradictory. Strategically, China can afford to express disdain for the United States as another superpower on the long cycle of hegemonic decline. However, the United States can greatly help or hinder China's modernization march. Hegemonic decline or not, the United States still has—and often exercises—its veto power in the global political economy. It still holds what post-Mao China regards as the master key to its modernization drive: science and technology, and it still enforces its will through substantial penalties and payoffs.

Ironically, the U.S. response to China's earlier call for a major arms buildup has turned out to be a mixed blessing. The renewed Soviet-U.S. arms race offers a degree of breathing space for China's modernization drive. At the same time, the intensification of superpower arms rivalry poses a clear and present danger to another sine qua non of the modernization drive—a peaceful and stable international environment.

It must be equally unsettling for the post-Mao leadership to realize that the Reagan administration is following China's earlier united-front strategy by subordinating everything—including North-South relations—to the cause of its unrelenting struggle with the Soviet Union. Although China rejects the thesis that a rising tide of recovery and revitalization in the U.S. economy would lift all boats in the global political economy, it has also bewailed the steady decline in U.S. economic aid, especially to multilateral financial institutions such as the IDA. The Reagan administration is criticized for increasing bilateral aid while decreasing multilateral aid, for concentrating bilateral aid on a few states regarded as critical to U.S. geopolitical interests, and for increasing military assistance and reducing economic aid.[56] In short, the United States is criticized for dominating the global political economy without assuming any corresponding obligations.

Clearly, post-Mao Chinese world policy faces a dilemma in accommodating external/systemic constraints. The global dominance system defines the permissible and the possible for those on the periphery and semiperiphery (including China) and imposes heavy penalties upon dissenters. The delinkage strategy of self-reliance is condemned in an interdependent world as an act of self-immolation.

Yet to fully embrace the global dominance system is ideologically unacceptable and politically risky. China's late entry into the global political economy at a time of declining payoffs (preferential aid, loans, and trade) and rising penalties (tariff and nontariff barriers) has highlighted the limits of the Trilateral interdependence model. However, Beijing cannot completely disengage from this game either. China's current strategy is to compete with other Third World nouveaux riches on an equal footing and beat them at their own game by emulating their strengths in export strategy while avoiding their mistakes in the management of domestic unrest and heavy external debts.

Third World dominance of the politics of collective legitimation and delegitimation is important to China's normative world policy but not essential to China's security and development needs. The use of normative concepts and principles to legitimize and enhance its symbolic capability in world politics has been moderated. China's full entry into the world economy has accentuated Sino–Third World competition for capitalist investment, credit, technology, and markets. The call for South-South cooperation is designed to blunt and disguise the competitive edge of Sino–Third World relations.

As shown by China's entry into the MFA but not the parent body, GATT, the neorealist world policy has sliced global reality into individual pieces for a more differentiated, case-by-case approach. The neorealist world policy has not fully resumed the Maoist revisionist challenge of seeking new rules, new values, and new norms as part of an overall struggle of the Third World for "redistributive justice." Instead, China has become more selective in accepting the existing rules, structures, and processes of the present international order. Beijing has diversified its bets and stakes in the global political economy. Above all, post-Mao China has renewed its Maoist dialectics of synthesizing two contradictory forces (theory and practice, norms and interests), seeking the best of both worlds.

FUTURE PROSPECTS AND DIRECTIONS

How long will China remain committed to its current neorealist policy? The projected image of Chinese foreign policy as one of principled constancy and continuity notwithstanding, specific policies involving a broad array of issues and global actors have changed frequently and unpredictably. Chinese foreign policy readjustment and reorientation is most likely to occur periodically, say on a five-year cycle. This cycle more or less corresponds to the periodicity of domestic and world politics (e.g., U.S. presidential elections, Chinese Party congresses, the election of the UN secretary-general, nonaligned summit conferences, UNCTAD, and five-year economic plans).

The future stability of the neorealist policy depends upon how well it is accepted and institutionalized at home, and on its success in maximizing systemic opportunities and payoffs and minimizing systemic constraints and penalties. By the end of the current five-year cycle (mid-1986) the success or failure of this policy can be assessed with greater confidence. The early signs are mixed. Despite the centrist balancing act to rectify both leftist and rightist errors, persistent intraelite strife hangs over Chinese foreign policy like the sword over Damocles.[57]

More positively, the national economies of China and India stand out as exceptions in having successfully weathered the adverse systemic impact of the recent global recession.[58] China has overcome the world trade recession better than most countries, emerging as a major Third World exporter. The value of foreign trade as a proportion of China's gross domestic product (GDP) has doubled from 8 percent in 1977 to over 16 percent in 1981.[59] China's foreign trade deficit of US$1.1 billion in 1978 turned into a US$1 billion foreign trade surplus in 1983. Only six other Third World countries had exports in 1982 of more than US$20 billion—Saudi Arabia, Hong Kong, South Korea, Singapore, Brazil, and Mexico. Against the backdrop of the Third World debt crisis (approaching US$700 billion in 1983), Beijing's foreign exchange reserves increased from US$2.6 billion in 1979 to US$13.2 billion in 1983. This, along with China's avoidance of large debts, lends credibility to the Chinese assertion that the open door is supplementary to self-reliance.

A crucial question remains for those concerned about the shape of things to come in international life. With the steady rise in China's international status and capability, will it become more or less faithful to its repeated pledge never to act like a superpower? Once every five years, promised Hu Yaobang in a recent interview with Taisuke Yamaguchi, president of *Mainichi shimbun* (Tokyo), China will hold a people's congress and a Party congress to reiterate its antihegemony policy and to disclaim any superpower ambition.[60] Only time will tell whether post-Mao China can ultimately live up to this promise. All we can say for now is that in contrast with the entente period (marred by China's invasion of Vietnam), the neorealist foreign policy of the readjustment period has perceptibly shifted post-Mao China toward a position of greater normative propriety and behavioral prudence.

NOTES

I would like to thank William Feeney, Harry Harding, Donald Klein, Steven I. Levine, and Allen S. Whiting for their helpful comments on an earlier draft of this chapter.

1. For an excellent and thoroughgoing analysis of China's dual status, see Kim Woodard, *The International Energy Relations of China* (Stanford, Calif.: Stanford University Press, 1980).

2. Ruth Leger Sivard, *World Military and Social Expenditures 1983* (Washington, D.C.: World Priorities, 1983), p. 38.

3. See *Beijing Review* [hereafter cited as *BR*], No. 1 (January 5, 1981):12, and No. 10 (March 9, 1981):3.

4. For this line of analysis by Indian specialists on Chinese foreign policy, see V. P. Dutt, ed., *China: The Post-Mao View* (New Delhi: Allied Publishers, 1981).

5. *Selected Works of Mao Tse-Tung*, Vol. 4 (Peking: Foreign Languages Press, 1961), p. 415; emphasis added.

6. For a detailed analysis of the evolution of Mao's image of contradictions in the international system, see Samuel S. Kim, *China, the United Nations, and World Order* (Princeton, N.J.: Princeton University Press, 1979), pp. 73–82.

7. See *Renmin ribao* [People's daily, hereafter cited as *RMRB*], November 1, 1977, pp. 1–6; English trans. in *Peking Review*, No. 45 (November 4, 1977):10–41.

8. UN Doc. A/32/PV.13 (29 September 1977), p. 56.

9. For a complete English text of the speech, see UN Doc. A/34/PV.11 (27 September 1979), pp. 63–92; the full Chinese text can be found in *RMRB*, September 29, 1979, pp. 5–6. Emphasis added.

10. See UN Doc. A/35/PV.9 (25 September 1980), pp. 26–46.

11. "On Questions of Party History," *BR*, No. 27 (July 6, 1981):24, 29. This 30,000-word document deals almost exclusively with domestic politics, exempting the history of China's foreign relations from public criticism.

12. Ibid., p. 34.

13. Cited in Wang Qi, "Inheriting and Developing Mao Zedong Thought," *BR*, No. 52 (December 26, 1983):20.

14. See Shen Yi, "China Belongs Forever to the Third World," *BR*, No. 39 (September 28, 1981):23; Mu Youlin, "Opposing Hegemonism," *BR*, No. 32 (August 9, 1982):3; and Wang, "Inheriting and Developing Mao Zedong Thought," p. 21.

15. For a more detailed analysis of NIEO politics, see Samuel S. Kim, *The Quest for a Just World Order* (Boulder, Colo.: Westview Press, 1984), Ch. 5, pp. 135–194.

16. This point is based on a qualitative content analysis of the articles published in *Hongqi* [Red flag] and *Beijing Review* between January 1977 and December 1981 (corresponding roughly to the entente period). See Friedrich W. Wu, "Socialist Self-Reliant Development Within the Capitalist World-Economy: The Chinese View in the Post-Mao Era," *Global Perspectives* 1 (Spring 1983):8–24. According to my own account, the number of articles bearing the NIEO title in the *Renmin ribao* also dropped from twenty-one in 1977 to seven in 1978.

17. Hu Yaobang made his point clear in his interview with the Italian Communist Party daily *L'Unità*. See Foreign Broadcast Information Service, Daily Report, China [hereafter cited as FBIS-China], August 30, 1983, p. A2. For the quote, see *BR*, No. 17 (April 26, 1982):8.

18. For a Chinese assessment of NIEO politics, see Tan Feng, "The Struggle for the Establishment of a New International Economic Order," *RMRB*, April 1, 1983, p. 7.

19. See Xu Mei, "South-South Co-operation," *BR*, No. 26 (June 28, 1982):10–13, 15; Premier Zhao Ziyang's speech at the Beijing South-South Conference in *RMRB*, April 5, 1983, pp. 1, 4; and You Zhongwen and Zhen Bingxi, "The Third World's Debt Problem and Its Impact," *Guoji wenti yanjiu* [Journal of international studies], No. 3 (1983):50–58.

20. *BR*, No. 38 (September 21, 1981):4.

21. *RMRB*, September 29, 1983, p. 4. The Five Principles were codified in the 1982 Constitution of the People's Republic of China, and a variant set of four principles—independence, full equality, mutual respect, and noninterference in each other's internal affairs—were put forward by Hu Yaobang in 1982 as the only acceptable basis for interparty relations.

22. For a more detailed analysis and documentation, see my *China, the United Nations, and World Order*, pp. 227–229.

23. FBIS-China, October 21, 1982, pp. A1–2; emphasis added.

24. See "Co-Chairman's Summary of Conclusions," in a special document section of *BR*, No. 16 (April 18, 1983):iii–viii; quote in the text at p. viii.

25. See Commentator, "The Current Danger of War and the Defense of World Peace," *Hongqi*, No. 11 (1979):53–58; and Chen Youwei, "Why Recall the Year 1939?" *RMRB*, July 16, 1980, p. 7. For further analysis of the Chinese global policy during the entente period, see my "Wither Post-Mao Chinese Global Policy?" *International Organization* 35 (Summer 1981):433–465.

26. For this figure, see Commentator, "The Correct Path Toward Realizing Nuclear Disarmament," *RMRB*, November 30, 1983, p. 6.

27. "Modernization of National Defense and Building of People's Army—Interview with Yu Qiuli," *BR*, No. 31 (August 1, 1983):15.

28. A public declaration to this effect was made by Ambassador Wang Shu at the twenty-seventh annual conference of IAEA on October 11, 1983. During his state visit to the United States, Premier Zhao Ziyang also stated: "We do not advocate or encourage nuclear proliferation. We do not engage in nuclear proliferation ourselves, nor do we help other countries develop nuclear weapons." Cited in the *New York Times*, January 13, 1984, p. A6.

29. For the leak of this secret arrangement, see Murrey Marder, "Monitoring: Not-So-Secret Secret," *Washington Post*, June 19, 1981.

30. Harry Harding, "China and the Third World: From Revolution to Containment," in Richard H. Solomon, ed., *The China Factor: Sino-American Relations and the Global Scene* (Englewood Cliffs, N.J.: Prentice-Hall, 1981), p. 291; emphasis in original.

31. See *RMRB* editorial, January 17, 1982, p. 1; Li Dai, "Independence and Our Country's Foreign Relations," *Shijie zhishi* [World knowledge], No. 19 (October 1, 1981):2–4.

32. Chen Muhua, "Developing Trade with Other Third World Countries," *BR*, No. 38 (September 19, 1983):15–18.

33. For details, see U.S. Central Intelligence Agency, *China: International Trade, Third Quarter, 1982*, EA CIT 83-001 (March 1983).

34. *Development Forum* 10 (March 1982):8.

35. *New York Times*, December 25, 1983, p. 6F; January 9, 1984, pp. 1, D2.

36. Editorial, "On the Questions Concerning Our Country's Foreign Economic Relations," *Hongqi*, No. 8 (April 16, 1982):2–10.

37. See Zhang Zongji, "China's Economy: Achievements in 1983," *BR*, No. 8 (February 20, 1984):17.

38. Cao Guanlin, "Construction Contracting and Labour Co-operation Abroad," *BR*, No. 52 (December 26, 1983):27–29.

39. Harding, "China and the Third World," p. 274.

40. FBIS-China, September 26, 1983, p. A2.

41. Ibid.

42. For a detailed analysis of Chinese behavior in the World Bank Group, see William Feeney, Chapter 11 in this volume.

43. *BR*, No. 40 (October 4, 1982):14.

44. *New York Times*, January 15, 1984, p. 13.

45. *Hanyin cidian* [The Chinese-English dictionary] (Beijing: Shangwu yinshuguan, 1978), p. 464. This dictionary was prepared during the Maoist period.

46. In an essay completed before the onset of the readjustment period, though published in early 1982, I made a conditional prediction about the coming of another rectification campaign. This prediction came true a few years earlier than I had anticipated. I wrote: "Unless the Chinese expectations aroused by Deng's overselling of American payoffs are met by about the mid-1980s, Deng or his chosen successors could easily encounter another rectification campaign. The Maoist quest for an egalitarian social order is dormant but not dead. It is waiting for an opportune historical moment for a comeback." See Samuel S. Kim, "The Sino-American Collaboration and Cold War II," *Journal of Peace Research* 19, 1 (1982):11–20; quote at p. 19.

47. Zhou Yan, "On China's Current Class Struggle," *BR*, No. 33 (August 16, 1982):17–19; quote at p. 18.

48. See Xing Bensi, "The Alienation Issue and Spiritual Pollution,'" *RMRB*, November 5, 1983, p. 5.

49. Zhou Yang, "An Inquiry into Some Theoretical Problems of Marxism," *RMRB*, March 16, 1983, p. 4.

50. For a scholarly rebuttal of the socialist alienation thesis following the latest party line, see Xing Bensi, "The Alienation Issue and Spiritual Pollution," *RMRB*, November 5, 1983, p. 5; Wei Jianlin, "Socialist Practice and the So-Called 'Socialist Alienation,'" *RMRB*, November 13, 1983, p. 5.

51. *BR*, No. 40 (December 12, 1983):12.

52. Edmund Lee [pseud.], "Beijing's Balancing Act," *Foreign Policy*, No. 51 (Summer 1983):28.

53. See *Guoji xingshi nianjian 1982* [Yearbook of international affairs, 1982] (Shanghai: Zhongguo dabaikequanshu, 1982) and *Guoji xingshi nianjian 1983* (Shanghai: Zhongguo dabaikequanshe, 1983).

54. Huan Xiang, "Economic Trend of Western Capitalist Countries," *BR*, No. 13 (March 29, 1982):14.

55. Zong He, "Changes and Developing Trends in the International Situation," *Shijie zhishi*, No. 11 (1983):5.

56. Zhang Ruizhuang, "Ronald Reagan's North-South Policy," *BR*, No. 34 (August 22, 1983):19.

57. For an acknowledgment and discussion of the factionalism problem, see *RMRB*, November 8, 1983, p. 5.

58. See World Bank, *World Development Report 1982* (New York: Oxford University Press for the World Bank, 1982), p. 7, and *World Development Report 1983* (New York: Oxford University Press for the World Bank, 1983), p. 2.

59. Michael Yahuda, *Towards the End of Isolationism: China's Foreign Policy After Mao* (New York: St. Martin's Press, 1983), p. 143.

60. *RMRB*, October 10, 1983, p. 4.

Part 3
Policies and Issues

CHAPTER 9

SOLDIERS AND STATESMEN IN CONFLICT: CHINESE DEFENSE AND FOREIGN POLICIES IN THE 1980s

Paul H. B. Godwin

INTRODUCTION

This chapter will analyze the relationship between Chinese defense and foreign policies in order to determine the role the defense establishment is expected to fulfill in achieving Chinese security objectives in the 1980s. The focus on defense and foreign policies rather than security policy is necessary because the concepts of security, national security, and security policy are vague and subject to widely differing interpretations.[1] Nevertheless, security objectives are established and broadly defined. They are the ultimate purpose behind both defense and foreign policies.

Because security objectives are usually set in broad terms, they can become a source of disagreement between defense and foreign policy strategists.[2] Although these strategists are charged with pursuing presumably common objectives, their different training and experience in dealing with external powers leads them to view security objectives quite differently. Soldiers are primarily concerned with military coercion. They tend to be more sensitive to discrete components of the military "balance" and to estimate an adversary's capabilities within quite specific scenarios. Soldiers are often not as sensitive to the relatively abstract terms within which foreign policy is formulated and its objectives defined. Foreign policy strategists are primarily concerned with the more abstract political components of security objectives. They think and plan in terms related to influencing behavior and manipulating global trends.

It should not be surprising, therefore, that soldiers and politicians differ over the relative importance of military force and political strategies in influencing the behavior of adversaries. This divergence of views is given greater importance because foreign policy usually sets the parameters of defense policy; defense policy does not often set the parameters of foreign policy. China is no exception to this rule.

Lest the above argument be viewed as too simplistic an interpretation of the sources of disagreement over foreign policy, I should emphasize that this chapter focuses on the relationship between defense and foreign policy, not on foreign policy formulation. Thomas Gottlieb[3] and Kenneth Lieberthal,[4] among others, have carefully detailed the complexity of factions and coalition formation in Beijing's internal disputes over foreign policy. The dichotomy I suggest is not intended to override the complexity of factional foreign policy disputes, but simply to focus on a potentially divisive issue that arises once foreign policy has been determined.

CHINA'S USE OF FORCE: DETERRENCE AND COERCIVE DIPLOMACY

The Chinese armed forces have been used with some frequency to achieve Beijing's foreign policy objectives, and the Chinese People's Liberation Army (PLA) has had considerable experience with military operations designed to achieve specific and limited political objectives.[5] A continuing problem facing the PLA when planning these military operations is that its military capabilities have been significantly lower than those of its major adversaries. Furthermore, the United States and the USSR have been the major sources of political, economic, and military assistance for the lesser powers Beijing has sought to coerce. This situation has required China to seek a careful balance between the risks involved in coercion and the gains to be made if the venture is successful.

Because China has been willing to use coercion in spite of its overall military weakness, the psychological or "demonstration" effect has been greater than the actual military balance might otherwise have permitted. Tactically, the Chinese have sought to offset the implications of the overall military balance by achieving battlefield superiority whenever possible. Nonetheless, Beijing has not shrunk from facing either the United States or the USSR when convinced that military coercion was necessary. China's willingness to use force in Korea influenced U.S. decisions in conducting the war against North Vietnam,[6] and China's 1979 incursion into Vietnam may even now influence Hanoi's policies toward Bangkok.

China's restraint in using military force and its consistent attempts to fit the level of force to the political objectives sought indicate that Beijing sees a major role of the defense establishment as supporting strategies of *coercive diplomacy*. Coercive diplomacy requires that military force be used in "an exemplary, demonstrative manner, in discrete and controlled increments, to induce the opponent to review his calculations and agree to a mutually acceptable termination of the conflict."[7] Even so, there have been significant differences among the major examples of China's use of coercive diplomacy. Strategies of deterrence have not always been successful, and Beijing has had to shift to the more forceful end of the coercive diplomacy spectrum.[8]

The Korean War and the expansion of U.S. military involvement in Vietnam were probably seen by Beijing as the most serious threats to Chinese security until the Soviet buildup along the Sino-Soviet border. In both conflicts there was the distinct possibility that neighboring Communist states would be eliminated, placing U.S. client states directly on China's borders. Beijing's objective was to preserve North Korea and North Vietnam. China was unable to deter an invasion of North Korea by its threats to enter the war; the Chinese had to cross the border to persuade the United States and the United Nations to abandon the objective of unifying the Korean peninsula. During the Vietnam War, Beijing's deterrence strategy was more successful: Even though the United States used its airpower over the north, the Democratic Republic of Vietnam was never invaded by the ground forces of either the United States or the Republic of Vietnam.

During the Taiwan crises (1954–1955, 1958, 1962)[9] the perceived threat was a potential invasion from the island, supported by the United States. Beijing sought to demonstrate the gravity with which it viewed the emerging situation and to convey to the United States the dangers inherent in supporting any invasion plans the Republic of China might have. Carefully controlled force seemed designed to convince the United States to restrain Chiang Kai-shek and restrict the conflict to diplomatic processes. These efforts were successful largely because the PRC's actions supported what was in fact already Washington's policy.

The Sino-Indian Border War and the PLA's invasion of Vietnam in 1979 present quite different issues from those involved in the Korea, Vietnam (1964–1968), or Taiwan crises. Neither conflict posed a major threat to China's territorial integrity. The border war with India was fought after diplomatic efforts and threats of military coercion failed to deter New Delhi from placing troops in disputed territory or to persuade the Indians to withdraw them once they were in place. As in Korea, China compelled its adversary to change its policy by defeating New Delhi's forces and forcing them to retreat to uncontested territory. The 1979 invasion of Vietnam was due not to a major threat to Chinese territory or a boundary dispute, but to the perceived threat to China's image as a military power. A client state of the USSR, in Beijing's eyes, had defeated China's client government in Kampuchea. China believed it had to demonstrate that Soviet forces deployed along its northern borders had not rendered Beijing militarily impotent. As with India in 1962, there was no strategic requirement to defeat Hanoi, therefore a limited punitive expedition was all that was required to demonstrate China's willingness to use force.

Nevertheless, the 1979 invasion differed significantly from the Indian case. In 1962 China could not deter India, therefore it had to use force to compel a policy change. In 1979, Beijing could neither deter Vietnam from invading Kampuchea, nor could it compel Hanoi to withdraw. China could only use its troops to "punish" Hanoi. Within the narrow perspective of Sino-Vietnamese relations, China's armed forces had only limited utility.

The militarization of the Sino-Soviet dispute raised quite different issues for the Chinese leadership to consider. Deterrence took on a new meaning when a military superpower was poised aggressively along China's longest border. What Beijing had fought so hard to avoid in Korea and had successfully deterred in Vietnam had come to pass. It was of little comfort that the USSR was a Marxist-Leninist state—even though the Chinese Communist Party denied the legitimacy of the Soviet claim. In the late 1960s, China's military weakness demanded a critical review of Beijing's defense and foreign policies.[10] The need to deter the USSR (coercion was out of the question) ultimately caused Beijing to reject the policies that had left China in self-imposed isolation, weak and vulnerable. Rapprochement with the United States led ultimately to Beijing's sponsorship of a loose coalition of states opposed to the "hegemonistic" goals of the USSR. The process of shifting from rapprochement with the United States to a global coalition was not without its own divisive disputes,[11] but in 1979 China had essentially aligned itself with the United States in global competition with the USSR. Beijing's military weakness, itself a reflection of China's failure to develop its technological and industrial base, had compelled China to align itself with the United States.

In its search to deter the USSR, Beijing recognized the limits of its own capabilities. The security objective it sought could not be achieved within its past practices of coercive diplomacy. Beijing's analyses of the path to security—seen primarily as constraining Soviet power—became more complex. As they did so, the role of the United States in Chinese foreign policy shifted once again.

CHINESE FOREIGN POLICY IN TRANSITION

Beijing's willingness to enter into "consultations" with Moscow in the fall of 1982 is part of a distinct tactical change in Chinese foreign policy. For much of the past decade China has leaned toward the United States and the Western powers in an effort to block what it sees as the predatory objectives of Soviet global strategy. Eventually, China sought to participate in an "antihegemonistic" front based upon the United States as "the best qualified country" to challenge Soviet objectives.[12]

By 1981, even while the advantages of this strategy were being proclaimed by the Chinese press, Beijing had become sensitive to charges that China was dependent upon the United States for its security against the USSR,[13] and that its links with the United States and the Western powers had undermined its commitment to the Third World.[14] Over the past two years it has become evident that these charges entailed political costs the Chinese are unwilling to pay in order to sustain their close ties with the United States. The dissension between Beijing and Washington created by U.S. arms sales to Taiwan and the problems associated with technology transfers and trade restrictions exacerbated the growing suspicion in Beijing that China's relations with the United States were becoming increasingly burdensome and counterproductive. Beijing now believes that its relations with both the United States and the USSR need to be modified.

China has restructured its relationship with Moscow and Washington by seeking to reduce the level of tension with the USSR and by distancing itself from the United States. Under the rubric of an "independent foreign policy," Beijing now classifies the United States as a hegemonic power along with the Soviet Union and regularly catalogues its differences with Washington.[15] These attacks on U.S. policy undermined Beijing's earlier analyses, notable for their explicit statements of the common interests it shared with the United States in opposing the global expansionism of the USSR.[16] Beijing now charges that Moscow and Washington are competing hegemonists.

This concept of superpower competition has been integrated into a revised interpretation of the dynamics of global politics. According to this interpretation, in the 1980s and 1990s the influence of the United States and the USSR will continue to decline, and the trend toward multipolarity will become stronger. Competition for spheres of influence will weaken the superpowers, but the balance of power between them will remain unchanged. The importance of their economies to the world will also continue to decrease as those of Western Europe, Japan, and the Third World become stronger. With this increasing economic strength will come greater military capabilities. These increased capabilities will permit greater resistance to the hegemonistic goals of the superpowers, both in the Third World and among the allies of the superpowers.[17]

This pattern of multipolarity, however, has its own dangers. Whereas the unchanging balance of power between the Soviet Union and the United States will reduce the probability of a world war, the growing military capabilities of lesser powers will increase the incidence of local wars. These wars will flare up not only because individual countries will be more capable of determining their own goals without reference to the superpowers, but also because competition for spheres of influence between the United States and the Soviet Union will lead to their continuing interference in the affairs of other countries.[18]

By opposing both the USSR and the United States on selected issues, Beijing's revised foreign policy implies a selective nonalignment. Beijing now believes it can engage both Washington and Moscow in either dialogue or confrontation—whichever posture fits its purposes. It may also pursue policies parallel with either Moscow or Washington when that fulfills Beijing's purposes. Maneuvering space and flexibility may therefore be improved by a judicious selection of issues with which to confront or support the positions of either of the global military and political powers.

There is, however, an element of optimism in these revised analyses of the future patterns of international politics. Specific military security issues are not discussed in these evaluations, but they are areas of obvious concern to Beijing. In its consultations with Moscow, Beijing insists that progress in Sino-Soviet normalization can be achieved only if the USSR reduces its force levels deployed along the northern borders of China, including those in the Mongolian People's Republic; withdraws its occupying forces from Afghanistan; and ceases its support for Vietnamese aggression in Southeast Asia. Yet there is no plausible military action China can take that would compel either the USSR or Vietnam to change their policies. In terms of direct military confrontation, the gap between Chinese and Soviet military capabilities along the Sino-Soviet border may have widened rather than narrowed over the past decade.[19] In the south, improvements in Hanoi's defensive positions along its border with China[20] would make a second expedition into Vietnam a far more difficult undertaking than the first.

Within this context, China's insistence that the USSR change its military posture in the north, withdraw from Afghanistan, and curtail its support for Vietnam must be seen as diplomatic pressure designed to increase the political cost to Moscow of sustaining its current policies. Beyond giving assistance to the guerrilla forces operating in Afghanistan and Kampuchea, militarily there is little that Beijing can do.

Nonetheless, China's interpretation of the constraints on Soviet power has changed little since 1980. At that time, Beijing was arguing that the military balance in both Europe and Asia had created a stalemate in the global situation, leaving only the Gulf/Indian Ocean area open to possible Soviet aggression. Even here, Chinese strategists argued that the Soviet invasion of Afghanistan had verified China's interpretation of the Soviet threat and that this blatant projection of military force had alerted the world to the true nature of Soviet aggression.[21]

China's analysis of the global strategic situation enabled Beijing to argue that the USSR was bogged down by its global military commitments. Vietnam, the "small hegemonist" and "Asia's Cuba," was in similar straits, with its puppet in Phnom Penh unrecognized by the United Nations and its troops engaged in an unwinnable guerrilla war.

China's optimistic interpretation of the constraints on Soviet power is not new. What is new is the assertion that these restraints will continue into the 1990s and that the USSR will be unable to break its military stalemate with the United States. The USSR will remain isolated by its threatening foreign policies, weakened by its internal problems and its deteriorating relations with Eastern Europe, and subject to a debilitating global conflict with the United States. The United States faces similar problems, but does not present a military threat to China, although Washington's continuing arms sales to Taiwan are viewed as "meddling in China's internal affairs." China's isolation from military threats, Beijing now argues, is assured by trends in global politics that will remain in force through the 1990s. This interpretation permits Beijing to de-emphasize the military component of its foreign policy and focus on political strategies that are consonant with the enduring trends of world politics.

DEFENSE AND FOREIGN POLICIES: A CLASSICAL CONFLICT?

Beijing's optimistic view of China's security environment supports current military modernization policies, which continue to place the defense sector of the economy quite low in investment priorities. As in the recent past, both the optimistic interpretation of China's international environment and the investment priorities it supports continue to be challenged, most recently in the Communist Party's principal journal, *Hongqi.* One essay contrasted the distinction between domestic and foreign affairs by arguing that whereas China could control its domestic environment and settle on policies designed to modernize its society, "international affairs are not determined exclusively by us."[22] The essay describes the immediate international environment, in which the USSR still presses on China's northern borders, has occupied China's "neighbor" Afghanistan, and continues to support Vietnam's expansionist policies in Southeast Asia. Thus "China's security is seriously threatened."[23]

Within this environment, author Shao Huaze maintains that as the national economy improves, "national defense should be supplied with increasingly better material conditions and with even better weapons and equipment which it needs."[24] Zhang Aiping, the newly appointed defense minister, has recently raised similar concerns. He insists that in order to "defend" China's domestic construction programs, "in addition to carrying out necessary political and diplomatic struggles we must build a powerful defense behind us. The stronger our national defense, the bigger the guarantee for our peaceful construction and the possibility of suspending and preventing war."[25] Although, like Shao, Zhang expresses support for current policies, he states that "if the proportion of spending on national defense is too small and we miss our opportunity (to strengthen national defense in time of peace), we will be put in a passive role if an unexpected event occurs and our losses will be inestimable."[26]

Neither essay challenges current policy directly, and Zhang Aiping is quite specific in his opposition to modernizing the armed forces with foreign weapons. It would be too expensive; it would make China dependent upon foreign sources; and it would ultimately be self-defeating, because foreign suppliers will not sell China the very latest military technology.[27] Both essays do, however, demonstrate serious concern that the current interpretation of the international environment is too optimistic. As Shao Huaze put the problem: "We must guard against the misunderstanding among some comrades who seem to think that national defense construction is no longer important. Our construction must as far as possible strive for a peaceful international environment. However, we cannot, because of a peaceful life, adopt the attitude of lowering our guard and slacking our vigilance."[28] Both authors argue that a strong military capability is essential for a successful foreign policy and that the international environment is difficult to predict and control.

It is evident that issues of defense and foreign policy remain divisive in China, as they do elsewhere. One major cause of disagreement between defense and foreign policy establishments is common to all security policies. Foreign policies are usually couched in abstract terms; defense policy, seen through the eyes of soldiers, is viewed in concrete terms.[29] Foreign policy strategists can think of armed force being used to deter or even compel an adversary, whereas the soldier is trained to think in terms of planning, organizing, and employing military forces. The soldier must think in quite precise terms in order to specify to the command structure the military objectives and the forces available for employment.[30] In short, the soldier prefers to defeat, not "influence," an adversary. As Zhang Aiping has noted: "The principle of war is to achieve the greatest victory at the smallest cost."[31]

The issue raised by these essays, however, goes beyond the need to define the role of the military establishment and the armed forces in foreign policy in more precise terms than foreign policy establishments usually do. Shao directly challenges the underlying optimism upon which Beijing's revised foreign policy is based: "World peace can be maintained provided the people of the world are truly united and struggle resolutely against hegemonism and expansionism of all kinds. However, possibility is not reality."[32]

Current Chinese evaluations of the constraints on Soviet power may well be too optimistic, as Jonathan Pollack has suggested.[33] The objections raised by members of the defense establishment may be based upon the largely unstated argument that there have been no major changes in the global strategic environment that led to China's support for an antihegemonistic coalition in the late 1970s. In the Asian context, which is the most direct source of threats to the People's Republic, U.S.-Soviet rivalry and long-term Soviet interests will require a continuing and growing Soviet military presence. Consequently, it is extremely unlikely that there will be a dramatic drop in Soviet military deployments in the foreseeable future. China's talks with the USSR may well reduce the atmospherics of their disagreements, but the strategic logic that drove the USSR to its present policies remains in force. A major reorientation of Soviet objectives in Asia and its global strategy does not seem plausible, yet without it the core of discord between Beijing and Moscow will remain.

Looking at China's current defense posture, there is little to indicate that any major changes have occurred or will occur in the near future. Its central feature remains the creation of a stable deterrent against a massive Soviet attack across China's northern borders, especially into Manchuria. The core of this deterrent is now formed by China's nuclear weapons. Although few in number and of questionable reliability and accuracy, they threaten the USSR with a punitive retaliatory strike. Current testing programs indicate that China's nuclear forces will become more numerous, better protected, and more accurate over the coming years. The testing of a solid-fuel ballistic missile launched from a submerged submarine (SLBM);[34] the reported launching of a nuclear-powered ballistic missile submarine (SSBN);[35] the launch of three earth satellites from a single booster;[36] and the initial deployment of full-range intercontinental ballistic missiles (ICBM)[37] all raise serious problems for Soviet defense planners. In the coming years a disarming first strike will become ever more difficult for the Soviets to execute, and a Chinese second strike will become ever more probable.

Beijing's nuclear deterrent is backed by large ground and air forces, admittedly armed with outdated equipment, whose basic strategy is designed around a more modern version of protracted war. The PLA still substitutes mass for mobility and lethality even as these forces are gradually modernized. Incapable of blocking a determined Soviet attack, the PLA plan would be to conduct a strategy of attrition warfare.

The essence of China's deterrent posture is to deny Soviet forces the opportunity to gain the quick military victory they are designed to achieve. The combined capabilities of the nuclear and conventional forces will, the Chinese believe, raise the potential cost of an attack to the point that it will outweigh any possible Soviet gains. The core of China's military deterrent has now shifted to its nuclear forces, but the threat of a protracted conventional war remains a formidable component of the Chinese strategy.[38]

Although Beijing's confidence in its deterrent posture seems established, the military hierarchy is less certain of the PLA's capability to conduct conventional military operations. The seventeen-day war with Vietnam raised serious questions about the PLA's capability to conduct such operations within the confines of coercive diplomacy. Following the ambiguous results of China's punitive expedition across the border, the military hierarchy has reported extensive efforts to improve the armed forces' capabilities in combined arms operations, to increase their logistical and combat support proficiency, and to improve the quality of the officer corps.[39] If these reports are accepted at face value, the time and effort now devoted to training and professional military education is designed to build a more effective combat force without heavy investment in new weapon systems and battlefield equipment. The long-term need for training and for the reorganization of the PLA's military system to make it both more efficient and competent is unquestionable. The short-term cost of making do with equipment based upon designs of the 1950s and 1960s—suitable for clear air and easily identified targets—is what has the defense establishment concerned.

The defense establishment could well agree that deterrence against the USSR, except under extreme conditions, has been achieved. However, the conventional forces, no matter how capable they may be of fighting a defensive protracted war of attrition, are seriously deficient in their ability to conduct offensive operations even limited distances across China's borders. This was the lesson the military hierarchy learned from their war with Vietnam. The PLA may now be less capable of successfully supporting a strategy of coercive diplomacy than at any time since 1950. It therefore faces the 1980s best prepared for the least probable war. Presenting a reliable military deterrent against the USSR is no mean achievement, but within the defense establishment China's military options are seen as extremely constrained.

It is possible that the military hierarchy is now questioning its deterrent capability against the USSR as the technology of contemporary conventional weapons makes them more lethal. Even as China focuses its deterrent capabilities on nuclear weapons, Chinese interpretations of Soviet military strategy are beginning to stress that the USSR is preparing for victory with the use of conventional arms. Analysts suggest that the Soviets now plan to use their "superiority in conventional weapons to gain the initiative in the war and to even win the war before the enemy has made the decision to use nuclear weapons."[40] If some members of the defense establishment blame the poverty of the conventional forces on the cost of the nuclear weapons program, resource allocation between nuclear and conventional forces could divide the military hierarchy. The focus on improving the capabilities of the conventional forces may therefore extend beyond the need to improve offensive operations in coercive diplomacy to basic issues of defense against the USSR in a nonnuclear war.

DEFENSE AND FOREIGN POLICIES IN THE 1980s

Even though members of the defense establishment are questioning the underlying optimism of China's current foreign policy, Soviet-American rivalry continues to provide China with a tacit security umbrella. The United States does not present a military threat to China, and its defense policies are designed to constrain the USSR's use of military power. Beijing may not be especially confident that the United States will be firm in opposing the USSR, or that its strategies will always be successful,[41] but Washington's opposition to Moscow and the defense strategies it adopts to contain and frustrate Soviet objectives will continue to serve China as they did in the 1970s.

U.S. defense policy complements Beijing's efforts to create a credible deterrent against the USSR. The risk of a nuclear exchange and a protracted conventional war make a Soviet attack on China extremely unlikely. With NATO forces in the west, U.S. deployments in the east, and China preparing for both nuclear and conventional warfare, Moscow's defense planning remains extremely complicated. A major war with China would seriously erode the USSR's capabilities against the United States and its NATO allies, and would require an extreme escalation of Sino-Soviet tensions before a war would be worth the risk. China's foreign policy strategists believe they can safely assume not only that U.S. defense policy will continue to emphasize the need to block Soviet power projection, but also that Soviet defense planning will continue to view the U.S. threat as central. China's forces are not modern, but neither are their capabilities negligible, given the complexity of Soviet defense problems.

Under these conditions, Beijing may well believe that it can safely downgrade its relations with the United States. This strategy communicates to Washington Beijing's dissatisfaction with recent developments in Sino-American relations, while gaining increased credibility with the Third World through the creation of an image of an evenhanded treatment of the two superpowers. Similarly, by agreeing to reopen talks with the USSR, Beijing may believe that it can exert greater leverage on U.S. policy toward China.

Two recent developments in Sino-American relations could indicate that China's shift has been beneficial to Beijing. The United States recently agreed to accelerate the sale of "gray area" high-technology items to China that had been delayed by internal disputes within the Reagan administration.[42] In addition, Defense Secretary Caspar Weinberger visited China in September 1983 to discuss arms sales and reopen the Sino-American dialogue on the military situation in Asia, especially the Soviet threat to China and Soviet assistance to Vietnam.[43]

South Asia

It should not be assumed, however, that China's restructuring of its relations with the United States and the USSR indicates a sharp break with policies China developed in the latter part of the 1970s. In South and Southeast Asia China has been mixing military coercion and diplomacy in opposition to the USSR for some time. In South Asia, China began its search for rapprochement with India in 1976, when Beijing and New Delhi exchanged ambassadors after a break of some fourteen years. These initial efforts were confounded by a series of problems. While the Indian foreign minister was visiting Beijing in 1979, China invaded Vietnam. The parallel with the Sino-Indian Border War no doubt prompted New Delhi to cut the visit short. Beijing then scheduled a visit by its foreign minister, but this was canceled in response to New Delhi's recognition of the Phnom Penh government installed by Hanoi. By 1981, both India and China found it appropriate to rekindle the process of rapprochement, and they began a dialogue that led to a reconstruction of Beijing's policies in South Asia.

Several factors contributed to this process. With the invasion of Afghanistan, India became uncomfortable with its pro-Soviet tilt. Rapprochement with China would demonstrate to the USSR that India was capable of determining the course of its relations with China. Furthermore, many in New Delhi were worried that as a result of the Soviet occupation of Afghanistan, a Pakistan-China-U.S. axis was forming that could cause India to become more dependent on the USSR than was desirable. Thus India began to seek better relations with both China and the United States. Pakistan's position in India's security concerns also changed as New Delhi began to fear that a permanent occupation of Afghanistan by the USSR would leave Islamabad exposed to Soviet threats and open to destabilization by Soviet manipulation of ethnic unrest in Baluchistan. New Delhi, therefore, recognized Islamabad's right to modernize its armed forces when Foreign Minister P. V. Narasimha Rao visited Pakistan in 1981. This recognition, however, did not extend to the F-16, which India continues to perceive as too threatening to its own defense.[44]

By 1982, the diplomatic environment in South Asia had thus changed dramatically. No longer were China and Pakistan aligned against India and the USSR. A set of mutually reinforcing security interests were drawing India, Pakistan, and China closer together. They were joined by the United States, which sought to improve its diplomatic position in South Asia by attempting what had heretofore been impossible: close relations with both India and Pakistan.

Even given the six-year process of improving Sino-Indian relations, the move toward greater balance in China's relations between Moscow and Washington has not been irrelevant. In a 1982 interview, the Indian foreign minister could comment on New Delhi's improved relations with Beijing by referring to their mutual agreement in such areas as North-South relations, the problem of South Africa, and Israeli aggression in the Middle East.[45] All of these issues had been used by China to demonstrate its areas of disagreement with the United States.

Although diplomacy is the critical factor in China's recent policies toward South Asia, the military instrument of foreign policy has played a role. China has been a major source of weaponry for Pakistan and is no doubt pleased by Washington's agreement to boost Islamabad's military capabilities through the sale of high technology weapons. Similarly, it may be safely assumed that Chinese weapons are finding their way to Afghan rebels. Thus both diplomatic and military pressure is placed upon the USSR, making its presence in Afghanistan costly and seriously undercutting Moscow's political position in South Asia.

Southeast Asia

Southeast Asia has seen a mix of Chinese diplomatic action and military coercion for some years. China continues to exert military pressure on

Vietnam while fostering its diplomatic links with ASEAN. Although it supports ASEAN's efforts toward a negotiated settlement to the Kampuchean dilemma, China has threatened a second invasion of Vietnam and is the major supplier of arms and equipment to the 20,000 to 40,000 Khmer Rouge who provide the major military opposition to the Vietnamese forces occupying Kampuchea. The situation in Kampuchea is in many ways similar to that of Afghanistan and has had similar results. The 1978 invasion of Kampuchea permitted China to establish closer ties to the ASEAN states, especially those on the mainland, by generating fears that Beijing could manipulate. China's own fears, however, are in some ways distinctly different from those of the ASEAN states.

Soviet use of the base facilities at Cam Ranh Bay and Danang give the USSR support facilities for operations against China, as Beijing learned during its expedition into Vietnam.[46] Continual pressure on Vietnam reinforces Hanoi's dependence on the USSR and almost guarantees continued Soviet use of Vietnamese bases. Yet the strategic value of these bases is not restricted to operations against China, for they also provide the Soviet Union with facilities of great value in countering the United States. These dual qualities give Hanoi leverage on Moscow and reduce Soviet incentives to pressure Vietnam into modifying its position on Kampuchea. Thus Chinese military pressure on Vietnam can be counterproductive, negating any chance for a diplomatic solution while giving Hanoi good reason to continue the Soviet presence.

Northeast Asia

Northeast Asia has been the least affected by the revision of China's foreign policy. Beijing has become significantly harsher in insisting on the withdrawal of U.S. forces from Korea,[47] but has sustained its now long-standing position that any reunification of the peninsula shall be peaceful. With Sino-Soviet talks under way, China may be reassuring Pyongyang that it fully supports North Korea while sending a message to the United States that China retains considerable influence over Kim Il Sung. To some extent this reflects Beijing's awareness that the United States credits China with urging restraint on Pyongyang during the crisis that followed the assassination of Park Chung Hee.[48]

Sino-Japanese relations remain both close and cordial, with each side recognizing the mutual benefits derived from their trade and commercial ties. China has, however, modified its past support for the modernization of the Japanese armed forces. As have other Asian states, Chinese officials now warn Tokyo that Beijing has no objection to Japan's military modernization programs if the increased capabilities are for defense and do not reach the level where they could threaten Japan's neighbors.[49]

Japan, in turn, may be concerned by Beijing's harsher position on the withdrawal of U.S. forces from Korea. Tokyo has high stakes in maintaining stability on the peninsula and would view any trend toward instability with alarm. However, bilateral relations remain focused on trade, and China has recently reassured Japan of the critical role it plays in developing China's economy.[50]

Along with Japan's important commercial relationship with China, one must also recognize the significant role that Tokyo plays in China's defense strategy. In the heyday of Beijing's push for an anti-Soviet coalition, Japan's security relations with the United States were an important aspect of China's global strategy. It is unlikely, therefore, that Beijing's defense analysts have failed to notice that the Reagan administration has changed past U.S. evaluations of the relative importance of Japan and China in U.S. defense strategy.

The Reagan administration has evidently concluded that the role Beijing can play in future U.S. strategies is limited, not only because of the known weaknesses of the Chinese armed forces but also because Beijing has demonstrated its aversion to being seen even as a quasi-ally of the United States. China's "independent" foreign policy, coming on the heels of increased criticism of U.S. policies, confirmed the Reagan administration's suspicions that China had only limited value. The United States now anticipates that over the next decade Japan will become a major player in opposing Soviet aggression in Northeast Asia. Japan's geostrategic location, industrial capabilities, and existing security treaty with the United States provide the initial underpinnings for an expanded strategic relationship. Whereas China can play a passive role in pinning down Soviet forces, only Japan shows any promise of becoming an active ally. Prime Minister Nakasone Yasuhiro's more positive views on defense and his willingness to discuss Japanese defense issues have also served to increase U.S. interest in expanding military ties with Tokyo.[51]

Japan's well-known political and constitutional obstacles to expanding its military capabilities hinder any early moves toward a wider defense relationship with the United States. Nevertheless, even with these problems, there is considerable hope in Washington that Japan will be willing to play a more active role in the defense of the northern Pacific than it has in the past.

China's cautious warnings about the potential revival of Japanese militarism have not, thus far, included any commentary on the U.S.-Japanese defense link. In part, this reflects Beijing's appreciation that closer and expanded U.S.-Japanese defense cooperation directed at the USSR serves Chinese interests. Whatever residual fears the Chinese may have about Japanese "militarism" will be ameliorated by the knowledge that any future expansion of U.S.-Japanese defense cooperation will occur within the confines of the 1960 security treaty and current political constraints. Prime Minister Nakasone presented this argument to the ASEAN states when he visited them in the spring of 1983, and it was effective.[52] Presumably China would be swayed by the same argument.

Beijing's patterns of diplomacy in Asia are designed to exploit what Chinese foreign policy strategists view as long-term Soviet weaknesses. Although coercion is used as a tool to pressure Vietnam, the major instrument of Chinese foreign policy is diplomacy. The primary focus of this diplomacy is on areas of Soviet sensitivity. Beijing's political strategy is nonetheless supported by its military posture toward the USSR and the complementary function performed by U.S. defense strategy.

Eastern Europe

China's political strategy of maintaining pressure on areas of Soviet weakness can also be seen in Eastern Europe. As in Asia, the current pattern originated before Beijing began stressing its independence in foreign policy. The present diplomatic initiative in Eastern Europe dates from 1978, when Hua Guofeng visited the maverick capitals of Bucharest and Belgrade. At the time, Beijing was returning the earlier visits of Ceausesc and Tito, reaffirming its long-standing ties to Romania and consolidating its new alignment with Yugoslavia. The link with Belgrade provided the final cut that severed China's relationship with Albania. The USSR responded strongly to Hua's visit, warning all that China was aggressive and a "threat to peace,"[53] yet Moscow was unable to exploit Beijing's break with Albania, even as China's relations with Yugoslavia became closer.

It was not until 1983, when Hu Yaobang led a large delegation to Eastern Europe, that Beijing began to expand its ties in the region. As secretary general of the Chinese Communist Party, Hu restricted his visit to Romania and Yugoslavia, with whom China has party-to-party relations. Other members of the delegation visited East Germany, Poland, Czechoslovakia, Hungary, and Bulgaria. Officially described as an embassy inspection tour, the delegations took the opportunity to meet with foreign ministry officials in each of the countries they visited.[54]

China's diplomatic foray into Eastern Europe caused some concern in the USSR, for it came at a time when the Polish crisis had thrown past Soviet problems in the region into renewed focus. The visits cannot be viewed as making serious inroads into Soviet control over the Warsaw Pact countries, but a continuing active Chinese presence in trade and diplomatic circles can make Moscow's relations with Eastern Europe even more difficult than they already are. For Sino-Soviet relations, the visit creates a more dynamic China for Moscow to deal with in yet another key area of Soviet interests. Beijing's decision to patch up its relations with Tirana after a discord the USSR was unable to exploit is but an additional warning to Moscow that the PRC's Eastern European policies are far from moribund.

Over the past two years China has modified and built upon a foreign policy strategy developed in the 1970s. Because of the patterns of continuity in the policy, the changing positions of the United States and the USSR in the overall strategy should be seen as tactical changes rather than strategic shifts. Barring a change in leadership and a radical shift in Beijing's interpretation of the global dynamics of international politics, the strategic content of China's foreign policy is unlikely to change for the remainder of the decade. Attitudes toward the USSR and the United States, determined by their degree of utility and threat to China's goals within the international system, will change. For the rest of the 1980s, however, China will continue to seek a favorable international environment in which to pursue its critical internal development goals without constraint by uncontrollable external pressures. The USSR and the United States, as the two global military and political powers, will remain at the center of China's evaluation of the international system. This will make them continuously susceptible to tactical changes in Beijing's foreign policy strategies.

CONCLUSIONS AND SPECULATIONS

Defense establishment fears that Beijing's current foreign policy overestimates both China's capabilities to control the international environment and the constraints on Soviet power reflect the narrow concerns of the military hierarchy and a wider foreign policy dispute. Some members of the military hierarchy are particularly concerned that by overestimating the constraints on the USSR's exercise of its considerable military power, the current minimalist approach to defense modernization could lead to a dangerous neglect of the PLA's needs. This worry reflects the continuing dispute over funding levels for defense modernization and over the proper allocation of available resources between the nuclear weapons program and the conventional forces. The ambiguous results of the PLA's Vietnam operations made the military hierarchy especially sensitive to the weaknesses of the general purpose forces, both for limited force projection and for a conventional war with the USSR.

The fears expressed by members of the defense establishment are typical of any military hierarchy involved in a dispute over resource allocation, but there may also be more critical issues involved that extend beyond the defense establishment into a wider dispute over foreign policy. China's basic strategy has not been changed by the new policy. Beijing has long sought to insulate China from Soviet power through political strategies, and rapprochement with the United States was part of this strategy. However, when Beijing openly drew back from the United States and became harshly critical of both bilateral issues and broad aspects of U.S. foreign policy, members of the military hierarchy and others may have questioned the utility of the tactic.

The Sino-American relationship included consultations on military-strategic issues, consultations that broadened into discussions of how the United States might assist China in modernizing its armed forces.

The deterioration of Sino-American relations during the Reagan administration ended these discussions, and in spite of U.S. agreement to sell China arms on a case-by-case basis, the defense link has atrophied. In the defense establishment's view, the military link with the United States was valuable, and if kept to an appropriate level, would not have unduly alarmed the USSR. However, the decline in Sino-American relations in 1981–1982 led the United States to conclude that Chinese military weakness combined with an unpredictable foreign policy made China a questionable partner.

China's current foreign policy apparently assumes that U.S. opposition to the USSR will continue to provide a tacit defense umbrella regardless of Chinese attitudes toward the United States. A tacit arrangement may be acceptable to foreign policy strategists, but military planners prefer firmer commitments. No matter how informal, the discussion of mutual defense issues that developed prior to the Reagan administration provided a far more confident basis for Chinese defense planning than the current assumption of tacit support. Although they probably agree that China should not be "locked in" to a close relationship with the United States, defense analysts may well view current policy as too disruptive of an important link in Chinese defense strategy.

Defense Secretary Weinberger's visit to China in September 1983 provided an opportunity for the Chinese and the Americans to explore their mutual interest in rekindling the severed defense consultations. Similar foreign policy explorations took place during Foreign Minister Wu Xueqian's visit to the United States, which occurred shortly after Weinberger's trip. In a very uncertain period for Sino-American relations, both sides will be evaluating the value of improving their defense and foreign policy ties. Whereas the 1979–1981 period may have been too close for the Chinese, in 1981–1982 Beijing and Washington drew too far apart for members of the defense establishment, and perhaps others involved in foreign policy strategy. As Jonathan Pollack has observed, a continued degeneration in Sino-American relations could reach the point where the USSR was able to act without concern "that its actions might provoke a serious, coordinated response from Washington and Beijing."[55] It is precisely this critical point that members of the defense establishment seek to avoid.

NOTES

1. Arnold Wolfers, "National Security as an Ambiguous Symbol," *Political Science Quarterly* 67, 4 (December 1952):481–502.
2. For a precise discussion of this problem in terms of soldiers and statesmen, see Thomas A. Fabyanic, "The Grammar and Logic of Conflict," *Air University Review* 32, 3 (March-April 1981):23–31. The following discussion is drawn from this analysis.

3. Thomas M. Gottlieb, *Chinese Foreign Policy Factionalism and the Origins of the Strategic Triangle,* R-1902-NA (Santa Monica, Calif.: Rand Corporation, November 1977).

4. Kenneth Lieberthal, *The Foreign Policy Debate in Peking As Seen Through Allegorical Articles,* P-5768 (Santa Monica, Calif.: Rand Corporation, May 1977).

5. Two excellent sources analyzing the manner in which Beijing has mixed military force with diplomacy are Allen S. Whiting, *The Chinese Calculus of Deterrence* (Ann Arbor: University of Michigan Press, 1975), and Melvin Gurtov and Byong-Moo Hwang, *China Under Threat: The Politics of Strategy and Diplomacy* (Baltimore: Johns Hopkins Press, 1980).

6. Whiting, *Chinese Calculus,* p. 222.

7. Alexander L. George, David K. Hall, and William E. Simon, *The Limits of Coercive Diplomacy* (Boston: Little, Brown and Co., 1971), p. 18.

8. The now classic distinction between deterrence and coercion is to be found in Thomas C. Schelling, *Arms and Influence* (New Haven, Conn.: Yale University Press, 1966), pp. 69–91.

9. On the 1958 crisis, see Gurtov and Hwang, *China Under Threat,* pp. 91–97; for the 1962 crisis, see Whiting, *Chinese Calculus,* pp. 85–86.

10. See Gottlieb, *Chinese Foreign Policy,* for a discrete analysis of the debate that led to Beijing's acceptance of rapprochement with the United States.

11. Jonathan Pollack has analyzed the complexities of this dispute in *The Sino-Soviet Rivalry and Chinese Security Debate,* R-2907-AF (Santa Monica, Calif.: Rand Corporation, October 1982).

12. Qi Ya and Zhou Jirong, "Does the Soviet Union Have a Global Strategy?" *Renmin ribao* [People's daily, henceforth *RMRB*], May 20, 1981, in Foreign Broadcast Information Service, Daily Report, China [henceforth FBIS-China], May 21, 1981, p. C2.

13. Li Dai, "Independence and China's External Relations," *Shijie zhishi,* No. 19 (1981), in FBIS-China, November 19, 1981, p. A4.

14. See, for example, Xinhua News Agency, August 20, 1981, in FBIS-China, August 24, 1981, p. A3, where opposition to the policies pursued by the United States toward "certain Third World countries" is clearly stated.

15. See, for example, Peng Di, "On 'Change'—On New Trend of Reagan Administration's Foreign Policies," *Liaowang* (February 20, 1983), in FBIS-China, April 13, 1983, pp. B1–4.

16. See, for example, Jiang Yuanchun, "On the Soviet Union's Strategy Toward East Asia," Beijing Domestic Service, February 18, 1981, in FBIS-China, February 19, 1981, pp. C2–5; and Qi Ya and Zhou Jirong, "Does the Soviet Union Have a Global Strategy?" *RMRB,* May 20, 1981, in FBIS-China, May 21, 1981, pp. C1–8.

17. Xing Shugang, Li Yunhua, and Liu Yingna, "Soviet-American Balance of Power and Its Impact on the World Situation in the 1980s," *Guoji wenti yanjiu,* No. 1 (1983), in FBIS-China, April 21, 1983, pp. A1–12.

18. Zong He, "Changes and Development Trends in the International Situation," *Shijie zhishi,* No. 11 (1983), in FBIS-China, July 21, 1983, pp. A1–5.

19. This can be determined by comparing the battle order for the Sino-Soviet border areas reported in *The Military Balance 1973–1974* (London: International Institute for Strategic Studies, 1973) with the battle order reported in the 1982–1983 edition.

20. Derek Davies, "Caught in History's Vice," *Far Eastern Economic Review* 114 (December 25, 1981):20.

21. See Paul H. B. Godwin, "China's Defense Modernization," *Air University Review* 33 (November-December 1981):4–8, for an analysis of Chinese threat perception in the late 1970s.

22. Shao Huaze, "A Reliable Guarantee for Socialist Construction," *Hongqi* [Red flag], No. 21 (1982), in FBIS-China, November 19, 1982, p. K22.

23. Ibid., pp. K20–21.

24. Ibid., p. K22.

25. Zhang Aiping, "Several Questions Concerning Modernization of National Defense," *Hongqi*, No. 5 (1983), in FBIS-China, March 17, 1983, p. K7.

26. Ibid., p. K4.

27. Ibid., p. K3.

28. Shao, "A Reliable Guarantee," p. K25.

29. Fabyanic, "Grammar and Logic," pp. 28–29.

30. Ibid., pp. 24–25.

31. Zhang, "Several Questions," p. K2.

32. Shao, "A Reliable Guarantee," p. K20.

33. Pollack, *Sino-Soviet Rivalry*, pp. 88–96.

34. Xinhua News Agency, October 16, 1982, in FBIS-China, October 18, 1982, p. K2.

35. David G. Muller, "China's SSBN in Perspective," *U.S. Naval Institute Proceedings*, Vol. 109/3/961 (March 1983):125.

36. Xinhua News Agency, September 20, 1981, in FBIS-China, September 20, 1981, p. K1.

37. U.S. Joint Chiefs of Staff, *United States Military Posture for FY 1983* (Washington, D.C.: Government Printing Office, 1982), Map II-2, p. 42.

38. See Godwin, "China's Defense Modernization," pp. 13–16, for a more detailed analysis of this strategy.

39. There has been continuous reporting of the PLA's revised training programs, changes in military education, and changing recruitment requirements for both officers and enlisted ranks. A typical example is found in the announcement of the November 1980 all-army conference on training by the Beijing Domestic Service, November 21, 1980, in FBIS-China, November 25, 1980, pp. L24–25.

40. Xue Hai, "Evolution of Soviet Military Strategy," *Shijie zhishi*, No. 6 (1983), in FBIS-China, May 6, 1983, p. C4.

41. See, for example, Zhang Yebai, "Commenting on the Contradictions in the Reagan Administration's Foreign Policy," *RMRB*, July 31, 1982, in FBIS-China, August 2, 1982, pp. B1–6.

42. Michael Weisskopf, "U.S. Vows Speedup in Sales to China," *Washington Post*, May 26, 1983, p. 1; and Peter Marsh, "U.S. Delays Sale of Space Technology to China, Citing Likely Military Use," *Christian Science Monitor*, April 14, 1983, p. 18.

43. Richard Halloran, "Weinberger Planning to Visit China in the Fall," *New York Times*, July 12, 1983, p. A10.

44. Nayan Chanda, "A Time to Make Up," *Far Eastern Economic Review* 117 (July 2, 1982), pp. 20–23.

45. Ibid.

46. For details of Soviet air and naval assistance to Vietnam prior to and during China's invasion, see Bruce W. Watson, *Red Navy at Sea* (Boulder, Colo.: Westview Press, 1982), pp. 138–140.

47. See, for example, "The Historical Tide of Korean Independent Peaceful Reunification Is Irresistible," *RMRB*, June 23, 1983, in FBIS-China, June 23, 1983, p. D3.

48. Charles W. Corddry, "China Would Discourage North Korean Power Bid," *Baltimore Sun*, May 28, 1980, p. 2.

49. Beijing quotes Foreign Minister Wu Xueqian on this point. Xinhua News Agency, February 18, 1983, in FBIS-China, February 23, 1983, p. D2. Kyodo News Agency (Tokyo), February 20, 1983, quotes Premier Zhao Ziyang on this same point. Ibid., p. D5.

50. Pei Monong, "China's Future Position in Asia," *Beijing Review*, No. 16 (April 18, 1983):15–19.

51. For an interesting discussion of these changes in U.S. evaluations of China and Japan, see Richard Nations, "Why Pentagon Plumps for Japan" and "A Tilt Towards Tokyo," both in the *Far Eastern Economic Review* 120 (April 21, 1983), pp. 36–40.

52. Susumu Awanohara, "The Nice Man Cometh," *Far Eastern Economic Review* 120 (May 19, 1983), pp. 14–16.

53. Hal Piper, "Hua Visit Draws Soviet Admonition," *Baltimore Sun*, August 25, 1978, p. 1.

54. Christopher S. Wren, "China Seeks Better East European Ties," *New York Times*, May 5, 1983, p. A3.

55. Pollack, *Sino-Soviet Rivalry*, p. 94.

CHAPTER 10

THE POLITICAL ECONOMY
OF CHINA'S TURN OUTWARD

Bruce Cumings

During the past five years China has, in quite unprecedented fashion, opened itself to the world economy and pursued an export development strategy that has increased its exports to the level attained by Taiwan, South Korea, and Brazil. Overnight, China has become the newest newly industrializing country (NIC), and in the process, has apparently jettisoned two previous models of development: the Stalinist model of the 1950s, and the Maoist model of the 1960s and 1970s.

The Maoist model was always thought to be sui generis, a Chinese product to be emulated by other revolutionary regimes. Analyses of this model therefore began quite properly with China, its leader, the historical course of its revolution, or its unique ideology. The Stalinist path was widely—and correctly—interpreted as a Chinese adaptation of an earlier Soviet strategy of development; therefore analysts turned first to the Soviet experience to understand China. Curiously, however, the adoption of an export strategy that is quite clearly modeled on the experience of other NICs—and just as clearly *not* the product exclusively of causes or processes internal to China—has been examined as if it were merely a product of Chinese debates and deliberations. It has not been placed in its proper comparative and international perspective. One can search the recent literature on China and find few references to the external sources of China's turn outward; instead, the emphasis is on a domestic Chinese search for a new strategy in the wake of alleged failure of the previous two. Here is a curious paradox: In U.S. studies of China between 1840 and 1949, the dominant school—sometimes called the Harvard or the Fairbank school—had taken as its primary focus the explanation of China's response to the West. Yet U.S. studies of China since 1949, when they consider the West or more particularly the United States, tend to frame the problem as the West's response to China. It is assumed that China is the active factor, and therefore one studies how to contain China (the 1950s), how to accommodate China (the 1960s), or how to get on the good side of China (the 1970s).

This chapter argues, to the contrary, that it is imperative to understand the West's structuring impact on China, "the West" being the hegemonic United States and the world economy that it shapes (if increasingly less effectively). I hope to show that China's turn outward can be better understood by analytically bringing China into the world and using techniques and models appropriate to China's relative position in the world system. China is a poor, Third World, but rapidly industrializing and therefore semiperipheral country.

THE PLANET DIVIDED INTO WORLDS

Perhaps because of the original clash between their traditional world order and the Western imperial system, the Chinese are especially attentive to distinctions between "worlds," and have based policies on such distinctions. Mao Zedong evolved a theory of three worlds: a First World of superpowers (the United States and the USSR) in contention and collusion; a Third World of dependent and developing countries; and in between, a Second World (Western Europe and Japan) that "put upon" the Third World and was "put upon" by the first. This conception grew out of the collapse of an earlier two-worlds theory. In the late 1940s, Mao theorized that the world consisted of a capitalist world system, led by Washington, and a socialist world system, led by Moscow; in between was an intermediate zone of conflict that China wanted to avoid. Thus the PRC would "lean to one side"—the socialist side.

No statement captures the reasoning behind China's later defection from the socialist world system better than Mao's remark in 1961 on Khrushchev's doctrine of peaceful coexistence and competition with capitalism: "This is changing two de facto world markets into two economic systems inside a unified world market."[1] Here Mao suggests (1) that China's lean-to-one-side policy was predicated on withdrawing from the capitalist market system and building an alternative socialist system, itself in conflict with and seeking to replace the other; (2) that Soviet revisionism was responsible for giving up this struggle; (3) that what was left of the alternative, socialist system was corrupt, fostered dependency, and had lost its original raison d'être; and (4) that a unifed world market remained. If these four points were valid, China could either go it alone through a self-reliant strategy (such as Stalinism in the 1930s, when Soviet Russia was the only socialist state), or join the world market on the best terms China could get. Generally speaking, China chose the first course in the mid- and late 1960s and the second course in the late 1970s and early 1980s. Both choices assumed a unified, capitalist world market; the first spelled *withdrawal*, the second spelled *enmeshment*.

The self-reliant withdrawal strategy of Stalin and Mao was biased toward class struggle and independent development, with great emphasis on class conflict, steel, or grain as "key links." The enmeshment strategy emphasized measures to develop productive forces, to enhance competitive efficiency, and ideally, to implement a mercantilist political-economic strategy of protected markets at home and open markets abroad. It might consider exports the key link. The choice of options would also depend upon timing: In some periods, self-reliance would be more advantageous; in others, enmeshment. Above all, the choice between strategies would require a determination of how strong and how enduring the unified world market was likely to be.

All industrializing states adopt one strategy or the other, or a mixture of both. Early arriving, hegemonic industrial powers will favor free trade for themselves and enmeshment for those still "developing" (the British throughout the nineteenth century and the United States since 1945). Others will find value in enmeshment at one time (Japan and Germany in the 1920s), withdrawal and self-reliance at another (Japan and Germany in the 1930s), in both cases for the purpose of "catching up" with the hegemonic power. Some particularly well-situated nations will be able to have their cake and eat it too, with protectionism at home and access to free trade abroad (Japan since 1950). To his great merit Karl Polanyi discovered in the extreme and varied politics of the 1930s, which ranged from fascism to liberalism to Communism, a variety of responses to a nation's comparative advantages in the world market. Immanuel Wallerstein has also understood that rising semiperipheral industrializing states may pursue Communist or fascist withdrawal, military outward leaps, or capitalist export development, all as a means of upward mobility within a world system.[2] In our time there is only one world system, a capitalist world market, and its great remaining strength places upon all nations the question of their relationship to this system. Nations will pursue "open" or "closed" strategies depending upon their perception of which strategy will best serve their interests.

But this is too abstract. In 1984, no nation can choose simply to "open" or "close" to enhance its comparative advantages. Such changes cannot take place quickly; there will be lags, diversions, misunderstandings, mistaken estimates of advantage, and formidable obstacles placed in the way of new strategies. Furthermore, nations, states, organizations, and people will cloak developmental strategies with definitions of their own interest and with ideal rendering of those interests (ideologies). To fully comprehend the process of choice we need to (1) estimate the strength of the First World or hegemonic powers at the global or world-market level; (2) analyze the interaction of nation-state systems and national markets in competition; (3) understand domestic forces and coalitions and how they shape external policy; (4) understand how international forces in turn shape domestic settings—or as Peter Gourevitch put it, how domestic structure itself "derives from the exigencies of the international system";[3] and finally, (5) determine what domestic and international interests identify with particular strategies of development. In other words, we need to erase the distinction between domestic and foreign policy, or between international relations and comparative politics. The study that comes closest to doing this successfully is Schurmann's *Logic of World Power*. His complex argument borrows heavily from Mao, Polanyi, Joseph Schumpeter, and Richard Barnet, among others.[4]

The deep structure of Schurmann's theory is to seek an understanding of world politics through attention to the *global* level of strategic conflict in which economic, political, military, and technical resources are deployed by the two central powers of the First World; attention to the *national* level, and in particular to coalitions of interests favoring, say, free trade or protection; and finally attention to *bureaucratic* levels at which dynamic leaders like Mao or FDR wage political battles with vested interests in various bureaucratic constituencies. Of particular note is Schurmann's suggestion that these levels are hierarchical, with changes at the global level reverberating down through the national and bureaucratic levels.

As the distinction between domestic and foreign policy is erased, we are able to see that for each "domestic" Chinese development strategy (the Stalinist model, the Maoist path, and the current mixture of plans and markets), there is a "foreign policy" corollary: alliance with the Soviets, self-reliance, and quasi-alliance with the United States.

In an earlier article[5] I argued that three broad conceptions of political economy, each with a foreign policy corollary, could be discerned in post-1949 China, and that the three competed in the 1970s. Political economy I ("accumulation in command") was the Stalinist model. It emphasized China's relative backwardness and its late industrialization (a very Stalinist perception of racing against time), and saw constraints and economic determinants everywhere. Political economy I focused on heavy industrialization, with steel as the key link, and on the use of China's raw material resources, mainly oil, to earn foreign exchange for an import-substitution program to purchase technologically advanced plants from the world market.

Political economy II ("politics in command") was preeminently and uniquely a Maoist political economy—as interested as political economy I in China's rapid development, its wealth and power, and in leaping ahead industrially, but using different methods: mass mobilization, moral or ideological incentives, close links between leaders and masses, the "campaign style," and a singular strategy of self-reliant withdrawal from the world market. This model took class struggle as the key link. Often, however, class struggle meant political struggle at the top, with the Maoists fighting for control in order to move China in the direction they favored. Mao was acutely attentive to relations between the United States and the USSR, and to the implications of Soviet domestic policy ("revisionism") for a foreign policy of accommodation rather than struggle with Washington.

Political economy III ("the market in command") took a world system perspective, arguing that the capitalist market remained the only unified world system, whose many strengths included economic dynamism and high technology. In the mid-1970s the U.S. hegemonic power, after a flirtation with neomercantilist strategies in the early 1970s, returned to a classic enmeshment strategy, the Trilateral vision. Political economy III was both highly attractive to China's modernizing leaders, who were desperate for new technologies for an industrial leap forward, and deeply threatening, for this was the political economy that had destroyed the Chinese world order and subordinated China until 1949. Chinese leaders had also had the least experience with this political economy, especially with its motive force, the market principle.

In essence, the preference of the immediate post-Mao leadership for political economy I and the preference of the hegemonic capitalist power for political economy III combined to cancel out political economy II. This also canceled the central ideological element in the Sino-Soviet split. China had to abandon its critique of Soviet revisionism as it became more revisionist itself, and this in turn deflated Mao's argument that Soviet domestic policy predicated Soviet "social-imperial" behavior in the world.

China pursued political economy I between 1976 and 1978, then shifted rapidly to political ecor.Jmy III in 1978–1981. The current leadership seeks to have the benefits of both political economies without the costs, causing continuing tensions. Since 1976, Washington and Moscow have played a critical role in pushing China along whichever path their leaders favor, with far greater success on the part of Washington. Political economy II is gone as a set of high-level policies, but it remains as a powerful subterranean constraint on the leadership, through career and bureaucratic interests promoted during the Maoist phase, and through the axiomatic thinking of millions of cadres and activists who learned their politics from Mao.

To see if this argument holds, I will briefly survey political economy I in the 1976–1978 period; then take a long look at political economy III, "the market in command"; and then examine U.S. policies and their structuring impact on Chinese choices.

1976–1978: THE "WAR OF ANNIHILATION IN CAPITAL CONSTRUCTION"

The argument here may be stated briefly: The first response of the post-Mao leadership to China's continuing economic backwardness was in fact to turn back to the allegedly halcyon days of the mid-1950s, when the Soviet model, high growth rates, and general political stability held sway. The first post-Mao program favored heavy industry over light; steel; and the import of complete plants to obtain the technical renovation clearly deemed necessary by the leadership. Ever-expanding oil recovery would supposedly provide exports to garner the foreign exchange necessary to pay for the imported plants. But the oil did not materialize; the program could not pay for itself; China's industrial problems proved unresponsive to panaceas and massive "leaps forward." A major shift away from political economy I occurred at the end of 1978.

The post-Mao regime developed 120 major projects at the core of this original program: 10 in iron and steel, 9 in nonferrous metals, 8 coal mines, 10 oil and gas fields, 30 power stations, 6 railroad trunk lines, and 5 harbors among them.[6] Close to 80 percent of PRC imports from Europe and Japan in the mid-1970s were for raw material extraction, to fuel heavy industry and pay for new plants. China imported oil rigs and exploration technology, coal-retrieving and dressing machinery, and petrochemical technology. Heavy industrial sectors are metal and energy eaters, and the new technology would feed the ravenous appetites of this new leap forward.

Always thorough when embarking on major new programs, the Chinese leadership made the requisite revisions in basic theory and assumptions. In place of the Maoist emphasis on class struggle and the relations of production, Hua Guofeng and Deng Xiaoping pushed the "theory of productive forces" and the epistemological doctrine of "seeking truth from facts." The motive force in history was not class conflict, but an all-round development of human and material productive forces; the problem of the relations of production had been solved in the mid-1950s, in the main, when socialist ownership of the means of production was established. Deng deemed science and technology to be politically neutral, contradicting Jiang Qing, who had argued that a socialist train running late was better than a capitalist train on time.[7]

The new "Great Leap" could easily be understood apart from socialism, however. It was a classic strategy of "late" industrial development, emphasizing *sequence* (others are ahead; we can copy them and catch up), *timing* (China is poised for a new dash forward), China's *relative backwardness* in industry (with its disadvantages but also advantages), a search for *panaceas* (the classic affliction of developing states, which had also plagued China's earliest industrializers in the late nineteenth century), and a *strong state* (to accumulate power, strengthen central planning, and discipline labor).[8]

One particular document seemed to summarize these emphases. "Some Questions on Accelerating the Development of Industry" was its innocuous title, but it spoke of a "new flying leap" in industry, speed campaigns, "taking steel as the key link," and a "war of annihilation in capital construction." It criticized the doctrine "of trailing behind others at a snail's pace," and argued for import-substituting industrialization through four principles: "first, use; second, criticize; third, convert; fourth, create." "It is by the adoption of the most advanced technologies," the document stated, "that the industrially backward countries catch up with the industrially advanced countries of the world. We must also do the same." The advanced countries "will supply complete sets of modern equipment required by us and then we will pay for them with coal and oil." As for labor discipline, it reiterated the Biblical doctrine (in Leninist guise): "He who does not work, neither shall he eat."[9]

At the Fifth National People's Congress in 1977 the leadership projected an annual industrial growth rate of 10 percent through 1985, and enormous state investment equal to the total invested from 1949 to 1977.[10] The program did produce high growth rates; what Dernberger calls China's "Stalinist big push" took the stagnant industrial growth rates of 1972–1976 and pushed them ahead at double-digit rates.[11] The PRC benefited from the rapid recovery made possible by conditions of slack growth, underutilized capacity, and political infighting during the previous few years.

Political economy I was really nothing new; only the mammoth growth targets envisioned by the "flying leap" were remarkable. The 1976–1978 strategy was a return to the industrial programs of the mid-1950s and early 1960s, with key planners like Chen Yun, who had directed the earlier programs, called back from the oblivion of the Cultural Revolution. More fundamentally, the strategy represented another cycle of centralization and decentralization schemes within the basic Soviet model of playing catch-up ball through investing in heavy industry. The principle of the system remained the administration of economic activity through central plans, although schemes for unit profits and material incentives were reintroduced.[12] Self-reliance remained the foreign policy corollary; independence in industrial structure the goal.

A typical Communist political coalition, well known in studies of the Soviet Union and Eastern Europe, was behind the 1976–1978 program. A military-industrial complex of six machine-building ministries, controlling more than 10,000 plants and millions of employees, received vastly increased budget lines; vertically organized national bureaucracies articulated the interests of particular industrial sectors. Regionally, the coalition represented inland provinces more than coastal provinces, as the heavy industrial sites (the Northeast provinces, the Wuhan area) were located inland.[13] As in the Soviet Union, the Chinese military tends to identify with heavy industry, which possesses the sinews of modern military capability. PLA leaders supported the emphasis on heavy industry, hoping that the military could pursue its own program of buying advanced technology abroad to be copied at home (military import substitution), and they liked the orthodox socialism of the program. The Hua Guofeng leadership mixed the concrete realities of the "big push" with Maoist rhetoric, thus allaying fears amongst the PLA's peasant mass base, where pro-Mao sentiments were the strongest.

During 1976–1978 two factions in Beijing symbolized these twin emphases: the "oil gang" (Parris Chang's term), and the "whateverism" faction.[14] The latter included Wu De, Wang Dongxing, Chen Xilian, and Ji Dengkui, and probably Hua Guofeng as well. These Mao loyalists presumably thought that "whatever Mao said was correct." The oil gang included Yu Qiuli, Gu Mu, Li Xiannian, and Chen Muhua. They promoted China's energy and heavy-industrial sectors (metal- and oil-eating sectors), and thought that politics in the petroleum industry meant producing more oil: For miners, "politics is extracting more coal."[15] The political line of the Eleventh Party Congress in August 1977 demonstrated the predominance of this outlook and these factions, but their influence waned after the critical Third Plenum in December 1978.[16]

The preferences of the oil gang seemed correct when China's oil and coal recovery leaped forward by 11 and 12 percent respectively in 1978, supporting a massive 36 percent increase in energy exports. Their program was foundering badly by early 1979, however, when oil production peaked (coal production actually fell in 1980) and a fundamental crack opened in the foundation of the Four Modernizations.[17] Whereas mid-1970s projections suggested that increases in oil recovery would be in the double-digit range for the next decade or so, the peaking of Chinese oil production now suggested an "energy-constrained" industrial structure that would probably only grow in the 3–5 percent range through 1985.[18] Although no single factor can account for the critical shifts that came at the end of 1978, the oil problem probably ranks high among the several causes. If oil recovery stagnated, Chinese industry and the foreign-exchange earnings necessary to complete the 120 projects would be held back; something else would have to be exported.

It so happened that the CIA had predicted that China's oil production would peak, and had suggested a remedy that was deeply in the U.S. interest: offshore oil production.[19] The United States and its multinational oil companies possessed the expertise, technology, and world market position best suited to help China out of its oil quandary. The world oil regime, still dominated by the major U.S. oil corporations, could help China and help itself: It could make China dependent on Western offshore technology and achieve the traditionally all-important result of influencing if not controlling new Chinese oil supplies coming on stream. At the same time, this would head off a worrisome coalition, with Japan providing China with industrial technology of all sorts (e.g., the Baoshan steel mill) in return for Chinese oil, thus also lessening *Japan's* external dependence on Middle Eastern oil and the U.S. oil companies.[20] There was also the potential, dimmer in 1978 than it is today, that the Soviet Union might help China with its onshore oil technology needs, where the Soviets excel. Another benefit of the offshore option was that oil recovery in significant amounts would take at least a decade, or what CIA analysts have called "an ever-receding timetable,"[21] before it would make a difference in the PRC's energy picture. Thus a Chinese commitment to offshore development might predicate a continuing orientation toward the United States for a long time to come.

As it happened, Chinese interest in offshore oil coincided with the peak of the oil gang's influence in the spring of 1978. The PRC invited a number of technicians from the major oil companies to visit and consult on offshore oil.[22] Deng Xiaoping then made a well-publicized visit in February 1979 to Houston, the U.S. oil capital, and toured several petroleum facilities. The World Bank added its opinion that without offshore exploitation, China would become a net oil importer within a few years.[23] In any event, the Americans convinced China that it had to involve multinational oil companies in offshore exploration; by the early 1980s, about half of the forty-six oil companies dealing with China were U.S. firms. Oil production figures have borne out the CIA estimates: Onshore recovery fell by 1 million tons from the first quarter of 1979 to the first quarter of 1981.[24]

Many other difficulties emerged amid China's "big push" program. The construction of the massive Baoshan steel complex had to be suspended after only its first phase was complete, revealing astonishing ineptitude in site location, capital and energy estimates for the mill, and bureaucratic planning. Opponents of the heavy-industrialization program used Baoshan as a symbol in attacking "China's entire history of Stalinist/Maoist development."[25] The oil and coal recovery problem, the Baoshan fiasco, external pressures, bureaucratic and transportation bottlenecks, an enormous waste of labor and raw material resources, and political tensions in the leadership all combined to bring the "heavy" phase and the "war of annihilation in capital construction" to a creaking halt.

LIGHT INDUSTRY, EXPORT DEVELOPMENT AND THE WORLD MARKET: 1979–1981

In 1979 China once again shifted course, this time toward light industry and exports of manufactured goods and oil to the world market. Unlike the "big push," this strategy has won high plaudits from Western advocates of political economy III as the answer to China's problems. As the *China Business Review* put it in a general review of this transition, "China's apparent success in reining in its heavy industrial interests is remarkable. Many developing countries lack such self-discipline, and manage to turn back from overly ambitious schemes only under the watchful supervision of foreign bankers."[26] As we shall see, China's new program certainly held the watchful *attention* of foreign bankers and capitalists, if escaping their direct supervision.

Before turning to the external sources of China's turn outward, let us survey the extent of the change. The Third Plenum of the Eleventh Central Committee in December 1978 began a general reorientation of China's economy, termed a program of readjustment and reorientation. It signaled a definitive end to political economy II, on the grounds that "large-scale turbulent class struggles of a mass character have come to an end." The Hua Guofeng leadership went into eclipse, with Hua no

longer termed China's "wise leader." Hu Yaobang, soon to become
general secretary of the CCP, later stated that the Third Plenum was a
turning point in CCP history comparable only to the changes in 1927
and 1935.[27] Three years of readjustment were decreed at the second
session of the Fifth National Party Congress in June 1979, with a call
for expansion of light-industrial exports; then at the Fifth Plenum of
the Eleventh Central Committee in February 1980, high-ranking critics
of the new reforms were removed and Liu Shaoqi was rehabilitated.
Later in the year Hua Guofeng was officially demoted, Zhao Ziyang
became premier, and in November 1980 the celebrated trials of the Gang
of Four were held. A new political leadership, led by Deng Xiaoping,
had established seemingly firm control of the Chinese state.

The logic of the light-industrial program was spelled out clearly by
Dong Fureng, an economist with the PRC Academy of Social Sciences.
Dong began by criticizing the emphasis on heavy industry between
1949 and 1970 and the Soviet model that underlay the strategy of
political economy I. Central planning could not rationally allocate a
whole nation's material, financial, and labor resources; products needed
by society were often in short supply while unneeded things were
plentiful. Individual enterprises had little say in, or responsibility for,
the use of capital; if the enterprise made a profit, the workers were not
paid more; if it operated at a loss, the workers were paid the same.
Wages were determined by the state and bore no relation to labor
performance. All this stifled incentive and created waste. Chinese attempts
at reform within this system mainly concerned readjusting relations
between the center and localities through decentralization schemes, but
the paradigm of central planning and allocation of resources was never
seriously challenged. Local initiatives produced chaos; central direction
was stultifying.

Dong did not shrink from the logic of this critique: instead of plans,
markets were better allocators of goods and services. Let the center
provide overall guidance, but let firms be independent in accounting
and management and responsible for profits and losses; let firms retain
profits and reinvest them. Instead of capital grants from the center, he
recommended interest-bearing loans for all forms of investment. The
state should use economic, not administrative measures to regulate the
economy, under the superior "internal logic" of the market. Dong also
spelled out the foreign economic policy appropriate to such reforms:
strengthen economic relations with advanced industrial countries and
use foreign capital, loans, aid; set up processing zones where imported
materials are assembled or finished; seek preferential trade agreements
such as most-favored-nation status and join the General Agreement on
Trade and Tariffs; lead from comparative advantage in producing goods
for the export market—particularly advantageous for China because its
enormous domestic market can take up the slack when the world economy
is in recession. As he put it, "By paying special attention to China's

comparative advantage in manpower and natural resources, we want to increase the relative share of mechanical equipment, labor-intensive and highly processed commodities in our total exports."[28] Furthermore, China should integrate its readjustment program and restructure its economy to suit "the needs of foreign economic relations," with special attention to light industry and textiles where start-up costs are low, energy use is less, and quick returns can generate needed foreign exchange.

Dong's arguments are commonplace in the Western developmental literature, but they are breathtaking in the Chinese context. Of special importance for our purposes is Dong's forthright argument that China's restructuring should be done with attention to the requisites of the world market. Chinese leaders at the highest levels have made quite similar statements in the past few years.

In April 1979, Foreign Trade Minister Li Qiang said China should seek technical help (instead of importing complete plants) in heavy sectors and then export light-industrial goods; he argued that China should accept foreign buyer specifications, trademarks, and materials, and should also make use of joint ventures and cooperative production in assembly manufacturing. The same month, Zou Siyi of the PRC Export Bureau was among the first to say that "There is no such thing as a completely autarkic country. Furthermore, there is no country that became modernized by closing its doors." Taken literally, Zou's statement was, of course, correct.[29] Placed in its socialistic context, however, Soviet industrialization in the 1930s and North Korean industrialization in the 1960s and 1970s produced rapid "modernization" under conditions of relative autarky; thus Zou strayed rather far from previous socialist orthodoxy.

In June and July 1979, Yu Qiuli and Hua Guofeng both put great emphasis on speeding the growth of textiles and light industry to produce rapid growth in exports.[30] In mid-1980, Liu Lixin of the People's Construction Bank said "top priority should be given to those enterprises that produce goods for export," with oil remaining an important export commodity but a secondary priority compared to light-industrial exports.[31] Xue Muqiao, among the most important of China's planners, came close to arguing for markets over plans: "In the past, we kicked aside the structure of market economy, which the capitalist world had built up over the past two or three hundred years [sic]. . . . We set up a completely different economic model of our own based on administrative orders. This weakened economic links between different trades and different places and, to some extent, held up the development of productive forces." China's "strong points," he said, were its big supply of labor and its low living costs (meaning low wages), along with its natural resources; "therefore, for quite some time to come, we must make use of our rich natural resources as well as develop more labour-intensive industries and less capital- and technology-intensive ones."[32]

Zhao Ziyang's report to the Fourth Session of the Fifth National Party Congress, probably the most important speech of 1981, urged a radical change away from one-sided emphasis on heavy industry toward labor-intensive light industry (both for export and for the home market) and called for an all-out utilization of world economic resources: "We must abandon once and for all the idea of self-sufficiency . . . all ideas and actions based on keeping our door closed to the outside world and sticking to conventions are wrong." He continued: "Greater exports are the key . . . we should boldly enter the world market." Zhao cited China's vast labor pool as its key advantage in world markets, and was not above waving the fabled China market in the face of Western businessmen: "Farsighted personages . . . abroad understand the enormous potentialities of the China market."[33] Zhao did not, however, go as far as Dong in arguing for market allocation. Planning was still to be primary, with market allocation "a principal part" of production, but still complementary to central plans.

Hungary and Yugoslavia have long experimented with reforms that introduce market principles and promote exports that suit world market tastes and competitive standards. But no socialist country has lurched so quickly and so deeply into free export zones, joint ventures, and light-industrial comparative advantages—particularly a country at China's level of development. Unlike Yugoslavia or Hungary, China's only real comparative advantage is cheap labor.

The Chinese have, of course, dressed this model up with appropriate Marxist theory,[34] but the real logic here, of course, is world market logic. China (or its coastal provinces) should be inserted into the world system at a point appropriate to its market advantage; China should be another NIC, following the path blazed by South Korea and Taiwan. As Dernberger says, this represents "a wholesale rejection of the Maoist economic ideology."[35]

The necessary political emendations have been made as well. Qian argued that China needed a "peaceful environment" internationally and a "cooperative image," so that foreign investors and powerful friends in the West will not be frightened off; the *Renmin ribao* argued in early 1981 that "turmoil . . . cannot promote democracy."[36] At home and abroad, "great order" had replaced Mao's "great disorder under heaven." China's leaders seem even to have read core theory on comparative advantage, the product cycle, and the beneficial role of multinationals. Citing a Harvard study that must be Raymond Vernon's, two economists noted how a firm first seizes a home market, then moves abroad, then establishes subsidiaries in poorer countries in search of lower labor cost, then finally gives up its product entirely to up-and-coming industrializers. Although multinationals are capitalist and exploitative, they "have had a lot to do with the economic development of Brazil, Mexico and capitalist countries in the Far East." Thus, as long as a policy of independence is maintained "within limits," multinationals "can play a positive role" in developing countries.[37]

Deng Xiaoping did not shrink from copying slogans pioneered in South Korea, pronouncing that China's per capita GNP would be $1,000 in the year 2000.[38] (Park Chung Hee had often the same figure for the Republic of Korea's projected per capita GNP by 1980). The two economists may well be right; Park's prediction came true, and so may Deng's. The point to remember is how far China has departed from its previous principles, and how far out on a very new limb it is today.

China has mixed its new theory with a concrete practice that has brought remarkable changes, at least to its coastal cities (once its old treaty ports). K-Mart and Sears sell Chinese textile products, Nike and Voit make athletic equipment in China for export, Honeywell and Hewlitt-Packard have helped with small computers for China's textile industries, and an Illinois firm already manufactures its copying machines in China. American Motors has signed an agreement to produce Jeeps, citing Chinese wages of US$0.60 an hour compared to US$20 in the United States and US$12 in Japan; R. J. Reynolds produces cigarettes; Volkswagen hopes to produce autos by 1988; and U.S. buyers of screws and nuts (the easiest market entry point for China's unskilled labor) are trooping to China.[39]

As with other NICs, new joint ventures ostensibly give majority power to the PRC; but in practice, decision making often remains in the hands of foreign companies. As an American Motors executive said about the Jeep plant, the chairman will be Chinese, but "basically, we will run the plant."[40] The legal framework for such production is now mostly in place, with laws on joint ventures, special export zones, and labor contracts worked out in 1979–1981. PRC currency valuation has been a bone of contention, however, for it goes to the heart of China's economics: Will plans or market prices govern? As the *China Business Review* put it, "As long as administrative mechanisms isolate China's economy from the world marketplace," determining appropriate exchange rates "remains an impossible task." Prices regulated by the world market, not administration, should hold sway.[41] As Chinese leaders know, this is another way of saying that China's new program cannot escape the enmeshment that will place part of China's economic autonomy in the hands of world bankers.

The problem of labor is particularly interesting. The *China Business Review* noted at the end of 1981 that Western businessmen "most anxiously anticipated" the promulgation of labor-management regulations for export zones promising "more control over labor matters for foreign investors."[42] Although the right to fire recalcitrant employees remains a problem for employers, it appears that labor in the export zones will cost less than the equivalent of US$1 per hour, that employers will be able to discipline workers, and that a Communist Party can also be an agency of labor discipline. Investor worries in the mid-1980s seem to center more on the productivity and skills of Chinese workers than on potential labor unrest.

Another corollary of the light-industrial export program is a re-markable de-emphasis of defense spending and the role of the PLA.

China reduced its defense expenditures in 1980, 1981, and 1982; there was a slight increase in 1983. Whereas the defense budget had risen by 22 percent in 1979, it fell by 16 percent in 1981. Furthermore, shopping for weapons in Western markets—a cardinal feature of the 1976–1978 program—has virtually ceased since the Third Plenum. All this in the face of a defense capability that is seriously deficient, outdated and weak in comparison to China's real and potential enemies. Throughout the past five years, there have been indications and rumors that the PLA leadership is unhappy about taking a backseat.[43] But, as any thoroughbred free-trading internationalist would predict, enmeshment soothes the soul, fosters and requires peace, and can do without large standing armies that eat up capital, steel, and energy.

It would take an unreconstructed determinist to have predicted, however, that the same treaty ports that fueled China's economy in the imperial era would now be touted as models to emulate. Yet in April 1981, the State Council called on everyone to "learn from Shanghai, the coastal provinces, and the advanced"—not the Shanghai that was a radical bastion in the Cultural Revolution, but the Shanghai that provides about 15 percent of China's exports and 70 percent of its textile and light-industrial exports (bicycles, clothes, sewing machines). Shanghai's per capita income of US$1,500 compares favorably with that of Taiwan and South Korea.[44] Greater Shanghai, with its 15 million people, is a productive, light-industrial city-state all in itself; it is the guiding star in China's coastal enclave, which includes Guangzhou (Canton), Tianjin, processing zones in Fujian, and apparently, also Hainan Island, now being turned into a center of mineral exports and tourism. A quarter of Tianjin's factories now produce for export, making watches, TV sets and various kinds of electronic equipment (watch exports alone quadrupled fron 1970 to 1981).[45] China's treaty-port region is becoming another country, a semiperipheral entity that will both fuel and benefit from the export program.

China's open-door policy was called a long-term strategy in 1981, and at this writing there is little to indicate a turn back from taking light-industrial exports as the new "key link." China has joined the World Bank and the IMF and received hundreds of millions in long-term loans from both. At the end of 1982, the open door was termed "absolutely correct," and was predicted to quadruple foreign trade by the year 2000.[46] More than 400 joint ventures and foreign enterprises of various types have been contracted, with a total value of more than US$2 billion. The leading light-industrial sector, textiles, has grown at double-digit rates since 1979, and China is now the fourth largest textile exporter to the United States.[47] Total Chinese exports reached US$21.6 billion in 1982, identical to South Korea's total; even by 1980, China's total merchandise trade of US$38 billion had reached Taiwanese and Korean levels and was only US$5 billion behind Brazil. No other non-oil producing NIC was close, and China's oil exports accounted for a rapidly declining proportion of its total trade.[48] The readjustment and consolidation phase that inaugurated the new program has been extended into the distant future, with Zhao Ziyang projecting it to 1990, after which China "should be in a position to take off from a new starting point—and catch up with the more developed countries."[49]

THE STRUCTURING IMPACT OF U.S. POLICY ON CHINESE DEVELOPMENT STRATEGIES

Throughout the 1970s, the United States sought to shape China's economic and strategic policies, with far greater success than most analysts have suggested. It is commonplace to observe that China developed the strategic policy the United States wanted it to have: opposition to hegemonism (the USSR) but not to imperialism (the United States). But China also adopted the economic strategy that the United States—or world agencies dominated by the United States, such as the World Bank—wanted it to have. The external sources of Chinese policies can easily be overemphasized; this was more a matter of conditioning and shaping, rather than determining, Chinese options. What is remarkable in the literature is the rarity of any focus whatsoever on the external sources of Chinese changes.

At the beginning of this chapter, I suggested that only an analysis at multiple (and usually hierarchical) levels—global, national, bureaucratic—encompassing both economic and strategic considerations could grasp the *total field* within which China and the United States have interacted. A new Chinese domestic strategy of development will usually carry with it a new ruling coalition, to the advantage of some bureaucracies and interests and the disadvantage of others. A new strategy entails a foreign policy corollary that is both political and economic: alliance with the USSR, self-reliance, and so on. But this analysis applies to other countries as well. Although China's shifts have been more thorough than any other big power's since the 1940s, a similar analysis can nonetheless reveal much about the United States.

Since World War II, U.S. strategic and economic policy has been shaped by the conflict with Communism, usually meaning the Soviet Union. Three broad strategies may be discerned: internationalism, containment, and rollback. The first seeks to enmesh and shape Communism through economic means; it is an American one-world theory. The second is a two-world theory, a world of blocs and lines drawn in the dirt, in which economic means are used to influence "free world" nations and political-military means are used to confine radical adversaries. The third strategy is also a one-world strategy: Its ideal is a world without Communism, and political-military means are used to deal both with adversaries and recalcitrant allies. Its economic content would be a peculiar U.S. brand of nationalist mercantilism. Franklin D. Roosevelt would be the archetypal internationalist, Harry Truman and George Kennan the model containers, and Douglas MacArthur or Curtis LeMay, the archetypal rollbackers. The modal U.S. policy has been containment; the other two have been extremes that have shaped the containment consensus, biasing it at times toward détente and enmeshment, at times toward intervention and counterrevolution. Each strategy would carry with it different sets of bureaucratic and economic interests and coalitions within the United States.[50]

With the U.S. defeat in Vietnam, Japan and West Germany's return to economic prowess, and above all, the emergence of the USSR as a superpower with a roughly equivalent military capability, the postwar foreign policy consensus came unstuck, and it has not been put back together. Instead, "great disorder under heaven" has marked U.S. strategies, and the three 1940s tendencies of internationalism, rollback, and containment have all returned in somewhat parodied and weak forms.

Nixon and Kissinger pursued détente and enmeshment toward the Soviet Union, neomercantilism toward Japan, and intervention in the Third World. Internationalist enmeshment had its heyday (and Indian summer) in the Carter-Trilateral program of 1977–1979; this was directed toward all three worlds, including Third World revolutionary regimes such as those in Nicaragua and Zimbabwe, which Carter sought to accommodate. Much of this dissolved in the new Cold War of 1979–1981. Reagan has abjured détente and emphasized containment, but has also pursued a rollback agenda toward selected radical regimes (Nicaragua, Grenada, Surinam, and perhaps Libya). If the Nixon and Carter administrations formed a coalition between internationalists and containers, the Reagan coalition has been between containers and rollbackers.[51]

The rapid shifts of U.S. policy in the past decade have deeply affected Sino-American relations; for purposes of brevity, we may isolate the following periods: growth (1970–1973), stagnation (1974–1976), retrogression (1976–1978), identity (1978–1981), and retrogression tending toward crisis (1981–1983). Our main concern will be with the influence of U.S. policy in shaping Chinese economic and strategic choices in two periods: the period of identity, 1978–1981, and the period of backsliding and crisis since 1981. We will find that, like China, the United States has its antihegemonists, its own "oil gang," its own export promoters, and its own protectionist coalition.

In the spring of 1978, the Carter administration made a basic decision to normalize its relations with China; at the same time, Zbigniew Brzezinski and his National Security Council triumphed bureaucratically over Cyrus Vance, his "new boy" network of liberals and "détenteniks," and the State Department. Normalization came in December 1978 with an explicit joint Sino-American commitment to oppose hegemonism on a global basis. A remarkable parallelism, verging on identity, emerged in Chinese and U.S. strategies toward the three worlds.

Toward the Soviet Union, both sought a joint containment of hegemonism. For China, there was now but one superpower worth talking about, and so it supported U.S. policies toward Europe and Japan (i.e., the Trilateral Commission's policy of moving the advanced economies ahead in tandem and requiring Western Europe and Japan to share defense burdens); toward Indochina (where both saw Vietnam as a Soviet proxy and where both came to support the Kampuchea of the Pol Pot in different ways); toward Afghanistan, where both opposed the Soviet-supported factions and the Soviet invasion with money and arms; toward the Middle East, where both spoke of Soviet designs on oil resources and where both supported the Shah as his rule crumbled; and toward Africa, where both opposed Soviet and Cuban activities in Angola, the Horn and southern Africa (especially Zimbabwe). Both powers spoke of an "arc of crisis" running from Indochina through South Asia, the Middle East, and around to the Horn of Africa. Brzezinski reveled in this policy parallelism, showing up at the Great Wall in 1978 to urge joint intervention in the Horn, and on the Afghan border in 1980 where he told "freedom fighters" that God, plus China and the United States, were on their side.

China was quite content to support all this, especially because it led to U.S. shipments of "dual use" (economic and military) high technology, shared intelligence on and monitoring of the Soviets, and something like a U.S. nuclear umbrella for China. As Geng Biao reportedly put it in a secret speech, "At this moment, just let the U.S. defend us against the influence of Soviet revisionism and guard the coast of the East China sea so that we can have more strength to deal with the power in the north and engage in state construction."[52]

If there were only a *strategic* content to the China card, then the United States would have been happy with China's 1976–1978 program of heavy industry, as it fueled China's war machine and tied down the USSR in the Far East. Indeed, a close reading of the Nixon-Kissinger years and of Nixon's recent statements on China[53] indicates that strategic logic dominated the early years of Washington's 1970s China policy. But by the mid-1970s there was a complementary *economic* logic as well, which sought not simply an anti-Soviet China, but also a China that would be, for the foreseeable future, enmeshed with and dependent upon the U.S.-managed world economy. Today, it is this economic logic that stands out, the strategic logic having lost its earlier luster for both China and the United States.

U.S. hegemony in the postwar world has been most successful, long-lasting, and beneficial when the United States sought not direct control and subordination of other nations, but a policy that ensured a continuing orientation toward U.S. interests at the outer limits of politics, economics, and global security. Japan and Western Europe are the biggest successes and the best examples. After the Second World War ended, the United States reoriented the domestic political economies of Japan and Germany, provided for their defense against the Soviets, oriented their trade toward U.S. interests, and shaped monetary and resource arrangements (mainly the dollar and oil) and transnational agencies (GATT, IMF, World Bank) that would, ideally, bring power and plenty for all. The success and longevity of this system cannot be attributed to any single individual (although Dean Acheson should be mentioned), nor to any particular plan (let alone conspiracy); instead it grew out of the unprecedented power of the United States amid a prostrate world, and its pursuit of classic internationalist, free-trade policies for getting the world economy moving again.

Japan is a particularly good example of how U.S. hegemony functions. Japan has had a highly productive and dynamic economy, political independence since 1952, generally liberal and stable politics at home, and extraordinarily rapid economic growth rates. Yet until the 1970s, Japan was remarkably dependent upon the United States for its security and its essential resources, mainly oil and food, but also for advanced-country markets. The United States maintained a light hold on the Japanese jugular, so to speak, possessing but never invoking a capacity to strangle Japan economically and dominate it militarily. The strong economy but weak defense of Japan was a great virtue when it helped fuel the postwar economic boom and when the United States could easily pay for defense in the 1950s and 1960s; by the 1970s, the obvious virtues had begun to look like vices, with Japan devastating U.S. industry and the United States unable to pay for its far-flung commitments.

Nonetheless, the structure of U.S-Japanese relations has remained essentially the same since 1950: The United States provides security, shapes the flow of resources to Japan, and hopes that Japan will manufacture those products no longer produced efficiently in declining U.S. industries (autos, textiles, steel). The economic basis of the relationship is imbedded in theories of comparative advantage and the product cycle: Japan moves from textiles and light-assembly industries in the 1950s, to cars and steel in the 1960s and 1970s, to electronics, computers, and "knowledge" industries in the 1980s. Although this international division of labor has been opposed in the United States by declining industries and protectionist interests, it has had the support of internationalists and free traders, and of those high-technology industries that compete well in the world markets. The model has been replicated in a somewhat different form and at a lower level in the product cycle in Taiwan and South Korea.[54]

The economic logic of the Sino-American relationship during the "period of identity" (1978–1981) had many parallels with the case of Japan, parallels perceived as such by U.S. and Chinese leaders. As with Japan, security and economic issues mingled. For China, the essential point was to minimize defense costs by allying with Washington and maximize economic benefits by opening its doors to foreign capital, corporations, and technology. Trade with the United States increased from US$375 million in 1977 to US$1.1 billion in 1978, US$2.3 billion in 1979, and US$5 billion in 1980. Rhetorically, the Chinese sided with U.S. policy around the globe. Just as Brzezinski was arriving in Beijing in 1978, the Chinese warned that "Moscow is stepping up its strategic dispositions along the arc from Africa through West Asia to Southeast Asia," and urged a united front of "all forces" against hegemonism— meaning the PRC, the United States, Western Europe, and Japan and any Third World countries that would go along.[55] By 1980, *Renmin ribao* found that "China and the U.S. hold identical views" on meeting strategic challenges in the 1980s.[56] Deng Xiaoping, it was argued, wanted to buy time for developing the Chinese economy by shoring up defenses by political and diplomatic methods, hoping that the United States would guarantee China from Soviet attack and that the PLA would be patient in the face of declining defense expenditures.[57]

The Chinese also moved toward U.S. definitions of the world economy. Whereas Huang Hua had likened the Trilateralists' pet concept of "interdependence" to that between "a horseman and his mount," in the late 1970s the PRC supported this conception and accordingly dropped its support for Third World demands to transform the relationships between the advanced and developing worlds.[58]

The period of identity between Chinese and U.S. political-economic conceptions of the world did not emerge spontaneously. It was the product of similar perceptions of mutual interest, helped along mightily by pressure from the U.S. side. The role of James Schlesinger, aided by Brzezinski, Senator Henry Jackson, and others, was critical. Schlesinger, like Deng Xiaoping, had an integrated conception of how U.S. economic and security resources could shape China's evolution and support U.S. global interests.

As secretary of defense, in 1974 Schlesinger urged the adoption of the conclusions of a detailed Rand Corporation study, *L-32*, that called for "a far-reaching defense relationship with China" against the Soviets. These plans outlined "virtually all the elements" of the defense relationship established by the end of the Carter administration.[59] China could tie down a substantial proportion of Soviet forces and defense expenditures (some estimates went as high as 30 percent), thus taking pressure off the key European theater. Schlesinger met with candidate Carter in August 1976, and the media reported that Carter was most impressed. A month later, within days of Mao's death, Schlesinger visited China and even toured the Lop Nor nuclear facilities. In October, he was quoted as saying the United States should not reject out of hand the idea of supplying China with weapons; in early 1978 he supported a pseudonymous article arguing that playing the China card was "the best game in town," and outlined an ambitious program of deploying China against the USSR.[60] But he also deployed an oil weapon to encourage China in the appropriate direction.

In late 1977 Schlesinger, by then secretary of energy in the Carter administration, saw oil as a major weapon in shaping Chinese and

Soviet behavior. He argued that Soviet oil supplies were tightening, which could force the Soviets "out into international markets"; another U.S. official argued that Eastern Europe, supplied mostly by Soviet oil, would also be affected: "This could mean a reorientation of these countries' whole economies . . . it could force these countries to become Western-oriented, and that's not bad politically."[61] The same, of course, was true of China, with its oil production about to peak.

In February 1978 Henry Jackson visited China, found "a new openness toward the outside," and argued that China wanted to buy U.S. offshore oil technology. A month later he argued further, noting that China had to have offshore oil but lacked the requisite technology. Stating that "energy gives us an important opportunity to move toward a better relationship with China," Jackson urged full normalization.[62] The New York Times reported a big power struggle in Washington over whether to transfer offshore oil technology and underwater surveying equipment (useful also to monitor submarines) to China. Carter's science advisor, Frank Press, went to China in July 1978 to discuss infrared scanning technology for geophysical exploration.[63]

What Schlesinger, Jackson, and others began in 1978, coterminous with the beginning of U.S.-Chinese identity, bore fruit in the early 1980s, when China let major contracts to oil firms, the majority of them U.S. firms or using U.S. technology, to explore and develop offshore oil. In 1982, a U.S. official from the Department of Commerce argued that offshore oil would assure "a big takeoff in Sino-U.S. economic and trade relations until the end of the century." "Offshore oil is the cutting edge of Sino-U.S. relations for the rest of the century. . . . Any time oilmen put iron in the water, they're talking about a long-term operation." Coal and hydropower would also develop with U.S. help: "The Chinese can pay for anything they put their mind to," the official said; "it just so happens that in these three areas, we have the best technology."[64]

Thus, in both defense relations and energy, the U.S. oil gang encouraged China to take a long-term path that would entail continuing, if subtle, defense, resource, and high-technology dependency. Precisely because such investments and relations were for the long term, and because China could not realize the foreign exchange from oil exports that it had hoped to in the late 1970s, the strategy of export growth through light-industrial products was essential. This strategy would enmesh China in the world economy's division of labor.

Here too, there was much advice and encouragement given from internationalists on the U.S. side. The World Bank sent a mission to China in late 1980; this survey was a precondition for a US$200 million loan granted in June 1981. Prescribing an export strategy, the summary report concluded that "given the shortage of foreign exchange . . . expansion of manufactured exports must have high priority. The outlook is promising, given the abundance of low-wage labor and the enormous potential for economies of scale."[65] The report noted that wage levels were well below those of Hong Kong and South Korea, and suggested that exports could grow by 10 to 15 percent in the 1980s "if suitable market policies are followed and if new markets are penetrated." It recommended levels of foreign borrowing that would quickly propel China into the ranks of the most indebted developing countries (US$79 billion by 1990); Western banks were eager to rush in, as China was little encumbered by debt, and had a strong reputation for fiscal prudence. The World Bank also encouraged China to de-emphasize heavy industry; from an internationalist perspective this was import substitution and therefore violated rules of comparative advantage and the product cycle. This advice was quite similar to that given to South Korea when it embarked on a deepening industrialization program in the early 1970s.[66]

A group of internationalists sponsored by the Council on Foreign Relations and others met at the American Assembly's Arden House in New York in 1981. Bringing together many of the themes described above, they agreed that "We should seek to bring about great involvement by the PRC in the international trading and financial system," and noted that it would be in the U.S. interest to help China develop its critical energy sector. The United States should also "actively promote the licensing of high technology" for the PRC. Strategically, the report noted that China is a regional, not a global power, that it had largely given up its support for Third World revolutions, and that it had "helped to limit the influence of the Soviet Union" and its "proxies."[67] Here, in essence, was a strategy for incorporating a key socialist state and former adversary into a mutually advantageous U.S. condominium, or joint domination. When China's food needs and U.S. food supplies are also considered, we see a full program quite analogous to U.S. relations with Japan, Taiwan, and South Korea. The United States provides security, technology, food, energy, and ideology in return for enmeshment in the world economy at the point most fitting to each nation's comparative advantage.

Major figures in the China field quickly blessed the late 1970s accommodation. Doak Barnett told Congress that China should be seen as "a large, developing country that happens to be ruled by a Communist Party";[68] Michel Oksenberg argued that whereas Mao had been a totalitarian, Deng was an authoritarian leader (and therefore, presumably, more acceptable). Richard Pipes, a strongly anti-Soviet national security advisor, asserted that China was really more "Chinese" than Communist.

DETERIORATION TOWARD CRISIS: THE REAGAN CONTINUITY, THE REAGAN DIFFERENCE, AND CHINA'S RESPONSE

The Reagan administration has curiously reversed the China policy sequence of the Carter administration. Under Carter, the first year of deterioration was followed by a prolonged period of parallelism; under Reagan, a first year of continuity and parallelism was followed by two years of degeneration. This shift occurred so rapidly that by February 1982, barely a year after Reagan's inauguration, the deputy foreign minister of the PRC said "it is no exaggeration to say that relations are facing a crisis."[69] Most analysts have attributed the deterioration solely to the Taiwan arms sales issue. In fact, changes occurred at the global, national, and domestic levels, and in both security and economic realms. They have not reversed the Sino-American relationship; there is both continuity and change. But the changes do suggest how a reversal might come about.

The continuity of the first year of the Reagan administration in China policy owed much to the efforts of Alexander Haig, a protégé of Nixon and Kissinger. During his June 1981 visit to China, Haig claimed to have arranged "a major expansion" of the relationship, while the Renmin ribao continued to call for a united front against hegemonism. The Soviets assailed the visit. Until Haig was ousted the next year, China policy wavered between Haig's desire to push forward and a strong opposition favoring a different policy. What was the nature of this opposition?

First of all, the right-wing elements of the Reagan coalition were nostalgic for the bipolar atmosphere in which Taiwan had been a symbol of anti-Communism. Arms sales to Taiwan were a key issue for this group. Second, Secretary of Defense Caspar Weinberger paid far more attention to Japan in the first two years of the administration. His five-year plan for a new U.S. defense policy, leaked by the New York Times, says little about China but calls for a major Japanese buildup to defend sea-lanes and airspace in the Pacific within 1,000 miles of the Japanese islands. It also calls for a "forward policy" or "global reach" for U.S. forces, especially the navy, and for "prevailing" over Communism, the new code word for rollback.[70]

For such a strategy, a China with little or no navy, an obsolescent air force, no capacity for high-technology weaponry, and doubtful reliability against non-Soviet but nonetheless insurgent forces, is no match for the potential of Japan. Japan, situated close to Soviet naval "choke points" and with excellent technological capabilities, looks far more valuable, and in this preeminently naval strategy, Japan and Taiwan could both be "unsinkable aircraft carriers"—the term MacArthur used for Taiwan in 1949, and that Weinberger has recently used for Japan.

Weinberger's trip to China in September 1983 began cooly, but ended on a note of warmth and restored vigor in the Sino-American relationship. The defense secretary sought to enlist the Chinese in "strategic cooperation" against the Soviet Union, but the Chinese seemed far more reticent than in the halcyon days of Carter and Brzezinski. Furthermore, the Chinese refused to approve U.S. policy in Grenada or Central America, sharply condemning U.S. invasions and threats to "roll back" Communism south of the border.[71] The relative warmth of Weinberger's China visit primarily reflected Chinese pleasure over the lifting of restrictions on certain types of advanced technology exports, which had in fact been negotiated on a previous visit by Secretary of Commerce Malcolm Baldrige. During President Reagan's visit in April 1984, the United States and China concluded a nuclear sharing agreement, despite disagreements on many foreign policy issues.

The *strategic* component of U.S. "grand strategy" no longer depends on the China card. The combination of a domestic Republican coalition biased toward Taiwan and anti-Communism everywhere and a new strategy based on control of sea-lanes, maneuverable forward postures, and high-technology war-fighting capability puts China in a secondary position to Japan, if not yet on the back burner. Has the *economic* logic of influencing Chinese resource and energy sources and promoting export development also changed?

The answer seems to be a qualified no. U.S. support for Chinese offshore oil exploration, coal recovery, hydroelectric development, and nuclear power facilities continues apace, and is probably the outer limit restraining the Chinese from more outcries against the Reagan administration. But the economic logic of export development has run into strong opposition because of problems at the world-market level and in the Reagan coalition. By the end of 1981 the *Wall Street Journal*, while noting that joint ventures were picking up rapidly, stated that Chinese labor-intensive exports were already "swamping the market."[72] This exaggerated the problem, perhaps, but it highlights the possibility that China's comparative advantage in exports might grow so rapidly that China might (1) edge out the exports and weaken the economies of other NICs, particularly Taiwan and South Korea; (2) hasten the already-rapid decline of U.S. textile and light-electronic industries; and (3) burden the entire world economy at a time when various developing countries must export if they hope to pay back loans to Western governments and banks, loans now totaling more than US$700 billion.

China's turn outward has exacerbated conflicts between free trade and protectionist interests on a world scale; the *China Business Review*, firmly on the free trade side, has written extensively about protectionist interests in the United States. U.S. producers of textiles, footwear, menthol, tobacco, and even mushrooms are "fearful of revenues and jobs being washed away by a rising tide of Chinese exports."[73] In January 1983 the PRC stopped purchases of U.S. soybeans and cotton to protest curbs on Chinese textiles. The problem came to a head when textile negotiations broke down and the U.S. imposed unilateral quotas after China had refused to be bound by U.S.-imposed growth limits on Chinese textile exports to the United States, which would tend to keep the PRC well below the levels allowed to Taiwan, Hong Kong, and South Korea for the next few years. Chinese textiles had grown to almost 40 percent of total sales to the United States, representing a 32 percent increase in

1982 alone. The chairman of the U.S. Knitted Textile Association spoke of an "onslaught" from the Chinese that would sink U.S. textile producers in "the sea of foreign products," thus threatening national security because the U.S. might have to clothe its armies in foreign uniforms![74] The old dream of adding an inch to every Chinese shirt had flown back in the face of U.S. industry.

For generations the deep South was a rock-ribbed supporter of free trade programs, primarily because of cotton sales abroad. In spite of the deep conservatism and anti-Communism of the region, during the heyday of McCarthyism and the "who lost China" debates Southern representatives were mostly silent; their hearts told them to support McCarthy but their heads and pocketbooks told them to go with free traders like Dean Acheson. But by the 1970s many declining industries, especially textiles, had moved to the South in search of low labor costs and freedom from trade unions. Now, with *Communist* China threatening to destroy U.S. textiles and light industries once and for all, some Southerners have united their anti-Communist sentiments with their pocketbooks. Jesse Helms, "the Senator from textiles," symbolizes this influence. Helms has remarkable weight within Reagan circles, and opposes almost everything to do with China.

When the sale of jets to Taiwan was announced in January 1982, Senator Helms was said to be behind it, leading the opposition to close relations with the PRC.[75] As chairman of the Senate Agricultural Committee he sought to block food aid to China, which would necessitate changing China's designation from an enemy to "a friendly country." Helms remarked that all the justifications for deepening relations with China could be wiped away in "one phone call between Peking and Moscow."[76] Helms and his allies blocked or delayed State Department appointments of people thought to be "soft on China." To read most accounts, one would think Helms acts out of an atavistic anti-Communism. In fact, much if not most of his obstructionism derives from his support of textile interests in the South.

Textiles are North Carolina's premier industry, employing 250,000 workers; almost half of all textile jobs in the United States are in the Carolinas. In the early 1980s one in five workers was unemployed. More than half of all textile plant shutdowns have been in the Carolinas, and major firms have reported large losses. Textile executives blame China, expected to be the world's largest textile exporter by 1985: "Unless imports are brought under control, unless something really dramatic is done soon, there won't be a textile business in this country at all in 40 years," one executive from Charlotte said. The Reagan administration has responded with what free traders have termed "shocking and unprecedented protectionist action"; some firms worry that as much as 30 percent of apparel imported from East Asia for the 1983 Christmas season may be blocked.[77] Trade conflicts such as this have affected trade volume significantly: U.S.-PRC trade fell 5.5 percent in 1982, and showed a "steep decline" to mid-1983.[78]

CONCLUSIONS: CHINA RESPONDS

As the period of identity in Sino-American relations reached its high-water mark in mid-1981, China responded with a major realignment of its basic foreign policy precepts. To date little concrete action has flowed from this realignment, and it is probably reversible. What is remarkable is the speed with which changes at the strategic and domestic-coalition levels in the United States reverberated through Beijing and Moscow. China has played a Soviet card and a Third World card, has dusted off a foreign policy of independence, and has threatened to return to political economy I, accumulation in command. Yet political economy III, the market in command, continues apace.

The Sino-Soviet conflict has now lasted a generation, and some U.S. scholars have become convinced that it is here to stay. Robert Scalapino writes that "no single event in twentieth-century international relations has more profoundly affected global policies. . . . Its impact, moreover, is accelerating rather than declining." Jonathan Pollack says: "By any measure, the Sino-Soviet rivalry ranks among the most enduring conflicts of the postwar era."[79] One wonders: more important than two defeats for Germany and one for Japan in this century? More enduring than Soviet-U.S. enmity or the Korean or Vietnamese conflicts? Few have actually died from Sino-Soviet conflict, when compared to many other clashes. Enduring, yes. Permanent, no. It could be scaled down and ended—precisely what a willing Moscow and a cautious Beijing have threatened since the summer of 1981, when Sino-American entente began to waver and degenerate.

The specifics of the many visits, hints, statements, and events of the warming between Moscow and Beijing have been described elsewhere. Donald Zagoria notes the big shift that occurred in the fall of 1981, heralding Chinese "distancing" from the United States, but he does not suggest, as I do, that Washington pushed a reluctant China into it. No analyst is willing to predict that relations between Moscow and Beijing will be patched up, and a second round of high-level talks in the spring of 1983 apparently produced no results.[80] In two capitals particularly affected by the split, Bucharest and Pyongyang, the thaw was welcomed with remarkable enthusiasm. In March 1983 Soviet officials said that the thaw was "irreversible, significant, and indisputable," and claimed that "substantial detente" had been achieved.[81] Earlier, U.S. officials found all this "cuddling up" to be rather "troublesome," and noted that Sino-American exchanges of intelligence information had slowed, and that the Reagan administration had approved only seven of fifty-five categories of weaponry that China had sought to buy.[82]

At the strategic level China has made several changes. In 1979 it dropped assertions that Soviet domestic policy was "revisionist" or tended in the direction of restoring capitalism; Soviet expansionism was linked not to "social imperialism," but to the history of tsarist expansionism and the requisites of a continental power strong militarily but weak economically and technologically.[83] After the "distancing" of 1981 the United States was once again described as a "superpower" contending (but not colluding) with Moscow; by mid-1983 both Moscow and Washington were described as superpowers that "commit aggression and intervene in other countries." The proper policy for the 1980s was identified as the "struggle to contain and weaken the two superpowers."[84] This was some months after China's new Party constitution spoke of uniting people "in the common struggle against imperialism, hegemonism and colonialism" (in that order, interestingly).[85] China also seemed to have increasing difficulty in justifying the growth of Japanese military power and the deepening of U.S.-Japanese military relations, something Beijing urged during most of the 1970s.

China's new "independent" foreign policy, Chinese analysts said, meant opposition to both superpowers, "keeping the initiative in our own hands," and not dancing "to any other country's tune." China once again "belonged to the Third World," a policy heralded by Zhao Ziyang's much-publicized tour of eleven African nations in the winter of 1982–1983. However, Beijing pledged to maintain its open-door policy in trade and investment.[86]

Because strategic and economic policies mingle so closely, Beijing has hinted that it might return to a heavy-industry-first program. Heavy industry did begin growing again in 1982, and Beijing reasserted the critical role of plans, with markets playing only a complementary role. There is little doubt that China's protectionist, import-substitution, orthodox (or Stalinist) coalition, which includes many PLA leaders, would favor such a course.[87] If a reversal were to take place, the Soviets would benefit. In the 1950s, they helped install or renovate much of China's heavy-industry base, and some 70 percent of Chinese machine tools are from the USSR or Eastern Europe.[88]

The Polish crisis has been a little-noted but possibly important influence on China. Poland has been in some ways the "Iran" of the socialist world, showing how a combination of economic involvement with the West, pivotal importance in the U.S.-Soviet conflict, and Western political pressures can combine to promote internal disorder (from the Communist point of view). Polish external dependency (US$27 billion in debts to the West) and internal *luan* (disorder) must frighten the Chinese. In 1983 the PRC paid off two-thirds of the external debt it incurred between 1979 and 1982, and Beijing has not supported U.S. economic sanctions against Poland, designed to persuade the regime to ease up on Solidarity. One analyst noted that U.S. sanctions caused much of the Eastern bloc "to abandon its efforts to become more integrated into the world economy."[89]

At this writing, however, a major economic shift seems unlikely. Zhao Ziyang's report on the Sixth Five-Year Plan in November 1982 projected a modest 5 percent growth in steel through 1986, but an increase in exports of more than 50 percent. Textiles and light-industrial goods were said to be particularly important, as were coastal cities such as Shanghai and Tianjin, which were to be given more autonomy. In March 1983 the PRC listed 130 projects for foreign investment in "a major new bid for Western capital and technology"; half the projects were in coastal cities.[90] In April 1984, the United States and China concluded an agreement on U.S. cooperation in developing China's nuclear power industry, with several billions of dollars of potential investment at stake.

China appears to be pursuing a dual track. Economics have priority over strategic security issues; China has said it needs a peaceful international environment for the next two decades and it has succeeded in lessening both the U.S. threat of the 1960s and the Soviet threat of the 1970s. It can pressure Washington with critical rhetoric and by periodically flashing its Soviet card, meanwhile deepening its economic ties with Western markets. This dual posture will be welcomed by enlightened internationalists, but opposed by inveterate anti-Communists and protectionists in the United States.

By diversifying suppliers of capital and technology, China can also play upon contradictions in the capitalist market. Beijing can pressure the United States by going to the French for nuclear technology; it can expect Japan to be ready for anything the United States is not; and it can play free-trade interests off against protectionist interests in the U.S. Congress. It can also utilize maverick firms who will trade with anybody— a strategy exemplified in the Jeep deal with American Motors, a weak but pliant auto firm. China signed a contract for the huge Pingshuo open-cut mine with Occidental Petroleum, the firm that helped break the hold of the major oil companies in the Middle East by dealing with Qaddafi, and whose venerable chairman, Armand Hammer, aided Soviet industries in the early years after the Bolshevik Revolution.[91] China has also frustrated U.S. oil firms by making exclusive contracts with national oil firms in Japan and France, firms that have themselves sought to escape from the U.S.-dominated world oil regime.[92]

Still, there remain the great attractions and subtle, yet ultimately powerful, influences of political economy III in a world market that commands far more resources than a developing China. There remains a remarkable naiveté in China about the market, which is uncharted terrain for the PRC. China has by no means elaborated a convincing ideology to explain how it can enmesh with the market and at the same time escape capture "by capitalism's powerful gravity," as Carl Riskin has put it.[93] Here, the jury is still out.

NOTES

I would like to thank Nicholas Lardy and Elizabeth Perry for their helpful comments and suggestions on an earlier draft of this chapter.

1. Mao Zedong, *Miscellany of Mao Tse-tung Thought, 1949–68* (Washington, D.C.: Joint Publications Research Service, 1974), Part 2, p. 297.

2. Karl Polanyi, *The Great Transformation* (Boston: Beacon Press, 1944, 1957); Immanuel Wallerstein, "The Rise and Future Demise of the World Capitalist System: Concepts for Comparative Analysis," *Comparative Studies in Society and History* 16 (December 1974):387–415.

3. Peter Gourevitch, "The Second Image Reversed: The International Sources of Domestic Politics," *International Organization* 32, 4 (Fall 1978):881–912.

4. Franz Schurmann, *The Logic of World Power: An Inquiry into the Origins, Currents, and Contradictions of World Politics* (New York: Pantheon Books, 1974).

5. Bruce Cumings, "The Political Economy of Chinese Foreign Policy," *Modern China* 5 (October 1979):411–462.

6. Of the many sources on this program, see A. Doak Barnett, *China's Economy in Global Perspective* (Washington, D.C.: Brookings Institution, 1981), pp. 38–41; Joseph Camilleri, *Chinese Foreign Policy: The Maoist Era and Its Aftermath* (Seattle: University of Washington Press, 1980), pp. 169–173; and "Some Questions on Accelerating the Development of Industry," September 2, 1975, in Kenneth Lieberthal, ed., *Central Documents and Politburo Politics in China*, Michigan Papers in Chinese Studies (Ann Arbor, Michigan, 1978), pp. 115–140.

7. Cumings, "Political Economy," p. 415.

8. The elements of this strategy could have been written by Alexander Gerschenkron, *Economic Backwardness in Historical Perspective* (Cambridge, Mass.: Harvard University Press, 1962). For a comparison with Latin America see articles by Guillermo O'Donnell and others in David Collier, ed., *The New Authoritarianism in Latin America* (Berkeley: University of California Press, 1979).

9. In Lieberthal, *Central Documents*; see also Ye Jianying, *Beijing Review* [hereafter *BR*], No. 40 (October 5, 1979):7–32, on the "liberation of productive forces" and "constantly rising laborer productivity."

10. Andrew Watson, "Industrial Development and the Four Modernizations," in Bill Brugger, ed., *China Since the 'Gang of Four'* (London: Croom Helm, 1980), p. 103.

11. Robert F. Dernberger, "The Chinese Search for the Path of Self-Sustained Growth in the 1980's: An Assessment," in U.S. Congress, Joint Economic Committee, *China Under the Four Modernizations*, Part 1 (Washington, D.C.: Government Printing Office, 1982), pp. 19–76.

12. One of the best surveys and analyses is to be found in Cyril Chihren Lin, "The Reinstatement of Economics in China Today," *China Quarterly*, No. 85 (March 1981):1–47. On Chen Yun, see Nicholas R. Lardy and Kenneth Lieberthal, eds., *Chen Yun's Strategy for China's Development: A Non-Maoist Alternative* (New York, M. E. Sharpe, 1983).

13. Susan Shirk, unpublished research proposal on Chinese political economy, 1983; also *Christian Science Monitor*, April 2, 1980.

14. Parris Chang, "Chinese Politics: Deng's Turbulent Quest," *Problems of Communism* 30 (January-February 1981):1–21.

15. *Renmin ribao* editorial in *BR*, No. 17 (April 27, 1979):10–13.

16. Chang, "Chinese Politics," pp. 4–10.

17. Robert Michael Field and Judith A. Flynn, "China: An Energy-Constrained Model of Industrial Performance Through 1985," in U.S. Congress, *China Under the Four Modernizations*, pp. 335–338; also Kim Woodard, "China

and Offshore Energy," *Problems of Communism* 30 (November-December 1981): 32–45.

18. Field and Flynn, "China," p. 357.

19. Central Intelligence Agency, *China: Oil Production Prospects* (Washington, D.C.: National Foreign Assessments Center, 1977).

20. The best study of the politics of the world oil regime is John M. Blair, *The Control of Oil* (New York: Vintage Books, 1978).

21. Field and Flynn, "China," p. 353.

22. *New York Times*, February 17, 1978; also Woodard, "China and Offshore Energy," pp. 38–41.

23. Woodard, ibid., p. 36.

24. Robert Michael Field and Helen Louise Noyes, "Prospects for Chinese Industry in 1981, *China Quarterly*, No. 85 (March 1981):96–106.

25. Martin Weil, "The Baoshan Steel Mill: A Symbol in China's Industrial Development Strategy," in U.S. Congress, *China Under the Four Modernizations*, pp. 365–392.

26. *China Business Review* 8 (January-February 1981):13.

27. Report to the Twelfth National Party Congress, September 1, 1982, *BR*, No. 37 (September 13, 1982).

28. Dong Fureng, "Some Problems Concerning the Chinese Economy," *China Quarterly*, No. 84 (December 1980):727–736.

29. Articles by Li Qiang and Zou Siyi, *BR*, No. 17 (April 27, 1979).

30. *BR*, No. 26 (June 29, 1979), and No. 27 (July 6, 1979).

31. *BR*, No. 34 (August 25, 1980).

32. *BR*, No. 36 (September 8, 1980).

33. *BR*, No. 51 (December 21, 1981).

34. Writing in *Hongqi*, Qian Junrui lauded "the great progressive role" that the capitalist world economy has played in development, setting the stage for "a unified world socialist economic system." Quoted in Richard Latham, "Science and Technology as an Instrument of China's Foreign Relations" (Seminar paper, University of Washington, Spring 1981).

35. Dernberger, "Chinese Search," pp. 48, 50, 53, 57.

36. *Renmin ribao* editorial, February 8, 1981, in FBIS-China, February 9, 1981.

37. Teng Weizao and Jiang Zhei, "Growth of the Multinationals," in *BR*, No. 7 (February 16, 1981):16–20.

38. *BR*, No. 43 (October 27, 1980).

39. *New York Times*, May 3, 1983; various articles in *China Business Review* 8 (November-December, 1981).

40. *New York Times*, May 3, 1983.

41. *China Business Review* 8 (November-December 1981).

42. Timothy A. Gelatt, "Doing Business with China: The Developing Legal Framework," in ibid., pp. 54, 56.

43. Harlan W. Jencks, "People's War Under Modern Conditions" (Paper presented at the University of Washington China Colloquium, March 3, 1983).

44. "Shanghai Leads in Modernization March," *BR*, No. 1 (January 4, 1982).

45. *China Daily*, January 7, 1983; on Hainan, see the report of a trip by Zhao Ziyang and Gu Mu, January 1983, *BBC Summary of World Broadcasts*, FE/7248/BII/1, February 3, 1982.

46. "Quarterly Chronicle," *China Quarterly*, No. 93 (March 1983):190; Huang Hua also pledged to continue the open-door policy at the United Nations, October 4, 1982. *BR*, No. 41 (October 11, 1982).

47. *New York Times*, January 14, 1983.

48. *BR*, No. 6 (February 7, 1983); World Bank, *World Development Report 1982* (New York, Oxford University Press, 1983), pp. 124–125.

49. *BR*, No. 51 (December 21, 1981).

50. Bruce Cumings, ed., *Child of Conflict: The Korean-American Relationship, 1943–53* (Seattle: University of Washington Press, 1983).

51. Bruce Cumings, "Chinatown: Foreign Policy and Elite Realignment," in Thomas Ferguson and Joel Rogers, eds., *The Hidden Election* (New York: Pantheon Books, 1981).

52. Cited in Camilleri, *Chinese Foreign Policy*, p. 180.

53. Henry Kissinger, *The White House Years* (Boston: Little, Brown and Co., 1979), Chs. 18, 19, 24; Seymour Hersh, *The Price of Power* (New York, Summit Books, 1983), Chs. 26, 27, 35; Richard Nixon, Op-Ed section, *New York Times*, October 11, 1982.

54. Bruce Cumings, "The Origin and Development of the Northeast Asian Political Economy," *International Organization* 38 (Winter 1983):1–40.

55. *Peking Review*, No. 26 (June 23, 1978); Jonathan Pollack, "Chinese Global Strategy and Soviet Power," *Problems of Communism* 30 (January-February 1981):54–69.

56. *Renmin ribao*, June 8, 1980.

57. Jonathan Pollack, "The Men But Not the Guns," *Far Eastern Economic Review* 114 (December 18, 1981).

58. Samuel S. Kim, "The Political Economy of Post-Mao China in Global Perspective," in Neville Maxwell and Bruce MacFarlane, eds., *China's Changed Road to Development* (Oxford: Pergamon Press, 1984), pp. 213–232.

59. Banning Garrett, "The United States and the Great Power Triangle," in Gerald Segal, ed., *The China Factor* (New York, Holmes and Meier, 1982), pp. 81–85.

60. *U.S. News and World Report*, October 18, 1976; Justin Galen [pseud.], "US' Toughest Message to the USSR," *Armed Forces Journal International* (February 1979):30–36.

61. Schlesinger, in the *New York Times*, November 21, 1977.

62. *New York Times*, February 23 and March 25, 1978.

63. Ibid., January 4 and July 9, 1978.

64. Ibid., October 14, 1982.

65. For a detailed analysis of the China report, see William Feeney, Chapter 11 in this volume.

66. Cumings, "Origin of Northeast Asian Political Economy."

67. American Assembly, "The China Factor" (Council on Foreign Relations, March 19–22, 1981).

68. Barnett, quoted in Chalmers Johnson, "What's Wrong with Chinese Political Studies?" *Asian Survey* 22, 10 (October 1982):927; Michel Oksenberg, "Economic Policy-Making in China: Summer 1981," *China Quarterly*, No. 90 (June 1982):170; Richard Pipes, lecture at the University of Washington, 1979.

69. *New York Times*, February 28, 1982.

70. See, among other sources, Richard B. Foster and William M. Carpenter, "Development of the Washington-Moscow-Peking Triangular Relationship During the Last Three Years," *Issues and Studies* 18 (June 1982):69–90.

71. *New York Times*, September 26, 27, 28, 30, 1983.

72. *Asian Wall Street Journal*, December 28, 1981.

73. See, for example, Carol S. Goldsmith, "Protectionism," *China Business Review* 8 (January-February 1981):19–22.

74. *New York Times*, January 20, 1982; January 3, 13, and 14, 1983.

75. *Far Eastern Economic Review* 115 (February 5, 1982).

76. *New York Times*, May 4, 1982.

77. Ibid., July 17, 1983; *News and Observer* (Raleigh, N.C.), November 25, 1982. (I am indebted to Thomas Ferguson for the latter source.)

78. *New York Times*, February 3, July 10, 1983.

79. Robert Scalapino, "Containment and Countercontainment: The Current Stage of Sino-Soviet Relations," in Douglas T. Stuart and William T. Tow, eds., *China, the Soviet Union, and the West: Strategic and Political Dimensions in the 1980s* (Boulder, Colo.: Westview Press, 1982), p. 159; Pollack, "Sino-Soviet Relations in Strategic Perspective," p. 275.

80. Donald Zagoria, "The Moscow-Beijing Détente," *Foreign Affairs* 61 (Spring 1983):853–872; a good review may be found in Yin Ch'ing-yao, "Communist China's Anti-Hegemony Policy." See also the report of French specialist Elisabeth Fouqoire, in FBIS-China, March 18, 1983, pp. 5–9.

81. *New York Times*, March 20, 1983.

82. Ibid., November 17, 1982.

83. Li Yuanming, "Historical Roots of Soviet Hegemonism," *Hongqi*, No. 17 (1981), pp. 21–25.

84. *BR*, No. 19 (May 9, 1983); the return to the phrase, "two superpowers contending for hegemony" came toward the end of 1981 (see the *New York Times*, December 28, 1981).

85. *New York Times*, September 9, 1982.

86. Wang Bingnan, "China's Independent Foreign Policy," January 30, 1983, in *BBC Summary of World Broadcasts*, FE/7246/A1/1, February 1, 1983.

87. See, for example, *Far Eastern Economic Review* 116 (June 23, 1982); heavy industry grew by 9 percent in 1982.

88. Lawrence Freedman, "Economic and Technological Factors in the Sino-Soviet Dispute," in Stuart and Tow, *China, the Soviet Union, and the West*, p. 80.

89. Frank Lipsius, *New York Times*, Op-Ed section, February 7, 1982.

90. *BR*, No. 51, December 20, 1982; *New York Times*, March 24, 1982.

91. *New York Times*, March 26, 1982; on Occidental and Qaddafi, see Blair, *Control of Oil*, pp. 213–234.

92. Woodard, "China and Offshore Energy," p. 41.

93. Quoted in Cumings, "Introduction," *China After Mao* (New York, M. E. Sharpe, 1983). On what one analyst calls "the shakiness of the ideological basis for [all] this activity," see David G. Brown, "Sino-Foreign Joint Ventures: Contemporary Developments and Historical Perspective," *Journal of Northeast Asian Studies* 1, 1 (December 1982):44–45.

CHAPTER 11

CHINESE POLICY IN MULTILATERAL FINANCIAL INSTITUTIONS

William Feeney

INTRODUCTION

As part of its domestic modernization program and foreign policy strategy, the People's Republic of China has recently expanded its participation in the global economy through greatly increased international trade and reliance on foreign investments, loans, and credits. This policy marks a significant departure from Maoist theoretical orthodoxy and an important milestone in the economic and political transformation of post-Mao China. In no way was that evolution better dramatized than by China's entry into the International Monetary Fund on April 17, 1980, and the World Bank (formally, the International Bank for Reconstruction and Development, or IBRD) and its affiliated agencies (the International Development Association and the International Finance Corporation), on May 15, 1980. For the first time since mainland China was seated in the United Nations in 1971, delegates from Beijing rather than Taipei represented China in the World Bank Group, or WBG (a collective term for the IMF, IDA, and IFC).

China's protracted exclusion from these autonomous UN specialized agencies had occurred largely because of Taiwan's continued economic and political importance to the United States, U.S. fears of economic and trade disruption for the island, a system of weighted voting in the WBG that accords extensive influence to the United States on major decisions, Beijing's long-standing ideological opposition to what were considered anti-socialist citadels of international capitalism and finance, and China's reluctance to accept many of the obligations of membership. The normalization of Sino-American relations in January 1979, greater U.S. confidence in Taiwan's economic viability, and especially the change in China's ideological and economic policy orientation paved the way for WBG membership.

This chapter will focus briefly on the Maoist principle and practice of self-reliance and on the reasons for the shift away from that approach during the 1978–1980 period. Major attention will be directed at China's economic and political role within WBG institutions, including an analysis of its borrowing and participatory behavior, and at possible PRC membership in other multilateral financial institutions. Finally, an assessment will be made of current Chinese foreign policy within multilateral financial institutions and the implications of Beijing's future participation for the world economic system.

CHINA'S DEVELOPMENT POLICIES, SELF-RELIANCE, AND MULTILATERAL FINANCIAL INSTITUTIONS UNDER MAO

China's decision in 1980 to join organizations that play an increasingly important role in the management of the capitalist world economy signaled a radical reinterpretation of Mao's long-standing economic development principle of self-reliance, in favor of a policy based largely upon foreign trade, investment, and credit. It acknowledged the reality and unity of a world economy dominated by developed capitalist states, for which there seemed to be no viable socialist substitute if China's modernization goals were to be achieved by the year 2000.

The roots of Maoist self-reliance can be found in a variety of Chinese traditions and experiences. These include: (1) the Sinocentric aspiration for political and economic independence; (2) the ancient conceptualization of China as the Middle Kingdom surrounded by a world of uncivilized and rapacious barbarians; (3) the modern legacy of depredation, exploitation, and national humiliation at the hands of foreigners from the Opium War to World War II; (4) the extreme adversities experienced by the Chinese Communist revolutionaries during the struggles of the 1930s and 1940s against the Nationalists and the Japanese, which inspired a survival strategy based upon decentralized resources and production; (5) the adverse Chinese experience with close economic ties and dependency on the Soviet Union during much of the 1950s; and (6) Maoist theory.[1]

Derived largely from the experiences described, Maoist theory stressed the need for balanced growth through local initiative, mass participation, and primary reliance on China's human, material, and capital resources. It denied any meaningful role to foreign economic assistance and trade in China's economic development process, and rejected both Western and Soviet economic foreign trade theories, which stressed the concepts of the international division of labor and comparative advantage. In Mao's view, if Western theory enabled the advanced capitalist states to perpetuate their domination of the world economy and exploitation of the Third World, the Soviet approach risked permanent Chinese trade and security dependency within the Soviet-dominated Council of Mutual Economic Assistance. Rather, China's interests could be safeguarded best through the formation of an anti-imperialist united front based upon closer economic ties with the Third World and following the principles of proletarian internationalism, equality, and mutual benefit.[2]

The Maoist self-reliance developmental strategy initially became operational during the Great Leap Forward (1958–1960) as an effort to emancipate China from dependence on the Soviet Union, and it reached its zenith during the Great Proletarian Cultural Revolution (1966–1969). During the Cultural Revolution this policy was characterized by xenophobia, autarkical self-isolation, and a significant decline in China's foreign trade.[3] Although the policy was broadened to some extent prior to Mao's death in 1976, foreign trade and economic ties were regarded as no more than temporary tactical measures to eliminate sectoral weaknesses in the economy, prevent any repetition of structural dependency on a foreign power, and strengthen existing links with the Third World. Foreign debt was viewed as detrimental to national independence and as a major factor responsible for the dependent and powerless plight of the Third World. In short, China simply would not permit foreign capital and trade to play any meaningful economic development role.

In keeping with this perspective, after 1971 China participated as a token donor nation in the United Nations Development Program, strongly supported the adoption and implementation of the New International Economic Order, and actively encouraged other Third World countries to develop their national economies independently and self-reliantly. Not unexpectedly, China continually disparaged the World Bank Group in UN speeches, largely on the grounds that the Taiwanese were "illegally" occupying the seat that rightfully belonged to the PRC. Speculation over China's membership interest was raised by a direct PRC communication in September 1973 to the annual joint IMF-IBRD meetings in Nairobi, Kenya, reiterating that charge. The message was considered by the executive boards of both bodies the following month, but no action was taken pending clarification of China's intentions. A similar telegram was received at the 1976 IMF-IBRD meeting in Manila, despite World Bank President Robert McNamara's offer two years earlier that China's application would be welcomed.[4] Finally, China declined an invitation to participate in the General Agreement on Tariffs and Trade in November 1971 after the Taiwanese representative was denied observer status.

DEVELOPMENT POLICIES, SELF-RELIANCE, AND FINANCIAL MULTILATERALISM AFTER MAO

The political economy of China experienced an extensive conceptual and policy transformation in response to circumstantial imperatives after Mao's death in 1976. If the need for an orderly succession prompted the continuity of Mao's domestic development and international NIEO policies, the new Hua-Deng leadership adopted a modernization strategy based less on the theoretical ideals and practice of self-reliance and more on the practical necessity of providing adequate domestic economic incentives and utilizing foreign ideas, technology, and trade. At this time, self-reliance was reinterpreted flexibly to permit the use, criticism, conversion, and creation of foreign contributions to serve China's needs. Learning from foreign countries and the principle of self-reliance were regarded as complementary rather than contradictory.[5] If official policy still rejected foreign assistance, investment, and loans, the dispatch of large numbers of technical missions and trade representatives to nearly all major industrial states and invitations to large numbers of foreign businessmen to visit China seemed to portend major practical changes. Aside from occasional denunciations of Taiwanese usurpation of China's seat in the World Bank Group, mostly in UN speeches, China made no overt efforts to alter its estrangement from the WBG.

In February 1978 Hua Guofeng officially announced the Four Modernizations program, which sought to raise production, productivity, and efficiency (a variety of market socialism) and to expand China's role in the world economy. This sweeping new approach resulted largely from a disappointing domestic economic performance. Problems included heavy losses and a serious decline in productivity and efficiency in state enterprises; a continued investment imbalance in heavy industry to the disadvantage of agriculture, transport, and light industry; a widespread lack of managerial and technical expertise aggravated by the severe damage inflicted upon the educational system by the Cultural Revolution; and the persistence of serious bottlenecks in raw-material supplies, transportation, and energy. China's response to this situation was the ambitious but largely uncoordinated and uncontrolled import of foreign factories, technology, and experts, and a significant increase in foreign trade and investment.[6] The result was an alarming budget deficit (US$11.5 billion) and a sharp rise in the inflation rate. Although China's level of foreign trade doubled (from US$14.7 billion in 1977 to US$29.3 billion in 1979), a US$342 million trade surplus was replaced by an alarming US$2.1 billion deficit. Although foreign debt remained relatively low, China was forced to draw down its foreign currency reserves to less than US$500 million.

This dismal performance prompted a broad retrenchment, which included cancellation or cutbacks in many large-scale projects involving foreign firms, capital, and expensive technology imports. A more cautious approach was adopted, one that stressed advanced planning and analysis, improved managerial and educational skills, adequate infrastructure preparation, the provision of raw materials and power supplies, and most importantly, an adequate payments mechanism. This reorientation was officially sanctioned in Hua Guofeng's Economic Report to the Second Session of the Fifth National People's Congress in June 1979. As the sixth of ten tasks, Hua stressed the need to "continue to do a good job in importing technology, [and to] make active use of funds from abroad and strive to expand exports."[7]

Accordingly, China developed new relationships with foreign businesses and restructured its foreign trade, banking, and financial system to facilitate the modernization strategy. Specific efforts to save scarce capital included joint operations and coproduction schemes in raw materials and light industry exports, cooperative production and processing, compensation (payback in kind), and barter arrangements. Of particular importance were joint ventures with foreign businesses, with contractual agreements stipulating investment periods, equitable rates of return, and capital and profit repatriation. Under the July 1979 Joint Ventures Law there was no upper limit on the foreign share of equity. Bèijing expanded the role of the China Council for Promotion of International Trade and the foreign trade corporations. It established the Export-Import Control Commission to coordinate foreign trade within the Ministry of Foreign Trade and with the State Planning Commission; a Foreign Investment Control Commission to review joint venture proposals; and in October 1979, the China International Trust and Investment Corporation (CITIC). CITIC's initial capital was 200 million yuan (about US$123 million). China's national and international banking system was modernized, and foreign banks were also encouraged to open offices in the PRC to facilitate the financing and business activities of greatly increased foreign trade and investment.[8]

An important symbolic change in China's policy was an unexpected request in November 1978 for UNDP technical assistance, a move officially described as supplementary to self-reliant efforts. China clearly had revised its status from an aid-giving to an aid-seeking state. The UNDP response was positive despite displeasure on the part of some Third World states and strong opposition from the Soviet Union and its allies. Two months later, the UNDP Governing Council approved an initial total of US$15 million for China through 1981, which included projects on the development of computer technology, weather forecasting, and automatic mail sorting. Later in November, China was granted US$20 million by the United Nations to aid in the resettlement of refugees from Vietnam, and in early 1980 received a four-year commitment for US$50 million from the UN Fund for Population Activities to help with a national census and population control program.[9]

But the most revealing and significant change was the abrupt shift in China's public attitude toward the World Bank Group between late 1978 and early 1979. Up until the end of 1978 and especially during the Thirty-third UN General Assembly session, China continued to attack the WBG, but beginning in January 1979, the Chinese press suspended its usual criticism, reports began to appear without the customary references to the illegal Taiwanese occupation of China's seats in these agencies, and leading PRC officials made statements regarding restored WBG membership. In January 1979 Feng Tianshun, acting general manager of the Bank of China, told a U.S. congressional delegation that he had "officially recommended" to the Foreign Ministry that China should rejoin the IMF. A month later Vice-Premier Deng Xiaoping declared in an interview in Tokyo that there would be "no hitch" on China's part in joining the IMF if the Taiwan issue were settled. In June Bu Ming, general manager of the Bank of China, in a meeting with the Japanese chairman of the Trilateral Commission, declared that China wanted to be reinstated in the WBG. Official confirmation of China's readiness to join the WBG and accept loans from these agencies came in July and September 1979 from former finance minister Zhang Jing-fu and Vice-Premier Gu Mu respectively.[10] China also dispatched a delegation to Romania to learn about that country's experience as an IMF member since 1972, and a PRC observer (Chao Mingde) attended the joint meeting of the IMF and IBRD in Belgrade in October 1979, though no official meetings occurred nor was the issue of Taiwan raised.

Perhaps the clearest indication of a change in policy was a February 1980 article by Deng Xiaoping entitled "Why China Has Opened Its Door." In a column entitled "Insight," Deng explained that China was at a turning point in its history and had to learn to "use this favorable international climate" to accelerate the advance toward the Four Modernizations. Deng declared that: "China has now adopted a policy of opening our doors to the world in a spirit of international cooperation. . . . To accelerate China's modernisation we must not only make use of other countries' experience. We must also avail ourselves of *foreign funding*."[11] The formal adoption of the open-door principle paved the way not only for far-reaching changes in China's international economic policies but also for membership in the WBG.

CHINA'S ECONOMIC POLICIES
IN MULTILATERAL FINANCIAL INSTITUTIONS

China's principal reason for joining the WBG in 1980 was to gain access to a large pool of capital resources to stabilize its monetary situation, expand its foreign trade, and finance the costly but fundamental infrastructure projects necessary for modernization. From a practical perspective, this action was made possible by diplomatic normalization with the United States and especially by U.S. extension of most-favored-nation (MFN) trade status to China in January 1980. But one complex economic issue had to be resolved first. When the IMF was established in 1946 to help stabilize the postwar international monetary system, each member country was required to pay in subscriptions, or quotas (25 percent in gold and 75 percent in each member's national currency), and each could borrow foreign exchange from the Fund in proportion to its overall quota. But for economically pressed countries like China after the war, a 10 percent foreign exchange holding in lieu of gold was permitted. Thus, Nationalist China paid in 15 percent of its original US$550 million quota in gold (about US$82.5 million), 10 percent in foreign exchange, and 75 percent in national currency, thus becoming the fifth largest IMF quota holder. In 1976 the Fund decided to sell part of its gold holdings to capitalize a trust fund from which members could borrow. As it was uncertain whether China would seek WBG entry, Taiwan's distribution from this sale (about US$100 million) was never made, and the original 15 percent gold quota was still held by the IMF.

When China announced its intention to join the IMF in early 1980, a compromise was needed on the interrelated questions of gold holdings, quota replacement, and outstanding loans. In early 1980 Taiwan had outstanding IMF special drawing rights (SDRs) totaling SDR 59.5 million (US$78.1 million),[12] seven long-term IBRD loans (with final payment due in 1995) with US$229.3 million outstanding; four IDA loans totaling US$15.3 million, and US$5.8 million in two outstanding IFC loans. In late March, IMF and U.S. negotiators worked out an arrangement under which Taiwan was allowed to repurchase the full 25 percent gold quota (470,700 ounces) at the old official rate of US$35 an ounce, provided that its outstanding obligations to the WBG were repaid (the IMF drawing immediately and the IBRD, IDA, and IFC loans according to the original terms). In return, Taiwan sold the gold at the market price of US$506 an ounce, and used a major portion of the proceeds to pay the IMF a total of SDR 107.6 million (US$139.9 million) to replenish about two-thirds of the market value of China's foreign exchange quota. The remainder, or about US$80 million, was kept by Taiwan as profit from the transaction.[13]

Economic Development and the Role of the IMF

The major function of the International Monetary Fund is to help its member-states stabilize their respective national currencies and overcome temporary balance-of-payments problems. Participation in the World Bank is conditional upon IMF membership. In marked contrast to its traditional policy of maintaining an initial low participatory profile in other UN specialized agencies during and after the Maoist period, China immediately adopted an activist role to expand its borrowing power in the WBG. At the time of China's entry, Beijing's initial quota was set at SDR 550 million, or about US$693 million. Because Taiwan had not taken part in the several general quota increases since the 1950s, the Chinese quota had slipped from fifth to seventeenth largest. In September the IMF Board of Governors authorized a special increase in China's quota from SDR 550 million to SDR 1,200 million, equal to some US$1,560 million and the eighth largest IMF quota. As part of a general 50 percent quota increase for all IMF members in December 1980 (total SDRs were increased from 39,766.5 million to 60,025.6 million), China's

TABLE 11.1
China's Comparative WBG Quotas/Shares/Subscriptions (1983)ᵃ

Country	IMF				IBRD			IDA		
	Rank	Present Quotasᵇ	New Quotasᵇ	Percent Total	Rank	Share Totalᶜ	Percent Total	Rank	Subsc Totalᵈ	Percent Total
United States	1	12,067.5	17,918.3	19.90	1	102,239	20.97	1	9,642.6	34.08
United Kingdom	2	4,387.5	6,194.0	6.88	4	26,000	5.33	4	2,918.7	10.32
West Germany	3	3,234.0	5,403.7	6.00	2	34,347	7.04	3	3,232.7	11.43
France	4	2,878.5	4,482.8	4.98	5	23,567	4.83	6	1,355.3	4.79
Japan	5	2,488.5	4,223.3	4.69	3	34,206	7.02	2	3,488.7	12.33
Saudi Arabia	6	2,100.0	3,202.4	3.56	17	4,899	1.00	10	774.0	2.74
Canada	7	2,035.5	2,941.0	3.27	10	13,962	2.86	5	1,493.5	5.28
Italy	8	1,860.0	2,909.1	3.23	8	19,592	4.02	8	809.6	2.86
China	**9**	**1,860.0**	**2,390.9**	**2.66**	**6**	**23,482**	**4.82**	**24**	**35.2**	**0.12**
India	10	1,717.5	2,207.7	2.45	7	22,633	4.64	21	50.9	0.18
Netherlands	11	1,422.0	2,264.8	2.52	9	15,117	3.10	9	782.5	2.76
Belgium	12	1,335.0	2,080.4	2.31	13	10,518	2.16	13	398.2	1.41
Australia	13	1,185.0	1,619.2	1.80	11	12,737	2.61	11	528.4	1.87
Brazil	14	997.5	1,461.3	1.62	12	10,706	2.20	19	52.7	0.19
WBG Totals		61,059.8	90,034.8			487,561			28,289.0	

ᵃBecause China has not utilized the IFC, these figures are omitted.
ᵇTotal SDRs equal to 1 million times quotas.
ᶜTotal SDRs equal to 1 thousand times shares.
ᵈTotal dollars equal to US$ 1 million times subscriptions.

Sources: "Present and New Quotas in the Fund," *IMF Survey,* December 5, 1983, p. 383; and World Bank,*The World Bank Annual Report 1983* (Washington, D.C.: IBRD, 1983), pp. 182-184, 200-203.

quota was raised a third time to SDR 1,800 million (US$2,340 million), ninth largest of total quotas (3.04 percent) (see Table 11.1). In February 1983 a 47.4 percent increase in quotas was proposed subject to ratification by member governments with a voting majority of 85 percent. This will further increase the Fund's basic lending pool to some US$90 billion. Thus with ratification, China's quota will soon rise by nearly 50 percent in 1983 to about SDR 2,390.9 million, or US$2,630 million at the 1983 conversion rate.

Prior to China's entry, there was considerable speculation that in theory China could demand special drawing rights in relation to its huge population, gross national product, and share of world trade, equal to perhaps one-third more than India's SDR 1 billion, with a commensurate loss to such large Third World borrowers as India, Bangladesh, Pakistan, Indonesia, and Brazil, unless new SDRs were created or drawing rights were significantly realigned. These losses have not materialized at least in the short term. China's level of borrowing from the IMF has not been excessive and has been related to its national economic situation and balance-of-payments needs. Initial difficulties did lead Beijing in December 1980 to make its first IMF drawing, amounting to SDR 218.1 million (about US$278 million). At present a country's IMF quota is divided into four credit tranches, each equal to 25 percent of the total. Easiest access is to the reserve tranche, which is the hard currency member contribution and which is payable in SDRs interest-free for an indefinite period to deal with balance-of-payments difficulties. With a quota at the time of SDR 1.2 billion, China's reserve tranche would normally have amounted to SDR 300 million. However, in line with a prior IMF ruling, China had been allowed to pay only half the amount in reserve currency it normally would have owed for the September 1980 increase in its quota.[14] In January 1981 China drew down the remainder of what had become a SDR 450 million reserve tranche (25 percent of SDR 1.8 billion).

In response to a sharp trade deficit for 1980, in March 1981 China utilized its first credit tranche of SDR 450 million (US$550 million) in the form of a one-year standby arrangement. In return for the loan, which was repayable in three to five years with maximum interest and service charges of 6.4 percent and 0.5 percent respectively, China pledged to readjust its modernization strategy, eliminate its 1981 budget deficit, control the growth of the money supply and inflationary tendencies, and reduce its trade deficit. As a low-income developing country, China received an additional loan of SDR 309.5 million (US$365 million) from the IMF Trust Fund, a now defunct account capitalized by earlier gold sales. That loan is to be repaid in ten years, in semiannual installments after the sixth year of the loan at an annual interest rate of 0.5 percent.

During its first year in the IMF, China borrowed nearly US$1.5 billion, and theoretically could have borrowed considerably more (as much as US$14.3 billion) from the higher credit tranches, the Extended

Fund Facility, and other special facilities up to a ceiling of 600 percent of its quota. This was not done for several reasons. First, because drawings on the higher credit tranches carry progressively stricter conditions relating to foreign debt targets, domestic credit, and government budgetary deficits, Beijing would have had difficulty accepting greater stringency. Second, IMF funds were limited, especially given the increasingly severe debt problems of many Third World countries. Finally and most important, it would have been difficult for China to convince Fund officials of its need for additional drawings, especially after the much-improved 1981 trade balance and foreign exchange reserve levels. In the event that the 1983 Eighth General Quota Review is approved and China's domestic economy and trade balance begin to falter, however, Beijing could be expected to draw the difference between its old and new reserve and first credit tranche limits.

The Role of the World Bank, the IDA, and the IFC

The primary purpose of the World Bank and the International Development Association is to channel financial resources from the developed countries to the less-developed countries to raise living standards in the Third World. These funds support a wide variety of infrastructure projects in agriculture and rural development, education, energy (electric power, oil, gas, and coal), industry, population planning, transportation, telecommunications, urban development, and water supply. The Bank also provides a broad range of technical assistance and training to Third World countries. Because the Bank obtains most of its funds on commercial terms, borrowers are charged the current market rate for twenty-year loans and since January 1982 a small variable front-end fee that may be capitalized and financed out of the loan. The IDA dispenses credits for a period of fifty years without interest except for a small service charge (currently 0.75 percent) to cover administrative expenses and since January 1982 a commitment charge of 0.5 percent on the undistributed amount of credit with repayment of the principal to begin after ten years. The bulk of IDA resources come from transfers of World Bank earnings, capital subscriptions in convertible currencies by IDA members, and contributions from the richer IDA members. The latter source has been replenished six times (most recently by thirty-three donor nations in January 1980 to cover the July 1, 1980, to June 30, 1983, period). Finally, the International Finance Corporation aids the growth of productive private enterprise—especially among Third World members—by investing in them in association with private investors.

China's entry into the three World Bank agencies similarly resulted in an upward realignment of its quotas, or stock subscriptions. Because these quotas are proportional to those in the IMF, the World Bank Board of Governors in September 1980 approved a special increase in China's subscription from its original 7,500 shares to 12,000 shares of the Bank's capital stock, then equal to 3.04 percent of the total (eighth place). The proposed 1983 increase will raise China's portion to 23,732 shares or 4.53 percent of the total (sixth place). Initially, China's subscription total in the IDA was set at 42,858 (or 0.22 percent), making it twentieth. In the IFC, China's subscription was 4,154 shares (or 1.36 percent), about thirteenth. By 1983 China's IDA total had been revised upward to 91,311 (or 1.93 percent), making it twelfth largest (see Table 11.1).

Before the disbursement of any WBG funds to China, an extensive economic survey was conducted by a thirty-member World Bank team during late 1980. In what was the most exhaustive study ever undertaken of the Chinese economy, the 1.5 million-word, nine-volume report issued in June 1981 examined five priority sectors: human resources (education, health, and population), agriculture, transportation, energy, and industry.[15] A major conclusion was that future Chinese economic growth would depend mainly on improved efficiency and resource use, and more specifically on medium- and long-term planning; gradual pricing deregulation of producer but not consumer goods; optimizing and decentralizing investment decisions; skilled labor reallocation; an increase in foreign trade; and trade reforms based upon greater freedom for importers, exporters, producers, and consumers and on cost-benefit analysis of trade options. Special attention was directed to a number of economic sectors: agriculture; energy (petroleum, coal, electricity/ hydropower) and its conservation; transportation; trade expansion; and the export role of both raw materials (especially oil and coal) and textiles and other light manufactures. Because of China's technological lag, advanced technology imports and education were deemed crucial to the development process and improved competitiveness for Chinese manufactured exports in the world market. Significantly, the report's conclusions strongly endorsed China's official economic priorities and policies.

Because projected export earnings, direct investment, and net transfers were judged insufficient to cover import financing requirements, the report also concluded that China would need to borrow foreign funds at a level commensurate to the desired rate of growth. The Bank postulated two economic growth scenarios for China during the 1980s. The high-growth model projected GNP increasing at 5 percent annually in 1980–1985 and 6 percent growth in foreign exchange earnings; a debt level of US$79 billion at 1990 prices (US$40 billion at 1980 prices) as against US$3.4 billion in 1980, and a debt-service ratio by 1995 of 10.3 percent of net foreign exchange earnings for concessionary credit terms and 13.8 percent for harder credit terms. Under the moderate-growth model, annual GNP growth would rise by 4 percent in 1980–1985 and 5 percent in 1985–1990. In this case there would be a lower debt level of US$41 billion (US$20 billion in 1980 prices) and a debt-service ratio of 7.6 percent with concessionary terms and 9.9 percent with harder terms by 1995.

Each projection has its pitfalls. The high-growth model assumed that population increase could be held to 1.2 percent annually, that manufactured exports would grow at 15 percent per year, coal exports would average 20 million metric tons, oil imports would not exceed 14 million metric tons by 1990, significant energy savings could be achieved, and foreign exchange earnings would expand by 6 percent in 1980–1985 and by 11 percent in 1985–1990. If a high borrowing commitment were made but some or all of these projections fell short, China could face a large increase in its debt-service ratio by 1995 (17.9 percent with concessions and 23.9 percent without). On the other hand, if China chose not to gamble on large borrowing, foreign exchange earnings would be insufficient to finance raw-material production and technological imports necessary to raise the real per capita income to US$1,000 by the year 2000.[16]

Even before the completion of the report, China presented a list of nineteen potential projects in July 1980. Tentative agreement was reached to begin work on six of these after World Bank President Robert McNamara's commitment to funnel large loans (some estimates ranged as high as US$9 billion) to China. Long before the usual preliminary studies had been completed, the World Bank agreed to allocate some US$800 million to China, divided equally between education, agriculture, transport, and energy. In May 1981 two IBRD representatives went to China to negotiate with a steering group over a package of World Bank (market-interest) loans and IDA (low-cost) credits acceptable to China. The Bank had assumed that based on China's creditworthiness, the mix would be 25 percent IDA money (US$200 million at 0.75 percent interest) and 75 percent World Bank money (US$600 million at 9.6 percent). However, the Chinese strongly argued that because of the difficulties imposed by internal reforms and economic readjustment the ratio could not exceed fifty-fifty. In the end, the Bank agreed to an even split.[17]

In June 1981 the World Bank announced the first project for China (see Table 11.2) a US$200 million loan/credit package to fund a four-year University Development Project as the first phase of China's higher-education development program for the 1980s. Estimated to cost some US$295 million, with China financing the remaining US$95 million, the project was aimed at increasing science and engineering enrollment from 92,000 to 125,000 by providing facilities and equipment to strengthen advanced training and research in engineering, physics, chemistry, and computer science in twenty-six universities. The project also would support research development programs at these universities by creating forty-six research and analytical centers; introduce techniques and procedures to improve university planning and management in five universities; and expand the managerial capacity of the Ministry of Education in the areas of statistics, accounting, monitoring and evaluation, and the preparation of subsequent investments in education.

China's second World Bank project, approved in June 1982, provided a US$60 million, fifty-year IDA credit for agricultural rural development in the North China Plain. The project would finance improvements in

TABLE 11.2
World Bank Projects, Loans, and Credits for China

Loan Project/Approval Date	Agency	Maturity Date/ Term	Interest Rate[a] (Percentage)	Principal Amount ($US mil.)
1. University Development Project/June 23, 1981	IBRD	2001 (20 yrs.)	9.60bc	100.0
	IDA	2031 (50 yrs.)	-- d	100.0
2. North China Plain Agric. Project/June 15, 1982	IDA	2032 (50 yrs.)	-- d	60.0
3. Three Ports Project/Nov. 2, 1982	IBRD	2002 (20 yrs.)	11.60bc	124.0
4. Agric. Education and Research Project/Nov. 2, 1982	IDA	2032 (50 yrs.)	-- d	75.4
5. Industrial Credit Project/Dec.21, 1982	IBRD	2002 (20 yrs.)	11.60ce	40.6
	IDA	2032 (50 yrs.)	-- d	30.0
6. Daqing Oil Field/Gaotaizi Reservoir Development Project/Jan. 25, 1983	IBRD	2003 (20 yrs.)	10.97ce	162.4
7. Zhongyuan-Wenlin Petroleum Project/Mar. 29, 1983	IBRD	2003 (20 yrs.)	10.97ce	100.8
8. Heilongjiang Land Reclamation Project/ April 19, 1983	IBRD	2003 (20 yrs.)	10.97ce	35.3
	IDA	2033 (50 yrs.)	-- d	45.0
9. China Polytechnic–Television University Project/ Technical Cooperation Project/Sept. 13, 1983	IDA	2033 (50 yrs.)	-- d	95.0
10. China Rubber Development Project/Nov. 29, 1983	IDA	2033 (50 yrs.)	-- d	40.0
	IDA Special Fund	2033 (50 yrs.)	-- d	60.0
Total Loans/Credits (To December 1983)				1,068.5

aPlus other charges, see following notes.
bThe first two IBRD loans were processed with a fixed interest rate.
cA commitment charge of 0.75% is applied to the amount of the principal of IBRD loans not disbursed.
dA service charge of 0.75% is applied to the disbursed and outstanding portion of all IDA credits, and beginning in January 1982, a commitment charge of 0.5% was applied to the undisbursed balance of IDA credits.
eBeginning in January 1982, a front-end fee was introduced for IBRD loans. For the Industrial Credit Project and the Daqing Petroleum Project, the fee was 1.5%. In March 1983 the fee was lowered to 0.75%. The interest rate given represents the initial rate charged at the time the loan was made. In 1982 a variable rate was introduced for IBRD loans and is applied twice annually for six months starting from the date of each loan's next interest period. The rate on all variable interest loans dropped from 10.97% in January 1983 to 10.47% in July 1983, and to 10.08% in January 1984.

Sources: World Bank, *World Bank Annual Report 1981* (Washington, D.C.: IBRD, 1981), pp. 191,196; World Bank, *The World Bank Report 1982* (Washington, D.C.: IBRD, 1982), p. 192; World Bank, *The World Bank Report 1983* (Washington, D.C.: IBRD, 1983), pp. 221, 226; and various IBRD press releases.

irrigation and drainage facilities to overcome soil salinity, waterlogging, and surface flooding for 325,000 hectares of farmland in the Huanghe flood plain covering nine counties in the provinces of Anhui, Henan, and Shandong. Agricultural inputs, rural electrification and roads, and training and other assistance will benefit about 280,000 farm families at a total cost of US$177.5 million.

China's third and fourth World Bank project loans, totaling nearly US$200 million, were approved in November 1982. The third was a US$124 million IBRD loan to increase the capacity and reduce the cost of cargo handling at China's three major ports (Huangpu, Tianjin, and Shanghai) by constructing additional berths, container facilities, high-productivity cargo handling equipment for bulk cargo, and coal wharf services for north-south coal transport. The estimated total cost of the project was US$235 million, with China assuming the balance of the commitment. Also announced in November, the fourth project, for agricultural education and research, was a US$75.4 million IDA credit designed to raise the quality of graduates and research work in the agricultural sciences, expand undergraduate and graduate enrollment and research capacity in these fields, and strengthen the organization and resource management at eleven leading agricultural colleges, six existing research institutes, and the new National Rice Research Institute.

In December 1982 the China Investment Bank (CIB) was authorized to borrow US$70.6 million to assist light industries with small- and medium-sized foreign-exchange-earning export projects. The following month the IBRD agreed to loan China US$162.4 million as part of a US$674.3 million project to introduce modern technology, including enhanced recovery techniques, into China's petroleum industry and to offset declining production in the Daqing oilfield. China would contribute US$445.9 million toward the local cost of the project; an additional US$66 million in foreign exchange costs would be shared by the government, export earnings, and suppliers' credits. A second petroleum project loan of US$100.8 million was approved in March 1983 to develop the production potential of the Zhongyuan basin 300 miles south of Beijing. The total cost of the project is US$499.8 million, with US$342.3 million financed by China and the remaining US$56.7 million financed in the same manner as the Daqing project. In April 1983 US$80.3 million was made available to China for extensive land reclamation and farm mechanization in Heilongjiang Province to increase the production of wheat, maize, and soybeans. Total cost of the four-year project is US$271 million with financing as follows: China, US$74.3 million; Heilongjiang General Bureau, US$49.1 million; and participating farms, US$67.3 million.

The ninth project financed by the World Bank was a two-part IDA credit. The first, for US$85 million, will support a US$206.2 million project to establish a new system of seventeen postsecondary polytechnic institutions (offering a broad range of specializations in engineering, science, business management, economics, social sciences, and the humanities) to serve some 45,000 students, and to update and expand the university television system. China will fund the remainder of the project cost. The second IDA credit, for US$10 million, is to fund the major part of a US$12 million series of twenty-five subprojects involving technical assistance and training for governmental institutions, including feasibility studies, project preparation work, and study tours. The tenth Bank project involves a two-part IDA credit of US$100 million to fund a US$301 million venture in Guangdong Province to expand rubber production by 72,000 metric tons annually, with China financing the remaining US$201 million. The five-year project will significantly reduce China's rubber imports, which now account for about half of consumption. By the end of 1983, the total value of all WBG loans and credits to China amounted to some US$1,068.5 million (see Table 11.2).

Although there was an acceleration of loans and credits to China in 1982–1983, that amount still represented a small percentage of total WBG financing made available to Third World countries (see Tables 11.2 and 11.3). A number of factors account for this situation. First, prior to China's entry a significant portion of lendable WBG resources and especially soft money funds in the IDA sixth replenishment (IDA-VI) had already been committed to specific projects in other recipient countries. Second, although the U.S. Congress at the end of July 1981 authorized the full US$3.24 billion U.S. share to IDA-VI for fiscal years 1981–1983, the Reagan administration stretched out that total for one additional year and "backloaded" the burden by graduating annual U.S. installments from US$504 million in 1981 to $1.09 billion in 1984. Third, during 1982, as a result of the severe and protracted global recession, a large number of Third World nations encountered severe debt service and balance-of-payments problems, which triggered a serious cash-flow crisis and necessitated an unprecedented rescheduling of nearly US$250 billion in debt. Finally, at a high-level CCP conference in December 1980, a decision was made to limit the rate of interest paid on foreign borrowings to 8.5 percent and to give priority to concessionary low-interest credits. High market interest rates during much of this period deterred the Chinese from opting for the more accessible but also more costly World Bank loans.

Some twenty additional projects came under active consideration for preparation and IBRD/IDA funding for the 1983–1984 period following extensive discussions in Beijing in October 1982 between Chinese officials and Munir P. Benjenk, World Bank vice-president for external relations. Because China is a socialist country that has only recently allowed joint ventures based on government and foreign private capital and because the IFC is committed to the expansion of the private sector in development, China has chosen not to seek IFC project funds, though technically eligible.

Since participating in the WBG, China has made notable progress in expanding its foreign trade, improving productivity and domestic

TABLE 11.3
Comparative Cumulative IBRD/IDA Lending Operations   **(June 30, 1983)**

Rank/Country		IBRD Loans (US$ mil.)	IDA Credits (US$ mil.)	Total Amount (US$ mil.)	Percent of Total
1.	India	5,553.3	11,529.2	17,082.5	14.27
2.	Brazil	8,337.3	–	8,337.3	6.97
3.	Indonesia	5,985.0	931.8	6,916.8	5.78
4.	Mexico	6,739.8	–	6,739.8	5.63
5.	Turkey	4,446.6	178.5	4,625.1	3.86
6.	South Korea	4,480.5	110.8	4,591.3	3.84
7.	Philippines	3,878.5	122.2	4,000.7	3.34
8.	Yugoslavia	3,787.7	–	3,787.7	3.16
9.	Colombia	3,681.1	19.5	3,700.6	3.09
10.	Thailand	3,313.5	125.1	3,438.6	2.87
11.	Egypt	2,029.0	981.2	3,010.2	2.51
12.	Pakistan	1,097.7	1,846.7	2,944.4	2.46
13.	Bangladesh	46.1	2,546.5	2,592.6	2.17
14.	Morocco	2,244.5	50.8	2,295.3	1.92
15.	Romania	2,184.3	–	2,184.3	1.82
16.	Nigeria	2,135.7	35.5	2,171.2	1.81
17.	Argentina	1,918.3	–	1,918.3	1.60
18.	Kenya	1,022.4	632.3	1,654.7	1.38
19.	Malaysia	1,610.0	–	1,610.0	1.35
20.	Peru	1,544.9	–	1,544.9	1.29
21.	Tunisia	1,211.7	74.6	1,286.3	1.07
22.	Iran	1,210.7	–	1,210.7	1.01
23.	Algeria	1,201.0	–	1,201.0	1.00
24.	Ivory Coast	1,088.3	7.5	1,095.8	0.92
25.	Tanzania	318.2	753.3	1,071.5	0.90
26.	Sudan	166.0	781.5	947.5	0.79
27.	Portugal	943.2	–	943.2	0.79
28.	**China**	**563.1**	**310.4**	**873.5**	**0.73**
29.	Japan	862.9	–	862.9	0.72
30.	Sri Lanka	136.6	654.6	791.2	0.66
Total Commitments		*$89,616.2*	*$30,078.9*	*$119,695.1*	

Source: World Bank, *The World Bank Annual Report 1983* (Washington, D.C.: IBRD, 1983), pp. 218–220.

output, and limiting inflation and balance-of-payments deficits. According to Chinese figures, by 1982 some US$10 billion in foreign capital had been received (US$7 billion in foreign contracts and US$3 billion in joint ventures and compensation trade), and more than 600 contracts for international construction projects and labor service had been signed, worth nearly US$1 billion. China's two-way foreign trade in 1982 totaled

US$38.6 billion, up some 87 percent since 1978. By 1985 it is slated to reach US$57.4 billion, or about 52 percent higher than in 1980. By the year 2000, the Chinese predict a trade volume of US$160 billion, a figure that suggests continued major participation in the global economy.[18]

CHINA'S POLITICAL POLICIES
IN MULTILATERAL FINANCIAL INSTITUTIONS

China has played a visible but low-key political role in the WBG. At the outset there was some Third World apprehension that the existing balanced voting structure might be undermined by a possible Chinese claim to one of the several elected seats reserved for Third World groups on the IMF and the IBRD boards and at least one Asian group directorship. However, a decision was made to award China an exclusive seat on both boards, thus raising the number of seats from 21 to 22 in the IMF and from 20 to 21 in the IBRD. This change has not had any significant political impact, as decisions are made on the basis of overall vote quotas, but China's acceptance of this revision within the larger WBG weighted voting system did represent a reversal of its earlier premembership advocacy of egalitarian decision making.

The current WBG voting system provides that important decisions must have an 85 percent (80 percent before 1975) majority, which confers veto power on the United States exclusively and the other Western industrial countries collectively.[19] As a result of China's increased quota in the IMF, its vote total was raised from 5,750 (1.12 percent) to 12,250 and ultimately to 18,250 (2.82 percent), from seventeenth to ninth largest. Similar changes were forthcoming in the IBRD, from 7,750 (2.69 percent) to 12,250 votes (2.84 percent), and under the proposed share expansion, to 23,732 votes (4.53 percent). In the IDA, the increase is from 71,247 (2.64 percent) to 91,311 votes (1.93 percent). Despite these symbolic voting realignments, China could not hope to exert any meaningful political influence (even in alliance with other Third World members) on WBG decisions, not only because of the weighted voting system (see Table 11.4) but also because of the tradition of decision by consensus.

Throughout its WBG tenure, China's political goals have always been subordinated to its economic objectives. Yet Beijing has consistently identified with the positions of the Group of 24, the less-developed country (LDC) lobby in the WBG.[20] This group has advocated extensive reform of existing international monetary and financial institutions and processes and a major expansion of WBG financing facilities, including an upward revision of IMF quotas, a loosening of conditionality provisions for IMF drawings, and linkage between SDR allocations and development finance needs. Finally, the Group of 24 has called for debt relief and rescheduling for hard-pressed developing states and an increase in Third World participation in IMF decision making. China has supported these

TABLE 11.4
China's Comparative WBG Voting Power (1983)[a]

Country	IMF Rank	IMF Vote Total	IMF Percent Total	IBRD Rank	IBRD Vote Total	IBRD Percent Total	IDA Rank	IDA Vote Total	IDA Percent Total
United States	1	126,325	19.52	1	102,489	19.58	1	873,571	18.51
United Kingdom	2	44,125	6.82	4	26,250	5.01	4	336,440	7.13
West Germany	3	32,590	5.04	2	34,597	6.61	2	342,586	7.26
France	4	29,035	4.49	5	23,817	4.55	5	175,147	3.71
Japan	5	25,135	3.88	3	34,456	6.58	3	338,756	7.18
Saudi Arabia	6	21,250	3.28	18	5,149	0.98	10	106,443	2.25
Canada	7	20,605	3.18	10	14,212	2.17	6	165,730	3.51
Italy	8	18,850	2.91	8	19,842	3.79	8	123,671	2.62
China	**9**	**18,250**	**2.82**	**6**	**23,732**	**4.53**	**12**	**91,311**	**1.93**
India	10	17,425	2.69	7	22,883	4.37	7	157,108	3.33
Netherlands	11	14,470	2.24	9	15,367	2.94	11	96,098	2.04
Belgium	12	13,600	2.10	13	10,768	2.06	16	58,076	1.23
Australia	13	12,100	1.87	11	12,987	2.48	15	69,115	1.46
Brazil	14	10,225	1.58	12	10,956	2.09	13	81,496	1.73
Total WBG Votes		647,098			523,561			4,720,646	

[a]Because China has not utilized the IFC, these figures were omitted.

Sources: International Monetary Fund, *Annual Report 1983* (Washington, D.C.: IMF, 1983), pp. 177–179; World Bank, *The World Bank Annual Report 1983* (Washington, D.C.: IBRD, 1983), pp. 182–184, 200–204.

positions, but as a nonmember of the Group of 24 and the Third World lobby (the Group of 77) in the UN General Assembly, has not assumed a leading role in this campaign.

On the contrary, China has on occasion pursued patently self-serving policies in the WBG. Upon entry, China had submitted data to the WBG which estimated its per capita GNP, a crucial determinant for access to IDA soft money credits, at US$230, a figure later raised to US$240 in the Chinese press. Even though previous WBG estimates published in the *1979 World Bank Atlas* placed China's 1977 and 1978 per capita GNP at US$410 and US$460 respectively, and the *Financial Times*, using figures released by the PRC Foreign Trade Ministry, put the 1979 value at US$650, the World Bank accepted without question the lower Chinese estimate and revised its total downward.[21] Third World reaction was strongly negative and intensified LDC suspicions that Beijing was out to maximize its WBG "take" at their general expense. Although later WBG measures were raised to US$260 in 1979 and US$290 in 1980, because the IDA "poverty ceiling" for the "Group I" (least-developed countries) was US$411 in 1980 dollars and 82 to 90 percent of all IDA credits were made to that group between 1980 and 1983, China still fell well within the most credit-eligible category.

China's political rhetoric in WBG meetings has reflected its Third World identity, but initially the tone of the speeches was strikingly conciliatory and emphasized negotiations and mutual benefit over confrontation. During the 1980 and 1981 joint IMF-IBRD meetings, PRC representatives called for reasonable solutions to North-South differences through "dialogue and negotiations on an equal footing" (a thinly-veiled criticism of weighted voting), and for the developed countries to abolish restrictive trade barriers, improve LDC terms of trade, and increase concessionary economic and technical assistance to developing countries. A key argument was that the LDC economic downturn would have "grave consequences" for both the developing and developed countries, and "might lead to social and political unrest and provide openings to hegemonistic [the Chinese code word for Soviet] expansion— a development that cannot but cause grave concern to the international community."[22] However, at the joint meetings in Toronto in September 1982, PRC Finance Minister Wang Bingqian muted the anti-Soviet theme, strongly identified with the Third World, and criticized "the failure of a major developed country [i.e., the United States] to honour fully and on schedule its commitments to the IDA," a reference to the decision of the Reagan administration to stretch out and backload its contributions to IDA-VI.[23] Even in this instance, the Chinese response was regarded as measured, low key, and consistent with its Western cooperative development posture.

This was decidedly not the case when the IMF Executive Board approved a US$1.1 billion loan to South Africa in November 1982. As an IMF member with severe temporary economic problems, South Africa had the right to draw on the Fund. Yet Third World opposition to the loan was very strong, with charges that South Africa's economic problems have derived in large part from heavy military spending and government subsidies to white farmers. Citing formal UN disapproval, the Chinese charged that the loan was a form of military assistance that would "bolster South Africa's racist and aggressive policies" at home and in Namibia, and strongly criticized U.S. support for the loan under the weighted voting system.[24] China was also outspoken when the IMF refused to extend the second-year portion (US$244 million) of a three-year US$976 million loan to Zambia, because the latter would not agree to devalue its currency by 30 percent and close some of its money-losing copper mines. The Chinese pointed out that the IMF had not required South Africa to take similar measures and suggested that superpower pressure had prompted this differential treatment.[25]

China has thus recently become more vocal in championing the views and objectives of Third World WBG members. In the general context of cooler Sino-American ties, particularly over the Taiwan question, and the partial thaw in Sino-Soviet relations, China probably feels that a more assertive WBG posture is more in keeping with its own foreign policy perspectives and might sensitize the United States and the other developed members of the "Group of 10" to the plight of the Third World. These appeals reinforce China's LDC advocacy image but may not defuse potential Third World criticism if subsequent WBG lending to China soon reaches the projected annual level of US$2 billion (a figure still well below India's present borrowing totals) and if fewer resources are provided under the seventh IDA replenishment (IDA-VII). In leaner times, therefore, China is seeking to have its own squeaky wheel greased on the basis of both economic need and political expediency.

PROSPECTIVE PRC PARTICIPATION IN OTHER MULTILATERAL FINANCIAL INSTITUTIONS

Speculation has surfaced recently regarding possible Chinese participation in both the General Agreement on Tariffs and Trade and the Asian Development Bank. The Taiwan representative was formally excluded as an observer to the GATT in November 1971, but PRC observers chose not to attend GATT sessions until November 1982. In 1966, Taiwan (as the Republic of China) was an original founding member of the ADB.

In 1979 China began to express a public interest in GATT participation. The principal advantage would be acquisition of preferential trade treatment for exports to the United States beyond the most-favored-nation status granted to China in February 1980. This new status, termed the Generalized System of Preferences (GSP), allows certain goods from developing countries to enter the U.S. market with zero tariffs, as compared to the MFN provision that automatically extends the lowest prevailing importing state tariff rate on a given product. Under Title V of the U.S. Trade Act of 1974 (PL 93-618), GSP status is linked to membership in both the IMF and the GATT. Even if China formally joins the GATT, the granting of GSP is discretionary for the U.S. president, a decision that might well be opposed by U.S. business and labor groups. Other benefits for China would be automatic extension of MFN status in trade with all eighty-eight members of the GATT (except in the case of regional trade arrangements) and protection against discriminatory trade practices including subsidies, countervailing duties, quantitative restrictions, and dumping. Finally, China would gain a more neutral mechanism than the national courts of its trading partners to settle trade disputes.[26]

In exchange for greater access to the world market through the GATT, China would have to liberalize its own trade procedures and import policies by (1) harmonizing national tariff rates with levels reached during the Tokyo Round of GATT trade negotiations (1973-1979), entailing significant reductions on a wide range of goods; (2) resolving the question of the alleged dual renminbi exchange rate system, which subsidizes exports and penalizes imports in violation of GATT rules; (3) devising a formula for China to avoid charges of dumping and the imposition of countervailing duties if a two-tiered pricing system is maintained for goods priced higher domestically and lower on the export market; and (4) acquiescing to periodic GATT trade reviews and disclosing a broad range of trade data and statistics. Although the cumulative effect of these measures might reduce China's control and flexibility in planning and managing its foreign trade and economy, a prospective member is able to negotiate with the GATT on the specific mechanisms and timetable by which its trade practices are brought into compliance with GATT rules.[27]

China would enter the GATT as its seventh socialist member. As a state with renewed Third World leadership aspirations, China is aware that less than half of the Group of 77 (about 125 states) are members of the GATT, which like the WBG is strongly dominated by the developed countries. Traditionally, the less-developed countries have faulted the organization for its failure to support concessionary agreements, preferential treatment, and export market access, and to provide protection for infant industries. Should China decide to enter the GATT, Beijing no doubt will join with other Third World members to push for these objectives, but with limited prospects for success.

Far more serious obstacles hinder chances for China's participation in the ADB. As early as February 1979, Deng Xiaoping expressed an interest in joining the bank, and by early 1983, the pressure from Beijing had become intense. But China faces two basic difficulties. The first is a minor economic problem. Because Taiwan has been a capital guarantor for ordinary ADB loan funds, member states that draw ordinary loans from the bank (made at prevailing market rates) and concessional loans (at no interest with a service charge of 1 percent) from the bank's soft-loan agency, the Asian Development Fund (ADF), have not been overly enthusiastic in welcoming what could become the bank's largest borrower. This reluctance undoubtedly has been reinforced by the Reagan administration's expressed preference for bilateral rather than multilateral lending and its probable parsimonious attitude to the third replenishment of the ADF.

The second difficulty is a major political one. The Reagan administration insists that Taipei has an inherent right to its present ADB seat, drawing a fine legal distinction between the WBG precedent and the ADB case. In the former, Taiwan as the Republic of China was the legal government of all China when it served as a founding member of the WBG in 1945. But because the Nationalist Government as an ADB founding member in 1966 only controlled Taiwan and some offshore islands, the U.S. position has been that Beijing has no right to usurp Taiwan's seat. This position, which appears to violate the one-China principle, has the approval of the U.S. Congress. In 1979 and 1980 the House adopted amendments to the International Finance Institutions Act to prohibit future U.S. contributions to the ADB unless Taiwan were allowed to retain its membership. Ultimately, House-Senate conferees recognized that Taiwan could be isolated from participation in the world economy, but agreed to soften the final language to provide for a "serious review of U.S. participation" in the ADB. Because of a weighted voting system, the United States has preponderent influence on all important decisions but is under strong pressure by the Taiwan lobby to set membership terms that Beijing cannot accept.[28]

In November 1983 the U.S. Congress added an amendment to the IMF appropriations bill recommending that Taiwan remain seated in the ADB, even if the PRC is admitted, and referred to the island by its official name, the Republic of China. This action placed the Reagan administration in a serious political dilemma. Failure to sign the bill would jeopardize IMF funding at a level supported by the administration, whereas signing it would imply official endorsement of a two-China policy, thereby risking cancellation of the president's forthcoming April trip to China. In the end Reagan signed the bill with reservations, meanwhile issuing a statement reaffirming U.S. recognition of the PRC as the sole legitimate government of China. The November 1983 legislation provided US$8.4 billion in U.S. support for the IMF and will help to boost IMF reserves by more than US$40 billion.

CONCLUSIONS AND PROGNOSIS

China's modernization strategy has been greatly assisted by participation in the WBG for several important and interrelated reasons. First and foremost, membership has enabled China to cope with a temporary adverse monetary situation and to finance an array of essential but costly and initially unprofitable infrastructure and development projects. Second, the WBG contributed valuable professional foreign economic expertise to analyze the strengths and weaknesses of the Chinese economy, jointly draft a long-range development blueprint, and provide advanced training for Chinese personnel through the World Bank Economic Development Institute. This interaction represents a significant socializing experience for Chinese economists and financial experts, which may foster the development of productive relationships with their foreign counterparts and help to influence China's political leadership in favor of continued economic pragmatism and global involvement. Third, the WBG provides a useful structured economic negotiating framework within which China can communicate and bargain with the advanced capitalist states to its best advantage. Finally, WBG membership confers a large measure of legitimacy on China's modernization program, raising international business confidence and facilitating more extensive foreign investment and trade arrangements.

However, there is growing doubt whether China's future multilateral funding needs can be even partially accommodated by probable available resources. A recent projection by the UNDP forecasts a sizable cutback in its financial support for Asian and Pacific countries over the next five years (1982–1986) because of the failure of major developed-state donors to increase their pledges to offset inflation and adverse shifts in exchange rates. Similar resource pressures are probable for the IMF. Despite prospects for a 50 percent increase in SDR quotas, a massive and growing Third World and Eastern European debt estimated at some US$700 billion (due largely to the rise in world oil prices, low commodity prices, high interest rates, a protracted global recession, and increasing protectionism) must be serviced with the ever-present risk of large and progressive default. Though it has been careful to limit its total borrowing and has not been caught in the debt squeeze, if its gamble on much higher levels of export production should fail, China, along with other relatively prudent Third World debtor states, could be forced to seek greater IMF borrowing.[29]

The ability to finance this massive international debt, the extent of global economic recovery, future interest rates for IBRD loans, and the level of replenishment of soft-loan funds under IDA-VII (1985–1987) will have a cumulative impact on China's IBRD/IDA borrowing prospects. To date, the debt crisis has been contained and a modest recovery appears to be under way. Interest rates have declined somewhat, but this advantage has been offset by a marked drop in world oil prices, and hence in hard currency earnings China had counted on to finance its import requirements. IDA-VII will be the first replenishment in which China's needs will be specifically considered. The key decisions will be made in 1984–1985, when the major donor states are likely to take a long hard look at their respective economic circumstances and what they can afford. It is known that the Reagan administration will seek a cut from the US$12 billion level of IDA-VI to only US$9 billion, and has pushed the idea of graduation. Graduation means raising the per capita GNP eligibility level for both IBRD loans and IDA credits to exclude certain recipients altogether and force many others to take market-rate IBRD loans rather than interest-free IDA credits. Should global economic stagnation persist and present U.S. policy continue, development funds most certainly will be in shorter supply and requirements will be more stringent, even if other Group of 10 states boost their contributions.

In predicating its modernization drive heavily on a global economic orientation, China could become far more vulnerable to uncontrollable and unpredictable external forces and trends and to the deepening structural problems plaguing the world market.[30] The *World Development Report 1982* offers a measure of hope for China to achieve substantial income growth under favorable conditions. But it also realistically assesses the prospects of low growth and underscores the need to create productive employment for the well over 100 million persons who will enter the labor force during the 1980s. The report advises China to import high-technology capital goods to improve efficiency, to increase agricultural production to prevent food imports from absorbing export gains, and to modernize manufacturing production.[31] The adoption of the open-door principle improves the odds that these goals can be achieved. In the process, the orthodox Maoist development model has been largely replaced by the classical capitalist growth pattern of savings, loans, investment, incentives, rewards, and profits. For China's moderate leaders, participation in multilateral financial institutions could be regarded as an important hedge against their monumental modernization bet. By relying on the essentially competitive nature of the capitalist world to provide ample investment capital, technology, expertise, and markets, they hope to preserve an acceptable level of national autonomy, underwrite part of the cost of the modernization program, and in the process, advance the national interest as well as their own political futures.

Accordingly, China has operated more as a Group of 1 within the WBG to maximize its own advantages, rather than as a leading member of the Group of 24 seeking to transform existing norms and rules along NIEO lines. The Chinese no doubt would welcome greater resource access, easier conditions, and more equitable LDC decision-making input. However, there is a recognition that substantive changes are not possible without the concurrence of the Group of 10 states, that China is in an inherently competitive relationship with the other Third World states for available financial resources, and that leading an NIEO assault to transform the system would seriously undermine vital national goals. If China promises to become a model beneficiary nation,[32] its overall

WBG policies have proved mildly revisionist in words but eminently pragmatic in deeds.

NOTES

1. See especially Edward Friedman, "On Maoist Conceptualizations of the Capitalist World System," *China Quarterly*, No. 80 (December 1979):807–821; Alexander Eckstein, *China's Economic Revolution* (London: Cambridge University Press, 1977), Chs. 2, 7; and Friedrich W. Y. Wu, "From Self-Reliance to Interdependence? Developmental Strategy and Foreign Economic Policy in Post-Mao China," *Modern China* 7 (October 1981):452–457.

2. Friedman, "On Maoist Conceptualizations," pp. 830, 834–835.

3. Eckstein, *China's Economic Revolution*, pp. 125–126; and Robert F. Dernberger, "Economic Development and Modernization in Contemporary China: The Attempt to Limit Dependence on the Transfer of Modern Industrial Technology from Abroad and to Control Its Corruption of the Maoist Social Revolution," in Frederick J. Fleron, ed., *Technology and Communist Culture* (New York: Praeger, 1977), p. 245.

4. Leo Goodstadt, "IMF: A Place for China," *Far Eastern Economic Review* [hereafter cited as *FEER*] 82 (October 8, 1973):47; and James B. Stepanek, "China, the IMF, and the World Bank," *China Business Review* [hereafter cited as *CBR*] 7 (January-February 1980):56.

5. Friedrich W. Y. Wu, "Socialist Self-Reliant Development Within the Capitalist World-Economy: The Chinese View in the Post-Mao Era," *Global Perspectives* 1 (Spring 1983):23–24.

6. See A. Doak Barnett, *China's Economy in Global Perspective* (Washington, D.C.: Brookings Institution, 1981), pp. 132–149.

7. Hua Guofeng, "Report on the Work of the Government," *Beijing Review* [hereafter cited as *BR*], No. 27 (July 6, 1979): 18.

8. Barnett, *China's Economy in Global Perspective*, pp. 141–143; Colina MacDougall, "Policy Changes in Foreign Trade Since the Death of Mao, 1976–1980," in Jack Gray and Gordon White, eds., *China's New Development Strategy* (New York: Academic Press, 1982), pp. 166–168; and Paul D. Reynolds, *China's International Banking and Financial System* (New York: Praeger, 1982) Chs. 2, 3.

9. Samuel S. Kim, "Whither Post-Mao Chinese Global Policy?" *International Organization* 35 (Summer 1981):450–451.

10. Ibid., p. 455.

11. "Deng Writes on Four Modernizations," Foreign Broadcast Information Service, Daily Report, China [hereafter cited as FBIS-China], February 27, 1979, p. A1, cited in Wu, "Socialist Self-Reliant Development," p. 27. Emphasis added.

12. The SDR (special drawing right) is the composite value of a weighted basket of selected national currencies, whose value is expressed in dollars and varies over time.

13. Reynolds, *China's International Banking and Financial System*, p. 144; and Anthony Rowley, "Compromising on the Gold Cache," *FEER* 108 (April 25, 1980):85

14. See Lynn Feintech, *China's Modernization Strategy and the United States*, Overseas Development Council Paper No. 31 (Washington, D.C., August 1981), p. 57; and Karen Berney and Dori Jones, "China's Activities in the IMF and the World Bank," *CBR* 8 (March-April 1981):47.

15. The China report has not been officially released by the World Bank, but summary reviews can be found in Berney and Jones, "China's Activities," p. 48; Robert Delfs, "A New Kind of Planning," *FEER* 113 (August 14, 1981):48–50; and Nicholas H. Ludlow, "World Bank Report: China's Options in the 1980s Hinge on Saving Energy," *CBR* 8 (July-August 1981): 6–8.

16. See Delfs, "A New Kind of Planning," p. 50; and Ludlow, "World Bank Report," p. 8.

17. Dinah Lee, "Trade Follows the Loans," *FEER* 112 (May 29, 1981):49.

18. See "Chen Muhua Describes Foreign Trade Situation," FBIS-China, September 23, 1982, pp. K1–6; "Chen Muhua Discusses Foreign Trade Policy," FBIS-China, October 7, 1982, p. K11; and Chen Muhua, "Prospects for China's Foreign Trade in 1983," *BR*, No. 6 (February 7, 1983):14.

19. See Joseph Gold, "Weighted Voting Power: Some Limits and Some Problems," *American Journal of International Law* 68 (October 1974):687–708; and Stephen Zamora, "Voting in International Economic Organizations," *American Journal of International Law* 74 (October 1980):576–577, 595–596.

20. Organized in 1972 within the IMF, the Group of 24 includes the finance ministers from eight selected countries in Asia, Africa, and Latin America. Though not a formal member, China has been invited to attend the semiannual meetings since May 1981.

21. Cf. World Bank, *1979 World Bank Atlas*, p. 14; and *1980 World Bank Atlas*, p. 14 (Washington, D.C.: IBRD/World Bank, 1980, 1981).

22. See International Monetary Fund, *Summary Proceedings Annual Meeting 1980*, pp. 99–103, and *Summary Proceedings Annual Meeting 1981*, pp. 110–113 (Washington, D.C.: IMF, 1981, 1982).

23. See "Minister Speaks at IMF, World Bank Meeting," FBIS-China, September 9, 1982, pp. A1, A2.

24. Chen Gong, "IMF's Unreasonable Loan," *BR*, No. 47 (November 22, 1982): 11. By a vote of 121 to 3 (United States, United Kingdom, West Germany), with 23 abstentions, the UN General Assembly adopted a resolution (A/RES/37/2) on October 21, 1982, requesting that the IMF refrain from granting any credits or other assistance to South Africa.

25. Xinhua Commentary, "IMF's Unjust Treatment of Zambia," *BR*, No. 49 (December 6, 1982): 15.

26. Barnett, *China's Economy in Global Perspective*, pp. 543–546; Feintech, *China's Modernization Strategy*, pp. 26–27; and "After MFN: GSP, GATT and IMF; Duty-Free Treatment for Chinese Goods?" *CBR* 6 (July-August 1979): 31–32.

27. Robert Delfs, "Flirting with Freer Trade," *FEER* 117 (September 24, 1982):126; "After MFN," p. 32.

28. See Bernard Gwertzman, "U.S. Backs Seat for China in Asian Bank," *New York Times*, March 22, 1983, p. 39; and International Financial Institutions Act of 1980 (S.662), PL96-259, Title II, Section 25; cited in Jonathan E. Sanford, *U.S. Foreign Policy and Multilateral Development Banks* (Boulder, Colo.: Westview Press, 1982), p. 232, n31; p. 251, n91.

29. Recently, the Chinese have estimated their foreign debt at US$17.3 billion (including loans from international financial institutions), with annual loan payments of less than 10 percent of average export income, well under the 20 percent figure generally considered overindebtedness. See Cai Jing, "China to Continue Seeking Foreign Investment," FBIS-China, September 27, 1982, p. K12.

30. See Samuel S. Kim, "The Political Economy of Post-Mao China in Global Perspective," in Neville Maxwell and Bruce McFarlane, eds., *China's Changed Road to Development* (Oxford: Pergamon Press, 1984), pp. 213–232.

31. World Bank, *World Development Report 1982* (New York: Oxford University Press for the World Bank, 1982), p. 37.

32. Nicholas H. Ludlow, "China and the World Bank: A Model Beneficiary in the Making?" *CBR* 9 (November-December 1982):13.

CHAPTER 12

THE ROLE OF SCIENCE AND TECHNOLOGY IN CHINA'S FOREIGN RELATIONS

Denis Fred Simon

INTRODUCTION

Science and technology (S&T) have had a pervasive and pronounced effect on the conduct of international relations during the postwar period. Along with the oft-noted impact on the military, advances in S&T have influenced both foreign policy and the traditional notions of national power. Autarky as a foreign policy option has been rendered somewhat, if not totally, problematic by the emergence of new and complex global and regional issues requiring technical as well as political cooperation. Examples include such wide-ranging problems as the management of space and global population control. Bilateral and multilateral exchanges of information and cooperative approaches to problem solving are becoming a more necessary and prevalent part of the international scene, greatly limiting the viability of unilateral and isolationist strategies for handling foreign policy matters.[1]

Achievements in science and technology have also contributed to a redefinition of traditional notions of national power. No longer is a nation's prestige and importance merely premised on its military might, particularly in situations where the use of force remains impractical or irrelevant. Economic power, supported and advanced by scientific and technological progress, has become a growing source of global influence. This is not to downplay the continued efficacy of military power in world affairs or the significant linkages between progress and military advance. It is meant to highlight the critical role of science and technology in fostering sustained economic growth and international competitiveness. This "civilian" dimension of S&T underscored by the momentous rise of Japan as a global power and the strident demands by the Third World for greater access to science and technology resources, promises to be an important source of wealth and power in the years ahead.[2]

Faced with the effects on their country of these various trends, Chinese leaders have paid increasing attention since the late 1970s to their own technological shortcomings and to the critical need for revitalizing their indigenous science and technology system. This recognition applies to both the domestic and foreign policy arenas. In fact, since the inception of the Four Modernizations program in the mid-1970s, science and technology have moved to center stage in the conduct of Chinese foreign policy. Never before in the history of the Communist regime has the Chinese leadership been as actively engaged in bilateral and international S&T activities.

Motivated primarily by a combination of national security concerns and economic needs, China has signed cooperative S&T agreements with all the major industrialized nations and has reaffirmed its interest in strengthening relations with the Eastern bloc countries and the Soviet Union. Beijing has also become actively involved in international scientific and technical activities, particularly through the United Nations. These formal agreements have been complemented by a myriad of nonofficial, informal cooperative relationships involving large numbers of PRC and foreign universities, commercial firms, and professional societies. This emergence from the self-imposed isolation of the past promises to have important consequences for the evolution of the international system as well as for Beijing's future external behavior.

The purpose of this chapter is to examine the breadth and focus of China's S&T relations, highlighting the implications that these rapidly expanded interactions will have for the direction of Chinese foreign policy during the 1980s. Although China has come far in recognizing the benefits of increased interaction with the world scientific community, traditional Chinese concerns regarding the actual and potential loss of political control over their affairs will continue to produce caution and apprehension within Beijing. And in spite of the merits of proceeding in a more moderate and gradual fashion, Chinese leaders will be unable to effectively manage the expanding levels of foreign influence on China's political economy and social system.

CHINA'S GREAT LEAP OUTWARD

On the surface, China's desire to acquire technology from abroad is attributable to a fundamental reordering of Chinese goals and priorities since the end of the Maoist era. In deciding to alter the closed-door policies of the past, China's current leadership has acknowledged on several occasions the central role that international scientific and technical cooperation will play in Chinese economic and military development. Specifically, the Chinese see technology imports as making five important contributions to their modernization program. They help accelerate the technical transformation of firms and strengthen the capacity for self-reliance; they assist in the rapid expansion of exports; they shorten the time it takes to carry out experiments or conduct research, thereby saving money and time; they offer learning opportunities regarding the management of technology; and they provide a context for training new technical personnel.[3]

Chinese leaders have recently acknowledged that as much as half of the gains toward achieving their goal of quadrupling the value of agricultural and industrial output by the year 2000 will have to come from increased application of science and technology.[4] A new science and technology development program, replacing the March 1978 S&T modernization program, was jointly formulated by the State Economic Commission, the Planning Commission, and the Science and Technology Commission in early 1981.[5] This plan includes the following principles: (1) the development of science and technology should be closely linked and coordinated with the development of the economy; (2) emphasis should be placed on the research and development (R&D) of production technologies; (3) greater efforts should be made to popularize and diffuse scientific results and research information; (4) basic research should receive stable but gradual support; and (5) the acquisition and assimilation of foreign S&T is to be regarded as an integral part of China's overall modernization effort.[6]

Rather than "catching up and surpassing" the West by the end of the century, which had been China's announced goal at the March 1978 National Science Conference, Beijing's revised goal is to attain the 1970s and 1980s technological levels of the advanced nations.[7] At present, however, the Chinese recognize that their current scientific and technical skills will remain far behind those of the West for the immediate future. Deng Xiaoping and his cohorts attest that the current open-door policy, exemplified by China's unparalleled willingness to import foreign technology and equipment, is an essential part of China's long-term development strategy and foreign policy.

In many important respects this is an accurate portrait of Chinese policy, yet it is also true that science and technology have been a focal point of Chinese development efforts over the last 130 years. China's current attempts to harness foreign science and technology as a means to catapult itself into the modern world provide a point of historical continuity with previous policies that date back to the "self-strengthening" movement of the Qing dynasty. In the post-Mao period, building once again on a modified version of the *ti-yong* equation, present leaders hope to establish a distinctly Chinese path to modernization by applying Western know-how to China's specific circumstances and culture. But as in the past, the precise formula and strategy needed to achieve this objective remains elusive.

Recognizing the efficacy of both change and continuity in Chinese foreign policy, we must also acknowledge the importance of the prevailing international environment within which Chinese leaders must act. As with any nation-state, the external environment provides both opportunities and constraints on Chinese behavior. Given the close interplay between "internal" and "external" in China's foreign policy, it also significantly affects the Chinese domestic policy agenda in such key issues areas as science and technology and national defense.

The world that Chinese leaders faced when they embarked on the insular policies associated with the Cultural Revolution of the mid-1960s has undergone a remarkable political and economic transformation. New issues have emerged, and uncertainty in global political and military alignments has increased, particularly as the Cold War era has given way to a world of shifting coalitions and growing transnational intercourse. The revolution in communication and transportation technology and the increasing sophistication of conventional and nuclear armaments have created an entirely new and dynamic setting for China's present activities. The "environmental uncertainty" engendered by these changes has generated a sense of urgency in China to better cope with the associated problems at both the national and international levels.

As suggested earlier, we now live in an era of increasing interconnectedness and, in some cases, interdependence. Cooperative development and application of scientific and technical information will entail significant cross-penetration of societies by widely disparate national groups and organizations. According to Inkeles and Keohane and Nye, one of the major consequences of the rapid and sustained increase in the level of interdependence is that as the channels of contact among nations multiply, there will be a blurring of the boundaries that have traditionally separated domestic and foreign affairs.[8] As contacts between national S&T communities within other nations expand, centralized control and coordination becomes more difficult to implement. Additionally, expanded communication and exchange with other members of the world scientific community may broaden the outlook of many Chinese scientists and technicians, but perhaps at the risk of generating greater sensitivity to the priorities and goals of their counterparts in the industrialized world than to the societal needs of China.[9]

Viewed from this perspective, science and technology do not only constitute a primary source of potential national power and prestige for China, they are also a vehicle through which Chinese society will become increasingly integrated within the world community. The long-term impact of these and related interactions on China's foreign policy remains uncertain at best. One likely result is that China's growing involvement in world scientific and technical affairs will give it a greater stake in supporting and preserving the established international order. Because of the possible rewards of active participation in selected international S&T fora and deliberative bodies, future Chinese S&T and economic progress could become more intimately tied to developments in the industrialized world, especially because these nations form the focal point for China's current outreach programs.

Yet, though the positive impact on Chinese development and foreign policy could be considerable, there are no guarantees that the intraelite conflicts of the past will not reemerge to influence China's future external outlook. For example, the current drive to curb "spiritual pollution," although ostensibly not aimed at the open-door policies of the Dengist regime, is a weapon that could be used by those who question the value or utility of relying on foreign technology and expertise. If a stable modernizing China can be thought of as a possibly more responsible international actor, a politically or economically unstable China could be prone to extremist behavior. More importantly, if the Chinese reap the anticipated benefits of their increased interactions with the world community, a stronger, more self-confident China could become a more assertive actor in regional or world affairs. The development of science and technology can promote cooperation and harmony between China and the rest of the world, but it could also generate serious domestic and foreign policy conflicts within China as the imperatives of interdependence come into conflict with the traditional Chinese concerns of self-reliance, independence, and national interest.[10]

To suggest that China will readily accommodate the sociopolitical intrusions that come with the open door to expanded science and technology relations would be to ignore both the critical role of domestic factors vis-à-vis Chinese foreign policy behavior *and* the continued legacy of past political turbulence. Despite their political differences, Deng Xiaoping has been almost as obsessed as Chairman Mao and his cohorts with liberating China from its economic and technological backwardness and avoiding excessive dependence on the outside world. According to pronouncements in the Chinese press, the open-door policies may represent a major tactical shift, but the goal of national self-reliance remains China's long-term objective. This suggests that the strategic dimension of China's international S&T relations may be more apparent than real.

THE ROLE OF S&T IN CHINESE FOREIGN POLICY

China's decision to significantly expand its S&T relations with the industrialized world is an extension of domestic science and technology policy rather than a major foreign policy initiative.[11] In a move designed to support the country's modernization objectives, China signed bilateral science and technology cooperation agreements with almost all the major industrialized nations.[12] These programs quickly superseded, in importance and size, the science and technology relationships China had built with the Eastern bloc and the Third World during the 1950s and 1960s. A radical departure from past practices of "politics in command," Beijing's unabashed willingness to enter into what has become a complex web of exchange programs and cooperative research projects reflected a belief that domestic science and technology capabilities were insufficient to meet the pressing demands of the economy and defense sector.

Beijing does stand to reap considerable political gains from its growing involvement in bilateral and multilateral S&T arrangements.

Politically, science and technology relations have added substance and cohesion to China's rapidly expanding relations with the West and Japan. Economically, they have helped to forge stronger commercial links as various development projects spin off from S&T cooperation. On a broader scale, growing involvement in S&T activities has provided a vehicle for Beijing to obtain greater international recognition and legitimacy. Acceptance as a full-fledged member of over 110 world and regional S&T organizations not only gives the Chinese access to scientific and technical resources but also provides acknowledgment of Beijing as the sole government of China—a high priority in Chinese leadership circles since 1949.

The fact remains, however, that the demands of internal scientific and technological modernization have provided the major impetus and direction for Chinese foreign policy in this area. Without a drastically modernized science and technology base, China will be unable to achieve its dual objectives of catching up with the industrialized world and attaining its desired status as a powerful state.[13] In perhaps the most important reflection of Beijing's new pragmatism, Chinese leaders have realized that China's claims as a world power are quite analogous to the "paper tiger" image that it had tried to associate with the United States—except that China is a *real* paper tiger.[14]

The primacy of domestic factors is demonstrated by China's willingness to maintain its S&T ties with countries such as the United States, even though relations in other important areas (e.g., Taiwan and textiles) have at times soured.[15] Because the Chinese see the United States as the fountainhead of advanced technology, gaining and maintaining access to U.S. S&T resources and data was a major factor in Beijing's decision to normalize relations with Washington and look the other way when political obstacles obstructed development of closer strategic relations. By touting the advantages of newly developed relations in the S&T area, supporters of the open-door policy were able to persuade more skeptical peers of the value of stronger links with the United States as well as with Western Europe and Japan. Had Beijing believed that its modernization goals could be achieved without such initiatives, it is likely that the scope and breadth of China's S&T ties with the United States and the rest of the world might be significantly more limited.

Since 1978, the highly publicized Chinese effort to promote the development of high-energy physics (HEP) also reflects the salience of domestic factors. China has devoted large amounts of extremely scarce financial and skilled labor resources to support activities in this field. Deng Xiaoping and China's leading S&T administrator, Fang Yi, have been strong supporters of an enhanced Chinese capability in the HEP field. Several reasons have been cited by Chinese leaders to explain the special status accorded to HEP, including a reference to Chairman Mao's own desire to see China make progress in this area. The two primary reasons, however, appear to have been the extensive influence that Chinese physicists had on the formulation of national science and technology policy since 1977–1978 and the key role played by overseas Chinese physicists when China was just beginning to revitalize its indigenous S&T system. Not only was HEP seen as having many possible scientific spin-offs into other critical fields; it was also viewed by many within China's physics community as a research vehicle to reintegrate themselves into the world scientific community after almost thirty years of isolation. The rapidity with which cooperation in HEP became a central element in the Sino-American S&T program after 1979 supports this argument.[16]

Of course, at the time Beijing was contemplating whether to enter into a more sustained program of scientific exchange and technology acquisition, the major issue on the agenda of Chinese leaders was the Soviet Union.[17] The large numbers of Soviet troops on China's northern border, combined with growing Soviet influence on China's southern border via the Soviet-Vietnam connection, made the Chinese leadership realize that a more credible deterrent might be necessary to stave off a potential military encounter with Moscow. This factor cannot be ignored in assessing the calculus of Chinese foreign policy decision making during the period in question. Here again, however, the evidence seems to point to domestic imperatives—the need to rebuild the country's shattered science and technology system—rather than foreign policy alliance building as the principal source of Chinese actions.[18]

The special role of domestic factors in stimulating China's push outward for science and technology should not be interpreted as suggesting that S&T have subsumed in toto other traditional political and cultural factors in guiding Chinese foreign policy. As Jonathan Pollack has suggested in the defense area, "China's security needs do not seem to be driven by a technological imperative."[19] At the same time, science and technology cut across so many dimensions of China's modernization program that Chinese leaders have been forced to grant S&T a high priority in laying out foreign policy objectives. This recognition has prompted Beijing to seek out foreign policy relationships that could be fruitful in helping China to fill some of the country's increasingly critical, and in many cases growing, technological gaps.[20]

Depending on the specific context, S&T relations have been viewed by Beijing as both separate from and integral to political relations with various friendly states.[21] At times, Beijing has viewed political relations as distinct from the realm of science and technology, particularly during the process of normalizing relations with a new country. This was the practice in the early 1970s before China had official diplomatic relations with several major countries, including the United States and Japan.[22] It also appears to be the case with Sino-Indian relations today.[23] Moreover, even though the large number of high-level Chinese delegations sent abroad during the late 1970s sought to heighten Western appreciation of the Soviet threat, the associated shopping spree for technology and equipment (military and civilian) was not accompanied by a massive effort to build a formal strategic alliance with any one or several nations. When such possibilities were raised by Western Europeans or the United States, the Chinese tended to retreat, clearly stating that their desire for access to science and technology did not necessitate such formalized foreign entanglements.

At other times, the Chinese have viewed the level and scope of S&T programs offered by any one bilateral partner as symbolic of the political strength of that specific relationship. For this reason, the Chinese have frequently pressed hard for additional technical assistance, expanded bilateral cooperation programs, and increased transfers of technology as a measure of goodwill by the U.S., British, or German governments. In these cases, politics—not potential technology sales—has been used by China as the leverage point. But when these expressions of political commitment have not been forthcoming, the Chinese have been unwilling to discount the benefits of science and technology relations because of problems in the political area. The exception that proves the rule was the downgrading of diplomatic relations with the Netherlands over the Taiwan issue. However, the level and scope of S&T exchanges with the Dutch was minor in comparison to Sino-American exchanges.

China views access to and use of science and technology as an essential part of its rights as a sovereign nation. Its willingness to carry on scientific and technical exchanges with other nations is premised on mutual adherence to the three principles of independence, equality, and mutual benefit. This reflects the continued concern of current and previous leaders about the dangers of becoming overly dependent on external actors for meeting its critical needs.[24] As mentioned earlier, self-reliance continues to be the watchword for China. Although Chinese leaders have moved away from the Maoist radical autarkic interpretation of the self-reliance concept, they still hold to three basic underlying principles: avoidance of excessive dependence on all external actors, including overconcentration of activities with any one nation; active promotion of indigenous capabilities, especially in areas with strategic military application; and resistance to those foreign influences on Chinese culture and society that accompany scientific exchange and technical cooperation. The current interpretation of self-reliance was contained in the March 14, 1983, issue of the *Beijing Review:* "Self-reliance means that a country relies on its own strength, uses its own resources, materials, and technology, and independently draws up a strategy for economic development according to its own conditions."[25]

China's approach to the development of its offshore oil reserves exemplifies both its apprehensions and its strategy for meeting self-reliance objectives. Lacking adequate equipment or the scientific and technical personnel to undertake a project as large and complex as the offshore development program, the Chinese have granted foreign firms opportunities to assist in the exploration and exploitation of these potentially oil-rich areas. With the goal of eventually assuming full responsibility for the management and operation of the rigs, China's petroleum officials have gone to great lengths to insure that Chinese nationals receive adequate technical training and are given appropriate managerial experience so that there will be no need to maintain long-term dependence on the foreign petroleum companies.

Publicly (in such fora as the United Nations), China has claimed that science and technology are "part of [the] universal human heritage, which should be shared by all countries, particularly developing countries."

> Science and technology is a shared asset for all of mankind. It should serve the social and economic progress of all countries and work for all people on earth. . . . China stands for the lifting of unreasonable restrictions on scientific and technological exchanges. She is opposed to the practice of using economic and scientific and technological superiority to bully weaker or smaller states or to undermine their interests.[26]

The Chinese have strongly supported Third World NIEO demands in the science and technology area, though efforts in this policy arena have not been as visible as other Chinese initiatives toward the Third World since 1981.[27] Because Chinese views of science and technology have been so intimately tied to their concerns about national sovereignty, they have tended to view matters such as technology transfer or control over technology as major issues in the context of recent bilateral relations with the industrialized world. Efforts by technology suppliers to apply export controls or to impose end-user restrictions dealing with the use and diffusion of technology once it has entered China's borders have been strongly resisted by the Chinese.

These Chinese responses reflect both a naive understanding and somewhat paradoxical view of science and technology. From an economic standpoint, the Chinese position reflects a lack of appreciation for the costs associated with research and development activities *and* for the value of proprietary knowledge as a commercially marketable good. From a governmental standpoint, domestic or multilateral regulations adopted by other nations to control technology outflows to protect their own perceived security interests have been poorly received in Beijing. Yet China has used the national sovereignty issue to protest the attempted imposition of limits on its intended use of certain technologies or to curtail opportunities for study and field research by foreign scholars in the natural and social sciences.

An excellent example of Beijing's hard-line attitude is its position on the acquisition of nuclear energy technology from abroad.[28] Throughout its negotiations with the United States, the Chinese have consistently refused to allow outside inspection of its facilities as required by the nuclear nonproliferation guidelines, even though some foreign scientists have reportedly visited several of China's nuclear weapons–related or other sensitive facilities.[29] The Chinese have claimed that China is already a nuclear weapons state, and that such inspections would violate its rights as a sovereign nation-state.

The Chinese continue to express three major concerns regarding the potential consequences of extensive borrowing of technology and foreign involvement in their domestic affairs: excessive penetration of their society by capitalist forces, destruction of domestic industry, and corruption and crime.[30] Apprehension about the impact on China's domestic industry has been particularly strong, especially as many Chinese enterprises and consumers are willing to forgo domestically made items, such as Chinese-made computers or consumer goods, to buy the generally more expensive and prestigious foreign products. An April 1982 editorial cites the presence of large numbers of foreign automobiles, trucks, and buses in China while the country's "Number One Automobile plant" does not have enough work.[31]

There also has been criticism voiced over the actual contribution of advanced foreign technology imports. In many instances, China has imported state-of-the-art or extremely sophisticated items when somewhat older and less complex imports or more importantly, domestic alternatives would have sufficed. A study of the textiles industry conducted in early 1981 concluded that imported technology and equipment made less of a contribution to increased productivity than domestically made items.[32] The study noted that the imported items cost more, consumed more raw materials, used greater power, had a higher depreciation cost, and demanded more operating personnel even though the number of unskilled laborers declined.[33]

The Chinese clearly recognize the costs, but it is doubtful whether they can effectively limit the damage and take what they want. They have shown no intention to "close the door." As one Chinese publicist has remarked concerning the possible problems associated with foreign technological borrowing, "you do not give up eating for fear of choking." To discourage corruption, the Chinese have used the threat of strong punishment. To ensure more effective use of imported technology equipment, they have tried to differentiate between "technically backward" and "technically advanced" recipients, with the latter given preference in receiving imported items.

As a result of their increased understanding of the prerequisites for successful acquisition and assimilation, the Chinese continue to seek out additional technology imports. According to an authoritative *Hongqi* article in April 1982, there are four major reasons that widespread involvement with other nations in the S&T area is now more feasible than in the past. The first is domestic political stability and a high degree of national integration; the second is rectification of ideology and Party attitudes and practices; the third is a strong national defense; and the fourth is a favorable international environment for China, as reflected in its broad spectrum of contacts with over 150 nations.[34]

THE CONTENT OF CHINA'S EXTERNAL S&T POLICY

Since the revision of the February 1978 Four Modernizations program and the announcement of the economic readjustment program at the Third Plenum in December 1978, China has significantly modified its technology acquisition policies. Chinese leaders have cited four main errors in their previous technology import strategy: (1) excessive reliance on whole plant and equipment imports; (2) widespread duplication of imports; (3) a tendency to import items without adequate knowledge to operate or maintain them; and (4) failure to analyze imported technology to understand and diffuse it to others.[35]

Recognizing that little actual technology transfer took place in the past, China has de-emphasized the acquisition of whole plants and equipment as a major means to secure desired know-how. The import of complete plants may have helped lay a foundation for industrial development, but it also weakened investment in R&D and stifled scientific and technological creativity.[36] As a result, new stress has been placed on the more "intangible" forms of technology acquisition.[37] This is true in both military and civilian areas. Beijing has encouraged the acquisition of advanced management methods; new skills and scientific rules of operation; new design principles, data, and know-how; new and sophisticated materials; and selected advanced equipment and components.[38]

With the shift away from whole plant imports and large equipment purchases, the Chinese have laid out several stipulations for their policies on technology imports, spelled out in October 1982 by Xu Deen, deputy managing director of the China National Technical Import Corporation. China will not sign technology transfer contracts that restrict it from undertaking R&D or innovating with imported items; reserves the right to use technology after the expiration of the contract; and will not return documentation after a contract expires. Agreements must guarantee that the specified technology will be suitable to Chinese needs, and China will not accept any tie-in agreements requiring additional purchases. China will not approve any agreements that limit its ability to use other suppliers if desired; the supplier must provide information on any improvements or modifications in the technology; and the Chinese will reject any arrangement that contains extraterritoriality provisions.[39]

These stipulations though strongly worded are quite consistent with the attempts of the Third World in general to increase its bargaining leverage in negotiations for the acquisition of technology from the industrialized nations. They also reflect China's increased sophistication in the international marketplace for technology. At the same time, however, that China has imposed these requirements on foreign suppliers, it has been reluctant to offer reciprocal protection to overseas companies in such areas as patent infringement. Even though the Chinese claim to recognize the need for a patent law and have in fact drafted a preliminary set of codes for protecting the technology of foreign firms, they apparently have proceeded reluctantly. Reverse-engineering, copying, and imitation are common practices in China,[40] and at least on the surface, the enactment of a comprehensive patent law would put a severe damper on these activities.

Within the above context, the following forms of cooperation are being emphasized by Beijing: bilateral or multilateral agreements for S&T cooperation; bilateral and multilateral academic seminars; mutual exchanges of scientists and technical personnel for lectures; joint research projects; establishment of joint research centers; establishment of "sister" relationships with research institutes having similar interests; student exchanges; exchanges of scientific and technical information; and the provision of technical assistance and technology transfers with specific industrial or agricultural applications. In all cases, both official and nonofficial contacts are acceptable to Beijing. The latter include academy-to-academy or university-to-university relationships that exist outside of formal government-to-government agreements.

China's academic exchange programs with the West and Japan assume special importance in the context of Beijing's foreign science and technology relations. Because the mainstay of the technology transfer process is the individual, these exchanges have already helped China to build a much stronger and better-qualified labor pool from which to draw scientific and technical talent. According to the *China Daily,* by the end of 1982 China had sent 12,000 to 15,000 students overseas for education and advanced training.[41] The Sixth Five-Year Plan calls for sending another 15,000 students. The majority of Chinese students and scholars abroad are studying the natural sciences and engineering, though over the last year or two more students have been entering fields such as management and the social sciences.

The PRC government has also made a special effort to cultivate the Overseas Chinese community to assist with science and technology modernization.[42] In May 1980, for example, a major scientific and technical magazine was launched with the help of Dr. Chien Ning, a citizen of China who was conducting physics research in the United States. This magazine, *Science and Technology Review,* was distinguished by the number of high-level Chinese-American scientists serving on the editorial board.[43] Deng Xiaoping announced a massive drive to secure the assistance of Overseas Chinese to take advantage of their knowledge and expertise as China attempts to sustain its economic and S&T modernization program.[44] One has merely to review a list of the foreign visitors that have had an audience with Deng, Fang Yi, and Premier Zhao Ziyang over the last several years to recognize the importance that the leadership attaches to the Overseas Chinese scientific community around the world.[45]

In spite of the shifts in China's external S&T policy, there has not been widespread agreement on the extent to which China should rely on foreign imports of technology and equipment or send large numbers of students overseas.

At present, some people maintain that the less foreign technology we import, the more self-reliant we are. These people have dared not emancipate their thinking nor have they actively imported advanced technology, particularly since the time when the sets of equipment we imported cause some mishaps. Their viewpoint is wrong. . . . We must not let ourselves be bound by the outmoded idea of self-sufficiency, but must embrace a broader view of global strategy and integrate our country's vast material and manpower resources with the huge international market, thereby finding a better way for our development.[46]

There have also been disagreements on whether to give know-how or whole plants primary emphasis. According to one analyst critical of extensive reliance on "software," "judging from the present state of our country's scientific and technical level, as well as our power to absorb and digest, we cannot yet introduce too many single items of technology. It is certain that we must import complete sets of equipment."[47] Other factors have also affected China's ability to implement its technology acquisition policy. One of the major problems has been excessive departmentalism and continuous wrangling among ministries.[48] A February 1983 article in *Shijie jingji daobao* (World economic herald) complained that there is no clear delineation of which agencies have the necessary authority to and responsibility for signing contracts.[49] Moreover, even when deals are signed, many acquisitions have not been preceded by adequate feasibility studies, often leading to problems later on down the line.[50]

All of these shortcomings have led to serious problems with the assimilation and application of technology. The importance of the assimilation task was highlighted in a January 1983 editorial in *Renmin ribao*:

We must direct great efforts towards solving the problem of assimilation. This is a weak link in this work. We must strengthen leadership, make overall arrangements, seek energetic cooperation in all fields, and change the situation marked by the lack of communication between those units importing technology, scientific research units, and units producing equipment. We must do a good job of assimilation, so that the fullest play can be given to imported technology in our production and construction.[51]

Given the significance attached to the acquisition and use of foreign know-how, continued examples of assimilation problems could lead to questions about the viability of the open door to foreign science and technology.[52]

As far as the student/scholar exchanges are concerned, they have also raised several important issues for Chinese political leaders. First and perhaps most sensitive has been the issue of defections. Some restrictions have been imposed on the children of high-level officials to avoid possible embarrassment.[53] In addition, self-supporting students must now work for two years before they are allowed to go overseas.[54]

Second is the problem of reassimilation. Students that return after being trained in advanced laboratories in the West or in Japan may find that settling back in China is difficult.[55] Research institutes lack similar equipment, may have different research priorities than their Western counterparts, or simply do not have the funding to support expensive research efforts.[56] This raises the question of whether or not the Chinese being sent abroad are learning the right skills to accord with China's specific conditions.

Last, along with their role in technology transfer, students serve as a transmission belt for bringing both desirable and undesirable foreign ideas and culture to China. Life in the West for many Chinese, despite their limited means, is often exciting and highly thought provoking. Accordingly, the supply of people wanting to go abroad is quite high. In late 1982 this led *Renmin ribao* to harshly criticize those who "crave" to go abroad.[57]

DEFENSE MODERNIZATION AND THE ACQUISITION OF FOREIGN TECHNOLOGY

China's efforts since 1978 to assess and in some cases, acquire military equipment and technology have been well documented. The plethora of military delegations that have traveled to and from Beijing have discussed possible purchases of weapon systems ranging from the French-manufactured Mirage 2000 jet fighter to the U.S.-built TOW missile. These delegations have served as an effective mechanism for acquiring state-of-the-art information about foreign weapon systems and Western technological achievements. Over the last five years, academic, government, and business hosts to visiting Chinese groups note a substantial improvement in the technical sophistication and knowledge of each new delegation. In the commercial area, the improved qualifications of delegation members have aided in the selection and negotiation of specific technologies and pieces of equipment. At the same time, many business leaders have been angered when Chinese purchase agreements have not been forthcoming.

In many cases, the Chinese have come up against constraints of their own that have prevented large sales from taking place. These constraints have included foreign exchange limitations, indecision over which items to acquire, uncertainty regarding the relationship of acquired items to existing doctrine, and doubts about China's own absorptive capacity. China's decision in early 1983 to cancel a US$170 million agreement with Great Britain to upgrade the electronic and missile capabilities of their LUDA destroyers is suggestive. Although the agreement had been signed in November 1982, it was allowed to lapse past the date when it needed to be ratified by the Chinese government.[58]

At other times, the Chinese have faced constraints beyond their own system. The most pervasive have been the export-control regulations in the United States and their counterpart controls administered by the Coordinating Committee of the Consultative Group (COCOM), the multilateral body composed of NATO members (minus Iceland) and Japan responsible for monitoring and controlling exports of critical technologies and equipment to Communist countries. Some nations have been reluctant to acquiesce in China's desire for military purchases for fear of aggravating relations with the Soviet Union or opening the door too wide for other nations who may be more willing to accept higher levels of risk associated with weapons sales to the Chinese in order to expand commercial exchanges.

One of the key factors that has constrained Chinese access to dual-use technologies—those with both civilian and military applications—has been the structure of China's industrial and R&D organizations. There is a high incidence of military work being done jointly by both civilian and defense research institutes or factories.[59] This close overlap in functions and the Chinese tendency to obscure rather than delineate military-civilian distinctions have run up against the end-user evaluation process that frequently accompanies many requests for export licenses. In most cases, the dual structure in China is not a matter of deception; it reflects the scarcity of financial, equipment, and personnel resources. The result is that some Chinese requests have been delayed or denied on the basis of unacceptable end users. The Chinese have made it clear that they find these determinations unacceptable. They characterize attempts to distinguish end users as interference in their internal affairs.

In other instances, export control and COCOM decisions to deny certain sales to China are based on the level of technology and its potential application as well as on end-user considerations. Under the "two-times" rule that was inaugurated in mid-1981, the U.S. government indicated that it would approve technology sales to China at "twice the level that would have been sold to the Soviet Union prior to the invasion of Afghanistan"—a rather inexact measure in all respects except perhaps in political intent. This China "differential" clouded the low end of the technology spectrum: It was easy to see which technologies went beyond the limit, but far less easy to specify the initial benchmark.

Since Secretary of Defense Harold Brown's visit to China in January 1980, Washington has steadily relaxed its controls over the export of critical technology to China. The first move in this direction occurred shortly after the Brown trip, when U.S. firms were notified by the State Department—which administers the Munitions Control List—that non-lethal dual-use military gear could be sold to the Chinese.[60] The decision to relax existing controls coincided with the visit of Zhang Wenjin, the Chinese vice–foreign minister, who had come to the United States to discuss strategy for countering the Soviet intervention in Afghanistan. These regulations were further refined in May 1980 to coincide with the visit of former Chinese defense minister Geng Biao to the United States.[61]

Perhaps the most significant movement in the technology area took place in September 1980 with the visit to China of William Perry, director of research and engineering in the U.S. Defense Department. The Perry visit provided the first real opportunity for comprehensive and substantive discussions on specific pieces of equipment and technology.[62] Movement toward this end, however, was interrupted by the reemergence of Taiwan as a major issue in the context of the Sino-American relationship.

In June 1981, Secretary of State Alexander Haig ventured to China in the hope of providing a breakthrough in the deadlock over both Taiwan and the technology transfer issue. In spite of U.S. commitments to open up technology transfer channels in areas desired by Beijing, the Chinese began to feel that Washington was unwilling to meet its demands for advanced items. One prime example cited by China was Washington's refusal to clear the way for export of several IBM computers to be used in the Chinese census project. The Haig visit therefore provided an opportunity to rectify the Chinese perception that they were still being denied access to U.S. technology. In June 1981, just prior to the Haig visit, China was moved out of the same export control category as the Soviet Union and a new "P" category was inaugurated just for the Chinese.[63]

The "P" category significantly expanded the level and type of technology that could be sold to China. Under the terms of this export control legislation, "licenses may be approved even when the end-use is military or the end-user engages in military activity." The regulation states that "potential use of equipment or data in design, development, or manufacture of military tactical items will not necessarily preclude approval." The major limits of the "P" category were reflected in the identification of five special mission areas: nuclear weapons; nuclear weapons delivery systems; antisubmarine warfare; electronic warfare; and intelligence gathering systems. Although each request for an export license in the military area would be decided on a case-by-case basis, technologies and equipment that would make a direct and significant contribution to these five areas were to be denied.[64]

In spite of the enactment of more relaxed regulations, differences persisted, and in some cases grew. One of the reasons for this state of affairs was the stronger emphasis China placed on technology acquisitions than on purchases of hardware. A case in point involves the proposed sale of telephone equipment by the Belgian ITT affiliate, which included an advanced digital switching system and related technology.[65] According to the press, Washington expressed fears over the sale because of a belief that China could substantially benefit from the computer software and electronics technologies included in the agreement. Because of the broad nature of the five special mission areas, it was not too difficult to envision a present or future application to any one of them, particularly as electronics constitutes a "critical" technology. U.S. opposition to the agreement was only dropped after Belgium was able to work out a technology transfer arrangement with China that was acceptable to the United States and COCOM.[66]

The Haig visit apparently gave the Chinese reason to believe that existing bottlenecks in technology exports would be rapidly removed, opening up the opportunity for relatively unencumbered access to U.S. industrial and defense technology and equipment. When from Beijing's point of view this did not occur, Chinese disaffection steadily increased. A Xinhua News Agency editorial on the tenth anniversary of the Shanghai Communiqué noted that "as far as advanced technology is concerned, China has not received much from the United States since diplomatic relations were established."[67] In October 1982, Foreign Minister Huang Hua commented in a speech before the Council on Foreign Relations in New York on what he called continued discrimination against China by the United States.[68] He pointed to a lack of U.S. sincerity in its overall commitment to the Sino-American relationship.[69]

Chinese demands for a more forthcoming U.S. technology policy coincided with congressional testimony and press reports indicating growing PRC involvement in illegal and covert acquisition of U.S. technology. According to testimony provided by Lt. General James Williams, the director of the U.S. Defense Intelligence Agency, China had set up a series of dummy firms and related clandestine acquisition mechanisms, to secure technologies prohibited for export under the regulations.[70] Moreover, it was reported in the *Asian Wall Street Journal* that several firms in Hong Kong and the West Coast of the United States were investigated for training PRC technicians and engineers in sophisticated electronics areas.[71] These purported attempts by China to bypass existing regulations not only underscored the vital importance of technology transfers to the Chinese; they also raised further questions about Beijing's long-term intentions and its ultimate reliability as a "strategic associate" of the United States.[72]

In spite of the strong words coming out of Beijing, the Chinese may also have been posturing on the issue to secure a further loosening of controls. After all, S&T cooperation with the United States was proceeding rapidly. Over seventeen protocols for cooperation had been signed by mid-1982 and several thousand government-sponsored scientists, scholars, and students had come to the United States for education and advanced training.

Ironically, sustained pressure and discontent over the technology transfer issue did not fully surface until after the signing of Shanghai Communiqué II in August 1982. One explanation may be that the Chinese wanted to dissociate the Taiwan and technology issues. As long as the Taiwan issue generated uncertainty over the relationship, Chinese leaders may have felt uncomfortable about pushing this "strategic" side of the relationship. Moreover, by focusing on the technology issue prior to a resolution of the Taiwan issue, Chinese leaders may have felt that they would be acknowledging a strategic dimension to the Sino-American relationship that the Reagan administration had wanted to attach to it in words but not in deeds.

Another explanation for the harshness of the Chinese criticism may have been increasing pressure from domestic political factions skeptical of the long-term value of the Sino-American relationship. Certain segments in the military may have believed that unless the United States provided ample supplies of advanced, military-applicable technology, the relationship was not worth pursuing. This argument is supported by the new emphasis on defense industrial and technological modernization that was emerging at the time. Given the technologies under dispute—electronics and computers, there is ample reason to suspect some military concern about the continued "tightness" of U.S. export laws.[73]

In March 1983, Zhang Aiping, China's minister of national defense and former director of the National Defense Science and Technology Commission, published an important article on military modernization in *Hongqi*, the authoritative journal of the Chinese Communist Party. Zhang's article made three major points: the need to concentrate available resources on strategic weapons programs; the need for closer coordination between military and civilian research and manufacturing; and the "unreliability" of foreign suppliers regarding the transfer of desired technologies to China.

> We must soberly see that what can be bought from foreign countries will be at most things that are advanced to the second grade. This cannot help us attain the goal of national defense modernization, nor will it help us shake off the passive state of being controlled by others. Nor is dependence on modelling one's weaponry on others a way of realizing national defense modernization. At the outset it is necessary to import some technology and model some weaponry on that of others. However, if we are content with copying, we will only crawl behind others and will still be unable to attain our anticipated goals. The fundamental way is to rely on ourselves.[74]

Zhang's article underscored the expectation in parts of the Chinese military that foreign technology and equipment would play a vital role in defense modernization—and made clear that these expectations had not been fulfilled. Without dismissing the obvious utility of technology imports, Zhang stressed that in the long run, as in the case of China's development of advanced strategic weapons and its successful SLBM launch in late 1982, the technical requirements for further advance would have to be met internally.[75] This same message was echoed again in late July 1983 by Yu Qiuli, head of the PLA Central Political Committee.[76]

A third plausible explanation for the intransigence of some Chinese may have been the poor performance of the country's science and technology modernization effort. In October 1982, Zhao Ziyang made a special effort at the national Scientific Awards Conference to attach greater significance to scientific and technological advance and to criticize those who were merely paying lip service to the science and technology policies coming out of Beijing, particularly concerning the treatment of scientific and technical personnel.[77] Accordingly, in January 1983 a new supraministerial leading group directed by Premier Zhao was formed to strengthen support for S&T modernization and provide greater cohesiveness to S&T policymaking efforts.

The severity of the Chinese criticism is also surprising in view of increasing indications that Chinese S&T needs could be met by Western Europe and Japan. In the areas of bilateral cooperation and commercial technology transfer, Western Europe and Japan have indicated a strong willingness to serve Chinese needs. After all, the Sino-American S&T agreement was one of the last to be signed with the Chinese. It was preceded by agreements with the French in January 1978; the West Germans, Swedes, and Italians in October; and the British in November. In most cases, the governments in these countries have been willing to lend financial assistance to facilitate commercial technology transfers and the expansion of student exchange and cooperative research programs.[78] In addition, this potential for alternative sources also appears to hold true for COCOM, most of whose members have publicly indicated that U.S. policies are too restrictive.

According to a study conducted in the early 1980s, however, the Chinese have consistently expressed a clear preference for U.S. science and technology.[79] In the nuclear energy area, for example, they have twice retreated from purchasing the French Framatome reactor in the hopes of buying a U.S. system. And they have not pulled back from negotiations with the United States despite obvious disagreements over inspection. Discussions on a bilateral cooperation program in nuclear energy are also continuing. From the perspective of both parties, a failure to get some movement would only yield further damage to the Sino-American relationship, even though in the long run the Chinese might be the real loser.

Secretary of State George Schultz's visit in February 1983 and the Joint Sino-U.S. Science and Technology Commission meeting in May 1983 provided further opportunities for the Chinese to make their case. In both instances, however, even after seemingly productive discussions, the Chinese remained dissatisfied.[80] It was only in May and June of 1983, with the visit of Commerce Department Secretary Baldrige, that the Chinese felt some movement had been made and toned down their criticism.[81] The Baldrige delegation brought as promise that the red tape in the U.S. bureaucracy would be cleared up and that the controls on exports would be both better defined and further loosened.[82] The result was that in late June a new set of export guidelines was introduced. The provisions of this new set of controls were spelled out in the *Federal Register* in November 1983.[83]

The "P" category that had been specially created for China was abolished. Instead, China was placed in the "V" category, the same classification applied to U.S. allies, India, and Yugoslavia. Along with continued concern about the five special mission areas, limits were introduced on technologies that would contribute to Chinese air superiority or increased power projection capabilities. The new regulations also pay significant attention to the problem of reexport or diversion to other countries, both of which would be illegal under U.S. law. The new guidelines open up greater technology exports at the low-to-middle end of the technology spectrum, identifying for approval those items that fell in gray areas under the preexisting export regulations. A three-tier system—green light/yellow light/red light—has been established to speed up the processing of license requests. Although they clearly help to overcome the logjam at the low end of the technology spectrum, the new regulations actually do very little to clarify nonapproved technologies at the middle-to-high ranges. Rather than resolving the issues, the new law may in fact cause greater difficulty if the Chinese apply pressure at the high end of the spectrum.

Defense Secretary Weinberger's visit to China in September 1983 provided an excellent opportunity for both sides to pursue discussions on advanced technology sales, especially in the military area.[84] Premier Zhao Ziyang seized the moment to acknowledge U.S. movement on the export control issue, yet Weinberger's attempts to interest the Chinese in various acquisition possibilities were partially rebuffed.[85] The prevailing defense modernization priorities may allow for broader consultation, but Chinese technology and equipment purchases will continue to be modest as the rebuilding of the domestic S&T base moves at a gradual, deliberate pace.

CONCLUSIONS

If one thing is clear from China's foreign policy behavior during the last several years, it is that Chinese leaders have their own working policy agenda, especially in the area of science and technology. This is likely to continue well into the future. Even though this agenda may be influenced by outside forces, it can also be insulated from external factors when necessary. This working agenda and the objectives it contains reflect a Chinese view of the world, a combination of distinctly Sinocentric elements and inputs from the external environment in which China must exist. Any attempt to fully understand Chinese foreign policy in the future must focus on the increasing difficulty that Chinese leaders will encounter in trying to balance these two forces. The greatest risk to any leader will be to move too far in either direction.

China has had a difficult time managing its expanded relations with the outside world. In many cases, its managerial capabilities have been outstripped by the rapid and tenacious influence of the transnational forces that accompany science and technology relations. Yet without significant inputs of technical information and scientific data from abroad, China will continue to lag behind the industrialized world—a plight that post-Mao Chinese leaders have officially acknowledged, but find difficult to institutionalize in China's open-door policy.

We may see a growing disjuncture between policy pronouncements and policy implementation in the future. For the most part, China's willingness to maintain a broad base of sustained S&T contacts with the West and Japan will depend upon its ability to capture the benefits of these exchanges more effectively, while minimizing the impact of undesirable societal and political disturbances. If they are unsuccessful, this leadership and its successors will be unable to muster the necessary political support to keep the open door as "open" as it has been.

Of course, only a short time has passed since China made a decision to expand its foreign science and technology relations, and it may be too early to project far into the future. China has always been an enigma to the West as far as predicting Chinese behavior over a long period of time is concerned. The fact remains, however, that involvement in these activities strikes at the very heart of Chinese sensitivities. Consequently, as reports of uneasiness about dependence on foreign technology appear in the press, Chinese leaders have been constantly faced with the task of reassuring the outside world that receptivity to foreign know-how is not a temporary phenomenon. Despite these assurances, the Chinese press reports assimilation problems, and the foreign business community remains frustrated over China's inability to make acquisition decisions rapidly and in large numbers. With modernization demands remaining high and tolerance for undesirable foreign influence still low, it remains to be seen whether the search for "balance" that has escaped previous leaders can be achieved by the current leadership.

In a period in international affairs when the costs of interdependence are growing and the ability of governments to manage cross-national flows is decreasing, China is apt to experience the same "loss of control." Interdependence is mainly a phenomenon associated with the industrialized world, but China's intercourse with these countries is growing at a speed that will make the effects of closer interaction unavoidable. Yes, China can and will likely try to resist or at least minimize these effects, but always at the danger of creating too much of an arm's-length relationship to make technology transfers meaningful.

China has made great progress in overcoming many of the debilitating effects of the Cultural Revolution on its science and technology system. This progress promises to be a positive factor in helping China to derive optimal gains from expanded science and technology relations. The tradition of xenophobia, however, continues—a somber thought in view of the massive changes that have taken place in post-Mao China. In the final analysis, the Chinese must be prepared to accept the sociopolitical changes that accompany widespread application of science and technology—whether foreign or indigenously developed. Once these changes in attitude are made, there will be more certainty, more predictability, and, one hopes, more openness regarding the role that Chinese leaders assign to science and technology in China's foreign relations.

NOTES

1. Eugene Skolnikoff, *The International Imperatives of Technology* (Berkeley: Institute of International Studies, University of California, 1972). See also the special issue of *International Organization* 29 (Summer 1975).
2. For a discussion of the role of science and technology in the call for a New International Economic Order, see Ward Morehouse, *Science, Technology and the Social Order* (New Brunswick, N.J.: Transaction Books, 1979).
3. Chen Lianzhen, "A Breakthrough Is Necessary in Importing Advanced Technology," *Fujian ribao*, January 23, 1983, in Joint Publications Research Service [hereafter JPRS], 83440 (May 10, 1983), pp. 76–79.
4. For example, see "The Glorious and Historical Mission of Scientific and Technical Workers," *Renmin ribao* [People's daily, hereafter *RMRB*], October 23, 1982, in Foreign Broadcast Information Service, Daily Report, China [hereafter FBIS-China], October 27, 1982, pp. K6–8.
5. "Key State Science and Technology Projects Listed," in FBIS-China, August 4, 1983, pp. K9–10.
6. Lin Zixin and Wu Mingyu, "An Exploration of Some Questions Concerning China's Strategy for Technological Development," ST/BIC/PS/CH/01 (Paper presented at the Beijing International Conference on Science and Technology Policy and Research Management, sponsored by the United Nations Financing System for Science and Technology for Development, Beijing, October 4–8, 1983).
7. "Zhao on Technological Progress," FBIS-China, December 1, 1982, p. K6.
8. Robert Keohane and Joseph Nye, *Power and Interdependence* (Boston: Little, Brown and Co., 1977). See also Alex Inkeles, "The Emerging Social Structure of the World," *World Politics* 27 (July 1975):467–495.
9. For a discussion of the impact of these transnational interactions on the behavior of scientists within international organizations, see Ernst Haas, Mary Pat Williams, and Don Babai, *Scientists and World Order: The Uses of Technological Knowledge in International Organizations* (Berkeley: University of California Press, 1977).
10. For an examination of these problems in the context of China's behavior in the United Nations, see Samuel S. Kim, *China, the United Nations, and World Order* (Princeton, N.J.: Princeton University Press, 1979).

11. The role of domestic factors in the making of foreign policy is discussed in James Rosenau, ed., *The Domestic Sources of Foreign Policy* (New York: Free Press, 1967).

12. Richard P. Suttmeier, *Science, Technology and China's Drive for Modernization* (Stanford, Calif.: Hoover Institution Press, 1980). The major exception was Japan, which did not sign a formal S&T agreement until May 1980. However, Sino-Japanese S&T relations had been broadening since the early 1970s through the activities of the Japan-China S&T Exchange Association, formed in December 1977, and the cooperation agreement signed between the Chinese Academy of Sciences and the Japan Society for the Promotion of Science in September 1979.

13. Richard Baum, ed., *China's Four Modernizations* (Boulder, Colo.: Westview Press, 1980).

14. John F. Copper, *China's Global Role* (Stanford, Calif.: Hoover Institution Press, 1980).

15. Denis Fred Simon, "The Technology Issue in Sino-US Relations," (forthcoming).

16. The Sino-U.S. cooperation program in high-energy physics is discussed in Richard P. Suttmeier, *US-PRC Scientific Cooperation: An Assessment of the First Two Years* (Paper prepared for U.S. Department of State, Contract 1751-000372, June 1981).

17. Richard Solomon, ed. *The China Factor: Sino-American Relations and the Global Scene* (Englewood Cliffs, N.J.: Prentice-Hall, 1981).

18. A reading of both the Western and Chinese press during this period indicates that China's main motive was to solidify the Western alliance, not to join it.

19. Jonathan Pollack, "Rebuilding China's Great Wall," in Paul M. B. Godwin, ed., *The Chinese Defense Establishment: Continuity and Change in the 1980s* (Boulder, Colo.: Westview Press, 1983), pp. 3–20.

20. Leo Orleans, ed., *Science in Contemporary China* (Stanford, Calif.: Stanford University Press, 1981).

21. Harry G. Gelber, *Technology, Defense, and External Relations in China, 1975–1978* (Boulder, Colo.: Westview Press, 1979).

22. Charles Ridley, *China's Scientific Policies: Implications for International Cooperation* (Washington, D.C.: AEI, Hoover Institution Press, 1976).

23. China and India have been exchanging science and technology delegations over the last several years, though activities increased during 1982 and 1983. See "Lu Jiaxi Fetes Indian Science Academy President," in FBIS-China, November 23, 1982, pp. F1–2.

24. Thomas Fingar and Stanford Journal of International Studies, eds., *China's Quest for Independence: Policy Evolution in the 1970s* (Boulder, Colo.: Westview Press, 1980). See also "Science and Technology Exchanges with Foreign Countries," *Beijing Review*, No. 13 (March 29, 1982):21–28.

25. Zheng Hongqing, "Opening to the Outside World and Self-Reliance," *Beijing Review*, No. 11 (March 14, 1983):15–20.

26. State Science and Technology Commission, *Science and Technology in China* (Beijing, October 1982).

27. Harry Harding, "China and the Third World," in Solomon, *The China Factor*, pp. 257–295.

28. Robert Delfs, "The Balance of Power," *Far Eastern Economic Review* 120 (May 19, 1983):80–81. See also "US and China Discussing Export of Nuclear Technology to Peking," *New York Times*, June 2, 1982, pp. 1, 7.

29. "US Nuclear Scientist Lectures in China," in JPRS, 81028 (June 11, 1982), pp. 7–8.

30. Wang Yaotian, "Strategic Importance of an Open-Door Policy," *Guoji maoyi* [International trade], August 1982, in JPRS, 82457 (December 14, 1982), pp. 47–54.

31. "Protect and Develop Our National Industry," *RMRB*, April 24, 1982, in FBIS-China, April 26, 1982, pp. K3–5.

32. Wang Chiwei and Liu Mingdong, "Import of Foreign Technology and Economic Effectiveness," *Caijing wenti yanjiu* [Research on the problems of finance and economics], July 1982, in JPRS, 82364 (December 1982), pp. 23–28.

33. The main reasons suggested by Wang and Liu for the use of foreign over domestic items is the longer and more uncertain delivery time of indigenously produced items.

34. "On Questions Regarding the Country's Economic Relations with Foreign Countries," *Hongqi*, No. 8 (1982), in FBIS-China, May 11, 1982, pp. 4–16.

35. "On Questions Regarding the Country's Economic Relations."

36. According to one article, between 1950 and 1979 US$13.5 billion was spent on foreign technology acquisition, with 93 percent going for complete plants. The amount spent on acquiring technical information was less than US$200 million, even including royalty fees. See Guo Xinchang and Yang Haitian, "China's Unfavorable Position in International Technology Transfer Should Be Changed As Quickly As Possible," *Caimao jingji* [Finance, trade and economics], January 10, 1982, in JPRS, 80736 (May 5, 1982), pp. 31–40.

37. "China Switches Emphasis from Equipment Imports to Technology," *China Daily*, September 11, 1982, p. 4.

38. "On Questions Regarding the Country's Economic Relations."

39. "Technology Imports Official on Trade Policies," in FBIS-China, October 24, 1982, pp. K17–18. Some Chinese have criticized the agreement with Coca-Cola because of the tie-in clauses that obligate China to buy certain equipment and the cola formula only from the U.S.-based firm. See Wang and Liu, "Import of Foreign Technology."

40. "Patent Law Being Drafted and Patent Bureau Set Up," in FBIS-China, October 21, 1982, p. K13. See also "Americans Wary of Chinese Theft of Technical Know-how," *Chicago Tribune*, November 12, 1981.

41. "Another 15,000 to Study Abroad," *China Daily*, December 13, 1982.

42. Liao Chengzhi, "Strengthen Work Concerning Intellectuals Among Overseas Chinese and Dependents of Overseas Chinese Living Abroad," *Hongqi*, No. 15 (1983), in JPRS, 84444 (September 29, 1983):40–45.

43. "China Science Journal Starts," *Washington Post*, May 29, 1980.

44. Ibid.

45. A major gathering of Overseas Chinese scientists was held in Beijing in mid-1983. See FBIS-China, August 25, 1983, pp. A4–8.

46. "State Official Reports on Importing Foreign Technology," in JPRS, 79902 (January 20, 1982), p. 74.

47. Zhu Yuening, "Give Weight to the Importation of Technology and Machinery," in FBIS-China, August 13, 1982, pp. K12–15.

48. "Combating Departmentalism," *RMRB*, January 21, 1983, in FBIS-China, January 24, 1983, pp. K5–6.

49. "Problems in Technology Imports Analyzed," *Shijie jingji daobao* [World economic herald], February 28, 1983, in JPRS, 83413 (May 5, 1983):88–89.

50. Ma Hong, "On Economic Appraisals," *Guangming ribao* [hereafter *GMRB*], February 20, 1983, in JPRS, 83144 (March 28, 1983), pp. 21–24.

51. "Boldly Import Technology in Transforming Small and Medium Sized Enterprises," in FBIS-China, January 18, 1983, pp. K1–2.

52. Denis Fred Simon, "China's Capacity to Assimilate Foreign Technology: An Assessment," in U.S. Congress, Joint Economic Committee, *China Under the Four Modernizations* (Washington, D.C.: Government Printing Office, 1982).

53. "Chinese Leaders in a Dither Over Defections," *Kansas City Star*, October 24, 1982.

54. "Students Abroad Covered by New Regulations," *China Daily*, July 16, 1982.

55. "Nankai University Creates Conditions to Facilitate Scientific Research of Scholar Returning from Advanced Studies Abroad," *RMRB*, July 6, 1983, in JPRS, 84100 (August 11, 1983), pp. 114–115.

56. Lu Jiaxi, "Several Problems Concerning Current Scientific Research Management," *Keyan guanli* [Science research management] 3 (July 1982), in JPRS, 83240 (April 12, 1983), p. 173.

57. "People Craving to Go Abroad Criticized," *RMRB*, June 9, 1982, in JPRS, 81629 (August 25, 1982), p. 45.

58. "China Cancels Sea Missile Contract," *China Business and Trade* 4 (March 21, 1983):1. See also "PLA's Wu Xiuquan on Foreign Military Purchases," in FBIS-China, April 20, 1983, p. A3.

59. The Nanjing Radio Plant, for example, provided nearly 200 pieces of equipment and machinery for the testing of China's ICBM in 1980. See JPRS, 83790 (June 29, 1983), p. 5.

60. "Military Gear Sales to China Approved in State Department," *Wall Street Journal*, March 18, 1980, p. 8.

61. "US Clears Way for the Sale of Military-Related Products to Beijing," *New York Times*, May 30, 1980. See also "US Expected to Approve Military Goods to China," *New York Times*, May 20, 1980, p. 5.

62. *Aviation Week and Space Technology*, September 22, 1982, p. 10. See also *Aviation Week and Space Technology*, October 6, 1980, pp. 25–26.

63. For a complete explanation of the "P" category, see *Federal Register* 46, 249 (December 29, 1981), pp. 62837–62840.

64. Ibid.

65. "New Rows in Sino-US Relations," *Ming pao* (Hong Kong), in JPRS, 83854 (July 8, 1983), pp. 147–149.

66. "ITT Affiliate to Sell China Digital Gear," *Washington Post*, July 31, 1983, p. A20.

67. "Commentary on the Anniversary of the Shanghai Communique," in FBIS-China, March 2, 1982, p. B2.

68. "PRC Foreign Minister Analyzes Relations with the US," *Summary of World Broadcasts*, FE/7152/A1 (October 9, 1982), p. 1.

69. "China Hopes to Continue Developing Sino-US Relations," *China Daily*, October 8, 1982, p. 1.

70. "Allocation of Resources in the Soviet Union and China—1982: Testimony of Lt. General James Williams," U.S. Congress, Joint Economic Committee, Subcommittee on International Trade, Finance and Security Economics, June 29, 1982.

71. "US Export Crackdown Hits Another China-Linked Firm," *Asian Wall Street Journal*, June 15, 1982, p. 1. See also "US Expands China-Linked Export

Curbs," *Asian Wall Street Journal*, July 26, 1982, p. 1; and "China's Bid for US Technology Tests Government Export Rules," *Asian Wall Street Journal*, March 8, 1983, p. 1.

72. In retrospect, the possibility of defense interest in such activity was underscored by statements made by Minister of Electronics Jiang Zemin in August 1983. In highlighting the three strategic priorities of the electronics industry, he stated the following major objectives: (1) insure that electronics serves national defense; (2) develop large-scale integrated circuits; and (3) develop computers. See Wang Yuling, "Develop the Economy and Supply Advanced Electronics Equipment As Quickly As Possible," in FBIS-China, September 1, 1983, pp. K11–12.

73. "Zhang Aiping Stresses PLA's Modernization," in FBIS-China, December 27, 1982, p. K4.

74. Zhang Aiping, "On National Defense Modernization," *Hongqi*, March 1, 1983, in FBIS-China, March 1, 1983, pp. K8–9.

75. "Zhang Aiping Speaks on Defense Modernization," in FBIS-China, March 2, 1983, pp. K5–6. On China's SLBM launch see *Asia Research Bulletin*, November 30, 1982, Section 6, p. 989.

76. "Interview with Yu Qiuli," *Beijing Review*, No. 31 (August 1, 1983):13–16.

77. "Leaders Attend Science Awards Conference," in FBIS-China, October 25, 1982, pp. K3–12.

78. For example, in 1981 West Germany provided China with a grant of DM 15 million to support science and technology exchanges and training. See FBIS-China, October 8, 1981, p. G1.

79. "Survey Shows Chinese Prefer US Equipment and Technology," *Journal of Commerce*, July 21, 1980, p. 12.

80. "Zhao Discusses Sino-US Relations," *Beijing Review*, No. 7 (February 14, 1983):8–9. See also Frank Ching, "The Major Strains in US-China Relations," *Asian Wall Street Journal*, March 31, 1983, p. 4.

81. "Reportage on the Visit of Secretary Baldridge," in FBIS-China, May 25, 1983, pp. B1–2. See also "US Heightens High Technology Exports to the PRC," in FBIS-China, June 22, 1983, p. B1.

82. "China Says US Pledges Easier Technology Sales," *Washington Post*, May 25, 1983, p. A2.

83. *Federal Register* 48, 27 (November 23, 1983):53064–53071.

84. According to the *Christian Science Monitor*, Secretary Weinberger informed the Chinese that the list of high-technology items given to the United States in June 1981 had been reexamined and that a majority of the requests had been approved for export to China. See "China Woos Weinberger in Hopes of Technology Sales," *Christian Science Monitor*, September 27, 1983.

85. "Zhao Ziyang Holds Talks with Weinberger," *RMRB*, September 28, 1983, in FBIS-China, September 28, 1983, pp. B1–5.

Part 4
Prospects

CHAPTER 13

CHINA'S FOREIGN POLICY OPTIONS AND PROSPECTS: TOWARD THE 1990s

Allen S. Whiting

INTRODUCTION

There is no need to belabor the problems of predictability in human behavior, whether for China or any other country. The hazards of attempting to anticipate the precise course of foreign policy at specific points in time are formidable enough for one's own government, let alone for another society. The interaction of relevant variables, internal and external, affects the context as well as the content of decision making. Yet to the extent that political science can justify its claim to being a science, it must at least attempt, with what Harold Lasswell called "developmental constructs," to identify the key inputs and forecast the probability of differing outcomes dependent on the varying inputs.[1]

This effort is both facilitated and hampered when the object of inquiry is the People's Republic of China. On the positive side, the regime has maintained a relatively consistent leadership compared with most major powers, despite the dramatic interruption of the Cultural Revolution. Next in line is the Soviet Union, which has had four key leaders since 1949, with a fifth presently in charge. Mao's rule ended in 1976 with a nominal and transient successorship under Hua Guofeng. This was followed by a more dominant role for Deng Xiaoping, working through the formal heads of party and government, Hu Yaobang and Zhao Ziyang, respectively. Such continuity lessens the problem of idiosyncratic variables, whether in perception or style of decision making, commonly encountered in democratic regimes with a high turnover of top-ranking officials and their politically appointed associates.

Against this analytical advantage, however, stand several disadvantages. First and foremost is the paucity of direct evidence on the decision-making process. Except for two collections of Mao's unpublished speeches and memoranda, clandestinely published and acquired abroad during the Cultural Revolution, there is virtually no firsthand information on how foreign policy is made or on its rationale and implementation.[2] Published versions of major speeches often have suspiciously little detailed discussion of foreign policy, offering instead standard formulations of a highly generalized nature.[3]

This situation is in marked contrast with domestic policy. During the Cultural Revolution and the period of its subsequent repudiation, considerable material—albeit tendentiously released—provided a wealth of data and documentation on the politics and economics of the PRC since its inception. Personal memoirs (sometimes published post-humously), previously suppressed speeches, and statistical compilations offer insights and revelations on past politics and problems. Unfortunately, no such bonanza has enriched the understanding of foreign policy, nor does this seem likely in the near future.

A second disadvantage, parallel and somewhat related to the first, is the paucity of scholars studying China. During the 1950s, the impact of McCarthyism and the "who lost China" purge that swept through all sectors of American society seriously inhibited the study of contemporary China. In the 1960s the Ford Foundation generously allocated US$30 million to six university centers for the study of China, but most of the effort went to the internal aspects of Chinese society.

The relative lack of evidence and the paucity of scholars to develop the field has left a serious gap in empirical research and monographs on Chinese foreign policy in comparison with the growth of domestic policy studies. Yet it is only through the systematic cumulation of rigorous research that logic and inference can be tested to be disconfirmed or accepted.

A third handicap is the political impact of Sino-American relations on the perception and analysis of PRC foreign policy. For twenty years, from 1949 to 1969, the bitter public polemics exchanged between Beijing and Washington were intermittently matched by bloody confrontation, overt (Korea) or covert (Vietnam), and systematic subversion, indirect (through Taiwan) or direct (Thailand). Then for ten years, 1971–1981, Sino-American relations moved from détente to rapprochement and finally approached entente because of parallel strategic interests against the USSR. This prompted euphoria in the United States over the opening of China as a market for business and a mecca for tourists. The pendulum swing of passions and fashions induced a corresponding swing in the framing of research and analysis on China's foreign policy. Although scholars eschewed the more virulent "hate-love" vocabulary of politicians and public media, they were necessarily influenced by the context of the times.[4]

These problems notwithstanding, a projection of alternative options and prospects for Chinese foreign policy makes forecasting, rather than prediction, feasible. Our time frame is the latter 1980s. A shorter time span is less challenging, if one assumes that present policy priorities and outputs will remain fairly constant. For the 1980s, this assumption reflects the apparent stability manifest in the Twelfth Party Congress and Sixth National People's Congress programs and personal appointments. A longer time span becomes too speculative, subject as it is to the multiple impact of internal and external variables that cannot be calculated so far in the future.

Of these variables, two are potentially incalculable even within our five-to-seven-year frame, namely economic growth and elite politics. Given the importance of agriculture and its vulnerability to natural disasters such as flood and drought, forecasting can be fouled by successive years of widespread catastrophe. Although the PRC has accomplished much in flood control and grain reserves, it is still susceptible to severe economic disruption if disasters persist for three years or more. This can affect import programs as well as export capacity, ultimately influencing both consumer satisfaction and industrial growth. The gap between expectations and realization can trigger a regime crisis in which dissident factions, bureaucratic interests, and political opportunists may combine to oust the leadership. Fortunately, the likelihood of this set of developments is very low.

Although "worst case" scenarios can be scripted to identify a least probable but hypothetically possible contingency, the utility of this approach is rather dubious. Highly imaginative analyses can point toward specific foreign policy outputs that may be so extreme as to excite undue attention, quite disproportionate to the likelihood of such a development. Parsimony requires instead that sufficient probability exist for a particular eventuality to warrant research on early warning indicators and analysis of possible responses.

DOMESTIC AND FOREIGN POLICY LINKAGES

Before moving to selected issue areas, domestic politics deserves special attention for its potential effect on foreign policy, a phenomenon trenchantly addressed by Susan Shirk (Chapter 3). The relationship between internal tensions and externally directed hostility has been widely examined for other countries as well as for China, but with few conclusive findings to date.[5] A regime may try to divert internal dissent by channeling it against an external target and thereby mobilizing or uniting the populace, or it may adopt a less assertive posture to avoid raising external risks in addition to internal ones. But the main relevance for international affairs is behavior, not rhetoric. Research focused on domestic media images without examining actions abroad, for example, does not address the central linkage question.

A more pertinent problem for China is the political sensitivity of dependence on foreign technology and assistance in economic development. Its juxtaposition with reiterated assertions of self-reliance poses a dialectic whose inherent tension can affect foreign policy. For example, a short-run forecast of the Sino-Soviet alliance made in the winter of

1957–1958 would have emphasized the cohesive rather than the disruptive aspects, judging from the interaction between the two regimes during and after the Bolshevik Revolution celebration in Moscow that November. Problems that had surfaced previously seemed to be shelved or moderated by mutual compromise. In particular, suggestions of a possible nuclear sharing agreement, subsequently confirmed, seemed a harbinger of greater longevity to the alliance than had appeared likely during the more difficult days of Stalin.[6]

However, in early 1958 Mao Zedong specifically, albeit secretly, called for placing "self-reliance" ahead of "foreign aid" in determining the priorities and pattern for Chinese domestic and foreign policy.[7] The Great Leap Forward and the Quemoy (Jinmen) bombardment followed, both without consultation—much less agreement—with the Kremlin. These unilateral challenges to Soviet leadership of "the socialist camp," which had been so vigorously championed by Mao in Moscow, triggered a chain reaction in and between the two Communist capitals that quickly passed the point of no return for resolving differences on other issues. Seen in this perspective, the domestic variable proved to be the determining factor in foreign policy. Similarly, the import of whole plants and foreign technology in 1964–1966 provided no advance warning of the virulent xenophobia manifest in the Red Guard assaults during the Cultural Revolution in 1966–1967. The halt in construction of a major petrochemical project and the detention of foreign business executives on charges of espionage damaged the image of PRC reliability abroad. Once again the key variable was domestic politics.

There is a high probability that the reliance on foreign technology, advisors, credits, and markets as prime factors in China's economic growth and development will continue uninterrupted well into the 1990s. Publication of The Selected Works of Deng Xiaoping, 1975–1982 in mid-1983 canonized Deng's post-Mao speeches, most of which had not previously been publicly available. This cemented in place, at least for the tenure of Zhao Ziyang as premier, the acceptance of dependency that Deng had promoted vigorously, first in the mid-1970s and then more successfully after Mao's death and the downfall of the Gang of Four.[8]

In addition to elite politics, bureaucratic and interest politics are likely to perpetuate the open-door relationship with the international economic system. As William Feeney shows (Chapter 11), what Bruce Cumings (Chapter 10) terms China's "enmeshment" with the World Bank Group (WBG) weaves an intricate web of financial ties that benefit various government sectors responsible for industry, transportation, and energy. In addition to this increase in organizational power at the governmental center, the distribution of technological, financial, and human resources acquired abroad to various provinces, cities, and special economic zones builds up political interests that gain from extant policy. Because, as Susan Shirk points out (Chapter 3), these areas tend to coincide with the more populated parts of the country, any policy struggle that emerges between the economic centers and the periphery will favor the former over the latter.

However, two exceptions to this general principle must be noted. First, a singularly strong and charismatic leader who can coalesce opposing or opportunistic factions may successfully challenge established policy, much as Mao was able to do in launching the Cultural Revolution. So far, no such individual is visible, and the likelihood of one appearing in the near future is minimal. Hu Yaobang might conceivably challenge Zhao on the dependency issue once Deng is gone. But unless a genuine crisis were to hit the economy, an attack based purely on ideological charges of "bourgeois poison" and "capitalist restoration" would not seem promising enough to risk Hu's position as head of the Party.

The second possibility lies in the traditionally conservative military opposition to reform, especially where it conflicts with national values. A military move to restore Mao's principles and to reduce China's dependence on foreign, particularly capitalist, economic relations is conceivable, but this too seems unlikely in view of the various measures taken to prevent a coup, together with the promise of better weapons once economic modernization is attained. The wholesale retirement of older officers and their replacement by appreciably younger men has removed those whose claim to authority and whose beliefs were rooted in combat mastery of Mao's principles of "people's war" and "men over weapons." In their place is a generation whose military coming of age began with the humiliating Quemoy setback of 1958. This demonstrated the superiority of weapons over men, marked by the 12-to-1 kill ratio of Nationalist over Communist aircraft, thanks to the U.S. air-to-air missiles used by Taiwan. The lesson was reinforced during the Vietnam War, when China's refusal to provide air cover for Hanoi allowed Soviet surface-to-air missiles a virtual monopoly in shooting down U.S. bombers, including the vaunted B-52.

China's air force and navy cannot be modernized on indigenous technology for at least five years. Whether this capability can be acquired by the end of the decade is uncertain, but it is a credible goal for the 1990s. Under these circumstances there is no reason for the PLA to reverse the regime's reliance on foreign assistance prematurely in the name of self-reliance, regardless of how frustrating it may be in the meantime to go without the newer weapons available abroad.

Beyond the bureaucratic factions and interest groups that reinforce elite politics in support of present policy lies a possible modernization of mentality that may weight the argument over dependency versus self-reliance in favor of the former. By 1983 15,000 Chinese students were studying abroad, 10,000 of them in the United States. Overwhelmingly, they are advanced scholars in engineering and science, who seemed destined for key appointments in government, industry, and universities upon their return. Among them are many offspring or close relatives of high officials, including Politburo members. Their long-term impact on the thinking and decisions of key institutions and groups should not be underestimated, although their age and residence abroad will limit their immediate effect.

In addition, the wholesale translation of foreign books, together with the widespread study of English for coping with the flood of technical journals being acquired abroad, is opening the minds of millions who cannot leave China but who can learn how to apply much of what is available on the international shelf of knowledge. Meanwhile, the televised transmission of life abroad challenges the self-perception as well as the national expectations of nearly a billion Chinese, most of whom heretofore had an horizon of experience that was severely limited in time as well as place.

Against the gradual acceptance of dependency stands more than a century of argument and anxiety over how to preserve China's spiritual essence and societal identity while absorbing foreign ways and advice. Whether in the final decades of the Qing empire, the early years of the Republic, or the brief period of peace under the Nationalist rule, the search for an acceptable synthesis of the Chinese past and the Western present has confounded successive regimes and their opponents as well.

Even the proclaimed triumph of Marxist–Leninist–Mao Zedong thought failed in this regard, with the underlying tension of the Sino-Soviet alliance between dependency and self-reliance. Indeed, recent developments already noted—large-scale training abroad, massive transmission of technology by translation and foreign language study, military confrontation with superior weapons—also occurred during the heyday of the Sino-Soviet alliance in 1949–1959. Yet the alliance foundered, in part because of, rather than in spite of, these developments.

Was the Gang of Four an anachronistic last gasp of that "feudal mentality" against which Deng's associates have inveighed so vehemently? Probably, but it would be simplistic to exclude altogether the residual reactionary impulse as a possible constraint on dependency. Though it is not likely to transform general policy for the above-mentioned reasons, reactionary elements can inhibit options and at times compel postures in selected issue areas of foreign policy that deserve special consideration in forecasting the range of likely Chinese behavior.

Taiwan

First and foremost among issue areas is the question of Taiwan. This embodies a truly "worst case" dilemma for Beijing in the linkage of domestic and foreign politics. On the one hand, it involves nationalism at its most basic level: territorial unity and sovereignty. Unification of the island with the mainland was promised by joint Allied declarations in World War II, firmly accomplished by the Chiang Kai-shek regime in 1945, and publicly avowed as a goal by the PRC since its inauguration in 1949. Moreover, its separation has been overwhelmingly a function of foreign intervention on the island in 1950 and foreign protection of Taiwan by treaty from 1954 to 1980. Last but not least, the Taiwan regime continues to claim it is the sole legal government of China and is so recognized by twenty-one countries.

On the other hand, U.S. opposition to the use of force in resolving the Taiwan question, reiterated by presidents Eisenhower, Kennedy, Johnson, Nixon, Ford, Carter, and Reagan, raises the risk of military escalation at worst and economic sanctions at best should the PLA blockade or attack the island. This could critically affect China's offshore oil capability, which will be virtually dependent on U.S. companies for at least a decade and without which domestic needs may not be met, much less vital foreign exchange earnings. Tokyo's response is less certain, but any impairment of the major investment and technological imports from Japan would disrupt key components of China's economic modernization.

In addition to these countervailing intangibles of domestic and foreign politics is the practical problem of feasibility. A direct military assault might so damage Taiwan's economy and alienate its population as to make success a Pyrrhic victory. Attack also risks tremendous human and material costs, as well as possible embarrassment to China's military prestige should Taiwan hold out for any length of time. Alternatively, a blockade might not break the regime's resistance to negotiations for many months, but would trigger a flight of capital and personnel that could collapse the island's economy and bankrupt its potential as an asset to the mainland.

Finally, there is the imponderable question of what will happen once Chiang Ching-kuo is no longer the head of Taiwan. Eighty-five percent of the population are native Taiwanese, with the remaining 15 percent composed of mainlanders who came over after World War II and their descendants. The prospect of an independent Taiwan haunts Beijing as one of three contingencies that PRC officials claim would necessitate the use of force. The other two would be Taiwan's acquisition of a nuclear bomb or its alignment with the USSR. With no successor to carry on the Chiang line and no figure with his leadership talents, the possibility of an eventual Taiwanese takeover is real.

Beginning in 1981, Beijing's pronouncements of autonomy for Taiwan should it rejoin the mainland have been increasingly detailed and authoritative.[9] However, Taiwanese authorities have adamantly refused negotiations and any partial measures of reconciliation, such as permitting direct mail and family reunions. For the PRC program to convince a significant sector on the island that a negotiated union is advantageous there must be a prolonged period of political stability in Beijing and the successful implementation of economic reforms that upgrade private enterprise and productivity. Thus, in addition to the external constraints on the use of force, formidable internal obstacles to peaceful unification exist.

Recognition of these problems and the dilemma they pose has apparently prompted Deng to postpone the attainment of Taiwan. Having initially posited this as one of the major goals to be pursued during the 1980s, he subsequently slated the 1990s for their accomplishment.[10] Meanwhile, Beijing's pressure on Washington to fix a specific time to terminate arms sales to Taiwan aims at pulling the last U.S. prop out from under the Nationalist regime, guiding it toward negotiations.

An additional constraint on Beijing's options is the availability of the PLA for sustained or massive effort against the island. So long as Sino-Soviet confrontation along the 4,500-mile border preempts the largest and best air-ground components, they cannot be deployed along the Taiwan Strait. A lesser but nonetheless competing demand is posed by Vietnam. Détente on both fronts would allow an exclusive military focus on Taiwan. Then the comparative military capabilities of the two sides would have to be taken into account, especially in air and naval power.

On balance, there is little likelihood of Beijing moving to take Taiwan by force during this decade, given the status quo. If an independent Taiwan were suddenly to emerge, however, forecasting would be more problematic. Much would depend on the domestic politics in Beijing, the vulnerability of Deng's leadership or of his like-minded successors, and the priority given to economic dependency as compared with political sovereignty and national self-esteem. It will be difficult for any individual to have sufficient political power to finally write off Taiwan as Chiang Kai-shek wrote off Mongolia in 1946 when he accepted the terms forced on him by the Yalta accords. Emotion could prevail over reason to prompt a forceful response to the declaration of an independent Taiwan, but other priorities might obtain at that time, such as confrontation with the USSR and economic dependence on the United States and Japan.

Hong Kong

By comparison with Taiwan, the problem of Hong Kong is more amenable to resolution. It cannot be militarily defended by Great Britain, except perhaps for a few hours at most, so there is no need on either side to contemplate the use of force. The sole legal defense rests on "unequal treaties" commencing with the Opium War of 1839–1841, an approach that is firmly rejected by Beijing and only pro forma advanced by London. Within the legal framework, the lease to the New Territories expires in 1997, and without them the island of Hong Kong and the tip of Kowloon would not be viable as a separate economic entity.

Therefore, the problem for both London and Beijing is how to negotiate a transition and takeover so as to maximize the mutual payoff in national sensitivity and minimize the disruptive impact of Hong Kong's socioeconomic way of life. After an initial clash in 1982, the two sides settled down to a more deliberate exchange of views in which Deng, in mid-1983, foresaw agreement in principle by 1985.[11]

Beijing's assurance that Hong Kong's socioeconomic lifestyle will continue after the British leave seems credible on two counts. First, this is essential if foreign investment is to keep Hong Kong prosperous, for most of it comes from Overseas Chinese with alternative investment possibilities elsewhere. Second, such assurances have also been given to Taiwan, and therefore they must become reality if Taiwan is to accept them as a basis for negotiating union with the mainland. Whether in fact these promises will remain in effect ten years hence is impossible to predict. However, Beijing is likely to keep them alive at least until the 1990s so as to lessen the flight of capital that threatens to collapse the Hong Kong economy, through which China presently earns up to 30 percent of its foreign exchange. With much of this capital in five- to ten-year investments, there is still some room for maneuvering before 1997.

Gradually, however, the Hong Kong economy will decline as 1997 approaches. Concern in Beijing for the colony's economic welfare may also decline compared with the political imperative of reestablishing Chinese sovereignty and control. Presumably, the proportion of foreign exchange earned through Hong Kong will shrink as earnings from the special economic zones, expanded port facilities, joint ventures, and offshore oil expand. In particular, the development of Tianjin, Shanghai, Fuzhou, and Guangzhou may make Hong Kong much less important for entrepôt trade; Hong Kong may become an unwelcome competitor for local industry. Should these alternatives prove economically viable, they are likely to increase Chinese nationalistic pressures on Hong Kong and decrease concessions to capitalistic concerns.

Sino-Soviet Relations

Chi Su's comprehensive treatment of Sino-Soviet relations (Chapter 6) and their prospects limns the various factors that bear on the relationship, with proper emphasis on mutual perceptions. As he acknowledges, forecasting is particularly hazardous because of each country's interests in third countries and their development over time. For example, how Moscow and Beijing interact both affects and is affected by how each interacts with Hanoi, Washington, and Tokyo. This in turn introduces additional policy elites whose composition and priorities can change.

Focusing narrowly on the bilateral relationship, however, does permit us to address the key question of détente versus confrontation. Insofar as the outcome rests on Beijing's behavior, the prospects for a limited détente are good. This would involve a virtual freeze on military deployments by both sides and perhaps a modest reduction in troops, though the upgrading of air and ground defense systems would continue. The mutual benefit outweighs the risk with both sides seeking to limit military expenditures for the sake of civilian priorities. But this détente will not lead either side to seek a mutual security arrangement or to rely on assurances of nonaggression in lieu of a reasonably adequate defense against attack.

Economic exchange will also increase, particularly between north-eastern China and the far east of Siberia, where a natural complementarity coincides with local transportation systems. This is not likely, however, to develop the genuine interdependence envisaged in joint Sino-Soviet surveys of the Amur River Basin in the 1950s.[12] Overall trade will never rival that with Japan, the United States, and Western Europe for either China or the USSR. Their mutual reorientation precludes a return to the high level of the 1950s. Neither side has enough to offer the other that cannot be better acquired elsewhere.

A reduction of military confrontation would not necessarily bring about a Sino-Soviet alignment or eliminate Chinese rhetorical attacks on Soviet hegemony in those regions and countries where the two have competed for influence in the past. Having embarked on the path of becoming a global power, in word if not in deed, Beijing will be loathe to abandon it for a more limited role confined to Asia. This ensures a perpetuation of Sino-Soviet friction in the Middle East, Africa, and to a lesser extent, Latin America. It also ensures their working at cross-purposes in both Eastern and Western Europe, as well as in Northeast Asia. Whether Beijing aligns with or opposes Washington will depend on the particular circumstances in each case, but Beijing will continue to challenge Moscow at selected points of opportunity.

This global game serves several purposes. It enhances China's self-image as a major actor in world politics. It appeals to anti-Soviet interests in the United States and among U.S. allies. It gives China a role in the Third World, depending on whether local attitudes define nonalignment as neutrality toward both superpowers or sanction the singling out of one for greater attack. In this regard, though the PRC's economic relations will not be equidistant between the United States and the USSR, its public polemic against "superpower hegemony" is likely to strike a more even balance for Third World audiences.

Thus the ideological imperative of socialist solidarity will remain subordinate to the nationalistic necessity of power politics in determining China's relations with the Soviet Union. Already in the years of proclaimed "monolithic unity of the socialist bloc," circa 1954–1957, Beijing and Moscow competed for influence throughout much of what was then called the Afro-Asian world. Thirty years later, with most of the inter-vening period spent in open confrontation and intermittent border conflict, this rivalry has become psychologically rooted and bureau-cratically routinized. As such it severely constrains the ability of both sides to move beyond détente to rapprochement, much less entente.

Japan

Of all foreign powers, Japan has profited the most, literally and figuratively, from the post-Mao open-door policy. Commanding one-fourth of China's foreign trade, the formerly aggressive neighbor has become the chief source of financial and technological assistance in economic modernization. Beijing quietly acquiesces in Tokyo's efforts at developing a limited self-defense capability and publicly applauds Japan's potential resistance to Soviet domination of East Asia. Repeated assertions of "friendship" in Chinese pronouncements to visiting Japanese dignitaries belie the underlying resentment and residual hatred resulting from a half-century of territorial and material losses, political humiliation, and human tragedy resulting from Japanese expansionism.

This historical heritage has important implications for future PRC policy. It precludes China becoming dependent on Japan's military capability, at least for this decade. The alacrity with which Chinese media, visual and print, revived images and memories of "Japanese imperialistic militarism" in mid-1982 (in response to proposed history textbook revisions in Tokyo) vividly demonstrated subsurface attitudes and the regime's willingness to exploit them.[13] The Japanese villain is the favorite whipping boy of film and theater. His image is too firmly entrenched to become a military ally in the foreseeable future. Beyond the assertions of "independent foreign policy" and "self-reliance" that characterize official discussions of defense, Japan suffers a special liability as a possible political partner.

Within this constraint, however, the question arises as to what degree economic dependency will prevail over nationalistic assertiveness in handling conflicting claims on ocean resources and islands. During the 1970s, China formally protested Korean-Japanese exploration for offshore oil, claiming that the entire continental shelf under the East China Sea belonged to the PRC.[14] It also lays claim to the Senkaku Islands (Diaoyu Tai) northeast of Taiwan, which are administered by Japan. Deng Xiaoping refused to give up the latter claim despite the "China fever" that swept over Tokyo during his visit in 1978 to sign the Sino-Japanese Treaty of Peace and Friendship. Instead he said that perhaps the next generation could better settle the dispute, repeating this admonition as recently as mid-1983.[15] Their access to potential offshore oil makes the Senkakus of special interest to Japan as well as China.

As with Taiwan, China's handling of this matter will depend on the balance of interests and priority in Beijing. The nationalistic sensitivity of territorial sovereignty is heightened by Japan's aggression against China over much of the past century. But this conflicts with the economic imperative of dependency that makes Japan the best source of help because of its technological capability, its cultural compatibility, its geographical proximity, and its financial availability. So long as the latter considerations prevail, as has been true under Deng's direction, the former aspects of the relationship will be muted and the contentious issues postponed indefinitely. A shift of power and priority in Beijing, however, may make Sino-Japanese relations vulnerable to political exploitation of historic antagonism and its heritage of hatred.

Triangular Games and the Third World

Michael Ng-Quinn's theoretical modeling of bipolarity and his practical applications thereof to China's possible options and likely choices (Chapter 4) provides an explicit framework for aggregating our foregoing analysis, adding Japan as a quasi-independent subsidiary of the U.S. pole. China's willingness to exploit its advantage as a potential middle power capable of tilting in either superpower direction was symbolically manifested in the fall of 1983, when Beijing hosted Secretary of Defense Caspar Weinberger only days before receiving the Soviet deputy foreign minister for a third "discussion" of Sino-Soviet differences and possible détente.

However much this may appear to emulate the classic Chinese strategy of "using barbarian against barbarian," Samuel Kim's detailed analysis of Beijing's relations with the Third World (Chapter 8) is a cogent reminder that there is another dimension of policy that deserves attention. Whether supporting "national liberation struggles" in the 1950–1975 period or championing the New International Economic Order thereafter, Chinese policy has devoted considerable effort to that vast portion of the globe of which the PRC claims to be a contributing member.

As Kim points out, to a certain extent China's Third World orientation is a function of its relationship with the two superpowers. Unable to compete with them in military or economic reach, Beijing's rhetoric, sometimes implemented in revolutionary assistance or economic aid, offers an ideologically attractive and operationally feasible means of asserting a claim to global status. In addition, action can determine the outcome of particular situations. In 1950–1954, Ho Chi Minh's forces could not have overcome the French, particularly at Dien Bien Phu, without significant help from the PRC. In 1981 China's representatives on the Security Council vetoed successive candidates proposed or backed by the USSR and the United States, thereby securing eventual victory for the Peruvian candidate.

It would be wrong, however, to explain this Third World orientation, whether revolutionary or economic, as primarily opportunistic in motivation. There is a genuine historical affinity between China's "century of shame and humiliation" and the colonial experience suffered throughout the Third World. In both instances the advanced industrial nations exploited their material superiority to impose their own political and cultural values on indigenous cultures. China threw off its "semicolonial" yoke—so defined by Sun Yat-sen and Chiang Kai-shek as well as by

Mao Zedong—at the same time that colonialism was beginning to crumble in the aftermath of World War II. Symbolically, this association received dramatic emphasis in 1971 when the UN General Assembly voted to oust the Nationalist delegation and replace it with the Communist, whereupon Third World members cheered and some literally danced in the aisles.

Again, Kim's analysis shows that the Beijing leadership does not identify wholly with its Third World counterparts, nor will this association necessarily receive a greater priority in PRC policy over time. On the contrary, in strategic, economic, political, and psychological terms, the People's Republic will more often have its primary relationships and roles in what is often called "the North" in the North-South equation. The United States, the Soviet Union, Japan, and Western Europe will weigh far more heavily in Chinese calculations of security, development, and status than whatever Third World groupings emerge in the Asian, African, and Latin American regions.

The late Zhou Enlai once received an American visitor who praised China for having foresworn ever becoming a superpower, remarking how reassuring this pledge was for its future behavior. Zhou responded, "I hope you are right." His words suggested an awareness of how China's traditional role of regional hegemony might, consciously or unconsciously, shape his colleagues and their successors in viewing the world, despite the self-imposed normative proscription against this attitude. This attitude, for example, underlies much of Chinese resistance to Vietnamese control of the Indochina region.

It is appropriate to end this cursory review of likely and possible futures on a note of uncertainty. The experiential component remains central. All too often projections of foreign policy behavior, Chinese and otherwise, are unidirectional, from the subject outward. Yet Beijing, like all capitals, is the recipient of countless signals, messages, and stimuli from the outside world. How these are interpreted and responded to may be individually forecast from a fixed frame of reference but incremental changes over time through a "learning" process of interaction can cumulatively alter that frame. This is less important in our chosen horizon of five to seven years, yet the influence can nonetheless be felt during this period and certainly beyond it. How the world acts toward China will affect, positively or negatively, how China interacts with the world.

NOTES

1. Harold D. Lasswell, introduction to Ernst B. Haas and Allen S. Whiting, *Dynamics of International Relations* (Westport, Conn.: Greenwood Press, 1975; reprinted from McGraw-Hill, New York, 1956), p. xx.

2. *Mao Zedong sixiang wansui* [Long live Mao Zedong Thought], initially published in 1967 and 1969 in the People's Republic of China during the Cultural

Revolution by an unidentified source; photocopied and distributed by the Institute of International Affairs in Taiwan. Translated portions appear in Stuart Schram, ed., *Chairman Mao Talks To The People* (New York: Pantheon, 1974).

3. Despite the loosening of restrictions on published materials since the death of Mao, the paucity of public discussion on foreign policy is striking in the speeches released after the Twelfth Party Congress in 1982 and the Sixth National People's Congress in 1983. The omission is especially noticeable in *Deng Xiaoping wenxuan 1975–1982* [The selected works of Deng Xiaoping, 1975–1982] (Beijing: Renmin chubanshe, 1983), which covers a wide range of Deng's major statements on domestic issues.

4. For an exceptional self-criticism in this regard, see Jonathan Spence's introduction to the second edition of *To Change China* (London: Penguin Books, 1980). See also Harry Harding, "From China, with Disdain: New Trends in the Study of China," *Asian Survey* 22 (October 1982):934–958.

5. Useful reviews of the literature are contained in Michael P. Sullivan, *International Relations: Theories and Evidence* (Englewood Cliffs, N.J.: Prentice-Hall, 1976), pp. 121–132; also Kuang-sheng Liao, *Antiforeignism and Modernization in China, 1960–1980* (Hong Kong: Chinese University Press, forthcoming), Ch. 1.

6. An insightful analysis with documents concerning the November 1957 Moscow Conference may be found in John Gittings, *Survey of the Sino-Soviet Dispute* (New York: Oxford, 1968), Ch. 7.

7. Mao Zedong, "Talk at an Enlarged Central Work Conference," January 30, 1962, in Schram, *Chairman Mao Talks*, p. 178.

8. Deng Xiaoping ("Speech at a Meeting of the Military Commission of the CCP Central Committee, July 4, 1983," in Deng, *Selected Works*, pp. 363–367) asserts: "In carrying out socialist modernization it is necessary to practice the policy of promoting economic exchanges with foreign countries and enlivening the domestic economy." Translated in Foreign Broadcast Information Service, Daily Report, China [hereafter FBIS-China], July 27, 1983, p. K8.

9. The offers and their implications are analyzed in Allen S. Whiting, "PRC-Taiwan Relations, 1983–93," *SAIS Review* 3, 1 (Winter-Spring 1983):131–146. Deng Xiaoping went beyond the earlier offers in an interview with Professor Winston Yang on June 26, 1983; see Allen S. Whiting, "Peking's Bait to Taiwan," *New York Times*, August 23, 1983.

10. Wang Zhaoguo, "Studying the 'Selected Works of Deng Xiaoping' Is the CYL's Important Ideological Building," *Zhongguo qingnian bao*, July 2, 1983, in FBIS-China, July 15, 1983, p. K16.

11. "Deng Xiaoping's Latest Statement on Hong Kong's Future," *Ming pao*, July 10, 1983, in FBIS-China, July 18, 1983, p. W3.

12. For a fuller examination of the joint Amur survey see Allen S. Whiting, *Siberian Development and East Asia: Threat or Promise?* (Stanford, Calif.: Stanford University Press, 1981), Ch. 6.

13. This is examined at greater length in Allen S. Whiting, "Chinese Foreign Policy and Assertive Nationalism," *Asian Survey* 23, 8 (August 1983):913–933.

14. See Selig S. Harrison, *China, Oil, and Asia: Conflict Ahead?* (New York: Columbia University Press, 1977), Ch. 7.

15. See note 11 above.

BIBLIOGRAPHY

This bibliography has grown out of our teaching and research experience in Chinese foreign policy. It is presented here as a reference point of departure for serious research. With the exception of a few "classic" books, the bibliography takes up from where Roger Dial's *Studies on Chinese External Affairs: An Instructional Bibliography of Commonwealth and American Literature* (1973) left off. In addition, we include here most useful or relevant PRC sources, both in Chinese and English. The bibliography, though still selective, lists the range and type of materials that are now available for studying various dimensions of Chinese foreign policy, with main emphasis on the post-Mao era.

The Chinese publications listed below are available in most major research libraries in the United States. Subscriptions to such periodicals as *Faxue yanjiu, Guoji wenti yanjiu, Hongqi, Remin ribao,* and *Shijie zhishi* can be obtained through the China Books and Periodicals, Inc., which has retail centers in Chicago, New York, and San Francisco. The Foreign Broadcast Information Service's Daily Report, China (cited throughout the book as FBIS-China) is the most useful and widely consulted reference in English; it is easily available in paper and microfiche versions and includes English translations of important PRC newspaper and journal articles and monitored radio broadcasts on both domestic and foreign policy issues.

Secondary sources available in English are arranged topically, generally reflecting the organization of the book. For brevity and space, we have been highly selective on the inclusion of journal articles. Periodicals of particular value for the study of Chinese foreign policy include *Asian Survey, China Business Review, China Quarterly* (London), *Far Eastern Economic Review* (Hong Kong), *Foreign Affairs, Foreign Policy, International Affairs* (London), *International Organization, International Security, International Studies Quarterly, Orbis, Problems of Communism,* and *World Politics.*

CHINESE PUBLICATIONS

Beijing Review. (Weekly, English; March 4, 1958–   ; *Peking Review* before January 1, 1979.)
China Daily. (English, 1982–   .)
China's Foreign Economic Legislation. Vol. 1. Beijing: Foreign Languages Press, 1982.

Deng Xiaoping. *Deng Xiaoping wenxuan 1975–1982* [The selected works of Deng Xiaoping, 1975–1982]. Beijing: Renmin chubanshe, 1983.

Faxue yanjiu [Legal research]. (Bimonthly, April 1979–   ; edited by the Institute of Law, Chinese Academy of Social Sciences, Beijing.)

Guoji wenti yanjiu [Journal of international studies]. (Quarterly, July 1981–   ; edited by the Institute of International Relations, Beijing.)

Guoji xingshi nianjian [Yearbook of international affairs]. Shanghai: Zhongguo dabaikequanshu chubanshe. (Annual, 1982–   ; edited by the Shanghai Institute for International Studies.)

Hongqi [Red flag]. (Semimonthly; June 1958–   ; the official organ of the Central Committee of the Chinese Communist Party.)

Ma Hong. *New Strategy for China's Economy*. Beijing: Foreign Languages Press, 1983.

Mao Zedong. *Mao Zedong sixiang wansui* [Long live Mao Zedong's Thought]. Vol. 1. N.p.: 1967.

————. *Mao Zedong sixiang wansui* [Long live Mao Zedong's Thought]. Vol. 2. N.p.: August 1969.

————. *Selected Works of Mao Tse-tung*. 4 vols. Peking: Foreign Languages Press, 1961, 1965.

————. *Selected Works of Mao Tsetung*. Vol. 5. Peking: Foreign Languages Press, 1977.

————. Mao Zedong xuanji [Selected works of Mao Zedong]. Beijing: Renmin chubanshe, 1969. (The first four volumes in Chinese were published in one volume.)

Renmin ribao [People's daily]. (June 15, 1948–   ; official organ of the Central Committee of the Chinese Communist Party.)

Renmin ribao suoyin [Index to People's daily]. (Monthly; 1951–   .)

Shijie zhishi [World knowledge]. (Semimonthly; September 1934–   .)

Shijie zhishi nianjian [World knowledge yearbook]. Beijing: Shijie zhishi chubanshe. (Annual, 1952–1966, 1982–   .)

Social Sciences in China. (Quarterly, in English; 1980–   ; edited by the Chinese Academy of Social Sciences.)

Xiandai quoji guanxi [Contemporary international relations]. (Irregular, October 1981–   ; edited by the Institute of Contemporary International Relations, Beijing.)

Zhongguo baike nianjian [Chinese encyclopedic yearbook]. Beijing: Zhongguo dabaikequanshu. (Annual, 1980–   ; edited by the Chinese Encyclopedia Publisher.)

Zhongguo guojifa niankan [Chinese yearbook of international law]. Beijing: Zhongguo duiwai fanyi chuban gongsi. (Annual, 1982–   ; edited by the China International Law Society.)

PUBLICATIONS IN ENGLISH

The Study of Chinese Foreign Policy

Bobrow, Davis. "Old Dragons in New Models." *World Politics* 19 (January 1967):306–319.

Callahan, Patrick; Brady, Linda P.; and Hermann, Margaret G., eds. *Describing Foreign Policy Behavior*. Beverly Hills, Calif.: Sage Publications, 1982.

Cibulka, Frank. "China and the World in the 1970s." *Polity* 16 (Fall 1981):142–152.

Dial, Roger. *Studies on Chinese External Affairs: An Instructional Bibliography of Commonwealth and American Literature.* Halifax, Nova Scotia: Centre for Foreign Policy Studies, Dalhousie University, 1973.

Dial, Roger L., ed. *Advancing and Contending Approaches to the Study of Chinese Foreign Policy.* Halifax, Nova Scotia: Centre for Foreign Policy Studies, Dalhousie University, 1974.

Harding, Harry. "From China, with Disdain: New Trends in the Study of China." *Asian Survey* 22 (October 1982):934–958.

———. "The Study of Chinese Politics: Toward a Third Generation of Scholarship," *World Politics* 36 (January 1984):284–307.

Huck, Arthur. "Interpreting Chinese Foreign Policy." *Australian Journal of Chinese Affairs,* No. 6 (1981):213–217.

Johnson, Chalmers. "The Role of Social Science in China Scholarship." *World Politics* 17 (January 1965):256–271.

———. "What's Wrong with Chinese Political Studies?" *Asian Survey* 22 (October 1982):919–933.

Kim, Samuel S. "China's Place in World Politics." *Problems of Communism* 31 (March-April 1982):63–70.

Klatt, W. "Global China," *China Quarterly,* No. 89 (March 1982):105–109.

McGowan, Pat, and Kegley, Charles W., Jr., eds. *Foreign Policy and the Modern World-System.* Beverly Hills, Calif.: Sage Publications, 1983.

Murray, Douglas P. *International Relations Research and Training in the People's Republic of China.* A special report of the Northeast Asia–United States Forum on International Policy. Stanford, Calif.: Stanford University, 1982.

Ng-Quinn, Michael. "The Analytic Study of Chinese Foreign Policy." *International Studies Quarterly* 27 (June 1983):203–224.

Pollack, Jonathan D. "Interpreting China's Foreign Policy," *Problems of Communism* 29 (July-August 1980):84–88.

Rong Zhi, "Two Views of Chinese Foreign Policy." *World Politics* 34 (January 1982):285–293.

Whiting, Allen S. "Chinese Foreign Policy: A Workshop Report." *SSRC Items* 31 (March-June 1977):1–3.

Wu, Friedrich W. "Explanatory Approaches to Chinese Foreign Policy: A Critique of the Western Literature." *Studies in Comparative Communism* 13 (Spring 1980):41–62.

Yahuda, Michael. "Perspectives on China's Foreign Policy." *China Quarterly,* No. 95 (September 1983):534–540.

General Works: Historical Origins and Development

Camilleri, Joseph. *Chinese Foreign Policy: The Maoist Era and Its Aftermath.* Seattle: University of Washington Press, 1980.

Dutt, V. P., ed. *China: The Post-Mao View.* New Delhi: Allied Publishers, 1981.

Fairbank, John K. "China's Foreign Policy in Historical Perspective." *Foreign Affairs* 47 (April 1969):449–463.

Fairbank, John K., ed. *The Chinese World Order.* Cambridge, Mass.: Harvard University Press, 1968.

Gittings, John. *The World and China, 1922–1972*. New York: Harper and Row, 1974.

Harding, Harry. "Change and Continuity in Chinese Foreign Policy." *Problems of Communism* 32 (March–April 1983):1–19.

Harding, Harry, ed. *Chinese Foreign Relations in the 1980s*. New Haven, Conn.: Yale University Press, forthcoming.

Hinton, Harold C. *China's Turbulent Quest*. Rev. ed. Bloomington: Indiana University Press, 1972.

Hsiung, James C., and Kim, Samuel S., eds. *China in the Global Community*. New York: Praeger, 1972.

Mancall, Mark. *China at the Center: 300 Years of Foreign Policy*. New York: Free Press, 1984.

Reardon-Anderson, James. *Yenan and the Great Powers: The Origins of Chinese Communist Foreign Policy, 1944–1946*. New York: Columbia University Press, 1980.

Robinson, Thomas W. "Restructuring Chinese Foreign Policy, 1959–1976: Three Episodes." In K. J. Holsti et al., *Why Nations Realign: Foreign Policy Restructuring in the Postwar World*. London: George Allen & Unwin, 1982.

Teng, Ssu-yu, and Fairbank, John K. *China's Response to the West: A Documentary Survey, 1839–1923*. Cambridge, Mass.: Harvard University Press, 1954.

Yahuda, Michael. *China's Role in World Affairs*. New York: St. Martin's Press, 1978.

———. *Towards the End of Isolationism: China's Foreign Policy After Mao*. New York: St. Martin's Press, 1983.

Domestic and External Determinants

Adomeit, Hannes, and Boardman, Robert, eds. *Foreign Policy Making in Communist Countries*. New York: Praeger, 1979.

Armstrong, J. D. *Revolutionary Diplomacy: Chinese Foreign Policy and the United Front Doctrine*. Berkeley: University of California Press, 1977.

Bialer, Seweryn, ed. *The Domestic Context of Soviet Foreign Policy*. Boulder, Colo.: Westview Press, 1981.

Chan, Steve. "Rationality, Bureaucratic Politics and Belief System: Explaining the Chinese Policy Debate, 1964–66." *Journal of Peace Research* 16 (1979):333–347.

Copper, John Franklin. *China's Global Role*. Stanford, Calif.: Hoover Institution Press, 1980.

East, Maurice A.; Salmore, Stephen A.; and Hermann, Charles F., eds. *Why Nations Act: Theoretical Perspectives for Comparative Foreign Policy Studies*. Beverly Hills, Calif.: Sage Publications, 1978.

Fingar, Thomas, and the Stanford Journal of International Studies, eds. *China's Quest for Independence: Policy Evolution in the 1970s*. Boulder, Colo.: Westview Press, 1980.

Gottlieb, Thomas M. *Chinese Foreign Policy Factionalism and the Origins of the Strategic Triangle*. R-1902-NA. Santa Monica, Calif.: Rand Corporation, 1977.

Hiniker, Paul J. *Revolutionary Ideology and Chinese Reality*. Beverly Hills, Calif.: Sage Publications, 1977.

Kim, Samuel S. *The Maoist Image of World Order*. Princeton, N.J.: Center of International Studies, Princeton University, 1977.

Lee, Edmund [pseud.]. "Beijing's Balancing Act." *Foreign Policy*, No. 51 (Summer 1983):27–46.

Liao, Kuang-sheng. "Linkage Politics in China: International Mobilization and Articulated External Hostility in the Cultural Revolution 1967–1969." *World Politics* 28 (July 1976):590–610.

Lieberthal, Kenneth. *The Foreign Policy Debate in Peking As Seen Through Allegorical Articles*. P-5768. Santa Monica, Calif.: Rand Corporation, 1977.

Ng-Quinn, Michael. "Effects of Bipolarity on Chinese Foreign Policy." *Survey* 26 (Spring 1982):102–130.

O'Leary, Greg. *The Shaping of Chinese Foreign Policy*. New York: St. Martin's Press, 1980.

Pollack, Jonathan D. *China's Potential as a World Power*. P-6524. Santa Monica, Calif.: Rand Corporation, 1980.

Schram, Stuart, ed. *Chairman Mao Talks to the People*. New York: Pantheon, 1974.

Schurmann, Franz. *Ideology and Organization in Communist China*. 2d ed. Berkeley: University of California Press, 1968.

_____. *The Logic of World Power*. New York: Pantheon, 1974.

Solomon, Richard H. *Mao's Revolution and the Chinese Political Culture*. Berkeley: University of California Press, 1971.

Whiting, Allen S. *Chinese Domestic Politics and Foreign Policy in the 1970s*. Ann Arbor, Mich.: Center for Chinese Studies, 1979.

The Decision-Making Process

Bobrow, Davis B.; Chan, Steve; and Kringen, John A. "Understanding How Others Treat Crises: A Multimethod Approach." *International Studies Quarterly* 21 (March 1977):199–223.

_____. *Understanding Foreign Policy Decisions: The Chinese Case*. New York: Free Press, 1979.

Chan, Steve. "Chinese Conflict Calculus and Behavior: Assessment from a Perspective of Conflict Management." *World Politics* 30 (April 1978):391–410.

Gurtov, Melvin, and Hwang, Byong-Moo. *China Under Threat: The Politics of Strategy and Diplomacy*. Baltimore: Johns Hopkins University Press, 1980.

Oksenberg, Michel. "Economic Policy-Making in China: Summer 1981." *China Quarterly*, No. 90 (June 1982):165–194.

Tretiak, Daniel. "Who Makes Chinese Foreign Policy Today (Late 1980)?" *Australian Journal of Chinese Affairs*, No. 5 (1981):137–157.

Whiting, Allen S. *China Crosses the Yalu: The Decision to Enter the Korean War*. New York: Macmillan, 1960.

_____. "New Light on Mao: Quemoy 1958: Mao's Miscalculations." *China Quarterly*, No. 62 (June 1975):263–270.

China and the Soviet Union

Borisov, O. B., and Koloskov, B. T. *Soviet-Chinese Relations 1945–1980*. 3d supp. ed. Moscow: Mysl Publishers, 1980.

Ellison, Herbert J., ed. *The Sino-Soviet Conflict: A Global Perspective*. Seattle: University of Washington Press, 1982.

Gittings, John. *Survey of the Sino-Soviet Dispute 1963–1967*. London: Oxford University Press, 1968.

Griffith, William E. "Sino-Soviet Rapprochement?" *Problems of Communism* 32 (March-April 1983):20–29.

Pollack, Jonathan. *The Sino-Soviet Rivalry and Chinese Security Debate*. R-2907-AF. Santa Monica, Calif.: Rand Corporation, 1982.

Rozman, Gilbert. "Moscow's China-Watchers in the Post-Mao Era: The Response to a Changing China." *China Quarterly*, No. 94 (June 1983):231–236.

Stuart, Douglas T., and Tow, William T., eds. *China, the Soviet Union, and the West: Strategic and Political Dimensions in the 1980s*. Boulder, Colo.: Westview Press, 1982.

Su, Chi. "U.S.-China Relations: Soviet Views and Policies." *Asian Survey* 23 (May 1983):555–579.

Whiting, Allen S. *Siberian Development and East Asia: Threat or Promise?* Palo Alto, Calif.: Stanford University Press, 1981.

Wich, Richard. *Sino-Soviet Crisis Politics: A Study of Political Change and Communication*. Cambridge, Mass.: Harvard University Press, 1980.

Zagoria, Donald S. *The Sino-Soviet Conflict 1956–1961*. Princeton, N.J.: Princeton University Press, 1962.

_____. *Vietnam Triangle: Moscow/Peking/Hanoi*. New York: Pegasus, 1967.

_____. "The Moscow-Beijing Detente." *Foreign Affairs* 61 (Spring 1983):853–873.

China and the United States

Barnett, A. Doak. *US Arms Sales: The China-Taiwan Tangle*. Washington, D.C.: Brookings Institution, 1982.

Brzezinski, Zbigniew. *Power and Principle*. New York: Farrar, Strauss, Giroux, 1983.

Carter, Jimmy. *Keeping Faith: Memoirs of a President*. New York: Bantam Books, 1982.

Fairbank, John K. *The United States and China*. 4th ed. Cambridge, Mass.: Harvard University Press, 1979.

Garrett, Banning. "China Policy and the Constraints of Triangular Logic." In *Eagle Defiant: United States Foreign Policy in the 1980s*, eds. Kenneth A. Oye, Robert J. Lieber, and Donald Rothchild. Boston: Little, Brown and Co., 1983.

Hsiao, Gene T., and Witunski, Michael, eds. *Sino-American Normalization and Its Policy Implications*. New York: Praeger, 1983.

Huan Xiang. "On Sino-US Relations." *Foreign Affairs* 60 (Fall 1981):35–53.

Kissinger, Henry A. *White House Years*. Boston: Little, Brown and Co., 1979.

_____. *Years of Upheaval*. Boston: Little, Brown and Co., 1982.

Levine, Steven I. "China and the Superpowers." *Political Science Quarterly* 90 (Winter 1975/1976):637–658.

Oksenberg, Michel. "A Decade of Sino-American Relations." *Foreign Affairs* 61 (Fall 1982):175–195.

Oksenberg, Michel, and Oxnam, Robert B., eds. *Dragon and Eagle: United States–China Relations: Past and Future*. New York: Basic Books, 1978.

Segal, Gerald. *The Great Power Triangle*. London: Macmillan, 1982.

Solomon, Richard H., ed. *The China Factor: Sino-American Relations and the Global Scene*. Englewood Cliffs, N.J.: Prentice-Hall, 1981.

Starr, John Bryan, ed. *The Future of US-China Relations.* New York: New York University Press, 1981.

Sutter, Robert G. *China-Watch: Sino-American Reconciliation.* Baltimore: Johns Hopkins University Press, 1978.

Whiting, Allen S. "China and the Superpowers: Toward the Year 2000." *Daedalus* 109 (Fall 1980):97–113.

———. "Sino-American Relations: The Decade Ahead." *Orbis* 26 (Fall 1982):697–719.

China and the Second World

Boardman, Robert. *Britain and the People's Republic of China 1949–1974.* New York: Macmillan, 1976.

Hsüeh, Chun-tu, ed. *China's Foreign Relations: New Perspectives.* New York: Praeger, 1983.

Kapur, Harish. *The Awakening Giant: China's Ascension in World Politics.* Alphen aan den Rijn, Netherlands: Sijthoff & Noordhoff, 1981.

Lee, Chae-Jin. *Japan Faces China.* Baltimore: Johns Hopkins University Press, 1976.

Okita, Saburo. "Japan, China, and the U.S." *Foreign Affairs* 57 (Summer 1979):1090–1110.

Stuart, Douglas T. "Prospects for Sino-European Security Cooperation." *Orbis* 26 (Fall 1982):721–747.

Stuart, Douglas T., and Tow, William T. "China's Military Modernization: The Western Arms Connection." *China Quarterly,* No. 90 (June 1982):253–271.

Tow, William T. "Sino-Japanese Security Cooperation: Evolution and Prospects." *Pacific Affairs* 56 (Spring 1983):51–83.

Tow, William T., and Stuart, Douglas T. "China's Military Turns to the West." *International Affairs* 57 (Spring 1981):286–300.

Weinstein, Franklin B., ed. *U.S.-Japan Relations and the Security of East Asia: The Next Decade.* Boulder, Colo.: Westview Press, 1978.

China and the Third World

Abidi, A.H.H. *China, Iran, and the Persian Gulf.* Atlantic Highlands, N.J.: Humanities Press, 1982.

Bartke, Wolfgang. *China's Economic Aid.* Trans. Waldraut Jarke. London: Hurst, 1975.

Behbehani, Hashim S. H. *China's Foreign Policy in the Arab World, 1955–75.* London: Kegan Paul International, 1981.

Horvath, Janos. *Chinese Technology Transfer to the Third World: A Grants Economy Analysis.* New York: Praeger, 1976.

Johnson, Cecil. *Communist China and Latin America.* New York: Columbia University Press, 1970.

Kim, Samuel S. "Behavioural Dimensions of Chinese Multilateral Diplomacy." *China Quarterly,* No. 72 (December 1977):713–742.

———. "China and the Third World in NIEO Politics." *Contemporary China* 3 (Winter 1979):10–21.

Mortimer, Robert A. *The Third World Coalition in International Politics*. 2d ed. Boulder, Colo.: Westview Press, 1984.

Ogunsanwo, Alaba. *China's Policy in Africa, 1958-1971*. New York: Cambridge University Press, 1979.

Rubinstein, Alvin, ed. *Soviet and Chinese Influence in the Third World*. New York: Praeger, 1975.

Shichor, Yitzhak. *The Middle East in China's Foreign Policy, 1949-1977*. New York: Cambridge University Press, 1979.

Taylor, Jay. *China and Southeast Asia: Peking's Relations with Revolutionary Movements*. 2d ed. New York: Praeger, 1976.

Van Ness, Peter. *Revolution and Chinese Foreign Policy: Peking's Support for Wars of National Liberation*. Berkeley: University of California Press, 1971.

Vertzberger, Yaacov. "The Political Economy of Sino-Pakistani Relations: Trade and Aid 1963-82," *Asian Survey* 23 (May 1983):637-652.

Worden, Robert L. "China's Balancing Act: Cancun, the Third World, Latin America," *Asian Survey* 23 (May 1983):619-636.

Military and Strategic Policy

Dreyer, June T. *China's Military Power in the 1980s*. Washington, D.C.: China Council of the Asia Society, 1982.

Godwin, Paul H. B. "China's Defense Modernization." *Air University Review* 33 (November-December 1981):2-19.

Godwin, Paul H. B., ed. *The Chinese Defense Establishment: Continuity and Change in the 1980s*. Boulder, Colo.: Westview Press, 1983.

Jencks, Harlan W. *From Muskets to Missiles: Politics and Professionalism in the Chinese Army, 1945-1981*. Boulder, Colo.: Westview Press, 1982.

Marwah, Onkar, and Pollack, Jonathan D., eds. *Military Power and Policy in Asian States: China, India, Japan*. Boulder, Colo.: Westview Press, 1979.

Onate, Andre D. "The Conflict Interactions of the People's Republic of China." *Journal of Conflict Resolution* 18 (December 1974):578-594.

Pillsbury, Michael. "Strategic Acupuncture." *Foreign Policy*, No. 41 (Winter 1980/1981):44-61.

Pollack, Jonathan D. *Security, Strategy and the Logic of Chinese Foreign Policy*. Berkeley: University of California Institute of East Asian Studies, 1981.

Robinson, Thomas W. "Chinese Military Modernization in the 1980s." *China Quarterly*, No. 90 (June 1982):231-252.

Whiting, Allen S. *The Chinese Calculus of Deterrence*. Ann Arbor: University of Michigan Press, 1975.

Economic and Development Policy

Amin, Samir. *The Future of Maoism*. New York: Monthly Review Press, 1983.

Barnett, A. Doak. *China's Economy in Global Perspective*. Washington, D.C.: Brookings Institution, 1981.

Brown, Lester R. *State of the World 1984: A Worldwatch Institute Report on Progress Toward a Sustainable Society*. New York: W. W. Norton, 1984.

Cumings, Bruce. "The Political Economy of Chinese Foreign Policy." *Modern China* 5 (October 1979):411-462.

———. "The Origins and Development of the Northeast Asian Political Economy." *International Organization* 38 (Winter 1984):1–40.

Dernberger, Robert, ed. *China's Development Experience in Comparative Perspective.* Cambridge, Mass.: Harvard University Press, 1980.

Ding, Chen. "The Economic Development of China." *Scientific American* 243 (September 1980):152–164.

Friedman, Edward. "On Maoist Conceptualizations of the Capitalist World System." *China Quarterly,* No. 80 (December 1979):806–837.

Galtung, Johan. "What is Happening in China?" *Development: The International Development Review* 22, 2–3 (1980):17–22.

Gray, Jack, and White, Gordon, eds. *China's New Development Strategy.* New York: Academic Press, 1982.

Hooke, A. W., ed. *The Fund and China in the International Monetary System.* Washington, D.C.: International Monetary Fund, 1983.

Hsiao, Gene T. *The Foreign Trade of China: Policy, Law, and Practice.* Berkeley: University of California Press, 1977.

International Monetary Fund. *World Economic Outlook.* Washington, D.C.: International Monetary Fund, May 1983. (Annual.)

Kraus, Richard C. "Withdrawing from the World-System: Self-Reliance and Class in China." In *The World-System of Capitalism,* ed. Walter L. Goldfrank. Beverly Hills, Calif.: Sage Publications, 1979.

Lardy, Nicholas R., and Lieberthal, Kenneth. *Chen Yun's Strategy for China's Development: A Non-Maoist Alternative.* Armonk, N.Y.: M. E. Sharpe, 1983.

Maxwell, Neville, and McFarland, Bruce, eds. *China's Changed Road to Development.* Oxford: Pergamon Press, 1984.

Pye, Lucian. *Chinese Commercial Negotiating Style.* Cambridge, Mass.: Oelgeschlager, Gunn & Hain, 1982.

Reynolds, Paul D. *China's International Banking and Financial System.* New York: Praeger, 1982.

Selden, Mark, and Lippit, Victor, eds. *The Transition to Socialism in China.* Armonk, N.Y.: M. E. Sharpe, 1982.

Sivard, Ruth Leger. *World Military and Social Expenditures 1983.* Washington, D.C.: World Priorities, 1983. (Annual.)

U.S. Congress. Joint Economic Committee. *China Under the Four Modernizations.* 2 parts. Washington, D.C.: Government Printing Office, 1982.

Wang, George C., ed. and trans. *Economic Reform in the PRC.* Boulder, Colo.: Westview Press, 1982.

Woodard, Kim. *The International Energy Relations of China.* Stanford, Calif.: Stanford University Press, 1980.

World Bank. *World Development Report 1983.* New York: Oxford University Press, 1983. (Annual.)

Wu, Friedrich. "Socialist Self-Reliant Development Within the Capitalist World-Economy: The Chinese View in the Post-Mao Era." *Global Perspectives* 1 (Spring 1983):8–24.

Science and Technology

China's Scientific and Technological Modernization: Domestic and International Implications. Occasional Paper No. 11. Wilson Center, Washington, D.C., 1982.

Gelber, Harry, *Technology, Defense and External Relations in China, 1975–1978.* Boulder, Colo.: Westview Press, 1979.

Haas, Ernst B.; Williams, Mary Pat; and Babai, Don. *Scientists and World Order: The Uses of Technical Knowledge in International Organizations.* Berkeley: University of California Press, 1977.

Liu Jing-tong. *On Introducing Technology to China.* New York: China International Business Series, Columbia University, 1983.

Orleans, Leo A., ed. *Science in Contemporary China.* Stanford, Calif.: Stanford University Press, 1981.

Ridley, Charles P. *China's Scientific Policies: Implications for International Cooperation.* Washington, D.C.: American Enterprise Institute for Public Policy Research, 1976.

Simon, Denis Fred. "China's Capacity to Assimilate Foreign Technology: An Assessment." In U.S. Congress, Joint Economic Committee. *China Under the Four Modernizations.* Part 1. Washington, D.C.: Government Printing Office, 1982.

Suttmeier, Richard P. *Science, Technology and China's Drive for Modernization.* Stanford, Calif.: Hoover Institution Press, 1980.

———. "Politics, Modernization, and Science in China." *Problems of Communism* 30 (January-February 1981):54–69.

International Law, International Organizations, and World Order

Chai, Trong R. "Chinese Policy Toward the Third World and the Superpowers in the UN General Assembly 1971–1977: A Voting Analysis." *International Organization* 33 (Summer 1979):391–403.

Chang, Luke T. *China's Boundary Treaties and Frontier Disputes.* Dobbs Ferry, N.Y.: Oceana, 1982.

Chiu, Hungdah. *Agreements of the People's Republic of China: A Calendar of Events 1966–1980.* New York: Praeger, 1981.

Cohen, Jerome Alan, and Chiu, Hungdah. *People's China and International Law: A Documentary Study.* 2 vols. Princeton, N.J.: Princeton University Press, 1974.

Feeney, William R. "Sino-Soviet Competition in the United Nations." *Asian Survey* 17 (September 1979):391–403.

———. "Chinese Global Politics in the UN General Assembly." In *China in the Global Community,* eds. James C. Hsiung and Samuel S. Kim. New York: Praeger, 1980.

Hsiung, James C. *Law and Policy in China's Foreign Relations: A Study of Attitudes and Practice.* New York: Columbia University Press, 1972.

Johnston, Douglas M., and Chiu, Hungdah. *Agreements of the People's Republic of China 1949–1967: A Calendar.* Cambridge, Mass.: Harvard University Press, 1968.

Kim, Samuel S. "The People's Republic of China and the Charter-Based International Legal Order." *American Journal of International Law* 62 (April 1978):317–349.

———. *China, the United Nations, and World Order.* Princeton, N.J.: Princeton University Press, 1979.

_____. "Whither Post-Mao Chinese Global Policy?" *International Organization* 35 (Summer 1981):433–465.

_____. "Normative Foreign Policy: The Chinese Case." *International Interactions* 8 (1981):51–77.

Li, Victor H. "Reflections on the Current Drive Toward Greater Legalization in China," *Georgia Journal of International and Comparative Law* 10 (Summer 1980):221–232.

Lichtenstein, Natalie G. "The People's Republic of China and Revision of the United Nations Charter." *Harvard International Law Journal* 18 (Summer 1977):629–647.

_____. "China's Participation in International Organizations," *China Business Review* 6 (May-June 1979):28–36.

ABOUT THE CONTRIBUTORS

Davis B. Bobrow (Ph.D., MIT) is a professor of government and politics at the University of Maryland (College Park). His publications include *International Relations—New Approaches; Understanding Foreign Policy Decisions: The Chinese Case* (coauthored with Steve Chan and John A. Kringen), and he edited and contributed to *Weapons Systems Decisions; Computers and the Policy-Making Community;* and *Components of Defense Policy.* He has also contributed articles to numerous anthologies and to such journals as *World Politics, International Organization, Journal of Conflict Resolution, International Studies Quarterly, Public Opinion Quarterly,* and *Policy Sciences.*

Steve Chan (Ph.D., Minnesota) is a professor of political science at the University of Colorado, Boulder. He is author of *International Relations in Perspective,* coauthor of *Understanding Foreign Policy Decisions: The Chinese Case,* and coeditor of *Foreign Policy Decision Making.* He has contributed articles to *American Political Science Review, Comparative Political Studies, International Interactions, International Studies Quarterly, Journal of Conflict Resolution, Journal of Peace Research, Journal of Strategic Studies, Papers of Peace Science Society (International), Social Science Quarterly, Western Political Quarterly,* and *World Politics.*

Bruce Cumings (Ph.D., Columbia) is an associate professor of international studies at the Henry M. Jackson School of International Studies, University of Washington. He is author of *The Origins of the Korean War,* which won the Harry S. Truman Award in 1982 and the John K. Fairbank Award of the American Historical Association in 1983. He edited *Child of Conflict: The Korean-American Relationship, 1943–1953* and has contributed chapters to anthologies and articles to numerous journals including *Bulletin of Concerned Asian Scholars, International Organization, Journal of Korean Studies, Modern China, SAIS Review,* and *Problems of Communism.*

William Feeney (Ph.D., Johns Hopkins, SAIS) is a professor of government at Southern Illinois University at Edwardsville. He is coeditor of *U.S. Foreign Policy and Asian-Pacific Security* with William T. Tow; a contributor to *Sino-American Normalization and Its Policy Implications,* edited by Gene T. Hsiao and Michael Witunski; *China in the Global Community,* edited by James C. Hsiung and Samuel S. Kim; and *Sino-American Detente and Its Policy Implications,* edited by Gene T. Hsiao. He has published articles in *Asian Affairs, Current History, Korea & World*

Affairs, Asian Profile, Asian Thought & Society, Asian Survey, and *Current Scene.*

Paul H. B. Godwin (Ph.D., Minnesota) is an associate professor of Asian studies at the Air University, Maxwell Air Force Base. He is coauthor of *The Making of a Model Citizen in Communist China;* editor and contributor to *The Chinese Defense Establishment: Continuity and Change in the 1980s;* a contributor to *Civil-Military Relations in Communist Societies,* edited by Dale Herspring and Ivan Volgyes; and *The Small Group in Political Science,* edited by Robert Golembiewski. He has also published articles in numerous journals including *Comparative Politics, Studies in Comparative Communism, Small Group Behavior,* and *Contemporary China.*

Samuel S. Kim (Ph.D., Columbia) is a professor of political science at Monmouth College and a senior fellow at the World Policy Institute. His publications include *China, the United Nations, and World Order* and *The Quest for a Just World Order;* he is a coeditor and contributor to *China in the Global Community; The War System: An Interdisciplinary Approach;* and *Toward a Just World Order.* He has also contributed chapters in anthologies and articles to various journals including *Alternatives, American Journal of International Law, China Quarterly, International Interactions, International Organization, Journal of Peace Research, Journal of Political and Military Sociology, Vierteljahresberichte, World Politics,* and *World Policy Journal.*

Donald W. Klein (Ph.D., Columbia) is a professor of political science at Tufts University. He is coauthor of *Biographic Dictionary of Chinese Communism, 1921–1965* (1971) and coauthor of *Rebels and Bureaucrats: China's December 9ers.* He is an editorial board member of the *China Quarterly, Asian Survey,* and *Pacific Affairs.*

Steven I. Levine (Ph.D., Harvard) is an associate professor of international service at the School of International Service, American University, in Washington, D.C. A student of Chinese foreign policy and East Asian international relations, he has contributed to several conference volumes and to such journals as *Political Science Quarterly, Asian Survey, International Journal,* and *Problems of Communism.* His study of the Chinese civil war, entitled *World Politics and Revolutionary Power in Manchuria, 1945–1949* will be published soon.

Michael Ng-Quinn (Ph.D., Harvard) is an assistant professor of diplomacy at the Fletcher School of Law and Diplomacy, Tufts University. His articles have appeared in *Asia Pacific Community, Asian Survey, Asian Thought and Society, Far Eastern Economic Review, International Studies Quarterly, Qishi niandai, Survey,* and other journals. He is currently completing a book entitled *Perpetual Survival of an Empire in International Relations: Preliminary Hypotheses on Premodern China and Contemporary Implications.*

Susan Shirk (Ph.D., MIT) is an associate professor of political science at the University of California, San Diego. She is the author of *Competitive Comrades: Career Incentives and Student Strategies in China*. She has also contributed chapters to anthologies and articles to various journals on economic policy, industrial labor, educational policy, and political dissent in China.

Denis Fred Simon (Ph.D., Berkeley) is the Ford International Assistant Professor of Management at the Sloan School of Management of MIT. Prior to joining the MIT faculty, he was a research analyst specializing in technology transfer matters at the National Foreign Assessment Center in Washington, D.C. His publications include numerous articles on the problems of science and technology development in the PRC and Taiwan, including a forthcoming book entitled *Taiwan, Technology Transfer and Transnationalism: The Political Management of Dependency*.

Chi Su (Ph.D., Columbia) was a research fellow at the Center for Science and International Affairs, Harvard University, in 1983-1984 and is currently an associate professor of political science in the Department of Diplomacy, National Cheng-Chi University, Taipei. He has contributed articles to *Asian Survey* and *Journal of Northeast Asian Studies*, and is currently completing a book entitled *The Soviet Image of and Policy Toward China, 1969-1979*.

Allen S. Whiting (Ph.D., Columbia) was director of the Office of Research and Analysis, Far East, in the U.S. Department of State (1962–1966) and deputy consul general, Hong Kong (1966–1968), and is currently a professor of political science and director, Center for East Asian Studies, University of Arizona. He has authored many books, including *China Crosses the Yalu*, *The Chinese Calculus of Deterrence*, and *Siberian Development and East Asia*, and has also contributed numerous articles in leading professional journals on China and international relations.

INDEX

Acheson, Dean, 252, 258
ADB. *See* Asian Development Bank
ADF. *See* Asian Development Fund
Afanasyev, Viktor G., 138
Afghanistan, 23, 136–140, 150–153, 155–156, 182, 190–193, 205, 220–221, 226–227, 251, 307–308
Africa, 102, 168, 188, 251, 260, 330
Albania, 173, 189, 229
Algeria, 281
Alienation, 202–203
Alignment, 14, 95–102, 114, 117, 128–129, 178, 190, 249, 259, 300, 322, 326. *See also* Nonalignment
Alliance. *See* Alignment
American Institute in Taiwan, 118, 133(n28)
American Motors, 247, 261
Andropov, Yuri, 135, 138–139, 150
Angola, 189–190, 251
Anhui, 62, 279
Antigua-Barbuda, 189
Argentina, 281
Arms control and disarmament
   no-first-use principle, 150, 192–193
   nuclear proliferation, 9, 193, 210(n29), 302
   multilateral treaties, 192–193
ASEAN. *See* Association of Southeast Asian Nations
Asian Development Bank, 124, 285–287
Asian Development Fund, 287
Association of Southeast Asian Nations, 86, 102, 152, 170
Australia, 161–163, 165, 167, 169–170, 174, 176, 273, 283
Austria, 164
Autarky, 13, 17–18, 77(n12), 245, 268, 293

Babai, Don, 314
Baldrige, Malcolm, 257, 312
Bandung conference, 162–163, 179, 182
Bangladesh, 191, 274, 281
Bank of China, 58, 197, 271
Baoshan steel mill, 242–243
Barnet, Richard, 238
Barnett, A. Doak, 133(n23), 255
Behavioral science, 8
Beijing, 63–64, 74
Belgium, 162, 164, 273, 283, 309
Benjenk, Munir P., 280
Bernstein, Richard, 121
Bhutan, 16
Bialer, Seweryn, 157(n30)
Bipolarity, 85, 95–99, 203, 205, 332
Blair, John M., 263(n20)
Bobrow, Davis, 27(n9)
Brazil, 208, 235, 246, 248, 273–274, 281, 283
Brezhnev, Leonid, 25, 135, 137–138, 140–141, 149, 157(n10)
Brown, Harold, 116, 307–308
Brzezinski, Zbigniew, 122, 133(n21), 183, 250–251, 253, 256
Bulgaria, 173, 229
Bu Ming, 271
Bundy, McGeorge, 160(n160)
Burma, 16
Bush, Richard, 158(n40)
Butterfield, Fox, 121

CAAC. *See* Civil Aviation Administration of China
Cambodia. *See* Kampuchea
Canada, 16, 162–164, 169–170, 173–174, 176, 273, 283
Cancun summit conference, 187
Canton. *See* Guangzhou
Capitalism, 91–94, 203, 236–237

Capitalist world economy, 13, 89–95
Caribbean, 190
Carter administration, 115–118, 122, 151, 193, 250, 253, 255–256, 327
Carter, Jimmy. *See* Carter administration
CASS. *See* Chinese Academy of Social Sciences
CCP. *See* Chinese Communist Party
Ceausescu, Nicolae, 173, 229
Central America, 123, 190, 256
Central Intelligence Agency, 243
Chan, Steve, 27(n9, 12)
Chang, Parris, 241
Chao Mingde, 271
Chase-Dunn, Christopher, 89
Chen Muhua, 197, 242
Chenpao, 44, 46
Chen Xilian, 241
Chen Yun, 241, 262(n12)
Chiang Ching-kuo, 327
Chiang Kai-shek, 217, 326, 332
Chien Ning, 304
Chile, 16
China
   capabilities, 10–11, 20, 37, 84–85, 95, 101–103, 181, 215, 220, 223
   and capitalist world economy, 58, 75–76, 81(n68), 89–95, 128, 180, 236–239, 246–249, 255, 282, 296
   Constitution, 209(n21)
   and consumerism, 61
   and cultural exchanges, 115, 120–121, 126–127, 141
   as donor of aid, 11, 163, 174, 188, 197
   and EEC, 165
   and energy, 63, 71, 80(n56), 181, 242–243, 254, 261, 276, 278–279, 300, 311
   and exports, 75–76, 194, 207, 247–249, 270, 276. *See also* Export development strategy
   and foreign borrowing, 58, 255, 272–282. *See also* World Bank Group
   and foreign debts, 13, 58, 208, 255, 260, 268, 275–277, 288, 291(n29)
   and foreign investment. *See* Foreign investment
   and foreign trade. *See* Foreign trade
   grain imports, 163, 169, 195
   and India. *See* India
   and Japan, 170–172. *See also* Japan
   and joint ventures. *See* Joint ventures
   leadership, 37–39, 45, 114, 118, 136, 139, 142, 145–146, 148, 153, 180, 243–244, 293–294, 313, 321–323
   Ministry of Education, 277
   Ministry of Finance, 69
   Ministry of Foreign Affairs, 10, 23–24, 191, 271
   Ministry of Foreign Economic Relations and Trade (MOFERT), 68–70, 72–73
   Ministry of Light Industry, 68–69
   Ministry of Machine Building, 65, 68, 79(n36), 80(n52), 241
   and Mongolia. *See* Mongolia
   and NIEO, 186–188. *See also* New International Economic Order
   as recipient of aid, 165, 171, 175, 177(n11), 181, 188, 197, 270–290
   Science and Technology Commission, 295
   and state-sponsored overseas investment, 196
   and science and technology. *See* Science and technology
   and Second World, 161–177
   Soviet studies in, 147

and Soviet Union, 7, 21, 24, 32, 43–44, 85, 93, 95, 97–99, 114, 123, 135–156, 164, 175. *See also* Soviet Union
State Council, 71
State Economic Commission, 62, 66, 68, 295
State Planning Commission, 65–66, 68, 79(n35), 270, 295
and students and scholars abroad, 165–166, 177(n12), 304–306, 325
and Third World, 179–183. *See also* Third World
tourism, 165–166, 171
and United States, 7, 23, 26, 42–43, 85, 93, 95, 98–99, 113–133, 145, 154, 171, 175, 249–255, 282, 286–287, 288–289, 299–300, 307–312, 322, 326–328. *See also* United States
workers abroad, 197
China Business Review, 243, 257
China Construction Engineering Corporation, 197
China Council for Promotion of International Trade, 270
China International Trust and Investment Corporation, 69–70, 196, 270
China Investment Bank, 279
China National Metals and Minerals Import and Export Corporation, 196
China National Technical Import Corporation, 303
Chinese Academy of Sciences, 315(n12)
Chinese Academy of Social Sciences, 147, 159(n55), 191, 244
Chinese Communist Party, 8, 67–68, 136, 144, 155, 160(n84), 185, 187, 229, 244
Chinese foreign policy
  arms control and disarmament. *See* Arms control and disarmament
  behavioral properties of, 11–13
  behavior-centered approach to, 5–10
  bureaucratic conflicts, 67–70
  capitalist world-system approach, 89–95
  change and continuity, 3–4, 7, 16, 26(n2), 165, 167, 175, 179, 230, 249, 256, 295, 321
  cognitive processes, 40–41
  comparative analysis, 11, 12(matrix), 14, 16, 18, 27(n9), 34
  crisis behavior, 9, 21, 45–46
  covert activities, 9, 309
  data on, 9
  decision making, 9, 10, 22–24, 39, 74, 321
  definition of, 9, 22, 36
  dependent behavior of, 14–15. *See also* Dependency
  descriptive analysis, 10–15, 41–45
  diachronic analysis, 7, 11, 12(matrix)
  domestic factors on, 8, 16–18, 39, 57–81, 201–203, 237–238, 241–242, 296–299, 310, 315(n11), 323–326. *See also* Factionalism
  empirical analysis, 11
  explanatory analysis, 15–24, 42–45
  factional analysis, 16–17. *See also* Factionalism
  feedback process, 23
  forecasting, 24–26, 322–323, 328–329
  functional approach, 85–89
  goals, 36–37
  independent behavior, 140, 154, 260. *See also* Independence
  instruments of, 10–11, 28(n14)
  interdependent behavior, 14, 88, 102. *See also* Interdependence
  legal practice, 19, 121, 154, 270, 304
  legitimation, 25–28. *See also* Legitimacy
  linkage, 17, 22–24, 39, 43, 326
  model, 6(figure), 35(figure)
  negotiating style, 41–42
  nonevent, 44
  periodization, 4, 27(n4)
  prediction, 24–25, 45–47, 52, 321–323
  prescriptive analysis, 35(figure), 47, 54(n15)
  product, 41–49
  puzzles of, 7–8, 11–12, 33
  regional factors, 60–64
  sectoral conflicts, 64–67
  self-reliant behavior, 12–13. *See also* Self-reliance
  state-centric approach, 84–85
  status inconsistency, 21, 181, 208(n1), 298, 332
  study of, 3
  substance, 36–41
  systemic factors on, 18–22, 95–101, 203–207, 249–255

theory and practice, 8, 33, 183, 185, 188, 194, 200, 247
time perspective, 40
traditional, 16–17, 23, 134(n44), 295
uniqueness/commonness, 7, 34, 44, 46
voting behavior, 11, 157(n22), 189, 191
word/deed disjuncture, 7–8, 45–46, 53(n2), 138, 163–164, 194, 290, 313
Chinese Institute of International Studies, 22
Chi Su, 329
Chongqing, 74
Choucri, Nazli, 24
CIA. *See* Central Intelligence Agency
CIB. *See* China Investment Bank
CITIC. *See* China International Trust and Investment Corporation
Civil Aviation Administration of China, 121
Clausen, A. W., 199
COCOM. *See* Coordinating Committee of the Consultative Group
Coercive diplomacy, 216–218
Cognitive behavioralism, 22
Cognitive mapping, 10
collective self-reliance, 87. *See also* South-South cooperation
Colombia, 281
COMECON. *See* Council for Mutual Economic Assistance
Communist Party of the Soviet Union, 138, 142, 144, 149, 157(n32)
Comparative Research on the Events of Nations, 7, 14–15, 27(n9), 28(n14)
Coordinating Committee of the Consultative Group, 307, 309, 311
Council for Mutual Economic Assistance, 90–91
Council on Foreign Relations (New York), 255, 309
CPSU. *See* Communist Party of the Soviet Union
CREON. *See* Comparative Research on the Events of Nations
Cross, Charles T., 133(n28)
Cuba, 190, 205–206
Cultural exchanges, 139–141, 154, 304–306
Cultural Revolution, 13, 18, 44, 141, 148, 163–164, 169, 170, 176, 241, 248, 268–269, 296, 314, 321–322, 324, 333–334(n2)
Cumings, Bruce, 324
Czechoslovakia, 44, 94, 173, 229

Dadzie, Kenneth, 191
Dalian, 70
Dallin, Alexander, 25, 29(n29)
Daqing oilfield, 279
Deadline Data on World Affairs, 7, 27(n9)
Debt-service ratio, 276–277
De Gaulle, Charles, 164
De-Maoization, 136, 143, 185, 202
Deng Xiaoping, 22, 25–26, 27(n10), 31(n66), 44–45, 57–58, 71, 76, 117, 119, 128, 130, 135–136, 143–144, 150, 152, 160(n84), 167, 171, 173, 176, 184–185, 200, 211(n47), 240, 243–244, 246–247, 253, 255, 269, 271, 286, 295, 298, 304, 321, 324–326, 328, 331, 334(n3), 334(n9)
Deng Xiaoping wenxuan 1975–1982, 25, 157(n5), 201, 324, 334(n3)
Denmark, 161
Dependency, 13–14, 76, 87, 186–188, 201, 260, 267, 297, 313, 323, 325–326
Dernberger, Robert, 241, 246
Détente, 98–99, 149, 151–152, 192, 250, 322, 330
Deterrence, 216–218. *See also* Nuclear deterrent
Diaoyu Tai. *See* Senkaku Islands
Dien Bien Phu, 332
Diplomatic recognition. *See* Recognition
Diplomatic relations. *See* Recognition
Domes, Jurgen, 17
Dong Fureng, 77(n12), 244–246
Dos Santos, Jose Eduardo, 190
Dulles, John Foster, 41

East Asia, 102, 227–229, 330–332
Eastern Europe, 172–174, 205, 229–230, 254, 297, 330
East Germany, 173, 229
EEC. *See* European Economic Community
Egypt, 205, 281
Eight Principles for China's Aid to Foreign Countries, 188

Eisenhower, Dwight, 327
E su zhongguoxue gaikuang, 147
Eurocommunism, 153
European Economic Community, 7, 165
"Event data" movement, 5
Export development strategy, 235, 254–255
Export-Import Control Commission, 270

Factionalism, 16–17, 42, 74–75, 143, 184, 207, 211(n58), 216, 241–242, 296–299, 310, 323–326
Fairbank, John K., 16
Fang Yi, 298, 304
Feeney, William, 210(n43), 264(n65), 324
Feng Tianshun, 270
FEZs. *See* Free Trade Zones
Five Principles of Peaceful Coexistence, 8, 153, 179, 189, 209(n21)
Ford, Gerald, 327
Ford Foundation, 322
Foreign exchange earnings, 58, 61, 70–72, 166, 196, 208, 238, 239–240, 242, 245, 275–277, 327, 329
Foreign investment, 57–62, 72–73, 165–166, 196, 267
Foreign Investment Control Commission, 270
Foreign trade, 13, 57–59, 66, 69, 72–73, 76(n2), 93, 115, 120, 139–140, 163–165, 168, 173, 194–195, 208, 248–249, 267–268, 270–271, 280, 285–286, 330–331
Four Modernizations, 22, 142–143, 146, 153, 175, 182, 185, 192, 196, 242, 244, 267, 269, 271, 287–289, 294, 297, 303, 311
Four Principles for Sino-African Economic and Technological Cooperation, 188
France, 153, 162, 164–166, 173, 189, 261, 273, 283, 311, 332
Free export zones. *See* Free Trade Zones
Free Trade Zones, 196, 246–247
Friedman, Edward, 290(n1)
Fujian, 62, 64, 70–71 248
Fuzhou, 329

Gang of Four, 57, 93–94, 166, 170, 176, 240, 244, 324, 326
Gao Gang, 143
GATT. *See* General Agreement on Tariffs and Trade
Gelman, Harry, 157(n30)
General Agreement on Tariffs and Trade, 195–196, 207, 244, 252, 268, 285–286
Generalized System of Preferences, 285–286
Geng Biao, 308
Gerschenkron, Alexander, 262(n8)
Ghana, 191, 205
Gittings, John, 334(n6)
GNP. *See* Gross National Product
Godwin, Paul H.B., 233(n21)
Gottlieb, Thomas, 216
Gourevitch, Peter, 237
Great Britain, 162, 167, 189, 273, 283, 307, 311, 328. *See also* Hong Kong
Great Leap Forward, 45, 162–163, 268, 324
Greece, 162, 165
Grenada, 190–191, 250, 256
Griffith, William E., 157(n30)
Gromyko, Andrei A., 136
Gross National Product, 181, 276
Group of 77, 7, 87, 182, 186, 191, 284, 286. *See also* Third World
Group of 10, 289
Group of 24, 198, 282, 284, 289, 291(n20)
GSP. *See* Generalized System of Preferences
Guangdong, 61, 63–64, 70–71, 74, 79(n30), 280
Guangzhou, 70, 248, 329
Gu Mu, 62, 242, 271
Gurtov, Melvin, 232(n5)

Haas, Ernst, 82–83, 314(n9)
Haig, Alexander, 117, 123, 183, 256, 308–309
Hainan Island, 248, 263(n45)
Hammer, Armand, 261
Harding, Harry, 4, 50, 56(n34), 132(n4), 134(n44), 193
Hegemonism. *See* Hegemony
Hegemony, 93, 98–99, 137, 139–140, 147–151, 154–155, 172–175, 182, 185–190, 193, 222, 249–251, 253, 256, 330. *See also* Soviet Union; United States
Heilongjiang, 279

Helms, Jesse, 258
Henan, 279
Hewlitt-Packard, 247
Ho Chi Minh, 332
Hoffmann, Stanley, 85
Holbrooke, Richard, 133(n21)
Holdridge, John, 125
Holland. *See* Netherlands
Honeywell, 247
Hong Kong, 63, 73, 140, 169, 195–196, 208, 255, 257, 309, 328–329
Hua Guofeng, 167, 171, 173, 185, 240, 241, 243–245, 269, 321
Huang Hua, 14, 138, 153, 184, 189, 229, 253, 263(n46), 309
Huangpu, 279
Huguang bond case, 121, 154
Hu Na, 120, 124, 127, 154
Hungary, 72, 173, 229, 246
Hu Yaobang, 27(n10), 62, 103, 144, 153, 171, 173, 187, 208, 209(n17), 209(n21), 229, 244, 321, 325
Hwang, Byong-Moo, 232(n5)

IAEA. *See* International Atomic Energy Agency
IBRD. *See* International Bank for Reconstruction and Development
Iceland, 164
IDA. *See* International Development Association
IFC. *See* International Finance Corporation
ILO. *See* International Labour Organization
IMF. *See* International Monetary Fund
Imperialism, 137, 140, 149, 151, 249. *See also* Social imperialism
Independence, 15, 86–87, 98, 102, 117, 128, 140, 154, 156, 160(n84), 178, 182, 185, 259, 297, 313, 331
India, 44–45, 153, 175, 179, 217, 225–226, 273–274, 281, 283, 285, 299, 312, 315(n23)
Indonesia, 163, 179, 274, 281
Inkeles, Alex, 296
Institute of Contemporary International Relations, 149
Institute of Soviet and East European Studies, 147
Interdependence, 14, 88, 187, 253, 296–297, 313
Intermediate zones, 184, 236
International Atomic Energy Agency, 154–155, 193, 210(n29)
International Bank for Reconstruction and Development. *See* World Bank
International Development Association, 198–199, 206, 265, 275–282, 288–289
International Finance Corporation, 198, 275–276, 280
International Labour Organization, 181, 196
International law, 19–20, 86
International liberalism, 186
International Monetary Fund, 87, 124, 153, 191, 248, 252, 271–275
International organizations, 7, 11, 15, 19, 39, 86, 181, 198–199. *See also* United Nations
International regimes, 88–89
International structure, 19–20, 83
International system, 18–19, 82–83, 87, 180, 209(n6), 230, 236–239, 294
International values, 19
Intraelite conflict. *See* Factionalism
Iran, 281
Israel, 86, 151, 190, 226
Italy, 153, 164, 189, 273, 283, 311
Ivory Coast, 189, 281

Jackson, Henry, 253–254
Japan, 7, 32, 76, 78(n26), 86, 102, 124, 151, 154–155, 161–162, 164–168, 170–172, 189, 204–205, 227–228, 250–252, 255, 261, 273, 281, 283, 293, 299, 307, 311, 315(n12), 330–332
Japan-China S&T Exchange Association, 315(n12)
Japan Society for the Promotion of Science, 315
Jervis, Robert, 89
Jiang Qing, 240
Jiang Zemin, 318(n72)
Ji Dengkui, 241
Jinmen. *See* Quemoy
Johnson, Lyndon, 327
Joint Sino-U.S. Science and Technology Commission, 311
Joint ventures, 57–58, 60–61, 66–67, 71, 73–74, 76, 93, 134(n47), 166, 194, 196, 245–248, 270, 281

Kahn, Herman, 24–25
Kampuchea, 23, 86, 136, 152, 182, 190, 193, 217, 220, 227, 251
Kapitsa, Mikhail, 137–140, 145, 147
Kaplan, Abraham, 9
Kaplan, Morton, 82
Kaunda, K. D., 184
Kennan, George, 160(n75), 250
Kennedy, John F., 327
Kenya, 281
Keohane, Robert, 88, 296
Khmer Rouge, 227
Khrushchev, Nikita, 43, 141, 157(n10), 176, 236
Kim Il Sung, 227
Kim, Samuel S., 55(n23), 134(n44), 211(n47), 314(n10), 332–333
Kissinger, Henry, 122, 164, 183, 250–251, 256
K-Mart, 247
Korea
    North Korea, 38, 86, 91, 102, 172, 217, 227, 245, 259
    South Korea, 9, 38, 47, 76, 86, 124, 195, 208, 227, 235, 246–247, 252, 255, 257, 281
Korean Airlines incident, 139, 157(n22), 191
Korean War, 43, 45, 162, 217, 259
Krasner, Stephen, 88–89
Kringen, John, 27(n9)

Lasswell, Harold, 321
Latin America, 102, 262(n8), 330
"Lean-to-one-side" policy, 14, 97, 184, 236
Legitimacy, 153, 178, 180, 201–202
LeMay, Curtis, 250
Leninism. See Marxism
Lesotho, 189
Levine, Steven I., 160(n89)
Liao, Kuang-sheng, 334(n5)
Libya, 250
Lieberthal, Kenneth, 157(n30), 216
Lin Biao, 43, 45, 63, 163
Li Ni, 149–150
Li Qiang, 245
Liu Danian, 147
Liu Lixin, 245
Liu Shaoqi, 143, 148, 244
Li Xiannian, 139, 242
Lome Convention, 168
Lo Reqing, 43
Luxembourg, 162, 165

MacArthur, Douglas, 250
McCarthyism, 322
MacFarquhar, Roderick, 21
McNamara, Robert, 160(n75), 268, 277
Malaysia, 281
Maoism, 141, 143, 148, 180–183, 185, 201, 326
Maoist development model, 235, 238, 246, 267–268, 289
Mao Zedong, 17, 21, 29(n32), 44–46, 50, 57, 136, 142–144, 148, 155, 158(n40), 163–166, 172, 175, 184–185, 200, 209(n6), 236, 297–298, 321, 324–325, 333
Mao Zedong Thought. See Maoism
Marxism, 90, 141, 144, 148, 202–203
Matsu (island), 168
Mexico, 246, 281
MFA. See Multi-Fibre Arrangement
MFN. See Most-favored-nation status
Middle East, 102, 123, 150, 190, 226, 251, 330
MNCs. See Multinational corporations
Modernization drive. See Four Modernizations
MOFERT. See China, Ministry of Foreign Economic Relations and Trade
Mondale, Walter, 116
Mongolia, 47, 86, 136, 150, 155, 193, 220
Morocco, 281
Most-favored-nation status, 115, 244, 271, 286
MPLA. See Popular Movement for the Liberation of Angola
Mu Guangren, 152
Multi-Fibre Arrangement, 195–196, 207
Multilateral aid, 181, 271–285
Multinational corporations, 86–87, 92, 196, 242–243, 246–247, 261
Multipolarity, 99, 203–206, 219

Nakasone, Yasuhiro, 171, 228
NAM. See Non-Aligned Movement
Namibia, 190, 285
Nan Sha (island), 86
National interest, 21, 187, 193, 200, 289–290, 297
Nationalism, 90, 141–146, 176, 182, 326
National People's Congress, 63
National sovereignty. See Sovereignty
NATO. See North Atlantic Treaty Organization
Netherlands, 23, 153, 162, 169, 189, 273, 283, 300
New International Economic Order, 25, 86–87, 93, 182, 184, 186–188, 190, 209(n15), 209(n16), 209(n18), 268, 289, 314(n2), 332. See also North-South relations
Newly industrializing countries, 32, 195, 235, 247–249, 257
New Zealand, 162, 165, 167, 170
Ng-Quinn, Michael, 4, 332
Nicaragua, 250
NICs. See Newly indsutrializing countries
NIEO. See New International Economic Order
Nigeria, 281
Nixon, Richard, 164, 178–179, 250–251, 256, 327
Non-Aligned Movement, 7, 182–183, 187, 191, 205
Nonalignment, 13, 15, 178, 182, 219
North Atlantic Treaty Organization, 149, 162, 165, 167, 170, 225, 307
North-South relations, 93, 187–189, 206, 282–289
Nuclear deterrent, 149, 223–224, 232(n8)
Nuclear forces, 85, 99, 152, 181, 223, 230, 253, 310–311
Nuclear power plants, 63, 257, 261, 311
Nye, Joseph, 88, 296

Occidental Petroleum, 261
Ohira, Masayoshi, 171
Oksenberg, Michel, 54(n8), 122, 158(n40), 255
O'Leary, Greg, 50
Open Door (historical), 26, 201
Open-door policy, 22, 25–26, 58, 61, 63, 73–76, 128, 178, 187, 200–201, 208, 248, 260, 263(n46), 271, 289, 295, 297–298, 306, 313, 331
Opium War, 23, 267, 328
Overseas Chinese, 61, 166, 299, 304, 329

Pakistan, 9, 153, 162–163, 226, 281
Palestine Liberation Organization, 163
Pamir, 137
Pan American case, 121, 154
Park Chung Hee, 227, 247
Pei Monong, 22, 27(n10)
Peng Dehuai, 143
People's Liberation Army, 45, 67–68, 216–217, 223–224, 230, 233(n39), 247–248, 253, 260, 311, 325, 327–328
People-to-people diplomacy, 166
Per capita GNP, 181, 199, 246–247, 277, 284
Perry, William, 308
Peru, 281
Philippines, 162, 281
Pipes, Richard, 255
PLA. See People's Liberation Army
PLO. See Palestine Liberation Organization
Poland, 47, 123, 149, 173, 229, 260
Polanyi, Karl, 237–238
Polarity, 95–96, 154
Polarization, 96, 203–206
Political culture, 10, 16, 29(n29)
Pollack, Jonathan, 222, 231, 232(n11), 259, 299
Pol Pot, 251
Pool, Ithiel de Sola, 24
Popular Movement for the Liberation of Angola, 189
Population, 197, 276
Portugal, 281
Power, 20–21, 293
Press, Frank, 254
Pye, Lucian, 16, 41–42, 53(n2), 54(n8)

Quemoy, 45–46, 168, 324–325
Querrero, Manuel Perez, 191
Qian Junrui, 263(n34)

Rakhmanin, O. B., 144–145
Rand Corporation, 253
R&D. See Research and development
Rank disequilibrium theory, 21

Rao, P. V. Narasimha, 226
Reagan, Ronald. *See* Reagan administration
Reagan administration, 117–118, 121–124, 151–152,
    206, 225, 228, 231, 250, 255–259, 280, 284, 287,
    289, 310–312, 327
Realpolitik, 164, 183
Recognition, 162, 189–190, 225
Renmin ribao, 27(n9), 63, 184, 186, 209(n16), 246,
    253, 256, 305
Ren Zhongyi, 63
Research and development, 295, 298–299, 303, 307,
    315(n16)
Reston, James, 164
Revisionism, 136–137, 140–141, 143, 148–149, 151,
    236, 238–239, 251, 259
Riker, William, 97
Riskin, Carl, 261
R. J. Reynolds, 247
Robinson, Thomas, 3–4
Romania, 91, 94, 173, 229, 271, 281
Roosevelt, Franklin D., 238, 249–250
Rosecrance, Richard, 85
Rousseau, J. J., 18
Rozman, Gilbert, 158(n46)
Ruggie, John G., 85
Rusk, Dean, 163

S&T. *See* Science and technology
Saudi Arabia, 208, 273, 283
Scalapino, Robert, 259
Schelling, Thomas, 232(n8)
Schlesinger, James, 253–254
Schumpeter, Joseph, 238
Schurmann, Franz, 238
Science and technology, 92, 94, 137, 293–318
Science and Technology Review, 304
SDRs. *See* Special drawing rights
Sears, 247
SEATO. *See* Southeast Asian Treaty Organization
Second World, 38, 161–177. *See also* Japan; Eastern
    Europe; Western Europe
*Selected Works of Deng Xiaoping, 1975–1982. See Deng
    Xiaoping wenxuan, 1975–1982*
Self-reliance, 13, 57, 60, 77(n12), 86–87, 93–95,
    160(n84), 163, 165, 182, 185–188, 203, 206, 208,
    236–238, 249, 266–267, 269, 297, 300, 323, 325,
    331
"Self-strengthening" movement, 295
Senkaku Islands, 331
SEZs. *See* Special economic zones
Shandong, 279
Shanghai, 60–64, 70, 74–75, 79(n34), 248, 261, 279,
    329
Shanghai Communiqué, 149, 164, 309
Shantou, 196
Shao Huaze, 221–222
Shenzhen, 196
Shijie jingji, 149
Shijie jingji daobao, 305
Shirk, Susan, 262(n13), 323, 324
Shultz, George, 122, 139, 311
Sihanouk, Prince Norodom, 152
Singapore, 44, 195, 208
Sino-Japanese Treaty of Peace and Friendship, 331
Sixth Five-Year Plan, 166, 174, 260
Smith, Gerald, 160(n75)
Sobhan, Faruq, 191
Social imperialism, 137, 140, 149, 157(n10), 239, 260.
    See also Soviet Union
Socialist camp, 139–140, 184, 324
Solarz, Stephen, 124
Somalia, 205
South Africa, 9, 86, 151, 189–190, 199, 226, 284–285,
    291(n24)
Southeast Asian Treaty Organization, 162, 226–228
South-South cooperation, 87, 187–188, 191, 194, 207
South West Africa. *See* Namibia
Sovereignty, 98, 175, 300–302, 329
Soviet Union
    aid, 136
    cultural exchanges, 139–141, 193
    foreign policy, 16, 20, 23
    sinology, 141, 145
    social imperialism, 140, 149
    Soviet-Afghan Treaty, 137
    SS-20 missiles, 139, 141, 193

    trade, 139–140, 193, 330
Spain, 153, 165
Special drawing rights, 272–274, 282, 288, 290(n11)
Special economic zones, 60–63, 77, 77(n7), 78(n20),
    166, 196, 329
Spence, Jonathan, 334(n4)
Sri Lanka, 281
Stalinist development model, 235–236, 238–239, 241,
    243–244
State sovereignty. *See* Sovereignty
Strange, Susan, 89
Sudan, 205, 281
Sulian dongou wenti, 147
Sullivan, Michael P., 334(n5)
Sun Yat-sen, 332
Superpowers, 15, 38, 43, 46–47, 85, 93, 95, 98–99,
    114, 153, 164, 173–175, 178, 180, 183, 190,
    203–206, 250–251, 260. *See also* Soviet Union;
    United States
Surinam, 250
Suslov, M. A., 157(n32)
Suttmeier, Richard P., 315(n16)
Suzuki, Zenko, 171
Sweden, 162, 311
Switzerland, 162

Taiwan, 23, 44, 86, 117–118, 120–121, 123, 130, 140,
    145, 154, 161–162, 164, 168–169, 172, 175, 189,
    195–196, 235, 246, 248, 252, 255–258, 268, 271–
    272, 285–286, 300, 308, 310, 325–328, 334(n9)
Taiwan Relations Act, 118–119, 130, 140, 151
Tanaka, Kakuei, 171
Tanzania, 16, 281
Technology transfer, 127, 192, 219, 301, 303–304,
    306, 308–309
Terrill, Ross, 121
Territorial claims, 131, 138
Thailand, 9, 28(n15), 162, 281
Thatcher, Margaret, 167
Third World, 15, 19, 25, 87, 92–93, 98, 128–129, 140,
    149, 151, 153–154, 163, 168, 174–175, 179–183,
    203–208, 250–251, 259–260, 267–268, 275, 280–
    286, 293, 303, 330, 332–333. *See also* Group of
    77; Group of 24
Third World Foundation for Social and Economic
    Studies, 191
Thomas, W. I., 22
Three-world theory, 37, 172–173, 175, 179, 183–186,
    189, 236
Tianjin, 61, 64, 70, 248, 261, 279, 329
Tikhvinskii, Sergei, 138, 140, 158(n35)
Tito, Josip Broz, 173, 229
Transnational corporations. *See* Multinational
    corporations
Trilateral Commission, 250–251, 271
Tripolarity, 99–101
Truman, Harry, 250
Truman administration, 123
Tunisia, 281
Turkey, 281

UNCTAD. *See* United Nations Conference on Trade
    and Development
UNDP. *See* United Nations Development Programme
UNESCO. *See* United Nations Educational, Scientific,
    and Cultural Organization
UNICEF. *See* United Nations Children's Fund
United-front strategy, 114, 117, 141, 154, 180, 184,
    200, 206, 253, 256, 267
United Kingdom. *See* Great Britain
United Nations, 15, 18, 27(n10), 86, 162–164, 173,
    180, 191, 220, 263(n46), 270, 294, 301, 314(n10)
United Nations Children's Fund, 198
United Nations Conference on Trade and
    Development, 182, 187
United Nations Development Programme, 198, 268,
    270, 288
United Nations Educational, Scientific, and Cultural
    Organization, 180, 190–191
United Nations Fund for Population Activities, 198,
    270
United Nations General Assembly, 184, 270, 284,
    291(n24), 333
United Nations Law of the Sea Convention, 190
United Nations peace-keeping operations, 191

United Nations Security Council, 157(n22), 181, 189, 190
United States
  arms sales to Taiwan, 118–119, 124, 130, 151, 154, 168–169, 192, 219–220, 256, 258
  bilateral trade, 120, 195–196
  commercial air transport, 121
  Congress, 287
  cultural exchanges, 120–121
  Defense Intelligence Agency, 309
  Department of Treasury, 199
  grain exports, 163
  Huguang bond case, 121, 154
  Hu Na case, 120, 124, 127, 154
  imperialism, 151
  intelligence exchange, 259
  International Finance Institutions Act, 287
  missile monitoring facility in China, 9, 116
  nuclear sharing agreement, 257
  sinology, 235
  strategic relationship, 122–129, 150–153, 183, 211(n47), 255–258, 327
  and WBG, 199, 206, 273, 280–281, 283–287
U.S. Knitted Textile Association, 258
USSR. See Soviet Union

Values, 9, 19
Vance, Cyrus, 133(n21), 250
Van Ness, Peter, 8
Venezuela, 191
Vernon, Raymond, 246
Vietnam, 23, 42–43, 86, 102, 136, 152, 155–156, 163, 170, 175, 179, 191, 193, 205, 220–225, 227, 250–251, 259, 270, 328, 333
Vietnam War, 170, 325
Volkswagen, 247

Wallerstein, Immanuel, 18–19, 89, 183, 237
Waltz, Kenneth, 19, 82–83, 102
Wang Bingqian, 199, 284
Wang Dongxing, 241
Wang Ming, 143
Wang Shu, 210(n29)
Wang Youping, 24, 147–148
War, 152–154, 192, 219, 223–224
Wars of national liberation, 8–9, 28(n15), 189
WBG. See World Bank Group
Wei ch'i. See Weiqi game
Weinberger, Caspar W., 121, 123, 139, 225, 231, 256, 312, 318(n84), 332
Weiqi game, 45
WEIS. See World Events Interaction Survey
Western Europe, 150–151, 154, 161–162, 167–169, 204–205, 311, 313, 330

West Germany, 165, 250–251, 259, 273, 283, 311, 318(n84)
"Whateverism" faction, 184–185, 241
Whiting, Allen S., 34, 46, 133(n28, 29), 232(n5), 334(n9, 12)
Whitlam, Gough, 174
Wich, Richard, 44
Wiener, Anthony, 24–25
Williams, James, 309
Williams, Pat, 314(n9)
Wittfogel, Karl, 24
Wolfowitz, Paul, 125
Woodard, Kim, 47, 208(n1)
World Bank, 87, 124, 153, 174, 181, 243, 248–249, 252, 254–255, 272–273, 275–285
World Bank Economic Development Institute, 288
World Bank Group, 266, 272–273, 282–283, 324. See also IBRD; IDA; IFC; IMF
World Development Report 1982, 289
World Events Interaction Survey, 21
World-system approach, 18, 89–95, 183, 238–239
Wu De, 241
Wu Xueqian, 27(n10), 86, 92, 119, 144, 231, 234(n49)

Xiamen, 67, 196
Xiandai guoji guanxi, 149
Xi Sha (island), 86
Xu Deen, 303
Xue Muqiao, 62, 81(n68), 245
Xuexi yu tansuo, 159(n58)
Xueshu qingbao, 147
Xu Kui, 159(n55)

Yang, Winston L. Y., 119
Year 2000, 24–25
Ye Jiangying, 119, 136
Yugoslavia, 72, 76, 91, 173, 229, 246, 312
Yu Hongliang, 138, 140
Yu Qiuli, 245, 311

Zagoria, Donald, 42, 148, 157(n30), 259
Zambia, 199, 285
Zhang Aiping, 221–222, 310–311
Zhang Jingfu, 271
Zhang Peiji, 76(n2)
Zhang Wenjin, 308
Zhao Ziyang, 121, 167, 171, 188, 191, 209(n19), 210(n29), 234(n49), 244–246, 249, 260, 304, 312, 321, 324–325
Zhongnanhai, 148
Zhou Enlai, 41, 45, 164, 167, 173, 177, 185, 333
Zhou Yang, 202
Zhuhai, 196
Zimbabwe, 250–251
Zinnes, Dina, 21
Zou Siyi, 245

Other Titles of Interest from Westview Press

Misperceptions in Foreign Policymaking: The Sino-Indian Conflict, 1959–1962, Yaacov Vertzberger

China: The '80s Era, edited by Norton Ginsberg and Bernard A. Lalor

The Chinese Defense Establishment: Continuity and Change in the 1980s, edited by Paul H.B. Godwin

The China Quandary: Domestic Determinants of U.S. China Policy, 1972–1982, Robert G. Sutter

China's Financial System: The Changing Role of Banks, William Byrd

†*China in World Affairs: The Foreign Policy of the PRC Since 1970,* G. W. Choudhury

†*China's Economic Development: Growth and Structural Change,* Chu-yuan Cheng

†*The Government and Politics of the PRC: A Time of Transition,* Jürgen Domes

The Making of a Premier: Zhao Ziyang's Provincial Career, David L. Shambaugh

Three Visions of Chinese Socialism, edited by Dorothy J. Solinger

China as a Maritime Power, David G. Muller

†*China's Cultural Heritage: The Ch'ing Dynasty, 1644–1912,* Richard J. Smith

The Limits of Reform in China, edited by Ronald A. Morse

†*China Briefing, 1982,* edited by Richard C. Bush

†*China Briefing, 1981,* edited by Robert B. Oxnam and Richard C. Bush

†*China Briefing, 1980,* edited by Robert B. Oxnam and Richard C. Bush

†Available in hardcover and paperback.

About the Book and Editor

China and the World:
Chinese Foreign Policy in the Post-Mao Era
edited by Samuel S. Kim

How does China relate to the outside world in the post-Mao era? To what extent—and in what specific ways—has the nexus between China and the world changed, and why? With what future implications and prospects for both? Without being too rigidly bound by the requirements of any particular perspective and methodology, the authors of this collaborative work seek to answer these and related questions for various contexts and issue areas.

Within this broad range, the volume combines theory and generalizations with some specific empirical case studies. The chapters address several key questions and puzzles that are of theoretical and practical value to both students and policymakers. First, what are the wellsprings of Chinese foreign policy? Specifically, what is the relative weight of domestic/societal factors as opposed to external/systemic ones in influencing or circumscribing foreign policy options and directions? Second, what are the changes and continuities that characterize the Chinese foreign policy of the post-Mao era, and what are their sources? In Parts 2 and 3 of the book, the contributors identify the underlying patterns of China's interactions with the major global actors (the United States, the Soviet Union, the Second World, and the Third World) and China's policies on specific international issues and problems. Third, what is the extent of word/deed disjuncture in Chinese foreign policy? Several chapters probe and explain the discrepancies between ideal and real, between policy pronouncements and policy performance, and between intent and outcome in Chinese foreign policy. The concluding chapter identifies and assesses China's foreign policy options and prospects in the years to come.

Samuel S. Kim is professor of political science at Monmouth College and a senior fellow at the World Policy Institute. Dr. Kim's publications include *The Quest for a Just World Order* (Westview, 1983).